Cruising Cuisine

Fresh Food From the Galley

CRUISING CUISINE

Fresh Food From the Galley

Kay Pastorius
Illustrated by Hal Pastorius

International Marine
Camden, Maine

International Marine/
Ragged Mountain Press 
A Division of The ***McGraw-Hill*** *Companies*

10 9 8 7 6 5 4 3 2 1

Library of Congress Cataloging-in-Publication Data
Pastorius, Kay.
Cruising cuisine : fresh food from the galley / Kay Pastorius : illustrated by Hal Pastorius.
p. cm.
Includes index.
ISBN 0-07-048703-0
1. Cookery, Marine. I. Title.
TX840.M7P364 1997
641.5'753—dc21 97-17094
CIP

Questions regarding the content of this book should be addressed to:
International Marine
P.O. Box 220
Camden, ME 04843

Questions regarding the ordering of this book should be addressed to:
The McGraw-Hill Companies
Customer Service Department
P.O. Box 547
Blacklick, OH 43004
Retail customers: 1-800-262-4729
Bookstores: 1-800-722-4726

Cruising Cuisine is printed on 60-pound Renew Opaque Vellum, an acid-free paper that contains 50 percent recycled waste paper (preconsumer) and 10 percent postconsumer waste paper.

Cruising Cuisine is set in 10 point Adobe Bembo

Printed by R.R. Donnelley, Crawfordsville, IN
Design by Carol Gillette
Production by Deborah Krampf and Dan Kirchoff
Illustrations by Hal Pastorius and John Watts
Edited by Nancy Hauswald, Tom McCarthy, John Kettlewell

To my cruising partner, best friend, and husband, Hal Pastorius.

Without the encouragement of Hal, this book would never have been written. As we relaxed in quiet anchorages up and down the Pacific coast, Hal would ask if I had written down the recipe for the dish that we were eating. With more than 20 years of cruising and concocting meals in the galley, this book almost wrote itself.

Hal Pastorius was a well-regarded artist and we loved working on this project together. Many evenings at anchor found me at the computer and Hal, with drawing pen in hand, sketching for the book.

Hal passed away just weeks before our project was completed. The meals we have shared and the places we have cruised will be remembered through the pages of *Cruising Cuisine*.

Since I wrote this book before Hal's death, the anecdotes are in the present tense. Although I am no longer cruising aboard *SpiceSea,* we had intended to cruise for several years while I wrote this book. When I talk about favorite recipes of Hal's, or about what we were doing, I am referring to the time when we were cruising together.

Contents

INTRODUCTION ix

1. Philosophy, Provisioning, and Preserving 1

2. Essential Galley Equipment 20

3. Breakfast and Brunch Treats 26

4. Appetizers and Beverages 38

5. Seafood 57

6. Meat and Poultry 90

7. Pasta, Grains, and Beans 113

8. Fruits and Vegetables 131

9. Sauces and Marinades 157

10. Breadmaking 179

11. Desserts 198

INDEX 219

Acknowledgments

Creating this book would not have been possible without the help of many of my friends and family: my brother, John Watts; my parents, John and Pearl Watts; my sister-in-law Tricia Goldstein; my dear friends, Don and Linda Bryce, Tom Hayward, Susan Hamilton, Barbara Metz, John and Suzanne Pew, and Janice and Andy Sibert. I thank them and the many friends and acquaintances who made this book come together by making suggestions for its organization and for proofreading. I thank the cruisers who gave me lots of input, slip neighbors at Shelter Island Marina who were always obliging guinea pigs, and the many people who offered an upwelling of love and support when I needed it most. I also want to thank Bayliner Corporation for their enthusiasm for our cruising plans.

This book was a labor of love and I thank all those who helped make it possible.

Kay Pastorius

Introduction

This is a cookbook for those who enjoy good food. It is also a personal account of recipes invented while cruising from San Francisco, California, to Manzanillo, Mexico, aboard my 32-foot Bayliner, *SpiceSea*. The book features simple and exciting recipes for the galley chef, and includes menus for intimate dining and for entertaining on board. The recipes emphasize using fresh ingredients to supplement onboard staples.

I discuss the skills that are necessary for mastering fine cooking aboard; therefore, many of the recipes are presented as building blocks that teach a technique or style around which the cruising chef can improvise.

Eating well aboard while provisioning as seldom as possible has been an exciting challenge for me during my 20 years of cruising. *Cruising Cuisine* focuses on helping land-bound cooks adapt to the alien environment of a small boat. I include tips on setting up and customizing a galley, provisioning, and coping with supermarket separation syndrome.

I place a lot of emphasis on using fresh, locally obtained ingredients and discuss foods that are common to some of the most popular cruising grounds of Mexico, the Caribbean, and the South Pacific. The recipes included in *Cruising Cuisine* are modern, healthy, and designed to reduce your time, energy, and effort in the galley.

Main course selections include meat, chicken, pasta, grains, and, of course, seafood. Fishing, digging for clams, searching for mussels, and hunting for lobster are all part of the cruising experience. Knowing how to cook your catch is part of this book.

Cruising Cuisine also features tempting sauces that turn simple meals into elegant repasts, and great bread recipes that are easy to make. You'll also find a few sinful desserts along with some appetizers that will bring you fame as a boat cook. Read this book before you go, provision accordingly, and *Bon Appétit!*

CHAPTER 1

Philosophy, Provisioning, and Preserving

Philosophy of Cooking

I started cooking more than a quarter century ago with the enthusiasm and encouragement of a loving husband. Hal used to joke that he taught me everything he knew in one afternoon and that I took off from there. Having an appreciative audience was the best incentive I had as a fledgling cook. I honed my skills with frequent dinner parties and went on to open my own cooking school.

During those early years of marriage we fell in love with the sea. Although there is no more appreciative audience than the hungry boater, I refused to settle for canned Spam. I adapted my gourmet ideas to the confines of whatever boat we had at the time.

During our early boating years when we didn't even have a galley, cooking was a joint effort. I cooked over a one-burner alcohol stove, held on to the wok, and stirred. Whenever a boat wake rocked us, Hal grabbed the portable burner while I clung to the wok. We cooked pasta, sautéed fish, and made omelettes all in the same pot. We cruised for two weeks at a time with just an ice chest, and we enjoyed every minute. We ate fresh fish each day and began learning how to keep produce without refrigeration.

As our boats grew, so did the galley space. And so did my onboard cooking skills. Fine food afloat is not an oxymoron. I prepared many of the recipes in this book while anchored in deserted coves far from supermarkets. The keys to successful cooking onboard, I think, are keeping the menus simple and learning how to use ingredients that require little or no refrigeration. No one should spend time at sea worrying about whether or not the fresh strawberries and salad greens are going to spoil.

Although I do take a gourmet approach to cooking on the boat, emphasizing fresh ingredients, delicious flavors, and interesting textures, the ingredients I use are practical and storable. Since most galleys are sadly lacking in counter space, it is important to be very well organized when preparing a recipe. I first assemble all the ingredients, measure the appropriate quantities, and return the containers to the cupboard. Next, I chop, mince, dice, and set the ingredients aside, either on paper plates or in Ziploc bags. Then, I'm free to do the actual cooking on my limited counter space.

I've observed that few people drastically change their eating habits when at sea. As a matter of fact, I just threw away a huge amount of tofu that had been on the boat for three years. I had never enjoyed tofu while living on land—why in the world did I think I would enjoy it while cruising in Mexico?

Having a few recipes that you do well is a boon to the nervous cook. And, because boating calls for impromptu entertaining, it's a great confidence booster to have the ingredients for a few of your favorite recipes already packaged together in Ziploc bags. When unexpected visitors dinghy by and cocktails lead to dinner, grab one of your Ziplocs and cook a pot of bean soup or an easy pasta sauce. Above all, remember that boating is supposed to be fun—and so can cooking on board.

Breaking Away

We said our good-byes to family and friends, stowed the last of the produce, and found room for a few more spare parts as we headed out of San Diego harbor for our cruising odyssey. We had no itinerary.

Our boating friends were envious and our landlubber friends incredulous. How could we leave California for such a long period? How could we have sold 25 years of memorabilia and furnishings? How could we possibly be happy living for the next several years on a 32-foot boat? And more to the point, how could we afford to do it?

California was having its share of problems as we were getting ready to depart. Interminable rains, mud slides, fires, and a nearby earthquake made us relish the fact that we were living on a boat. We experienced a tremendous feeling of freedom when we winnowed our possessions down to what would fit in a small storage unit. We never realized how much time was involved in maintaining our acquisitions.

We knew that we liked the cruising lifestyle. We had cruised in Mexico for two, six-month seasons in the eighties in our 32-foot boat, spent a summer going north to the Sacramento Delta, and explored the islands off Southern California for many weeks—and no trip was ever long enough. We always felt that there wasn't enough time to investigate each anchorage thoroughly because eventually we had to return to our shoreside responsibilities.

Gradually, we realized that if we closed our businesses (the recession in California made this easier to do than we thought) and got rid of all the things that made it necessary to keep returning home, then we could go cruising until we tired of it.

I suppose that Hal and I have never been considered the average American couple. Purposefully childless, with no unpaid credit card bills, and being content to cruise in a small boat made it easier for us to take off. We contemplated buying a larger boat, but chose to stay with *SpiceSea* in part because she was paid for and equipped with most of the bells and whistles normally featured on larger boats: autopilot, watermaker, weatherfax, and single-sideband. We had cruised on her for several years and knew her to be safe.

Finally, my sister Tricia offered to take care of our finances for us while we were gone. Having a trusted family member or close friend to help you stateside is one of the most important factors in being able to depart. Tricia agreed to contact us once a week on the single-sideband radio. We had aging parents we worried about and they agreed to keep in touch with Tricia. Without her, we would have had to fly home and resolve problems that arose in our absence.

It's amazing how little one needs to spend when cruising. We were lucky, though, that Hal's mechanical skills helped us avoid expensive repairs. Our major expenses were fuel, food, laundry, and routine boat maintenance. Of course, the longer one cruises, haulouts and equipment replacement can become more expensive. We used credit cards to get cash advances and replaced our travelers checks on our trips back to the States.

We were able to earn some money while cruising, which greatly helped offset some of our expenses. We wrote, took photographs, and lectured about cruising, and Hal became a noted weather specialist whose weatherfax classes were in demand. I had completed a cruising cookbook and was working on this book; selling cookbooks and giving provisioning seminars helped support our lifestyle.

We tried to simplify our lifestyle and, although we may not have lived in luxury, we were doing what we wanted to do. All our experienced cruising friends had told us to go while we were still young enough to enjoy it. In retrospect, coping with Hal's illness and death, I echo this philosophy most emphatically.

Provisioning and Preserving

The tendency for the long-distance cruiser to overprovision is universal. You are nervous about leaving family and friends; you are nervous at the thought of not having a car to get to a grocery store; you are nervous about shopping in strange cities and countries; you are nervous about experiencing strange foods. The result? You shop 'til you drop!

The fact that people eat everywhere in the world is easily forgotten as your boat sinks lower and lower into the water under the weight of provisions. Here are a few provisioning tips I've learned:

- Ideally, you should have enough food on board to make a long passage or to make a prolonged stay in isolated anchorages. Estimate how long your longest passage will be and add an additional 20 percent. For example, if you think you can make the South Pacific from Mexico in 30 days, add an additional six days to your meal planning.
- Become familiar with the laws of the countries you will be entering. Just as you cannot bring raw pork and eggs into the United States, you can't bring meat (even canned) or seeds into New Zealand and Australia. New Zealand also prohibits honey. I have heard horror stories from cruisers who have had to throw away hundreds of dollars of food because they weren't aware of importing restrictions.
- Before you leave, try to learn which foods are especially expensive where you'll be cruising—and which are especially cheap. Many of the food items that we're accustomed to in the United States are not available in the Caribbean, where provisioning can be very

expensive. Food in Mexico, however, is very reasonable. (And so is certain liquor. Friends of mine recently bought several bottles of Ron Rico Rum in Mexico for $1.25 per liter. When they got to Bora Bora, the same rum was selling for $38.50 per liter.) Cruisers all over the world are happy to share their learning experiences. Take advantage of someone else's lessons.

- When stored for a long time, especially on a boat, dry foods get moldy, spices lose their flavor, cans rust, nut meats grow rancid, and bugs infest pasta, beans, and flour. The tropical sun helps to spoil food even more quickly than normal. The quality of most food starts to deteriorate when stored more than a year—so it's a good idea to write the purchase date on your packages and cans with indelible ink. (My friend Jane on *Stormy Petrel* marks every can left on the boat at the end of the year with that year's date. When she reprovisions, she knows that the unmarked cans are from the current year.) Always discard any cans that show signs of leaking or that bulge.
- Keep a master list of staples that you always want on board. When you deplete an item on the list, cross it off so you remember to replace it the next time you shop. The list might include such items as flour, sugar, baking powder, baking soda, bread crumbs, corn meal, cornstarch, dry milk, yeast, coffee, tea, cereal, pasta, beans, rice, oil, vinegar, mustard, pickles, mayonnaise, and catsup. These items are available worldwide so there's no need to overprovision with them. Instead, save valuable storage space for specialty items that probably won't be readily available, such as sun-dried tomatoes, dried cranberries, pesto sauce, Nori, mild green chiles, and white wine Worcestershire.
- Before you leave for a long trip, keep track of the items you use at home because you probably won't change your eating habits at sea.
- Try to find a cookbook that will help familiarize you with the cuisine of the area you will be cruising. Try local ingredients. Find out what the indigenous population is eating. In Mexico, beans are cheap, pasta is expensive. Ask a local person how to cook some-thing that you are not familiar with. Visit the hawker stands and watch carefully as they prepare the local specialty; have fun trying to duplicate the dishes when you get back to the boat. I fondly remember the Mexican woman in a market in La Paz who told me how to prepare verdolaga, an interesting green that I learned to enjoy south of the border, and I still use the batter recipe for fish tacos that I got from a hawker's stand in Ensenada. Worldwide, cooks are flattered when they're asked for their recipes and will usually share their secrets.
- Save small containers that will hold a week's worth of commonly used ingredients. When you need a tablespoon of powdered milk, it's much simpler to grab a margarine tub out of the cupboard than search for a gallon container under the V-berth.
- When cruising in Thailand aboard a friend's boat, I asked several long-term yachties who had been cruising around the world which products were the most difficult to find outside the United States. At the top of their lists were brown sugar, canned beef, canned chicken, canned tomatoes, canned bacon, and chocolate chips. Cereal is expensive everywhere, and Parmesan cheese is often hard to find. (Queso Anejo in Mexico makes a good substitute for Parmesan, by the way.)
- Make a list of which spices you use. I would be lost, for example, without Lawry's Lemon Pepper. I use it on fish, chicken, pork, potatoes, and green vegetables. But don't bring along too much of any one spice. Even when they are kept covered and in a dark place they are prone to molding or losing their flavor.
- Look for products that take up little space and keep well. Powdered Sweet and Sour Mix is sold in some liquor stores and is excellent for making mixed drinks. Dry taco and chili mixes are hard to find in foreign ports, but be careful of how much you bring—bugs love them. If you can, vacuum-seal dry mixes to preserve freshness and keep out the bugs.
- Cruising gives you the opportunity to try new recipes. When you read this book, keep a list of

ingredients that are new to you. Perhaps you've never cooked with Vietnamese rice paper (banh trang), which is used to wrap spring rolls. The paper is sold dry and keeps indefinitely, so it's an excellent item to keep on board.

- Learn which foods do not have to be refrigerated. Many items that all of us keep in the refrigerator at home can be stored at room temperature. Mayonnaise, pickles, mustard, and jelly will keep at room temperature, as long as you are very careful never to put a dirty spoon in the jars. If you lick the spoon and then scoop out some mayonnaise, bacteria will start growing and the mayonnaise will spoil.

Life Without Lettuce

In many places in the United States you can purchase most of the ingredients you want 365 days of the year. In many other countries, though, the only foods that you'll find readily available are the ones that are in season locally.

Learning to substitute is an important part of learning to be a cruising chef. Friends who have sailed halfway around the world mentioned that Thailand was the first place where they couldn't find string beans, but asparagus was available—what a nice substitution. When you can't find peaches, eat mangoes; when you can't find apples, try Asian pears. If you have a favorite abalone recipe, try substituting conch or squid.

Flexibility is the name of the game. There's no reason why you can't use pork instead of beef, or cauliflower instead of broccoli, or cabbage instead of lettuce in most recipes. I prefer fresh herbs, but that doesn't prevent me from using dried ones when that's all that is available.

When loading the boat in preparation for a long weekend away from the dock, the refrigerator becomes the focus of all of my planning. I store the meat and fish first, followed by a few beers. Then I get out the shoehorn as I start wedging in the dairy products. And there sits the shopping bag filled with fresh veggies.

There is never enough room in our small refrigerator for all of the fresh produce that I like to pack for a weekend away, let alone for an extended cruise. I have found, however, that with careful planning we can enjoy wonderful salads and save the refrigerator for storing only the most perishable of items.

For added shelf life, I wrap my vegetables in newspaper. When the paper begins to get damp, I rewrap it. If I'm short of paper, I hang the damp paper in the sun to dry. The paper helps to extend the life of lettuce, carrots, cauliflower, broccoli, and cucumbers.

Sometimes, no matter what you do, produce stays fresh for weeks—at other times, it spoils in just a few days. But anytime you can buy produce that's never been refrigerated it will keep much longer—especially when it's being stored at room temperature. For example, a head of napa cabbage that has been previously chilled will rot, usually from the inside out, within several days; a head of napa that has never been refrigerated will last up to two months.

I find, though, that even buying at farmer's stands doesn't always guarantee that the produce has never been refrigerated. Even in third-world countries produce is now coming to the market refrigerated.

For longer trips, it's critical to buy the very freshest products available. I scout out a nearby farmer's market where the growers do the selling because most of their products are picked that morning or the day before. I've had good luck keeping produce fresh by using a new, long-life produce-storage bag that's on the market from New Zealand. There is a special mineral impregnated into the bags that retards ripening and preserves freshness. Evert-Fresh Bags can be ordered from Evert Fresh Corporation, P.O. Box 540974, Houston, TX 77254-0974 (phone 713-529-4593; fax 1-713-529-4594). You can also order the bags from Downwind Marine, 2804 Cañon Street, San Diego, CA 92106. The bags are available in three sizes and cost about $5.00 for 10 bags. I have had good luck with these bags, but the produce must be very dry and stored air tight for best results.

My basic produce provisioning starts with cabbage, onions, potatoes, garlic, and tomatoes. These are available in most areas of the world and I try to keep a good supply of each on board. I buy the more perishable produce, such as avocados, peppers, cucumbers, and celery, in smaller quantities and try to use them first. The following is a list of some of the fresh ingredients that I try to keep on board.

Cabbage, if stored in a cool place, can keep for up to two months. I wrap large, unblemished heads in paper towels. Try to buy untrimmed heads; the outer leaves help protect the cabbage from drying out and can be discarded before using. Remove only the number of leaves that you need and avoid cutting through the entire head. Knife cuts eventually cause the cabbage to deteriorate and dry out.

Purple cabbage enhances a salad with its texture and color. To avoid its taste overshadowing more delicate salad ingredients, I cut it into very fine shreds.

Napa cabbage has firm, tightly packed light green leaves and a slight celery taste. The curly top part of each leaf gives a lettuce-like appearance in salads and the bottom half of the leaves is shiny and very crisp. When diced, it adds great texture to any salad; when cut in finger-sized portions, it's good as a vegetable for dips; and when stir-fried with garlic and onions, it's a delicious hot vegetable.

Lettuce comes along only on the very shortest of excursions. If you are determined to have lettuce on board, ask your greengrocer not to trim some of the heads—they will stay fresher if the outer leaves are left intact. Lettuce is very fragile, especially compared with cabbage, so it should be stored away from anything that can bruise it. Wrap each head in paper towels for storage.

Jicama (HEE-kah-mah) is a must for salads. A crisp, sweet, white root vegetable shaped somewhat like a turnip and covered with a brown skin, it needs to be peeled before eating. For salads, I cut jicama into ½-inch cubes; for appetizers, I cut finger-size portions to accompany a dip. Jicama makes a fun finger food when sprinkled with hot red pepper and a squeeze of lime, and you can make a delicious slaw with matchstick pieces of jicama, tossed with your favorite dressing, and sprinkled with poppy seeds. I have stored jicama on the boat for a couple of months. They can also be substituted for water chestnuts in any stir-fry recipe.

Carrots will keep for several weeks in an open plastic bag, and larger carrots keep much better than smaller ones. For longer-term storage, wrap each carrot in a paper towel before putting it in plastic. When the weather is exceptionally dry carrots will shrivel if not misted occasionally with water. On the other hand, if they are too moist, they will rot. To recrisp dried, limp carrots, peel and slice them and place them in a Ziploc bag with enough water to cover; chill until firm. I once purchased carrots with the tops on when provisioning for a trip to Mexico and wrapped them tightly in a long-life bag (the carrots were in the bag, the tops were outside) and they were still crisp and fresh after six weeks.

Onions will keep for months on board if you buy very firm ones—soft, mushy onions have already started to deteriorate. If any of my onions start to sprout, I cultivate this little bonus and encourage an onboard garden so that eventually I have green onions for a salad. The green sprout, or a little bit of shaved onion, greatly perks up a tossed salad.

Garlic, a member of the lily family, is related to onions and shallots but has a more potent flavor, so it is most often used as a seasoning. The easiest way to peel garlic is to use the flat side of your knife or cleaver to press each clove until it breaks; then simply slip the peel off. Remember that the longer you cook garlic, the milder it tastes—but be careful not to burn garlic because it will acquire a bitter taste. The entire bulb is referred to as a head of garlic; it consists of smaller cloves that are broken off individually. Although available for sale in dehydrated forms—garlic salt, garlic powder, and little jars and tubes of rehydrated garlic—they are not even close substitutes for fresh cloves. If you purchase firm heads of fresh garlic they will keep on the boat for two to three months.

Potatoes are part of my stores at all times. Leftover baked potatoes are great the next morning when sautéed in a little olive oil. They make good salads and are a key ingredient in my veggie packs. When kept in a cool dark place they will keep for many weeks. Don't store potatoes with onions, though, because the moisture in the onions will cause potatoes to sprout.

Tomatoes are the quintessential salad ingredient. I buy Roma tomatoes (sometimes called Italian plum tomatoes) for the boat since they keep well and don't bruise easily. The smaller ones can be stored in egg cartons—a safe place during rough seas. For long trips, purchase very green tomatoes and allow them to ripen on the boat. I have been able to keep tomatoes for six weeks when I've bought them in various stages of ripeness.

Avocados are an extremely versatile food. They add richness to a salad, make a wonderful filling for sandwiches, and are the key ingredient in guacamole. If purchased when very firm, avocados will keep a week without refrigeration. With any luck at all, the refrigerator will become a bit empty as the avocados ripen and you can chill a few ripened ones for later use.

Bell peppers ripen quickly at room temperature, but they add so much color to a salad and have such great flavor that I invariably bring along a couple of red and yellow bells and use them the first week that we are out. Look for very firm, unblemished peppers for best storage.

Cucumbers will keep for three to four weeks at room temperature and add great flavor and texture to a salad. The seedless, hothouse variety are my favorite—just make sure that they are very firm to the touch when you buy them. When hothouse cucumbers are not available, I peel and slice cucumbers down the center and scoop out the seeds before cutting them.

Celery keeps for about a week at room temperature before it dehydrates. Even though it may no longer be crispy, it's fine for cooking in stews and veggie packs. Make sure there's plenty of air circulation wherever you store celery.

Green apples such as Pippin or Granny Smith keep their crisp texture for one or two months when stored in a cool, dark place. They are delicious chopped up in a salad, cooked for dessert, or eaten out of hand. Fuji apples are my favorite eating apple; they also store well and retain their crunch for many weeks.

Bananas are the most frequently eaten fruit in this country. They are high in nutrition, inexpensive, easy to store, and they taste good. They are always on my weekly shopping list since Hal and I usually eat a banana every day.

At home, with a large refrigerator, I never worry about overstocking this favorite fruit. When provisioning SpiceSea, I try to buy the greenest bananas I can find. If none have started to ripen by the time I get them to the boat, I put a few in a brown paper bag. Doing so hastens the ripening process. Despite what Chiquita Banana used to sing, you can store ripe bananas in the refrigerator for several days. Their skin turns black but their taste and texture is still very good. Bananas also can be frozen. Slice and freeze them for a snack or freeze overripe bananas for making banana bread later. When we are out on the boat for more than a few days, a big bunch of bananas can start to ripen faster than we can eat them. Without the luxury of a large refrigerator and freezer, I've had to find some creative means for using an overabundance of bananas. Slightly green bananas are best for baking, broiling, or sautéeing. Once they become yellow, they're good when sliced on top of the morning cereal. When they become really soft and the skin has blackened and the fruit flies start to hover, it's time to make Hal's favorite quick bread, which features bananas. (See page 192.)

Plantains (see page 8 for more information) look like large bananas but can't be eaten raw. Curried plantains are delicious with boiled rice and barbecued meat or fish.

Fresh ginger adds great flavor to many vegetables, including carrots and squash. Powdered ginger is no substitute, but there is no reason that you can't keep fresh ginger on board—it keeps in a container of dry sherry for years without refrigeration. Peel and slice a firm, unblemished root and place it in a widemouth container with a tight-fitting lid. Cover with an inexpensive dry sherry and store at room temperature. An additional bonus to storing your ginger in sherry is that the sherry acquires a delicate ginger flavor and is excellent in any marinade that calls for wine. Even when I'm living on land I store ginger root in sherry.

Provisioning with Fresh Herbs

I have always told my cooking students that the single most important thing they can do to change their recipes from the mundane to the gourmet is to use fresh herbs. While I carry lots of dried herbs and spices on board, fresh is always better. Basil and cilantro are two of my favorite fresh herbs and I have learned through trial and error some ingenious ways to preserve their flavor.

I adore fresh basil. When I'm on land I use it

in copious amounts. Knowing how difficult it is to find basil in many parts of the world, I've experimented with ways of keeping it on the boat.

I've finally discovered that, by chopping fresh basil and completely submerging it in olive oil, it will keep for months in the refrigerator. One of my favorite recipes is Bruschetta (page 170), but there's no substitute for the fresh basil it requires. Since the recipe uses both olive oil and basil, my carefully preserved basil works well.

When basil is in season, I also make Basil Pesto Sauce (page 167), which keeps for months in the refrigerator and can be frozen. The flavor of the fresh basil, once again, is preserved.

I am always on the lookout for fresh basil to replenish my supply when I'm cruising and it crops up in the most amazing places. In Loreto, Baja California Sur on the Sea of Cortez, I visited the downtown farmer's market where you can pick your own produce. I was told that there really wasn't anything to buy, but when I strolled around the garden I found basil growing in profusion. In La Paz I found it growing in the planters at Marina Pamira, shaded by the potted palms.

Cilantro, also called Chinese parsley, is the fresh growth of the coriander seed. It is an aromatic herb with delicate green leaves that is an important ingredient in Mediterranean, Asian, and Latin American dishes. Grinding the coriander seed produces a pungent herb which in no way resembles the taste of the fresh greens. Although cilantro is sold dehydrated and freeze-dried, the products have very little flavor. I've never found anything that duplicates the flavor of fresh cilantro.

For the uninitiated, cilantro often is described as "that awful soapy tasting herb in Mexican salsa." Some people have a strong aversion to its flavor, but for me it enhances salsa, salads, and many Oriental and Mexican recipes. Cilantro is an important ingredient in the dishes I prepare and I really miss it when it's unavailable.

While spending a summer cruising Southern California's Channel Islands, I frequently asked friends to bring me fresh cilantro when they came to visit. It usually lasted two or three days before it got slimy and had to be thrown away. Sometimes it had already started deteriorating before I even got it aboard *SpiceSea*.

I tried storing it in paper towels in the refrigerator—and it still got slimy. I stored it with the stems in water at room temperature—and the stems got slimy while the leaves dried out. I tried chopping it and storing it in oil, like I do my basil—no flavor. Then my friend Jeri brought me a bunch of fresh unwashed cilantro in a jar and it kept for a month in the refrigerator. No more green slime! I've since discovered that if I occasionally open the storage container and dry it out, the cilantro keeps even longer.

Now I can keep a steady supply of fresh cilantro on board to make fresh salsa, guacamole, ceviche, and many other wonderful Mexican dishes. I store cilantro in a rectangular Tupperware container that easily fits into our small Norcold refrigerator; it works as well as Jeri's glass jar, but since it isn't transparent I have to remember to check it for excess moisture every few days.

I've created a few successful sauces with cilantro as one of the primary ingredients; all of them can be made in advance and stored in the refrigerator without the cilantro flavor deteriorating. (Green Chile Pesto, page 168, and Cilantro Garlic Marinade, page 177.)

What is That?

One of the challenges of cruising in foreign ports is knowing how to make use of ingredients that may be new to you. The following is a list of some fruits and vegetables that may not be common where you live.

Breadfruit is eaten like a vegetable, despite its name, and is most often cooked like a potato. It has a tough, yellowish green and bumpy or prickly skin and can weigh up to 10 pounds—an impressive sight hanging from a tree. It is an important food source in both the South Pacific and the Caribbean.

Breadfruit is often served boiled without any seasoning and has little flavor when eaten this way. It is, though, delicious when French fried or baked and served like mashed potatoes with butter. Try it cold with mayonnaise, onions, and some bell pepper, or make a mock potato salad. Use your favorite scalloped potato recipe for a special treat.

Diane on *Sorcery* dices and boils breadfruit and makes a sauce with ¼ cup of Dijon mustard, 1 tablespoon of vinegar, and 2 tablespoons of olive oil which she mixes with the warm vegetable.

My friend Linda on *Green Dolphin* has cruised for a number of years in the South Pacific and never throws away the porous center of the breadfruit after she cooks it. Instead, she suggests that you close your eyes and imagine that you are eating an artichoke heart. Dip it in mayonnaise—it's delicious.

The Tongans throw breadfruit in a fire and let them blacken on the outside for about 1 hour. They eat the breadfruit as is, but Linda always brings her own salt and pepper and a little butter to one of their feasts.

Callaloo, also known as elephant's ear, are the leaves of the taro plant. They can be up to 3 feet long and are heart-shaped. You always want to use the small, young leaves because the more mature leaves contain a great deal of oxalic acid, which burns your throat and makes it difficult to breathe. Callaloo tastes somewhat like spinach and can be used as a substitute for spinach in any recipe—just steam the leaves for 10 to 15 minutes. Callaloo isn't as watery as spinach, though, so always add a little extra liquid when using it as a substitute.

The leaves are also popular for wrapping fish or meat and cooking in the fire—they keep the meat moist and there's no aluminum foil to dispose of!

Chayote, christophene, or mirliton is a small, pear-shaped squash that varies in color from white to pale green. It has a very mild flavor that is enhanced when combined with onions and garlic. (Of course, there aren't many vegetables that aren't enhanced by adding onions and garlic!) Peel the tough outer skin, slice it in half, and remove the pit. Cook it like you would zucchini.

Coconut is a familiar fruit to most of us in its dried state. For the cruiser in tropical waters, however, it can be a challenge to expose the delicate white meat inside the husk. Hal loves to "go native" and shinny up a coconut palm, pick the mature fruit, and open it. The easiest method is to dig out two of the eyes with a sharp instrument. Drink the thirst-quenching water inside before continuing.

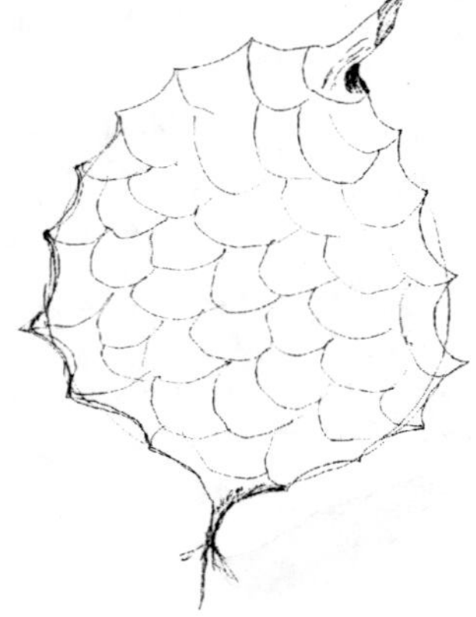

Strike the large fruit onto a rock and break away the thick husk. Continue banging the outside until the husk comes free and the meat is exposed. Vigorously tap the entire surface of the shell with the flat side of a cleaver or a flat rock. Then split the shell with a sharp blow from a hammer or rock. Pry the meat from the shell using a spoon or knife.

To make coconut milk, a delicious ingredient in many tropical drinks and curries, it is not necessary to remove the thin brown outer skin on the coconut meat. Break the coconut into 1-inch pieces and process in a blender with an equal quantity of hot water. Purée until fairly smooth, stopping the blender and scraping the sides frequently. (You can also grate the meat by hand, stir in hot water, and allow to steep for five minutes.)

Strain the coconut milk through a cheesecloth and then wring the last drops of the liquid out of the pulp. One cup of coconut pulp and 1 cup of water yields about 1 cup of coconut milk.

Guava are small, pear-shaped fruit that are native to tropical America. They are between 2 and 5 inches in diameter and can be eaten raw or stewed. They make excellent preserves and jelly.

Mango is one of my favorite fruits. It has a peachlike consistency and an excellent flavor. To peel a mango, stand the fruit with its stem end up. Make two cuts down the length of the fruit as close to the flat sides of the seed as possible. Score these two halves into cubes, cutting almost through the skin, and lift out with a spoon, leaving the skin behind. The flesh left around the seed can be peeled and eaten with the juice dripping down your chin and onto your hands! Messy, but delicious.

Nopales or cactus leaves. (See page 150 for information on nopales.)

Plantains, which look like large bananas, are more versatile, but not as sweet. In Latin America, where the name for banana is *plantano,* the plantain is called *plantano macho.*

When a plantain is not ripe you can cook it like a potato—boiled in salted water. It is difficult to peel, however, when it is not ripe. Try slicing off the ends and cutting it in half through the width. Then make four lengthwise cuts in each half through the skin. Lift the skin away from the fruit, a strip at a time, pulling off the skin on the diagonal rather than trying to pull it off down the length.

Plantains, when either ripe or not, make great fried chips. Deep-fat fry a few slices at a time, until golden. Sprinkle with salt and serve warm.

Pickle weed and sea spinach, although not available in markets, can be found near the shore of many beaches. Sea spinach has a robust spinachlike flavor, but use only the green leaves and soak them well to get rid of excess salt and any sand. Cook like you would fresh spinach.

Pickle weed grows a little farther back from the beach. Its tubular leaves look like miniature pickles. Run your fingers up the stalk to gather the leaves; rinse well and discard any of the yellowish unripened leaves. Eat only the jade-green colored leaves. Sauté in garlic and olive oil or butter.

Soursop is a large, dark green, heart-shaped fruit with spiny skin. Huge black seeds inside soursop make it difficult to eat. The juice, though, is excellent in drinks. Try it with rum.

Taro is a tuberous plant root about the size of a baking potato. It is covered with a dark brown barklike skin. The firm flesh has a mild, nutty taste and, when cooked, can be white, green, gray, or violet. You can substitute taro in breadfruit recipes.

Tomatillo or tomate verde resembles a small green tomato enclosed in a papery husk. The vegetable is a member of the eggplant family. Remove and discard the husk before washing it. The slightly tart flavor makes an excellent sauce when cooked (see Tomatillo Sauce, page 166) and is excellent raw, sliced in salads. Tomatillos keep for several weeks without refrigeration.

For a delicious salad, dice ½ pound of tomatillos with ½ pound of jicama. Season with ¼ cup of lime juice and a finely chopped jalapeño chile. Or, serve equal quantities of tomatillo and tomato with a little chopped onion and a vinaigrette dressing.

Verdolaga or purslane is a low-trailing succulent herb sometimes used in salads. I first discovered verdolaga in a market in La Paz where a busy housewife patiently explained how to cook it. I had never heard of purslane, which is the English word for this mildly tart green, but a friend told me that her grandmother used to dig it up when it grew between the paving stones in her yard. It is a sprawling weed that grows vigorously in the west in the late spring.

Verdolaga is delicious chopped up and sautéed in olive oil with garlic, onion, and cilantro. It can also be lightly steamed and served with a little lemon juice and olive oil.

Emergency Salads

Delicious salad makings can be part of your onboard emergency rations. As you walk along the gourmet aisle of any large supermarket you can fill your cart with salad items that are good for long-term unrefrigerated storage. Here are a few emergency salad suggestions:

- Garbanzo beans, pickled cauliflower, sun-dried tomatoes packed in oil, and sliced black olives make a lovely salad. Use some of the oil from the tomatoes and some of the vinegar from the cauliflower for the dressing.
- Combine cans of cut green beans, whole kernel corn, and roasted red peppers with thinly sliced fresh onions and bottled Italian salad dressing.
- Cans of julienne cut beets and sliced water chestnuts make an attractive presentation and will satisfy a craving for a salad.
- For a gourmet salad presentation, combine canned marinated artichoke hearts and button mushrooms with a can of sliced carrots. Or, try dilled green beans and baby corn for a cold veggie fix.

- If you hunger for tuna salad and are out of fresh veggies, mix 4 ounces of chopped Ortega chiles, 4 ounces of chopped ripe olives, 16 ounces of stewed tomatoes, and 14 ounces of tuna. Spice it up with a little red chile salsa if desired, and you have a Mexican-style tuna salad made totally with canned ingredients.
- Roasted nuts and seeds add great flavor to salads and store well on board. Shelled sunflower seeds, peanuts, pine nuts, and walnuts are my favorites and can be sprinkled on canned vegetables to provide some crunch.
- Eggs keep on board for many weeks in the refrigerator. They can be hardboiled and chopped and sprinkled on the top of a salad for a great taste.

When you have just a few fresh ingredients, you can improvise all kinds of salads by adding some cans or jars of "fun" food:

- Tuscan Chicken Salad: Sliced grilled chicken breast, shredded cabbage, canned roasted peppers, and penne pasta with vinaigrette dressing.
- Tostada Salad: Place shredded cabbage, cheese, canned black beans, guacamole, and salsa on a crisp corn tortilla.
- Mediterranean Salad: Chopped greens, salami, mozzarella, black olives, artichoke hearts, tomatoes, and roasted peppers in Lemon-Garlic Dressing (page 174).
- Salad Supreme: Sun-dried tomatoes, sliced pears, roasted walnuts, and blue cheese with vinaigrette dressing.
- Roasted Eggplant Salad: Slices of grilled eggplant, mozzarella, fresh basil, mixed greens, and roasted pine nuts in Tomato Vinaigrette (page 175).

Sprouts

I literally have an onboard garden. Sprouts are an ideal boat food because they are high in nutrition, they take up very little space, and the seeds will survive for years. Although I don't use my sprouter every time we go boat ing, I do keep seeds and my sprouter on board and get it out when the veggies start dwindling.

You can buy seeds in health food stores. Downwind Marine, 2804 Cañon Street, San Diego, CA 92106 (619-224-2733) has a wonderful assortment of seeds and sprouters and they will mail order. Never use seeds from a garden shop or catalog because they are treated with a fungicide. Health food stores also sell perforated lids that fit over a standard canning jar. Or, you can make your own lid from a piece of cheesecloth.

General sprouting directions

1. Pick over the seeds and throw away any debris and broken seeds.
2. Soak 1 tablespoon of seeds with enough water so they are completely covered in a clean glass jar for 6 to 8 hours; drain.
3. Rinse the seeds twice a day and drain well. I have had problems in the tropics with the seeds rotting due to excess moisture, so I lay the jar on its side and prop up the bottom so that any water can run out of the lid. There are lots of nutrients left in the soaking and rinsing water, so you may wish to drink it or use it when making soup.

Alfalfa sprouts, mung beans, and sunflower sprouts are the most popular and easiest to grow. Alfalfa are great in sandwiches and salads; 2-inch sprouts take about five days to grow. Mung beans can be stir-fried or used in salads; they grow to 2 inches in three to four days. Sunflower sprouts are a tasty addition to salads; they take five to six days to grow to 4 inches in length. Rinse off the black sunflower hull before using.

Don't grow any sprouts in direct sunlight—but once they've grown to harvesting size, do place them in sunlight to encourage chlorophyll to develop. Mist them lightly with fresh water to prevent them from wilting.

After you have some experience growing sprouts, branch out and experiment growing different kinds. I've had luck sprouting garlic, dill, onion, flax, fenugreek, and chia. Each variety has its own sprouting schedule, so each seed should be sprouted separately.

Wine Vinegar

This is a hard-to-find item in many cruising ports outside of the United States and Europe. Check the cap of the bottles for rust and deterioration, though, because the acid in the vinegar and the moisture in the boat can combine to eat away a metal can quickly. All vinegars keep indefinitely, but I prefer the milder flavors of wine vinegar.

Besides being useful in salad dressings and marinades,

wine vinegars are invaluable when you suddenly have too many fresh vegetables on board. To preserve fresh vegetables, pickle them with vinegar (see Chapter 8, page 151, for directions).

Never Running Out of Fresh Bread

It's hard enough keeping fresh bread on board for a weekend getaway, let alone for an extended cruise. Sandwich bread stales quickly and molds in the marine environment even faster than it does at home.

Unsliced bread will keep for two weeks if sprayed with white vinegar. Spray all of the cracks and crevices, allow to dry thoroughly, and wrap in plastic. The taste of vinegar disappears once the bread is dry.

If bread is stored in a plastic bag, keep it out of direct sunlight because the sun will cause moisture to form in the bag. (If this happens, open the bag and allow the bread to dry out.) Bread kept in the refrigerator quickly becomes dry and hard. If stored in the freezer, though, it stays fresher.

If you don't have the time or inclination to make yeast breads, the following breads offer quick solutions.

- Quick Loaf is an instant bread that takes 30 seconds to make and 50 minutes to bake. All you do is add 12 ounces of club soda or beer to the mix, stir, and bake. Nothing could be easier. The result is a fragrant loaf that tastes like old-fashioned homemade bread. It is crunchy on the outside and chewy on the inside. Quick Loaf is available in several flavors including Garlic and Herbs, Hearty Cracked Wheat, Cinnamon Raisin, Honey Oatmeal, Onion Dill, and Nine Grain. There are no preservatives, no artificial ingredients, no fat, and no cholesterol.

  Unlike most quick breads, Quick Loaf slices easily and holds together well, making it an excellent bread for sandwiches; it also makes great toast. Quick Loaf is available at many chain stores, or you can order it by calling 1-800-635-5668. The manufacturer's address is P.O. Box 1091, Port-smouth, NH 03802-1091. A three-loaf sampler, including postage, is $10.50. The price for a 12-bag case, including shipping, is $38.00. The shelf life is at least one year.

Two other long-lived bread products are Mediterranean Magic Pizza Bases and Focaccia (a thicker bread round), imported from Italy by Ferrara Foods. There are two thin pizza bases in each pizza package and one thick round in each focaccia package. Both items are vacuum-sealed in aluminum foil packages that keep at least a year and are perfect for the boat.

I brush the rosemary-flavored focaccia with a little olive oil and bake it until slightly crisp. You could also rub the bread with some fresh garlic and sprinkle it with Parmesan cheese. It's an especially delicious bread with soups and stews. For boats without ovens, the bread can be heated with a little olive oil in a shallow frying pan until it's lightly browned on each side. Because so many traditional pizza toppings keep well on a boat, I can whip up a pizza at a moment's notice as long as I have plenty of pizza bases on board.

The bread and pizza come in cartons of 10 for $31.50 plus shipping. You can order them from Marbella Farmers' Market at 31109 Rancho Viejo Road, San Juan Capistrano, CA 92675. To order by phone, call 714-248-0838, or you can fax them your order at 714-248-3450. If you order via fax, include your credit card number, mailing address, number of cartons, and type of bread desired.

Reduced Cream

I always keep a few containers of reduced cream on board. A popular dairy product in many parts of the world, it is like a very thick evaporated milk. I was first introduced to reduced cream in Mexico where it is called Crema, but I have also found it in Australia, New Zealand, and all over the South Pacific. Both Carnation and Nestle package it in cans or in an irradiated form in what is called a soft can. To make sour cream add a few squeezes of lemon or lime juice and allow to rest for 30 minutes before using.

Crema can also be used right out of the can as a topping for enchiladas, tostadas, and other typical Mexican dishes, or it can be used in casseroles and desserts. When chilled for several hours it can be beaten to the consistency of soft whipped cream which, when spooned over fresh strawberries and sprinkled with brown sugar, makes a delicious and easy dessert that everyone will love.

Butter

Canned butter from New Zealand and Ireland is fabulous. Look for it in the South Pacific, in former English colonies, and in many third-world countries where butter is not produced in much quantity.

Cheese

Many types of cheese store well on board. Following is a list of some of the best, and some tips on how to store them.

Cheese Food/Velveeta stores for about a year with no refrigeration. Although this is my least favorite cheese, it does make a quick appetizer if you melt it with a jar of salsa or chili and serve with chips.

Canned Brie or ***Camembert*** can be purchased in some stores. Check inside the package that the cheese is actually inside a can and not in a cardboard container.

▲ **WASHINGTON STATE UNIVERSITY CREAMERY**, Food Quality Building, Pullman, WA 99164-6392, offers a variety of excellent quality canned cheeses. For an easy hors d'oeuvre, serve slices of their smoky cheddar, sweet basil, hot pepper, or dill-garlic cheese. They also sell Cougar Gold cheese, which has a nutlike flavor similar to Swiss, and Viking cheese, which is a semisoft, mild white cheese much like Monterey Jack.

As they get older, the flavor of the university's canned cheeses becomes more pronounced. The creamery staff recommend storing their cheese in a cool place—preferably at about 40 degrees. We cruised for two years in Mexico, however, with the cheese stored in a compartment below the waterline and had no problem, even in that warm climate.

The cheeses come in 30-ounce tins and sell for $10.00 each; shipping is extra. Write for an order form or call 509-335-4014.

Parmesan cheese, when of good quality, can be vacuum-sealed and will keep without refrigeration for a couple of years.

Cheddar cheese, as well as other firm cheeses, can be preserved by placing as much of the cheese as possible into a clean jar with a tight fitting lid. Cover the cheese with vegetable oil (it must be completely submerged in the oil). Close the jar and store at room temperature for up to six months. Do not reuse the oil for more cheese, but it is fine to use it for cooking.

Cream cheese is one of the most convenient foods to have on hand for appetizers. Its flavor blends well with many ingredients and it's great as a spread on crackers or bread. It keeps for several months in the refrigerator or up to one year if vacuum-sealed.

Yogurt cheese is a good substitute for cream cheese. It has a short shelf life but can be made on board (see page 37).

Feta cheese can be used as a topping for salads, pasta, vegetables, and fruits. Stir it into hot cooked rice, sprinkle it on baked potatoes and pizza, blend it into tomato sauce, and crumble it into stuffings.

The principle difference between feta and other cheeses is that feta is cured in a brine solution. It is during this "pickling" process that the high acid level develops in feta that gives it its long shelf life. The brine that feta is packed in prevents molding and drying—both of which spoil cheese. I recently opened a package of feta that had been stored for more than a year on board (in the refrigerator) and it tasted great! Although the stated shelf life is normally six months, I can attest that in some cases it lasts much longer.

▲ **NEW ENGLAND CHEESE MAKING SUPPLY CO.**, Box 85, Main Street, Ashfield, ME 01330, has a catalog of products available to help you make cheese on board, including cheese presses, cheese starters, and mold powders. The yogurt cheese funnel (see Chapter 3, page 37) is available for $9.95. Call 413-628-3808 or fax 413-628-4061 to order a catalog or to place an order using Visa or MasterCard.

Eggs

The egg is one of nature's most nourishing foods; it contains everything needed for life except vitamin C. Eggs are a useful food source

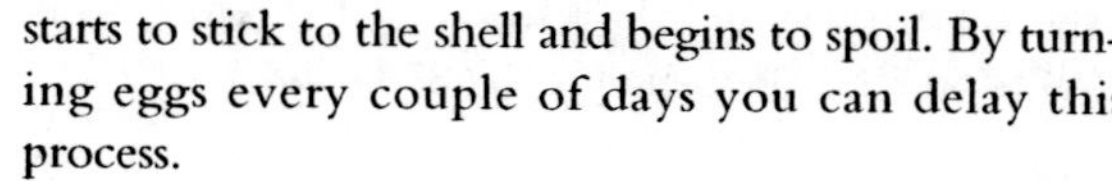

on a boat because they are inexpensive, versatile, and fairly long-lasting.

I buy the freshest eggs available and, whenever possible, I purchase them unwashed because there is a natural preservative on the outside of eggs that is destroyed when washed. (Eggs in third-world countries are almost always sold unrefrigerated and unwashed.) When I'm in the States I order my eggs from an egg ranch. I turn the eggs over every couple of days to keep the yolk from sticking to the shell and have had a lot of luck keeping them for as long as six weeks. I always break an egg in a separate container and give it the sniff test if it looks questionable. You can test an egg for freshness by placing it in a pan of water. If it sinks, the egg is fresh; if it floats, toss it out.

Freshly laid eggs may have salmonella bacteria on their shells. (Eggs that are sold in U.S. supermarkets have been carefully washed.) If you buy unwashed eggs, take special precautions to be certain that you do not contaminate your food. Always wash your countertops, utensils, and hands in hot, soapy water and be very careful that the eggshells do not come in contact with the contents of the eggs.

Salmonella reproduce rapidly in foods between 40° and 140° F. If foods containing uncooked eggs are held between these temperatures for more than one hour, the bacteria can multiply to hazardous levels. Symptoms of salmonellae poisoning are abdominal cramps, fever, headaches, nausea, vomiting, and diarrhea. Although the attacks are usually of short duration and rarely fatal, they can be more severe in the elderly, infants, and those with compromised immune systems.

Since salmonella is killed when food temperatures reach 140° F, thoroughly cooked foods such as baked goods, hard-boiled eggs, custards, and casseroles are safe. When preparing eggs and egg dishes that do not reach 140° F—scrambled, poached, soft-cooked and soft-fried eggs, cream pies, soft meringues, uncooked salad dressings, ice-cream mixtures, and raw egg drinks—you should be very careful to wash unwashed eggs just before using and to use eggs with no cracks.

Following are a few tips about handling eggs:

- An egg white holds the yolk in suspension. As the egg ages, the white gets thin and watery and can no longer suspend the yolk. As the yolk settles to the bottom of the egg, it starts to stick to the shell and begins to spoil. By turning eggs every couple of days you can delay this process.
- When an older egg is opened the yolk will not hold together, which makes it impossible to fry older eggs sunny-side up. They work fine, though, for scrambling and mixing with other ingredients.
- It is easier to separate a chilled egg than one that's at room temperature. When the egg is chilled, the fat in the yolk makes the yolk firmer and less likely to break.
- If there is even a speck of fat (egg yolk) in egg whites, they will not beat to firm peaks. Beat egg whites in a glass or stainless steel bowl—plastic or wooden bowls tend to absorb fat. Any film or residue on the bowl will keep the whites from obtaining a high volume.
- Sprinkle salt over a spilled egg for easier clean-up. The salt toughens the protein and firms the egg.
- An excellent way to preserve eggs is to hard-boil and then pickle them. (See page 26.) They will keep in the pickling solution for several weeks without refrigeration.

Powdered Eggs

With the scare of salmonella bacteria infecting eggs in the United States, it is no longer considered a safe practice to store eggs at room temperature. As a convenience item, Wakefield Brand Scrambled Egg Mix, packed in 6-ounce pouches (30 per case), is hard to beat. The product is a mixture of whole eggs, nonfat dry milk, vegetable oil, and salt. It is homogenized, pasteurized, and spray-dried, and has a shelf life of two years. Each package is equivalent to twelve eggs. The product can be used either as a replacement for liquid eggs in cooking or as a scrambled egg product. Two tablespoons of the mix and three tablespoons of water equals one egg.

You can make an incredibly easy quiche with a package of Wakefield's, some additional milk, and five cups of grated cheese.

A case of the Wakefield Scrambled Egg Mix is $29.95 plus $4.95 for shipping. Call 1-800-344-5463 to place your order and ask for a copy of their recipes.

Or, you can write to the Milton Waldbaum Company, P.O. Box 573, Wakefield, NE 68784-0573.

Chicken

Chicken seems to be the protein of choice in the United States these days. According to *Prevention* magazine, the average American eats almost seventy pounds of chicken per year. My father said recently that he consumed so much chicken that he no longer went to bed at night, but instead went to roost! Low in fat, cholesterol, and calories, a boneless skinless chicken breast is also a space saver on a boat.

Chicken's versatility is another reason for its popularity. It can be steamed, fried, boiled, broiled, stewed, poached, barbecued, and roasted. It combines well with vegetables and sauces but stands on its own sprinkled with just a little salt and pepper.

Chicken is extremely perishable and should be kept frozen or stored in the cold tray immediately under the freezer compartment. If no refrigeration is available, store chicken in the cooler, next to the ice, to keep it as cold as possible.

Because of the possibility of salmonella (see page 13) contamination, it is important to clean all of the surfaces and knives that come in contact with raw chicken with hot soapy water before using them in other food preparation tasks. Do the same with any containers that are used to marinate raw chicken. Once the chicken has been removed from the marinade, discard the marinade and wash the container thoroughly before reusing. A potentially dangerous practice when barbecuing chicken is to place the cooked chicken back in the unwashed container that was used for marinating. Don't do it! Bacteria can contaminate the cooked chicken.

Because chicken cooks quickly, stir-frying is an ideal way to prepare it. I use boneless, skinless breasts and find that it is much easier to cut them into bite-sized pieces if they are still partially frozen.

Goat

Although goat meat and the more tender kid is not popular in the United States, it is quite delicious. In many cruising areas it might be the only meat available. It is very common in parts of the Caribbean and in Latin America.

As I write this, we are anchored in the Sea of Cortez at Bahia Agua Verde, and the goats are making their daily pilgrimage across the foothills. Most cruisers assume that fresh meat is unavailable in this remote community, but in fact the ranchers would be happy to sell one of their goats, dressed and ready for the barbecue.

Young kid is delicious; it's tender and juicy like suckling pig. Older goat meat needs a lot of marinating. Jerked Goat (page 177), which is popular in the Caribbean, is a powerful marinade that both tenderizes the meat and adds lots of flavor.

Roasted Goat

John and Suzanne Pew, who owned the Sea Breeze Nautical Bookstore in San Diego before beginning their cruising life, once provisioned their Moorings charter boat in Mexico with a freshly dressed baby goat. Even though the goat was quite small, they said that the hardest part of preparing it was storing it in the refrigerator. Every time they opened the cold box for a beer, little legs would pop out and had to be stuffed back inside before they could secure the lid.

John and Suzanne marinated the meat in a large plastic trash bag. They made a vinegar and oil dressing (one part vinegar to two parts oil), flavored it with whatever herbs were around, added lots of black pepper and salt, and tossed it in the trash bag with the goat. Each night they dumped any wine that was leftover from dinner into the marinade and carefully turn the kid.

Finally, the big day arrived. They went ashore, built a fire, allowed it to burn down, and covered it with a grill. They placed the goat on the grill and roasted it, turning it frequently until it was golden and tender, basting the meat with the marinade throughout the cooking process. The goat was delicious and John and Suzanne freed up considerable space in the refrigerator!

Seafood

When buying seafood, always insist on the very freshest. Your nose is the best guide—there should be no fishy smell or ammonia-like odor. When you press the flesh of fresh fish it should feel firm and elastic. If the head is on, you can check for freshness by looking at the eyes. They should be clear, not cloudy. Also look for bright red gills; if they are a muddy gray the fish is not fresh.

If a fish is brought aboard alive and unbruised, and is immediately bled, cleaned, packed in ice, and kept at 32° F, it still tastes fresh after a week of storage. We have been given "fresh fish" by Mexican *pescadors* that was caught in the morning and allowed to sit in the sun during the day—by afternoon, the fish had already started to smell.

Fresh frozen seafood is often the best way to guarantee that the fish you are buying is of the best quality. Commercial fishing operations freeze many kinds of seafood immediately upon catching, and it often reaches the customer in better condition than seafood that is sold as "fresh." For the best flavor and texture, cook frozen fish without first thawing it.

On board *SpiceSea* we enjoy fresh seafood whenever possible. I never have to worry about checking the seafood for freshness, because Hal is an avid angler and frequently brings in enough fish for dinner.

Stocking Up

When stocking up for long-range cruising, it's a good idea to buy many of the convenience products you want in large quantities at discount stores before leaving home. Paper products, which make life so much easier, are expensive and often of inferior quality once you leave the States. Paper towels seem to dissolve in your hands, paper plates leak after a few seconds of use, and aluminum foil is tissue-paper thin.

The following is a list of supplies I keep on board *SpiceSea* and stock in quantity whenever we are leaving for Mexico.

Aluminum foil (heavy duty). A 75-foot roll lasts for six months to a year, depending on how many foil-wrapped dinners I prepare.

Disposable roasting pans. These are great for potlucks and beach parties.

Paper plates. Buy the ones that are somewhat water resistant. (It will say so on the wrapping.) I use about 1,200 plates a year. In small galleys, paper plates are very useful for food preparation. When assembling ingredients for a stew, for example, chop the onions and garlic on a plate and set it aside. Chop the carrots and celery on another plate and set it aside. Dredge the meat in seasoned flour on a paper plate and set it aside. Stack the plates on top of each other in the order of use, and then begin your cooking.

I don't like washing dishes in salt water. To conserve water on long passages I use paper plates for breakfast and lunch. If you have a microwave oven, paper plates can be used for reheating leftovers, cooking fish and chicken, and steaming vegetables (cover with a damp paper towel).

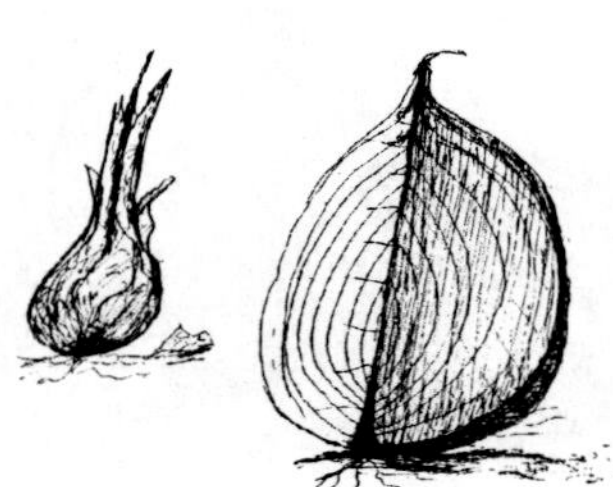

Paper towels and Handi-Wipes. These two items are indispensable on my boat. Thin paper towels are of little use, so I bring about twelve rolls of Bounty along (rationing one roll per month) and supplement them with reusable Handi-Wipes. The Handi-Wipes can be washed a few times, so they last much longer than paper towels. When passagemaking or when I'm far from laundry services, I use Handi-Wipes instead of dish towels to cut down on the amount of laundry that I am accumulating. Some cruisers hang only half a roll of paper towels at a time. Using a heavy knife, they cut through the towels and the cardboard roll.

Parchment paper. I use parchment paper to line baking sheets and save on clean-up. While you are waiting for one batch of cookies to bake, simply assemble the next batch on a precut piece of parchment paper the size of your baking sheet. There is no need to cool the cookies before removing them. Slip the baked cookies and parchment paper onto the counter and slip the next batch onto the baking sheet. The baking goes faster and there is no need for a second baking sheet. I use one-to-two rolls per year. Reusable Teflon baking sheets work even better and you can cut them to fit your baking sheet.

Ziploc bags. These are difficult to find in third-world countries. I use about 75 each of the quart and gallon sizes per year. To save space, you can fit two packages of bags into one box. If you don't like to keep boxes on board, store baggies in a large plastic bag, secure with a twist tie, and then remove a month's worth or so to keep handy in the galley.

Garbage bags. Any experienced cruiser will tell you that garbage bags on boats do more than simply stow garbage. They are essential when doing your laundry entails dinghying through choppy salt water. I remember Diane and Clyde on *Sorcery* getting flipped in the surf at Mexico's Bahia Chamela while all of their clean laundry floated away! On the next laundry day they brought garbage bags ashore and tied them tightly shut before negotiating the surf.

Garbage bags also double as quite fashionable outerwear. While cruising aboard *Green Dolphin* in Thailand, the wind blew spray every time we went ashore at Patong Beach. When it was time for me to leave for the airport, I wrapped up in a garbage bag and we put my duffel bag in one as well. I tried buying garbage bags in Patong and couldn't find any. I was glad that Linda was well supplied. A box of 48 garbage bags should last about a year. Get the heavy-duty ones—picking up old garbage because a bag has split is not fun.

Oven roasting bags. One box lasts me a couple of years. The bags are handy for doing roasts and stews in the oven.

Toothpicks. Bring along a box of toothpicks because you might only be able to find the really thin ones that break easily. Food that is steamed or fried can be held together with a piece of raw spaghetti rather than a toothpick. The pasta cooks and there is no toothpick to remove before eating!

Joy dishwashing detergent. Joy, or any coconut oil -based soap, cuts grease and will lather in salt water. If you wash your dishes in salt water you will use about 32 ounces of Joy per month for two people.

Nonskid. When underway, cover your table with nonskid. It's also useful in the galley when the seas are rough or the boat is heeled over.

Plastic dishpans. These are handy for many uses. I wedge one into the top of the galley sink, stow dirty dishes underneath it, and use the dishpan as a preparation area when seas are rough. You can also store bottles and cans in plastic dishpans in the bilge. The pans keep the cans dry and, if they rust, or a bottle breaks, the mess will be contained. I was glad I stored my supplies this way when a plastic bottle of cooking oil leaked. It was a mess, but at least the mess was contained in the dishpan and didn't spread throughout the bilge.

Canning jars and extra lids. These are difficult to find in many countries. If you have a pressure cooker, you might find yourself canning extra fish or ground meat when heading to the South Pacific. You can reuse the jars, but the lids must be replaced each time you can.

Trash Disposal and Trash Burning Fiesta

The accumulation of trash on a boat—even during a weekend at anchor—is a neverending problem. Returning to the marina with heavy sacks of trash and lugging them to the trash cans is a pain. At least in most parts of the States you are fairly certain that the trash will be correctly recycled and that the remainder will be disposed of properly.

That is not the case in many third-world coastal communities. I have seen cruisers carefully bag their trash for two weeks and then come ashore at a small town. After much searching, they finally find a trash receptacle and place what will fit into the container. The remainder is plopped near the trash bin. Before any municipal service comes along, stray dogs tear open the bags and scatter the contents. Then the afternoon wind comes up and plastic and paper blow down the streets. If there is someone responsible for disposing of the trash in these small communities, the contents of the trash receptacle and the loose bags are taken to a hill overlooking the ocean and dumped into a ravine where it eventually washes out to sea.

With this scenario in mind, Hal and I try to dispose of as much of our own trash as possible when we're not anchored near a major city. We save glass bottles until we are at least 12 miles out to sea, then fill them with sea water and drop them over the side. We dispose of our garbage when we're three miles out to sea. (By law, it must be in pieces smaller than an inch.)

In most third-world countries it is much cheaper to buy soft drinks and beer in returnable bottles, so we usually don't have a lot of aluminum cans to dispose of. (In Mexico you pay as much for the bottle as you do for the beer.)

We save disposable propane bottles, CO_2 cartridges, and aluminum foil until we find an appropriate disposal site.

I keep all burnable trash separate and when we get enough together, we plan an evening ashore at a deserted island or cove. With luck, Hal has caught a big fish and we can invite other cruisers to join us. We build a campfire and enjoy a potluck with new or old friends. Downwind of the party Hal builds a separate fire below the high tide line and burns all the trash. Stove alcohol makes lighting the trash fire a cinch. Before we go back to *SpiceSea* for the night, anything that did not burn (aluminum foil is our biggest problem) is gathered and taken back to the boat.

We have turned this chore into a fun outing. We go ashore at cocktail hour and enjoying the beauty of the setting sun. If we are lucky we may even stay long enough to witness the rising of the moon— and then we don't need flashlights to get back to the boat.

Hot dogs roasted on a stick, a can of Stagg chili heating right in the fire, and a little coleslaw on the side—simple food that tastes great around the campfire. (For a special treat try my recipe for Better Than S'mores, page 215).

Purifying Water and Cleaning Veggies

Several years ago, I attended a lecture in Cabo San Lucas about purifying water. The physician who gave the lecture, said that if amoebas contaminate the water where you are cruising, the only sure way to purify it is to bring it to a rolling boil and boil for 20 minutes. Bleach and iodine cannot be used in high enough dosages to kill this harmful bacteria.

To clean vegetables and fruit, wash them with soap and purified water, and rinse with purified water. Before eating, soak the food in a solution of one drop of microdyne to 1 liter of water. Shake out the excess water before consuming.

The physician told us that she had been born and raised in Mexico and had never drunk a glass of tap water in a restaurant—she drank only bottled water. She cautioned vigorously about eating the street foods, particularly if it was uncooked. When I questioned her more closely about never eating fresh salsa on a tortilla prepared by a street vendor, she did hedge a little. I guess even the doctor takes her chances with some of the tempting street food in Mexico.

A few years later, Hal and I happened to be studying Spanish in Antigua, Guatemala, which was having a severe cholera outbreak then. The father of the family we were living with was the chief health inspector for the town. Every Monday he gave us the statistics of how many people had died from cholera over the weekend in the town where we had just been sightseeing.

He instructed us to wash everything edible in a strong chlorine bleach solution and allow it to air dry before eating. (The bleach eventually evaporates so you don't taste it.) Oscar even recommended washing fruits and vegetables that you normally peel (such as avocados and oranges) because the skin could be contaminated, and when you cut into the fruit you risk contaminating the interior.

We spent a month with this family. There were fourteen of us eating three meals a day and never once was hot water used to wash the dishes—and never once did anyone get sick! A lot of chlorine bleach was used in the washing process, however.

My Spanish teacher in Antigua cautioned me about reusing the plastic bags that we put produce in. She said that once you wash the produce you must discard the bag because it may be contaminated. And of course, both of these Guatámalans advised against eating the food of the street vendors.

Mail-Order Sources for the Galley

Whether cruising in local waters for a few days or setting sail for a couple of years, stocking the boat with some easy-to-prepare specialty items will make meal preparation a lot more fun. Finding interesting foods that you can store on the boat is no easy assignment, though. We all keep a few emergency cans of Dinty Moore—which I am sure my husband would relish—but I dread the day when I have to actually open the can and eat it. My tastes run more to sun-dried tomato and goat cheese pasta sauce served on a bed of basil-flavored noodles.

There is nothing I like better on the boat than to be able to put together a delicious impromptu meal when friends stop by. So I try to keep *SpiceSea* stocked with nonperishable gourmet items. The following addresses will give you access to some of my favorite foods that aren't readily available in the local supermarket.

A word of caution before purchasing any new food items. Be sure you try the products first before you order a large quantity. You can order a few items to try from any of the above mail-order sources before you purchase them in quantity.

▲ **W.J. CLARKE AND COMPANY**, 5400 West Roosevelt Road, Chicago, IL 60650, produces the Foodways Catalog that lists all of their many products, including dried shitake, porcini, morel, and oyster mushrooms in 0.87 ounce cello bags. Throwing a few dried mushrooms in your pasta sauce makes it special. At cocktail time, serve one of their wild mushroom patés with crackers; the Cepes Wild Mushroom Caviar spread is $4.25 for a 4.75 ounce jar.

W.J. Clarke's Creamy Italian Risotto is a northern Italian rice dish that can be served as a main course or a side dish. I also recommend their Sun-dried Tomatoes and Peas or Milanese with Saffron. The 4.3 ounce packages sell for $4.00 each. You can order The Foodways Catalog by calling 1-800-229-0090. Visa and Mastercard are accepted; shipping is extra.

▲ **JUST DELICIOUS GOURMET FOODS**, 2481 East Orangethorpe, Fullerton, CA 92631 makes 15 different main course soups. Unlike most packaged foods, Just Delicious has no preservatives, salt, sugar, or MSG, making their products a healthy choice.

Try their Black Bean Chili, Jamaican Island, or Spicy Chicken Vegetable soups if you like your food on the spicy side. One of my husband's favorite soups is the Gourmet Minestrone, a thick, delicious blend of five dehydrated vegetables, macaroni, beans, peas, natural herbs, and spices. All of these soups stand on their own, or you can add some meat. Just Delicious also makes a variety of bottled salsas; their corn relish or chowchow make good accompaniments to the soups. Most items sell for about $5.00 a package, shipping included. Write for an order form or call collect 714-871-6081. They accept MasterCard, Visa, and American Express.

▲ **BUCKEYE BEANS AND HERBS,** P.O. Box 28201, Spokane, WA 99228-8201, has a mail-order catalog for their products. I particularly like their breads and pastas. Their Whole Wheat Beer Bread is a great companion to soup, and the Northwest Style Cornbread goes well with chili.

We like their Orzo Thyme, a pasta pilaf that features sun-dried tomatoes and herbs. The colorful noodles and blend of poppy seeds, sesame seeds, and herbs makes Poppy Sea'd Pasta a delicious addition to any meal. As a side dish use as packaged; for a main course seafood dish, add some fresh vegetables and shrimp. They also sell pasta in the shape of dolphins, rabbits, hearts, and Christmas trees. What a fun gift for a friend, as well as a treasure to prepare in your own galley.

Prices range from $3.50 to $5.00; shipping is extra. Call their toll-free number 1-800-227-1686 for a copy of their catalog. Visa and MasterCard are accepted.

▲ **LA ESPAÑOLA**, 2020 Lomita Blvd., Bldg. 7, Lomita, CA 90717, is a meat processing company that makes a variety of delicious Spanish sausages, including chorizo, a Spanish sausage with garlic, paprika, and other spices. La Española makes several types of chorizo that will keep for many months without refrigeration. *Cantimpalo*-style is made with both pork and beef and seasoned with cayenne and cumin. It can be diced and added to cooked dishes, but to prevent it from drying out, add it to the dish just before serving. It's also good served sliced as a cold cut.

Their *Soria,* or Spanish Girl Sausage, is made of pork that is diced by hand and is milder in flavor than the Cantimpalo. Eat it sliced and in sandwiches or chop it fine and combine it with scrambled eggs. Prices range from $5.75 to $6.25 per pound, plus UPS charges.

Although Española vacuum-packs some of their meats, you may want to request that all of your order be treated this way for longer shelf life. The Lomo Embuchado is a cured pork loin, trimmed of all fat, and cured for up to 9 months. In thin slices and vacuum-sealed, it will keep for several weeks without refrigeration. For mail orders, call 310-539-0455, or ask for a copy of their catalog.

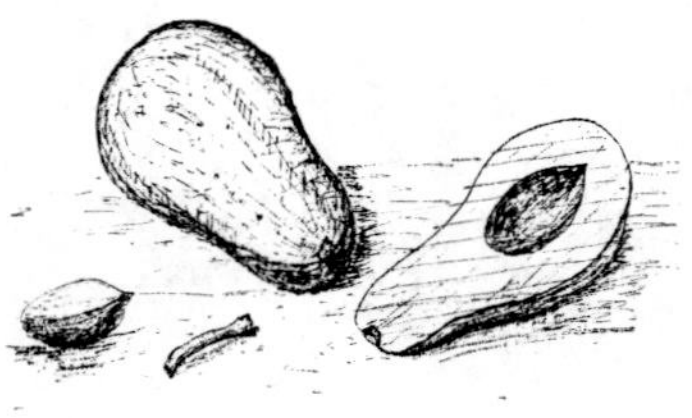

▲ **SHADE PASTA INC.**, 805 South Union, Fremont, NE 68025, makes instant lasagna noodles that need no precooking. You layer the raw noodles in the pan with sauce and filling, cover, and bake. The noodles come out light and delicate with no starchiness. You can also make manicotti rolls if you soak the noodles in warm water to soften, cut in half, spread with filling, and roll up. Not having to precook the pasta saves water, fuel, and work.

Pasta Defino No Boil Lasagna can be ordered for $16.50 per case (12 boxes), including shipping, by calling 1-800-662-645. Visa and MasterCard are accepted.

▲ **INDEPENDENT MICRO DIET ADVISOR,** P.O. Box 541, Keyport, NJ 07735, makes complete "instant" meals that come in mighty handy during rough passages, when cooking anything can be impossible. The meals contain one-third of an adult's daily nutritional requirements and all you need to do is rehydrate them with a little boiling water. (Keep hot water in a thermos.) The products are ideal for the on-watch crew when cooking is inconvenient or hazardous.

These products are similar to foods you can purchase in backpacking stores, but I think they are seasoned better and more nutritious. The entrée choices, which sell for $2.50 each, include Chili, Pasta Marinara, Pasta Tetrazzini, and Spanish Rice. Visa and MasterCard are accepted and orders can be placed by calling 1-800-578-1495.

▲

CHAPTER 2

Essential Galley Equipment

At times, Hal has accused me of trying to sink our boat. As a bachelor he needed only one pan in his entire bachelor pad—and that was to heat his Dinty Moore! Then he married me, a kitchen shop junkie. Although I'll never admit it to him, perhaps I do carry a few more pieces of cookware than the average cruiser—but as long as we can still see the waterline, I'll still stock my galley with what I consider the essentials!

I consider the following equipment to be essential aboard *SpiceSea:*

Flat-Bottom wok and bamboo steamers. If I could have only one cooking pot onboard, I would choose a wok. It is a triumph of Chinese engineering and has gone through few design changes during its many centuries of popularity. Its shape is ideal for boats since it makes economic use of whichever heat source you cook with: electric, alcohol, propane, or coals.

Although the three-burner propane stove that I now cook on is big enough for almost any pot, I still use the wok for much of my cooking. I prefer a medium-sized wok that's about 11 or 12 inches in diameter with a flat bottom and one long handle. That size stores easily (I keep mine in the oven), the flat bottom provides greater stability on board, and having only one handle takes up less space on the stove top. (Find a wok handle made from a nonconducting material to avoid burning your hand.)

The traditional material for a wok is cold-rolled steel. It is inexpensive and conducts heat fairly well but must be kept coated inside and out with oil or it will rust. Circulan makes an anodized aluminum wok with a Teflon coating that's ideal for a boat. The aluminum spreads heat better, the anodizing is permanent, and the Teflon makes a wonderful, easy-to-clean nonstick surface.

Bamboo steamers are excellent for reheating foods and steaming meats, fish, and vegetables. The stacking steamers consist of bamboo rings with woven bottoms and are usually sold in sets of two with a bamboo lid. When you stack bamboo steamers over boiling water in a wok you can steam several dishes simultaneously with one heat source and a small amount of water. When you aren't using the steamers they are perfect for storing fresh fruit.

Choose a steamer that best fits into your wok and that allows enough space to add a couple of cups of water. (I use 10-inch steamers for my 12-inch wok.) I line the steamers with cabbage or lettuce leaves and steam them for a few minutes before adding the food that is to be steamed. The leaves pick up the flavor of the food, are delicious as a vegetable accompaniment, and make cleanup easier. When finished, simply scrub the steamers with a soapy brush, rinse, and allow to air dry before storing. If stored while damp, they will mildew and you will need to bleach them before you can use them again.

You can make your own steamer by removing both ends of an empty tuna fish can, placing it in a wok, and putting a foil pie pan that's been punctured a few times with an ice pick on the top. Add 2 cups of water to the wok, bring to a boil, place the food to be steamed in the pie pan, cover the wok, and steam as directed.

Six-quart heavy-duty pot with lid. This is my basic cooking pot. It is just the right size to cook stews, soups, pasta sauces, and vegetables, and large enough to cook pasta and steam lobsters. I prefer stainless steel (for durability and ease in cleaning) with a bottom that has a core of a good, even, heat-conducting metal such as aluminum or copper. If the heat-conducting material is aluminum, do not let the bottom soak in salt water because the salt will eventually erode the aluminum. If you have a pressure cooker on board, it can double as your deep pot.

Teflon skillets. Over the years I have gone through a lot of cheap Teflon skillets. All Clad, Ltd., makes anodized aluminum skillets with very durable Teflon coatings that are heavy enough not to warp. I finally invested in two of their skillets—an 8-inch and a 10-

inch—that should last a lifetime. I have a lid that fits on both the 10-inch skillet and on top of my wok. I also have a spatter screen that fits over the 10-inch skillet—it saves on cleanup when frying bacon and sautéeing chicken breasts. I use my 8-inch skillet for making omelettes and crêpes.

Cast-iron skillet or griddle. Hal and I enjoy cooking on the beach and a cast-iron skillet can go right in the fire. It is great for cooking blackened fish on the barbecue as well. (See directions for blackened fish on page 69.)

Propane barbecue. I prefer a covered stainless steel propane barbecue such as the Magma Marine Cuisine Barbecue. Magma sells a variety of fittings to mount the grill permanently and securely on most boats. Our barbecue is probably the most often used piece of cooking equipment on the boat. When we're in port we have it mounted in the fishing pole holder so it doesn't take up precious deck space. It doubles as an oven, keeps the heat and mess out of the galley, and is (usually) tended to by someone other than the galley cook. A glass of wine and a kiss turns Hal into a super chef on the outdoor grill. (They also keep him out of the galley where there's only enough space for one body at a time.)

Although charcoal barbecues work fine, disposing of the coals and ashes can be a problem. Propane barbecues heat up much faster and you never have to worry about the coals burning down too much while you visit with friends over cocktails. The small disposable propane cylinders can be expensive, but we invested in a 1½-gallon refillable propane tank. (The tank is made of aluminum so we can keep it outdoors where propane should be stored.) We keep one disposable tank on the boat just in case we run short.

A new barbecue—whether propane or charcoal—should be seasoned before you use it for the first time. Grilling a whole chicken, with its skin still on, works great—lots of grease to drip down, flare up, and generally fill the harbor with smoke. I remember cooking a chicken while anchored at La Playa and the San Diego Harbor Department showed up to see if the boat was on fire. I guess we were breaking in a barbecue! (Once the barbecue has been broken in, remove the skin from chicken and trim the fat from steaks before cooking so flare-ups are kept to a minimum.)

Following are some grilling tips:

- Preheat a propane barbecue for 5 to 10 minutes before each use to sterilize the grill and get the barbecue to the correct temperature. (With a charcoal grill, the coals are ready when uniformly covered with gray ash.)
- A wire brush or metal scraper is useful for removing any stubborn bits of food before cooking.
- To reduce flare-ups and minimize the use of propane, close the lid while cooking. If your grill doesn't have a lid, make a foil tent for the food.
- If you have grilled greasy food, allow the grease to cook off before storing the barbecue. (Keep the barbecue lid *open* while doing so!)
- To prevent food from sticking, coat the grill lightly with oil.
- If using bamboo skewers for kebabs, soak them for an hour in water to prevent them from catching on fire. Or, better yet, use metal skewers. They are much easier to turn and can be reused.
- To give an interesting flavor to grilled meats, seafood, and vegetables, soak some fresh herbs in water and place them on the grill with the food. They'll lend a flavorful accent to any food. Fresh rosemary is one of my favorites.
- Soak some wood chips, such as mesquite, in water and sprinkle on the coals just before cooking your entrée. The chips gives off a smoky aroma that is absorbed by the food.

The Burton Stove Top Smoker. This is an exciting piece of equipment. It is a 9×13-inch stainless steel pan with a lid that slides on and off. I like to scatter presoaked wood chips under the smoker's stainless steel rack, place the ingredients to be smoked on the rack, and slide on the lid. I place the cooker over my stove top burner or on a hot barbecue. Thirty minutes later, I'm ready to serve moist, smoked, delicious poultry, fish, meat, or vegetables. A word of caution: If you don't have a strong galley exhaust fan, don't use the smoker inside. To order the smoker, contact Max Burton, 2322 South Holgate Street, Tacoma, WA 98402; or, call 206-627-2665.

Knives. I need at least four good knives in my galley: a fish fillet knife, a boning knife, a paring knife, and a large chef's knife. I prefer the rust-free German Solingen knives. They are more difficult to sharpen than other knives, but keep their edges well. If you don't know how to use a sharpening stone, Chef's Choice Manual Diamond Hone Knife Sharpener is great. It has both a sharpening and honing stage and does a good job of keeping knives sharp.

Baking equipment. I use an 8-inch baking dish, a 9×13-inch baking dish, and a 9-inch pie pan. Whenever possible, I purchase dishes that can be used in both conventional and microwave ovens and that come with airtight lids for sealing the finished product. Tupperware once made such cookware and you may still be able to find some of it around.

I also have a Cushionaire baking sheet, which is insulated to help prevent burning the bottom of baked goods. The 12×14-inch size fits perfectly in my boat oven.

A loaf pan is necessary for bread baking and can also be used to make meatloaf and cakes.

A set of nesting mixing bowls completes my baking utensils.

Not So Essential (But Fun to Have)

Mini-muffin pans are a big help for the muffins I love to make (I usually use a package mix); I have 2 sets of mini-muffin pans. The miniature muffins are a fun size and have been known to improve the attitude of customs officials and inspire harbormasters to find an empty mooring.

A tea kettle is handy, but you can always heat water in a pan.

A soda siphon with lots of CO_2 cartridges makes sparkling wine, juice, or water. We carried cola syrup (for Hal's Cuba Libres) and diluted it with carbonated water from the seltzer bottle, saving lots of space and weight.

A six-cup stainless steel saucepan with a lid is great for sauces and rice, but a wok can also work.

A two-quart tin Charlotte pan is very useful when I want to make rice or Lemon Pudding Cake. I use one that fits into the pressure cooker and that doubles for making cakes and soufflés.

A wide-mouth thermos is useful for making yogurt and keeping food hot for the night watch. A pump thermos filled with ice keeps drinks cold all day and keeps you and your crew from constantly opening the refrigerator. In the winter, many boaters heat up water in the morning and keep it in a pump thermos all day for a quick cup of coffee or tea.

One-quart containers (I have a couple) are handy for reconstituting dry drink mixes.

Assorted small tools, such as the ones I carry aboard *Spice-Sea:* a pasta strainer, a grater, a citrus zester (for removing the outer peel of citrus), a can opener, measuring spoons and cups, a spatula, rubber scraper, kitchen scissors, a balloon whisk (for volume), a flat whisk (for sauces), a vegetable peeler, and a cooking thermometer. (Instant-read thermometers are very handy for deep-fat frying and for checking the internal temperature of meat.)

A stove top Belgian waffle iron is great if you like waffles. Try to find one with a built-in thermostat and with Teflon coating inside.

A propane torch, such as the one Hal keeps on board. I borrow it for the galley every now and then. It works better than most boat oven broilers for browning the tops of casseroles. Just make sure you use it on a nonflammable surface such as the top of your stove.

Dishes and Storage Space

I try to buy only dishes and pans that nest well together. For glassware, we keep insulated drinking glasses aboard because they don't sweat. Corelle Dinner Wear is popular with many boaters because it looks and feels like china but is nearly unbreakable. Plastic scratches and eventually looks terrible; pottery and china can break.

Like all boaters, I'm always on the lookout for new ways to stow gear. I store my pots and pans in the oven and my set of nesting plastic dishes in the microwave. We hang our stemmed wine glasses from a rack on the overhead. They have made many long passages and are still intact. I keep them bungied to the rack and use clothespins to keep them from banging together.

Rather than hang decorative items on the galley bulkhead, I've installed two heavy-duty magnetic bars that are specifically designed for kitchen use. They are excellent for storing knives and frequently used hand tools such as the can opener, scissors, and vegetable peeler. I've also hung an additional spice rack to hold small containers of condiments that get lost in large cupboards.

Both Tupperware and Rubbermaid make modular units that stack compactly in small spaces. I store baking powder, baking soda, corn starch, and salt in ½-cup containers; flour and sugar in 9-cup units; rice, barley, bulgur wheat, and popcorn in 2-cup units; dry cereal in a 12-cup unit; and powdered milk and brown sugar in the 4-cup size.

Counter space is at a premium on most boats, and ours is no different. Hal made a ½-inch thick plastic cover for the top of the stove that is an excellent chopping board, easy to stow, and greatly increases my preparation space. (He used plastic that has been approved by the FDA for cutting meat.)

I have an additional cutting board that fits over one of my sinks and I wedge a plastic dish pan into the other sink top. Dirty dishes can be piled under the dish pan, which holds the ingredients for whatever recipe I'm working on.

Electric Appliances

Hal installed a 1,000-watt Heart Interface Inverter on *SpiceSea* that allows me to have 110-volt AC any time I want it. I find the following electrical appliances very useful in the galley. They are by no means essential, but they are labor-saving devices and encourage me to try recipes that otherwise might be too much work.

Braun Hand Blender. I find this more useful than a normal blender because I can blend food in disposable cups, which saves on clean-up. It's great for blender drinks; it purées soups right in the pan, minces vegetables, and comes with a small spice and coffee grinder.

Orange juice squeezer. We became addicted to freshly squeezed orange juice in Mexico, and this handy appliance makes the job of making it much easier.

Hand mixer. A hand mixer is great for making cookie dough, cakes, and beating eggs.

Food processor. I have always used a food processor at home to reduce the amount of time I spend in the kitchen, and really enjoy the luxury of having one on board. I found a smaller model of my large Cuisinart—a 6-cup Little Pro,—that fits perfectly on *SpiceSea.*

Hal and I enjoy eating well and try to use as much fresh food as possible. That often means lots of cutting, chopping, slicing, and mincing. A small food processor greatly reduces the amount of time I have to spend doing those chores. In addition, it lets us make blender drinks in small quantities, puree vegetables for gazpacho, make pesto with fresh basil, and make an egg yolk-thickened hollandaise.

For boaters without 110-volt capacity, try The Food Chopper, a plastic-covered container with a crank handle that turns stainless steel blades. It will grind meat, make slaw, and cut, chop, dice, and mince fruits and vegetables. The Food Chopper is available through a catalog called Healthy Living, (item #22280), 6836 Engle Road, Cleveland, OH 44130. Their toll-free number is 1-800-800-0100.

Microwave oven. Because they draw so much current, microwave ovens are best used at the dock when you're plugged in to shore power, while the generator is running, or when underway (under power).

A microwave is especially great for cooking in the tropics because it doesn't heat up the galley. It is also a useful bug-control unit. If you microwave suspicious grains, pasta, and flour for about 30 seconds you will kill any weevils or eggs lurking about. We had a terrible infestation of weevils from imported Italian pasta while living in Mexico. The eggs got in the flour, hatched inside the pasta, and the weevils ate their way through everything on board! I threw away the infested stores and microwaved any grains and flour products that were destined for long-term storage. And that, I'm happy to report, was the end of the weevils.

FoodSaver. This appliance vacuum-seals food for long-term storage. You can package foods at home in handy quantities for the boat and keep the appliance on board when cruising. Staples such as flour, rice, brown sugar, and baking powder keep better when they are vacuum-sealed. You can buy special polycarbonate canisters to keep chips and crackers from being crushed while vacuum-sealing. The compact style FoodSaver sells for about $179.95 plus tax and shipping through the Dilia Corporation, 568 Howard Street, 2nd floor, San Francisco, CA 94105. Credit card orders can be placed through their toll free number: 1-800-777-5452.

Galley Fan

The galley can be a source of heat and steam that makes the rest of the boat uncomfortable. If your boat is not equipped with a stove exhaust fan, you can easily make a custom vent system.

Cut a piece of ¼-inch plastic a bit larger than the port opening nearest the stove. With the hot knife of a soldering iron, cut grooves to match the port latches. The notches match the twistlock "ears" on the port frame and will keep the plastic cut-out in place.

Buy a brushless equipment ventilating fan to mount on the plastic. (Radio Shack has a large selection of fan sizes.) It's sometimes possible to mount two fans side by side in a wide port. The fans come with ready made mounting holes in the fan frame.

Cut a round hole through the plastic to match the fan blades and drill four small holes for mounting the fan. The mounting holes can be drilled and tapped into the plastic to accept threaded bolts directly without the use of nuts, if you prefer.

Since the fan is not permanently mounted in the port, use a 12-volt DC cigarette lighter plug when you want to use the fan. An in-line switch in the wire leading to the fan makes a convenient way to turn it on.

The whole package can be quickly removed when getting underway or when rain threatens to blow into the galley through the fan opening.

Pressure Cookers

My introduction to pressure cookers came at a young age—I remember my mother cleaning split peas off the kitchen ceiling after the pressure relief valve had clogged and the cooker lid blew off, spewing green goo everywhere. That incident will be embedded in my memory forever.

I inherited a pressure cooker when I married my husband and promptly sold it in a garage sale. We weren't boating in those first years of marriage, but I remember that the gentleman who bought the cooker was leaving for the South Pacific and said he needed a pressure cooker for the galley. I envisioned split peas plastered all over his boat, but gladly parted with the cooker.

As I got involved in boating, I began thinking about the pressure cooker that I had so easily parted with several years earlier. I decided that maybe it would be nice to have a pressure cooker on the boat. As I searched for the perfect cooker, I learned that they had been greatly improved since the fifties. I finally settled on a Chantal Speed Cooker, which was state-of-the-art in the world of pressure cooking.

I carried my shiny new pressure cooker aboard *Spice-Sea* for months and never did anything more with it than boil water for pasta. Then, while cruising in Mexico, I saw just how handy a pressure cooker can be. While we were having a potluck on shore at Santa Maria Bay, the surf started to roll in and one of the dinghies flipped. Although its occupants got soaked, their stew, which was still sealed in a pressure cooker, survived just fine. It was time to learn how to use my cooker.

I soon learned that pressure cookers are ideally suited to life on the water. They cook food three to 10 times faster than conventional cooking methods. Thus, they are great energy savers.

I also have learned to appreciate the safety feature of cooking in a sealed container—nothing can spill out of it. An errant wake is not going to bother a pot of stew on the stove, even if the boat starts rocking excessively.

How a Pressure Cooker Works. When liquid boils it produces steam. A tightly sealed pressure cooker traps the steam, which then builds pressure inside the cooker. When under pressure, cooking temperatures can rise significantly higher than possible under normal conditions. The superheated steam created by these higher temperatures allows food to retain more of its vitamins, nutrients, aroma, and flavor. Pressure cookers, therefore, are ideal for cooking vegetables, tougher cuts of meats, and hearty soups.

Modern pressure cookers have safety locks that prevent the covers from being opened until the pressure has been safely reduced. The longstanding fear of exploding food is no more. The bottom line is that pressure cookers save time and fuel while improving the end product.

I no longer have to plan hours in advance when I want to cook beans—they cook in only 20 to 25 minutes under pressure. (Remember, of course, that old beans will take longer to cook.) Beef stew needs about 20 minutes under pressure, and a savory soup can be cooked from scratch in 30 to 60 minutes.

A few words of advice from a devoted fan of pressure cooking:

- Never fill the cooker more than ⅔ full and always check to make sure that the steam valve is clear.
- When cooking a variety of ingredients, cut the delicate ones into larger pieces to avoid overcooking.
- When cooking meat, brown it first to seal in juices and give color to the dish.
- The basic sequence for pressure cooking is simple: seal the cooker, set the pressure regulator, and start timing once the pressure has been reached. Lower the heat and maintain a heat that will barely keep the pressure constant. When the cooking time is over, turn off the heat and allow the pot to cool—or run it under cold water if you're in a hurry. Do not attempt to remove the lid until all of the pressure has been relieved.

How to Make Foil Straps. Certain foods, such as rice or Lemon Pudding Cake (page 211), are easier to cook in another pan that's placed inside a pressure cooker. I use a 2½-quart Charlotte pan that has its own lid and fits nicely inside my pressure cooker—that is, once Hal folded the little handles so the pan would slide in and out of the cooker. The trick is in removing a hot pan from inside the pressure cooker when it is filled with steaming rice or pudding cake.

I finally solved the problem by making two strips of heavy aluminum foil that can be crisscrossed under the pan and that are long enough to come up the sides and fold over the top. When I remove the pressure cooker lid I carefully grasp the foil straps and ease the pan out of the cooker.

To make the foil straps, cut two pieces of heavy duty foil into 6×30-inch strips. Fold the strips into thirds so that each strap is 2 inches wide. I store the straps in the pressure cooker when they are not in use, since they can be used repeatedly.

CHAPTER 3

Breakfast and Brunch Treats

During a normal shoreside day, breakfast for Hal and me often consists of a quick bowl of cereal or a container of yogurt on the fly. But in the more relaxed mode we adopt while living aboard *SpiceSea,* breakfast can become a focal point in our day. Often Hal gets up early to catch a few fish; while he's fishing, I have the time to experiment with a new recipe.

Over the years we have developed some favorite breakfast dishes: Pancakes with Fresh Fruit and Nuts, Stuffed French Toast, Papaya Quesadillas, and a delicious Chile Relleño Casserole.

Crêpes are another breakfast favorite. They are easy to make, can be prepared in advance, and can be reheated with a sauce. For really decadent dining, try them with Orange Butter Sauce (page 178), or make a filling with your favorite fruit.

I have also included recipes for making your own cottage cheese, ricotta cheese, and yogurt—ingredients that are handy to have on board, but that have a short shelf life.

Summertime cruising in tropical climates presents a breakfast challenge. When we wake up in a pool of sweat on those steamy mornings, we don't feel like eating. Instead, we enjoy cool, frosty slurpies. Orange juice pureed with bananas, powdered milk, and lots of ice instantly revives our spirits.

Eggs

You can prepare an endless variety of breakfast and brunch recipes if you have eggs on board. They keep well (see page 13) and are an inexpensive source of protein.

TO HARD BOIL EGGS: Place room temperature eggs in a single layer in a pan. Add enough tap water to cover the eggs by at least 1 inch. Cover, and quickly bring the water to a boil. Turn off the heat and let the eggs stand covered, in the hot water—15 to 17 minutes for large eggs. Immediately place the eggs in cold water to prevent the yolks from discoloring.

Older eggs are easier to peel than fresh ones. To remove a shell, tap it gently all over, then roll the egg between your hands to loosen the shell. Peel the egg starting at the large end and dip it in water to help release the shell. To find out if eggs have been cooked, spin them. Hard-cooked eggs spin; uncooked eggs topple over.

TO PICKLE 12 EGGS: Hard boil the eggs and peel. Bring 3 cups of vinegar to a boil and simmer for 10 minutes with 1 tablespoon of pickling spices and 1 teaspoon of salt. Place the eggs in a clean, wide-mouth jar and cover with warm pickling solution. Allow the eggs to marinate for at least three days before tasting. Pickled eggs will keep for several weeks at room temperature.

There are an infinite number of variations you can use with, or instead of, the pickling spices: 1 to 2 teaspoons of mustard seed; ¼ pound of jalapeño peppers; 1 tablespoon of chopped fresh ginger and some sliced onions; or 2 teaspoons of black peppercorns. For **GARLIC PICKLED EGGS,** simmer 2 teaspoons of dried tarragon, 8 cloves of slivered garlic, 2 teaspoons of sugar, 1 teaspoon of mustard seed, and 1 teaspoon of peppercorns with the vinegar and salt. For **PINK EGGS,** add several cooked beets and some beet juice to the pickling solution. When you buy pickles, save the leftover pickling solution and reuse it when pickling eggs.

POACHING EGGS is most successful when using very fresh eggs. For the best-looking poached eggs, cook them in lots of water that has been seasoned with vinegar and salt—the vinegar and salt make the egg whites set faster.

For 1 pint of water, use 2 tablespoons of vinegar and ½ teaspoon of salt. For more tender eggs, poach them at a slow simmer—the egg whites get very tough if you boil the eggs.

Serve poached eggs on a bed of creamy spinach with hollandaise sauce, or on a toasted English muffin with a slice of ham, topped with Béarnaise Sauce (see page 159).

Huevos Rancheros is a popular egg dish using fried eggs, served on fried corn tortillas on a bed of refried beans, topped with Mexican Salsa Fresca (see page 165) that has been puréed and simmered over low heat for 10 minutes. Add some grated jack or cheddar cheese if you like.

Huevos Mexicanos are eggs that have been scrambled with green onions and peppers, served on corn tortillas on a bed of black beans, topped with Tomatillo Sauce (see page 166), jack cheese, and sliced avocado.

Powdered Egg Mix

Wakefield Powdered Egg Mix (see page 13) is handy for cooking on board. You can make an incredibly easy **quiche** with a package of this mixture, 3 cups of milk, 2½ cups of grated cheese, and a little chopped onion and cooked bacon.

For **scrambled eggs,** use equal parts egg mix and water, season with salt and pepper, and cook in a little butter. Make an **egg salad spread** out of any leftover scrambled eggs by adding mayonnaise, pickled relish, mustard, and a little chopped onion.

For 6 slices of **French Toast,** use a ½ cup of the egg mix and ¾ cup of water.

A **baked custard** is easy to make by dissolving 1 package of the egg mix with 1½ cups of water, 3 cups of hot milk, ½ cup of sugar, and 1 teaspoon of vanilla. Bake at 300°F for 1¼ hours.

Omelettes

Omelettes are easy to make, can be filled with a variety of ingredients including yesterday's leftovers, and are an impressive dish for your boat guests. All you need are an 8-inch nonstick frying pan (the same one used for crêpes) and lots of imagination.

Basic Omelette

1 serving

2 or 3 eggs, at room temperature
1 tablespoon water
Pinch of black pepper
Herb of choice (cilantro, tarragon, basil, dill weed)
2 teaspoons unsalted butter
Salt to taste

1. In a bowl, beat the eggs with water until well combined. Add pepper and herb choice.
2. In an omelette pan, over high heat, melt the butter until bubbly. Pour in the eggs and stir with the flat side of a fork, shaking the pan with your other hand until the eggs form a creamy mass. Top with filling ingredients.
3. Salt to taste before serving. (Salt added during the cooking tends to toughen the omelette.)

Fillings

- Cream cheese, smoked salmon, sliced onion
- Avocado, mushrooms, green onion, tomato, and melted jack cheese
- Sun-dried tomatoes, asparagus, roasted peppers covered with Italian Sauce (page 171) and melted mozzarella cheese
- Sautéed mushrooms, tomatoes, zucchini, and onions with melted jack cheese
- Sautéed potatoes, onions, bacon bits, and cheese
- Spinach, mushrooms, and cheese

Chile Relleño Casserole

8 to 12 servings

This is a great brunch or light supper dish, and also a popular appetizer. If you are using it as a finger food, omit the tomato sauce. The casserole can be baked ahead and kept in the refrigerator until serving. Reheat briefly to return to room temperature.

2 (7 oz.) cans whole mild green chiles
8 eggs, lightly beaten
½ cup milk
1 teaspoon ground cumin
Salt and pepper to taste
1½ cups grated mild cheddar cheese
1½ cups grated jack cheese
1 (8 oz.) can seasoned tomato sauce

1. Rinse the chiles under cold water and remove all seeds; allow to drain and blot dry.

2. Combine the eggs and milk with seasonings.
3. Spread the chiles evenly into the bottom of a greased 9×13-inch baking dish. Cover with the cheeses. Pour the seasoned eggs over the filling.
4. Bake at 350°F for 30 minutes until the eggs have set. Pour the tomato sauce over eggs and bake an additional 10 minutes.

Puerto Vallarta Frittata

6 to 8 servings

Once, while cruising the coast of mainland Mexico aboard a friend's boat, we sailed all night and arrived in Puerto Vallarta with a famished crew. I scrounged through the galley until I found enough ingredients to feed this hungry group, and wound up inventing a frittata. It was a great breakfast dish, but also would have been good for dinner.

Frittatas are wonderfully versatile dishes and substitutions are quite acceptable. Use whatever vegetables you have on hand, or leftover meat, or make it meatless. You can serve leftover frittatas cold for lunch the next day.

8 ounces spicy lean sausage, cooked and drained
3 tablespoons olive oil
1 cup leftover baked potatoes, thinly sliced
½ cup chopped green onion
1 zucchini, thinly sliced
1 cup mushrooms, sliced
1 (4 oz.) can chopped green chiles
1 (4 oz.) can chopped black olives
2 cups grated cheddar cheese
8 eggs, lightly beaten
Salt and pepper to taste

Garnishes

Sour cream or nonfat yogurt
Canned salsa

1. In a 10-inch skillet, sauté the potatoes until golden. Layer the remaining ingredients in the skillet, except for the eggs. Pour the eggs over the top and begin cooking, gently lifting the potatoes so that the eggs flow underneath. Season with salt and pepper.
2. Cover the skillet and cook until the eggs are set, or place the skillet under the broiler and cook until the top is set—about 1 minute.
3. Cut into wedges to serve.

Variation
Onion and Tomato Frittata

Sauté 2 onions in olive oil and then add 1 cup of canned tomatoes. Cook until the liquid has evaporated. Add ⅓ cup of chopped prosciutto or cooked sausage and ⅓ cup of Parmesan cheese. Whisk in 8 eggs and season with salt and pepper. Cook as above.

Eggs Cesena

8 to 12 servings

On the beautiful yacht *Lady Nancy,* Nancy Cesena fixes a great brunch dish that is a variation of the Chile Relleño Casserole. The ingredients are flexible—any cheese or any meat will do. Nancy serves this dish with her homemade flour tortillas and garnishes it with avocado, sour cream, and salsa.

2 cups jack cheese
2 cups cheddar cheese
2 large baking potatoes, baked and sliced (or any type of leftover potatoes)
1 pound Italian sausage, bacon, or ham, sliced, cooked, and drained
1 bunch chopped green onions
1 cup chopped fresh tomatoes (or canned)
12 eggs, beaten

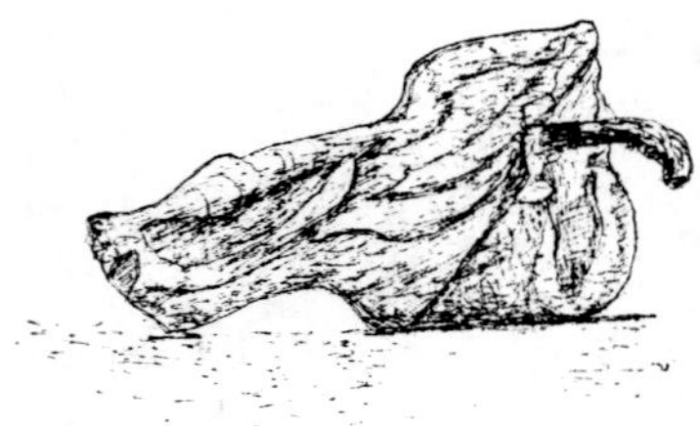

1. In a 9×13-inch greased casserole, layer half of the cheese, then the potatoes, meat, and vegetables.
2. Pour in the eggs and top with the remaining cheese.
3. Bake at 350°F for 30 minutes or until set.

Crustless Quiche

6 to 8 servings

Quiche is another delicious brunch treat. I usually make mine crustless because it saves time and calories. If you don't have a 10-inch quiche pan on board, use a shallow baking dish or a couple of small pie pans.

2 tablespoons olive oil
2 cups vegetables such as onion, bell peppers, mushrooms, broccoli, or zucchini
¼ cup flour
4 eggs
1 cup nonfat yogurt or sour cream
1 cup cottage cheese
½ cup Parmesan cheese
½ teaspoon Italian herbs or basil and oregano
Salt and pepper to taste
½ pound cooked seafood such as shrimp, crab meat, or salmon, or 1 pound cooked, drained, and chopped meat such as bacon, Italian sausage, or ham
2 cups grated cheese such as mozzarella, jack, cheddar, blue, or feta

1. Sauté the vegetables until tender. Mix together the flour, eggs, yogurt, cottage cheese, Parmesan cheese, and herbs. Stir in the vegetables, seafood, or meat and the cheese.
2. Pour into a buttered 10-inch quiche pan and bake at 350°F for 45 minutes. Allow to stand five minutes before cutting.

Arlene's Crab Quiche

4 servings

My sister-in-law Arlene owns the beautiful Pirate's Cove Bed and Breakfast on the coast of Oregon. Her pampered guests rave about this recipe, and it is so easy to make that it has become popular boat fare.

1 baked 9-inch pie crust (optional)
4 ounces cream cheese, at room temperature
3 tablespoons powdered buttermilk
¾ cup water
¼ cup nonfat plain yogurt
3 eggs
½ teaspoon Tabasco
1 ½ cups crabmeat or other seafood

Toppings

Toasted sliced almonds or Parmesan cheese and paprika

1. Combine all the ingredients *except* the seafood in a blender and blend until smooth. Stir in the seafood.
2. Place in a greased 9-inch pie pan or prebaked pie shell. Add a topping.
3. Bake at 350°F for 40 to 45 minutes.

Zucchini, Sausage, and Spinach Quiche

8 servings

1 pound Italian sausage
5 zucchini, thinly sliced
2 tablespoons oil
1 onion, thinly sliced
½ pound mushrooms, thinly sliced
2 cups finely chopped fresh spinach
4 eggs
1 ½ cups milk
Salt and pepper to taste
½ teaspoon thyme
½ teaspoon basil
½ cup freshly grated Parmesan cheese

1. In a nonstick skillet, cook the sausage until all traces of pink are gone. Remove from skillet and set aside.

2. Sauté the zucchini and onion in the olive oil for about 5 minutes. Place in a greased 9×13-inch baking dish, or a 1½-quart quiche dish.
3. Sauté the mushrooms for 3 minutes and mix with the sausage. Place in the baking dish. Quickly sauté the spinach, drain, and place in the baking dish.
4. In a medium-size mixing bowl, beat the eggs thoroughly with a wire whisk while slowly adding the milk. Stir in the salt, pepper, thyme, and basil and pour over the vegetables. Sprinkle with the cheese.
5. Bake at 375° F for 25 to 30 minutes. Serve hot, cut in wedges.

Easy Spinach Quiche

4 servings

1 cup cottage cheese
3 ounces cream cheese
3 eggs
1 teaspoon Tabasco
3 tablespoons flour
2 tablespoons butter, at room temperature
Salt and pepper
1 teaspoon dried mustard
1 (10 oz.) package frozen spinach, thawed and squeezed dry

1. Combine all the ingredients *except* the spinach in a blender and blend until smooth.
2. Combine the spinach with the egg mixture in a buttered, 1-quart casserole or a 9-inch square baking dish.
3. Bake at 350° F for 35 to 40 minutes.

Cheese Strata

8 to 10 servings

Stratas are a cross between a soufflé and a savory bread pudding. This is one of my favorite brunch dishes that serves equally well for lunch or dinner. There are many possibilities for varying the recipe: adding canned sliced mushrooms, sliced tomatoes, chopped green chiles, ham, crumbled bacon, cooked sausage, or leftover cooked vegetables. Any kind of cheese can be used, from cheddar and jack to blue cheese and Gruyère. Strata must be made in advance, which makes it ideal for entertaining in small spaces.

16 slices bread, crusts removed and lightly buttered
1 pound grated cheddar cheese
½ cup chopped green onion
6 eggs
½ teaspoon salt
¼ teaspoon pepper
3 cups milk
1 tablespoon Dijon mustard

1. Place half the bread, buttered side down, in the bottom of a greased 9×13-inch baking dish. Sprinkle the bread with half the cheese and onion and any meat or other vegetables that you are using. Repeat the bread layer, adding the remaining cheese, onion, and meat or vegetables as desired.
2. Mix together the eggs, salt, pepper, milk, and mustard and pour over the bread. Marinate in the refrigerator, covered, at least 3 hours or as long as overnight.
3. Bake at 350° F for 45 minutes or until a knife inserted in the center comes out clean.

Savory Soufflés

Soufflés are so versatile that you can serve them for breakfast, lunch, and dinner, and making them is quite simple. Choose your flavor (spinach, cheese, chocolate), make a white sauce, add egg yolks (optional), stir in stiffly beaten egg whites, season with herbs and spices (or sugar if it is a dessert soufflé), and bake. Most soufflé ingredients store well on board, they cook in 30 to 40 minutes, and the chef always gets rave reviews. I like to get my guests involved and have them help with beating the egg whites, which is a tiring task if you're doing it by hand.

Always use a very clean bowl for beating the egg whites. (I prefer stainless steel since I sold my copper bowl in the garage sale before we went cruising.) Although any ovenproof dish can be used for baking soufflés, I have a metal 2-quart Charlotte pan that I keep for dishes that I cook inside the pressure cooker. It is a perfect soufflé dish.

Basic Soufflé

4 servings

Parmesan cheese and butter for preparing soufflé dish
4 tablespoons butter
4 tablespoons flour
1 cup milk
Salt and pepper to taste
¼ teaspoon thyme
Flavoring choice (see list below)
4 eggs, separated
½ teaspoon cream of tartar

1. Preheat the oven to 375°F. Prepare a 1½- to 2-quart soufflé dish by generously buttering it and sprinkling with Parmesan cheese.
2. Make a white sauce by melting the butter in a medium saucepan and whisking in the flour. Cook over low heat, whisking constantly until the mixture foams. Whisk in the milk and bring to a boil. Season with salt, pepper, and thyme. Reduce heat and simmer for 5 minutes or until thickened.
3. Stir in your choice of flavoring. When slightly cool, beat in egg yolks to thicken mixture. Adjust seasonings. (Can be prepared ahead to this point.) If done ahead, rub top of sauce with butter to prevent a skin from forming. Cover and refrigerate. Bring to room temperature before using.
4. Beat the egg whites with the cream of tartar until stiff. Mix ¼ of the egg whites into the white sauce mixture to lighten it, then fold in the remaining egg whites. Spoon into a soufflé dish and bake 30 to 35 minutes

Soufflé Tips

- Fold the whites *gently* into the sauce base. Overfolding reduces the volume of the finished product.
- You can prepare a soufflé one hour before baking. Store it away from all drafts and place a large empty pot upside down over the soufflé.
- Serve soufflés immediately after baking because they will not hold.

Flavoring Ideas

- 1 cup of finely chopped or shredded, well-drained vegetables such as a 10-ounce package frozen chopped spinach or broccoli, thawed, drained well, and cooked
- 1 cup of shredded cheddar or Swiss cheese, stirred into the white sauce until the cheese melts
- 1 cup of finely chopped cooked meat (chicken, ham, turkey, or bacon)
- 1 (7 oz.) can tuna or salmon, drained and flaked
- 1 (8 oz.) can chopped mild green chiles

Chilaquiles in Salsa Verde

2 to 4 servings

Chilaquiles (chee-la-key-les) are made with stale tortillas that are cut up and lightly fried, then baked in a casserole with a red or green salsa. They are frequently served in Mexico for breakfast and are a tasty eggless recipe.

There is a saying in Mexico that no girl can get married until she knows how to make chilaquiles. *("Ninguna señorita se puede casar sin saber hacer chilaquiles.")* The reasoning is that chilaquiles make good use of tortillas, which are the most basic staple in Mexican cuisine—and to be a successful and thrifty housewife, one must know how to use even old stale tortillas.

While preparing to make chilaquiles aboard *SpiceSea* one morning, I unwrapped our corn tortillas and found that they were moldy. I decided to try using tortilla chips instead. The recipe turned out great and I saved myself the effort of frying the tortillas.

4 stale corn tortillas or 2 cups unsalted oven-baked crispy tortilla chips
1 cup Salsa de Tomatillos (page 166)
1 cup chopped leftover cooked chicken, beef, or pork
1 cup shredded mild cheese such as jack
Fresh cilantro leaves
Sour cream

1. In a 9-inch pie pan, spread 2 layers of broken tortilla chips or stale tortillas that have been broken up and lightly fried in oil.
2. Cover the chips with the salsa, sprinkle with the meat, and top with the cheese.
3. Bake in a 350°F oven for 20 minutes. If you have a broiler, it's nice to brown the top. We carry a propane torch on board, which comes in handy for all kinds of things—starting fires, lighting lanterns, and even browning the tops of recipes that are sprinkled with cheese!
4. Garnish with sour cream or cilantro and serve.

Dry Pancake Mix

6 cups

Having your own premade dry pancake mix on board saves a lot of time and expense—it's very cost effective to make the mix from scratch. To complete the mix, simply add water and oil.

1 ½ cups nonfat dry milk
4 ½ cups flour
2 tablespoons sugar
2 tablespoons baking powder
1 teaspoon salt
½ teaspoon baking soda
¾ cup powdered egg mix (This is the equivalent of 6 whole eggs. If you are not using powdered egg mix, add fresh eggs just before making each recipe of pancakes—1 egg per recipe. See page 13 for a powdered egg recipe.)

Combine all the ingredients and store in an airtight container.

Basic Pancakes

8 pancakes

1 cup dry pancake mix
½ cup water plus 2 tablespoons
1 tablespoon oil

Combine all the ingredients.

Banana Pancakes

8 pancakes

I make this recipe a lot. It's quick, delicious, and an easy way to use bananas that have gotten too soft. When you are faced with over-ripe bananas, don't throw them away. Instead, mash and freeze them in a Ziploc for a couple of weeks. Then, when you want to make banana pancakes, the bananas will be ready and waiting.

1 recipe Basic Pancake (above)
2 to 3 soft bananas, mashed

Mix the ingredients together. Use about ¼ cup of the dry mix for each pancake.

Do-Ahead Tip

Make a double batch of pancakes and refrigerate the leftovers. When you are passagemaking, it is easy to reheat the pancakes in a hot frying pan—you can even eat them cold.

WAFFLES

4 waffles

1 cup Dry Pancake Mix (page 32)
½ cup water plus 2 tablespoons
2 tablespoons melted butter
2 egg whites

1. Mix together the dry pancake mix, water, and butter. Beat the egg whites until stiff and fold into the batter just before making the waffles.
2. Spray a stove-top Belgian waffle iron thoroughly with a nonstick coating. Place the iron on a burner and heat one side. When it comes up to temperature, turn it over and heat the other side.
3. Pour ¼ of the batter onto the iron and cook until golden. Start checking the waffles when the steam disappears. Keep finished waffles warm in a 250° F oven until ready to serve.
4. Serve the waffles warm with butter and syrup or fresh fruit.

BASIC CRÊPE BATTER

12 to 16 crêpes

Crêpes are nothing more than thin pancakes. Any bits of leftovers can be placed inside them for a gourmet treat.

1 ½ cups flour
1 tablespoon sugar (for dessert crêpes only)
3 eggs
1 ½ cups milk
2 tablespoons butter

1. Combine the flour, optional sugar, eggs, and milk and beat until smooth. Allow the batter to rest for at least an hour.
2. To make the crêpes, use a nonstick 8-inch frying pan and heat over high heat until very hot. Add a ½ teaspoon of butter and swirl the pan until the butter is melted. Pour ¼ cup of batter into the prepared pan. Tip the pan from side to side very quickly so that the batter spreads evenly across the bottom of the pan.
3. Cook the crêpe for a minute or so, until the edges turn slightly brown. Turn the crêpe over with a spatula and barely cook it on the inside. Slide the crêpe onto waxed paper to cool.
4. When the crêpes are cool they can be stacked together, wrapped, and frozen for a few weeks, or stored in the refrigerator for several days.

CRÊPE BATTER USING DRIED INGREDIENTS

6 tablespoons powdered egg mix (page 13)
⅓ cup powdered milk
1 ½ cups flour
2 cups water

Mix 3 or 4 tablespoons of water with the egg mixture and beat well to dissolve all lumps. Add the remaining dry ingredients and mix well. Stir in the remaining water and beat until smooth. Allow the batter to rest 1 hour before using.

PECAN CRANBERRY CRÊPES WITH FRESH PEACHES

6 servings

½ recipe crêpe batter (above), using only 1 egg
3 tablespoons chopped pecans or pine nuts
3 tablespoons dried cranberries
Powdered sugar for garnish
4 to 6 fresh peaches or other fruit in season, peeled, sliced, and sweetened if necessary

1. Make crêpes by following the recipe for dessert crêpe batter (above), using only 1 egg. Combine the nuts and cranberries. For each crêpe, measure ¼ cup of

the batter and add a ½ tablespoon of the nut mixture before pouring into the prepared crêpe pan.

2. Place sliced peaches (or other fruit) inside the crêpe and roll up.
3. Dust outside with powdered sugar.

Pear Crêpes

4 servings

2 firm pears (Bosc are good), peeled, cored, and sliced
2 tablespoons butter
4 tablespoons sugar
4 crêpes

1. Sauté the pears in the butter. Sprinkle with 2 tablespoons of sugar and cook until the sugar starts to caramelize.
2. Divide the pears into the crêpes and fold in half. Sprinkle with the remaining 2 tablespoons of sugar and bake at 450° F until sugar melts.

Variations

- Apple Crêpes—Use 2 tart cooking apples instead of pears.
- Banana Crêpes—Use 2 firm bananas and brown sugar instead of pears and white sugar.

Apple Pancakes

4 servings

This pancake, which is a special breakfast treat aboard *SpiceSea,* is made like a frittata—the Italian version of an omelette. The trick is to have a pan lid that is the same size as your frying pan, so that you can slip the omelette out of the pan, turn it over, and brown it on the other side.

2 green apples, peeled and chopped
2 tablespoons raisins soaked in brandy, bourbon, or other flavorful alcohol
2 tablespoons sugar
½ teaspoon cinnamon
½ cup flour
3 eggs
½ cup milk
5 to 6 tablespoons butter
An additional ¼ to ⅓ cup sugar for glaze

1. Combine the apples, raisins and their soaking liquid, sugar, and cinnamon. Allow to marinate as long as 24 hours.
2. In a bowl combine the flour, eggs, and milk; stir until smooth.
3. In a 10-inch, nonstick frying pan, heat 1 tablespoon of butter and add the apple mixture. Cook until the apples are crisp-tender.
4. Add an additional 1 tablespoon of butter and, when melted, add the batter. Cook over medium-high heat, pulling the sides of the pancake away from the edges and allowing the batter to flow under the apples and cook. Keep lifting the batter with a spatula to prevent sticking. When the pancake begins to firm, slip it—uncooked side up—on to a pan lid the same size as the frying pan.
5. Add an additional 1 tablespoon of butter to the frying pan. Holding the lid, flip the pancake over into the pan and cook until golden. Once again turn the pancake out onto the pan lid.
6. Add 2 more tablespoons of butter to the frying pan and sprinkle with ¼ cup of sugar. After the sugar begins to caramelize, slip the pancake back into the frying pan. Brown the bottom of pancake, adding additional butter if necessary.
7. Serve with the caramelized side up, scraping the melted sugar from the frying pan onto the pancake.

Dutch Babies

2 to 4 servings

Related to Yorkshire Pudding, Dutch Babies are a simple breakfast popover. Serve them sprinkled with powdered sugar and/or a little Orange Butter Sauce (see page 178).

3 eggs, lightly beaten
¾ cup milk
¾ cup flour
1 tablespoon sugar
1 tablespoon grated fresh lemon or orange peel
4 tablespoons butter

1. Preheat oven to 425° F.
2. Combine the eggs, milk, flour, and sugar and blend until smooth. Add the citrus peel.
3. In an ovenproof skillet, melt the butter until it sizzles. Carefully pour the batter into the skillet and place in a hot oven for 20 minutes or until brown and puffy.

Variations

- Add a ½ to ¾ cup of sharp cheddar cheese and a ½ teaspoon of cayenne to the batter; omit sugar and citrus peel.
- Add a ½ cup of jack cheese and 4 ounces of mild green chiles to the batter; omit sugar and citrus peel.

Puffy Fruit Clafouti

6 to 8 servings

Clafouti is a puffy French pancake that can be served for breakfast or dessert. You can use almost any fresh fruit, or try canned blueberries, peaches, pears, plums, pineapples, or cherries.

½ cup flour
⅓ cup sugar
3 eggs
1¼ cups milk
Grated peel of 1 lemon
1 tablespoon vanilla
1 tablespoon butter
2 cups sliced fresh peaches, pears or canned fruit
Powdered sugar

1. Combine the flour, sugar, eggs, milk, lemon peel, and vanilla. Coat a 9- or 10-inch quiche pan with the butter.
2. Pour half of the batter into the quiche pan, top with the drained fruit, and add the remaining batter. Bake at 350° F for 55 to 60 minutes or until set.
3. Allow the clafouti to rest 15 minutes before cutting. Sprinkle with powdered sugar just before serving.

French Toast

8 servings

Stale bread makes ideal French toast. (If the bread is fresh it will absorb too much of the egg mixture.) Try seasoning the egg mixture with grated lemon or orange peel, cinnamon, vanilla, or even a little Grand Marnier. For toppings, you can use cinnamon and powdered sugar, maple syrup, fresh berries and sugar, warm apple sauce, or warmed fruit preserves.

4 eggs
1 cup milk
½ teaspoon vanilla (or seasoning suggestions above)
8 slices stale bread
Butter
Choice of toppings

1. Combine the eggs, milk, and seasoning. Dip the bread into the egg mixture and cook on both sides in hot butter until golden.
2. Serve with one of the toppings suggested above.

Variations

- Stuffed French Toast—Place a sliced banana, fresh berries, or canned fruit and a generous layer of cream cheese sweetened with jam between two slices of French toast. Or, try a mixture of peanut butter, honey, and banana as a filling. Serve with warm maple syrup.

- Cheesy French Toast—Bake basic French Toast in a 350°F oven for 5 minutes. Top with grated cheese and a little chili powder. Toast until the cheese is melted and begins to brown.

SWEET BREAKFAST PUFFS

2 dozen

These light pastries are a quick substitute for donuts.

2¼ cups flour
⅓ cup sugar
1 tablespoon baking powder
½ teaspoon salt
½ teaspoon nutmeg
¾ cup milk
¼ cup oil
1 egg
Oil for frying
Cinnamon and sugar

1. Combine the dry ingredients in a bowl.
2. Combine the milk, oil, and egg in a separate bowl.
3. Stir the liquid ingredients into the dry ingredients.
4. Heat the oil in a wok and drop the mixture by tablespoons into the hot oil. Fry until golden.
5. Drain on paper towels and sprinkle with cinnamon and sugar.

ORANGE SLURPIES

2 servings

Part of the time I was working on this cookbook, I was cruising the Sea of Cortez during the steamy summer. On most days I did everything possible to avoid cooking in the galley and heating up the boat. Slurpies became standard breakfast fare. These drinks, which are almost like milk shakes, can be made with any fruit juice or canned beverage. We have even made root beer floats this way in a desperate attempt to simulate one of our favorite treats.

Juice from 5 oranges (or 1¼ to 1½ cups canned juice)
½ teaspoon vanilla
Ice cubes
6 tablespoons powdered milk
Cinnamon

1. In a blender, combine the orange juice, vanilla, and ice cubes.
2. Blend until the ice is puréed, then add the powdered milk. Blend until smooth and frothy. Pour into glasses and sprinkle with a little cinnamon.

Variations

- Add two bananas to the above recipe and blend well. For a more filling drink, add some powdered breakfast substitute such as Slim Fast.
- Try pineapple chunks, melon (a great way to use too-ripe melon), or any juicy fruit. Combine fruits for an infinite variety of flavors. If you have freezer space and are cruising in areas where fresh fruit is not easily available, you can use packages of frozen fruit.

MAKING YOGURT ON BOARD

We eat a lot of yogurt aboard *SpiceSea*—over fruit for breakfast, as a light lunch, and as a base for dips and sauces. Drained, we also enjoy it as a low-fat cheese spread. Until recently we always ran out of yogurt if we were gone from the dock for more than a few days. Our small refrigerator just doesn't have the space for more than a few cartons of yogurt.

I finally decided to experiment with making my own yogurt and found that it is easy, inexpensive, and fun. All you need are a wide-mouth thermos bottle, a meat thermometer, powdered milk, and some lactobacillus powder (available at pharmacies and health food stores), or some plain yogurt left from your last batch.

1. Fill a wide-mouth thermos half-full of powdered milk; add enough water to make the thermos about ¾ full. Stir, and add enough boiling water to nearly fill the thermos. Stir again.
2. Check the temperature—it should be between 110 to 120°F; add the starter and stir. Use ¼ teaspoon of lactobacillus powder or 1½ teaspoons of plain yogurt per pint for the starter.
3. Place the stopper in the thermos, wrap it in a towel to insulate, and allow to brew for about 4 hours. The consistency will be that of sour cream. The more powdered milk you use, the thicker the yogurt will be.

To make yogurt cheese, pour some yogurt (1 ounce of yogurt yields approximately a ½ ounce of yogurt cheese) into a funnel lined with either a disposable coffee filter or a funnel made especially for yogurt (see page 12). Allow to drain in a cup in the refrigerator until it reaches the desired consistency—8 to 12 hours for most uses; 14 or more hours for cheese.

Uses and Variations

- Try this spread on toast or muffins for breakfast, topped with your favorite jam.
- Mix unflavored yogurt with honey to taste, and serve over fresh fruit and granola for a delicious breakfast treat.
- For vanilla yogurt, add 2 to 3 tablespoons of sugar to the milk as it boils. Stir in a ¼ teaspoon of vanilla extract before placing in thermos bottle.
- For fruit yogurt, make vanilla yogurt. When the yogurt is the consistency you want, stir in pureed fruit such as peaches, mangoes, or pears.

Ricotta Cheese

1 cup

This is one of the easiest cheeses to make because it does not depend on fermentation. Besides using in lasagna, ricotta is a good substitute for cottage cheese. For a light breakfast, sweeten some ricotta with a little sugar and top with chopped fresh fruit.

1 quart milk (I use reconstituted nonfat dry milk.)
2 tablespoons white vinegar

1. Very *slowly* heat the milk and vinegar to 200° F. The heating process will take about a half hour. If you try to hurry, the milk might scorch on the bottom of the pan and you'll have brown spots in the cheese.
2. Cover the pan and set aside in a warm place (80 to 100° F) for about six hours. The cheese is ready to strain when a solid curd has formed.
3. Strain through a dampened cheesecloth or a fine metal strainer and discard the whey—the watery residue.

Cottage Cheese

Cottage cheese is another milk product that is easily made on board. To curdle the milk you will need rennet tablets, which are available at health food stores. Rennet is the membrane that lines the stomach of unweaned animals; the tablets keep for a long time. An extract of this membrane is used to make cheese and junket, a milk-based dessert. Start making your cheese in the afternoon, so that you can begin checking the consistency the next morning.

1 quart milk (I use reconstituted nonfat dry milk.)
½ cup buttermilk (I use reconstituted dry buttermilk.)
1 rennet tablet (dessert type)

1. Heat the milk to 100° F and add the buttermilk. Remove from heat.
2. Thoroughly dissolve 1 rennet tablet in a small amount of water. Add to the warm milk. Cover the pot and allow to remain undisturbed until a firm curd is formed—approximately 18 to 24 hours.
3. Drain off most of the whey and then gently pour the remaining curd into a fine strainer or through cheesecloth. When the cheese stops dripping (2 to 3 hours), season with salt, and chill.

CHAPTER 4

Appetizers and Beverages

One of the most enjoyable aspects of boating is the camaraderie found among boaters. People are taking time out from their busy lives to relax and enjoy their favorite hobby. Being around happy boaters is an addicting pastime and often leads to casual, impromptu entertaining.

When I provision our boat I always plan on having lots of snacks that can be quickly brought out when a dinghy full of friends pulls up to the transom. Simple standbys include cheese and crackers, roasted nuts, chips and dip, sliced apples, clusters of grapes, or crunchy carrot sticks. I like to keep cans of smoked oysters and sardines on board, as well as black and green olives—all are popular munching fare. I also enjoy looking in markets for canned specialty items such as roasted bell peppers (add olive oil and chopped garlic and serve with French bread or crackers), caponata (eggplant appetizer served on crackers), and Brie, which can be lightly heated, sprinkled with chopped roasted nuts, and served with bread.

Sometimes, though, the occasion calls for something more than opening a can of nuts. When you are going to a potluck and want to bring a special appetizer, or when you are planning ahead and inviting some favorite friends over, leaf through these recipes. I think you will find some great surprises.

The loaf of sourdough bread stuffed with artichokes, clams, or crab is easy and always a fabulous hit. Potato Nachos is a popular and fun appetizer—just be sure to give everyone plates. I've included recipes for wontons, which keep for months in the refrigerator and make impressive appetizers. Try the Spicy Corn Cakes for something unusual, or make one of the easy appetizer tarts if you happen to have small tart pans on board. Pluck some mussels off the rocks and serve them with my easy Orange Sauce, or fry some Spicy Pecan Chicken Chunks—they'll be devoured in minutes.

Above all, remember to have fun.

Easy Appetizers

- Alternate black olives, cubes of cheese, and green olives on toothpicks.
- Wrap a seedless prune in bacon and bake.
- Place pineapple chunks, slices of bacon, and water chestnuts on a skewer. Marinate in teriyaki sauce for 1 hour before baking or broiling.
- Mix a ½ cup of grated cheddar cheese with 2 tablespoons of chopped olives and 2 tablespoons of mayonnaise. Spread on English muffins, cut the muffins in quarters, and broil until golden.
- Heat 1 pound of Velveeta cheese with 8 ounces of Mexican salsa until the cheese melts. Serve with chips.
- Spread mayonnaise on party rye bread, top with an onion slice, and sprinkle with Parmesan cheese. Broil until golden.
- Mix together 8 ounces of cream cheese, some diced ham, chopped black olives, and jalapeño chiles. Spread the cream cheese mixture on flour tortillas. Roll each tortilla into a cylinder and wrap tightly in saran wrap. To serve, unwrap and slice.

Cheese Wafers

48 slices

½ cup butter, at room temperature
1 cup grated cheddar cheese
1 cup flour
¼ teaspoon Worcestershire Sauce
¼ teaspoon salt

1. Cream together the butter and cheese; add the remaining ingredients.
2. Divide the mixture in half, roll into 2 cylinders, wrap in wax paper, and chill until firm.
3. Slice the cylinders into ¼-inch thick slices and place on greased baking sheets. Bake at 375°F for 10 to 15 minutes.
4. Serve warm, or store in an airtight container for several weeks.

Hot Spiced Olives

Make up a big batch of these olives to have on hand to serve with drinks. They will keep for months in the refrigerator. Save the leftover marinade to serve with homemade bread right out of the oven.

10 cloves garlic, finely chopped
1 ½ pounds black olives (such as Kalamata)
2 teaspoons dried rosemary
Finely chopped peel from one orange
1 ½ teaspoons crushed red pepper
1 teaspoon black peppercorns
2 cups olive oil

Combine all the ingredients and add enough olive oil to cover. Marinate at least one week. Serve at room temperature. The olives should always be completely covered with olive oil to prevent mold from growing.

Bev's Favorite Party Appetizer

36 servings

One of my cooking classes was relaxing around the dining table in a French farmhouse sharing recipes. Beverly insisted that this was her husband's favorite hors d'oeuvre, so I had to try it. It is not very French, but it certainly is tasty.

1 pound hamburger
1 pound spicy sausage (such as Jimmy Dean)
1 pound Velveeta cheese, cubed
½ teaspoon garlic salt
½ teaspoon oregano
½ teaspoon Worcestershire Sauce
1 loaf party rye

1. Cook the meat and drain well. Add the cheese and seasonings and stir until melted.
2. Spread the mixture on bread and bake at 350°F for 12 to 15 minutes. Can be frozen and then reheated.

Spinach Dip

2 ½ cups

Yogurt cheese, a low-calorie cream cheese substitute, can be easily made on board a boat (see page 37).

1 package (10 oz.) frozen chopped spinach, thawed and squeezed dry
1 cup yogurt cheese or cream cheese
½ cup chopped green onions
½ cup chopped parsley
1 teaspoon seasoned salt
½ teaspoon dried dill
3 tablespoons lemon juice

Combine all the ingredients and allow to marinate in the refrigerator for 48 hours before serving. Serve with crackers or fresh vegetables.

Herbed Cheese Spread

½ cup

8 ounces yogurt cheese or cream cheese
1 clove garlic, finely chopped
1 tablespoon dehydrated parsley or 2 tablespoons fresh
½ teaspoon dried thyme
1 teaspoon freshly ground black pepper

Combine the cheese with the spices and stir well. Store in the refrigerator. The spread keeps for about two weeks.

Other Uses for Yogurt Cheese

- For a dip to be served with fresh vegies, combine 1 ounce of Hidden Valley Ranch Dry Dressing Mix with ⅔ cup of yogurt cheese and ⅓ of cup mayonnaise.
- For a seafood spread with crackers, combine yogurt cheese with chopped olives and minced clams.

Cream Cheese, Fast and Easy

Cream cheese is the quintessential emergency hors d'oeuvre. When friends stop by your boat to chat, an impromptu invitation to stay for drinks often results. When you need to fix a fast and easy hors d'oeuvre, reach for cream cheese and try one of the following combinations:

- Jalapeño pepper jelly, spicy Mexican salsa, or chutney can be poured over cream cheese for a delicious spread.
- Smoked salmon or dried beef, chopped and mixed into cream cheese, can be spread on focaccia (see page 187) and baked, or used as a spread on crackers.
- Stir some Sun-Dried Tomato Seasoning (see page 167) or a can of drained, chopped clams into softened cream cheese for a quick spread.

Sourdough Roll-Ups

This simple recipe is always a favorite with my cooking students. When cruising in foreign ports you might have to substitute another type of bread, but the hors d'oeuvre will still taste great.

Sliced bread, such as sourdough, crusts removed
Cream cheese
Thinly sliced bacon
Toothpicks
Whole, pitted black olives

1. Spread the cream cheese ¼-inch thick on the bread. Place 2 slices of the prepared bread together and cut into bite-size pieces.
2. Wrap each bread cube in a slice of bacon and secure with a toothpick.
3. Bake at 375°F until the bacon is cooked—about 10 minutes. Drain well.
4. To serve, place a black olive on each toothpick.

Burrito-Wrapped Sausages

12 servings

4 slices jack or cheddar cheese
2 (8-inch) flour tortillas
2 (8-inches long) precooked spicy sausages
1 tablespoon cooking oil

Layer the cheese in the tortillas, top with the sausage, and roll up, securing with toothpicks. Sauté in the oil until the tortillas are golden and the cheese has melted. Slice and serve with toothpicks. Serve with Mexican Salsa (see page 165) if desired.

Lemon Pepper Cream Cheese Spread

1½ cups

This peppery cream cheese spread is reminiscent of pepper-coated Boursin cheese.

8 ounces whipped cream cheese
2 cloves garlic, minced
2 teaspoons grated lemon peel
4 teaspoons freshly ground black pepper
1 tablespoon lemon juice

Combine the ingredients and use either as a dip or spread for crackers.

Mozzarella Prosciutto Spread

2 cups

If you don't have prosciutto, you can use any cured meat—ham, dried beef, or salami work well, too. If you don't have mozzarella cheese, substitute Roquefort, Parmesan, or smoked Gruyère. This spread is excellent on crackers, baked on focaccia, or as a stuffing for chicken breasts.

8 ounces cream cheese
4 ounces mozzarella cheese, grated
¼ cup finely chopped parsley
¼ pound prosciutto or other cured meat, finely chopped

¼ teaspoon freshly ground black pepper
1 tablespoon grated lemon peel
1 tablespoon fresh lemon juice

Combine all the ingredients.

Porcini Mushroom Dip

Serves 2 to 4

Porcini mushrooms have a dominant, earthy flavor that pairs well with cream cheese. Try this dip warm with homemade bread cubes as a type of fondue. It is also excellent spread on focaccia and baked.

2 tablespoons olive oil
¼ cup chopped shallots or other type of onion
1 ounce dried porcini mushrooms, soaked in water until soft (do not substitute fresh mushrooms)
½ teaspoon freshly ground pepper
¼ cup dry sherry
8 ounces cream cheese

1. Sauté the shallots in the oil until limp.
2. Drain the mushrooms, squeeze dry, and finely chop.
3. Add the mushrooms to the shallots, season with pepper, and cook with the sherry until moisture evaporates. Mix with the cream cheese.

Focaccia with Black Olives and Cream Cheese

1½ cups (enough for a 14-inch round of bread)

8 ounces cream cheese, softened
2 cloves garlic, finely chopped
2 (4 oz. each) cans chopped black olives
½ red bell pepper, finely chopped
1 stalk celery, finely chopped
1 tablespoon Worcestershire sauce
1 teaspoon Tabasco sauce

Mix all the ingredients into the softened cream cheese and spread on a large round of focaccia or Boboli Bread. Bake at 400° F for 10 minutes. Slice into wedges and serve.

Layered Cheese Appetizer

8 servings

8 ounces cream cheese, at room temperature
8 ounces unsalted butter, at room temperature
1 filling—recipes below
Thinly sliced baguettes or crackers

Beat together the cream cheese and butter and blend until smooth. Layer the butter mixture with the filling of your choice, several times, beginning with the butter and ending with the filling. Chill about 1 hour.

Fillings

- Sun-Dried Tomato—Drain a 4-oz. jar of sun-dried tomatoes (packed in olive oil). Finely chop or purée the tomatoes with 1 tablespoon of the olive oil.
- Pesto—½ cup canned or fresh pesto.
- Ripe Olive—Combine the following ingredients:

¼ cup finely chopped black olives
2 tablespoons finely chopped green olives
1 teaspoon anchovy paste
1 clove garlic, finely chopped
2 tablespoons capers, drained and chopped
1 tablespoon lemon juice
½ cup canned or fresh pesto sauce

If the filling is too thick, add a little olive oil to thin. You can also purée all the ingredients in a food processor if one is available.

Jalapeño Pepper Jelly

6 cups

Jalapeño Pepper Jelly can be spread over cream cheese and served with crackers as an easy appetizer. A few teaspoons in a marinade make a tasty accent, or try it as an accompaniment to meats and fish.

When I lived ashore, I canned several batches of this jelly at Christmastime each year to use as gifts or to store on the boat for an impromptu appetizer. Now that I am living on board, I make up a batch in a few minutes and store it in a container with a tight-fitting lid. It keeps for years on the pantry shelf because both the vinegar and sugar are preservatives. Don't ever, though, put a dirty spoon in the jelly.

¾ cup finely chopped green bell peppers (about 3 large), stems and seeds removed
½ cup finely chopped Jalapeño chiles, stems removed*
6 cups sugar
1 ½ cups cider vinegar
1 (6 oz.) bottle liquid pectin
Green food coloring

1. Mix the peppers, chiles, sugar, and vinegar in a large saucepan and bring to a rolling boil. Boil for one minute. Remove from the heat and allow to cool slightly before stirring in the pectin and 5 drops of the food coloring.
2. Strain the mixture into hot sterilized jars and seal, or allow to cool and store in Tupperware.

**See page 139 for hints on how to handle chiles.*

Nachos

6 to 8 servings

A popular finger food, you can also serve nachos for a casual dinner.

8 ounces tortilla chips
1 (16 oz.) can pinto or black beans, rinsed and drained
4 cups grated cheese (jack or cheddar)
1 (4 oz.) can chopped green chiles
½ cup chopped cilantro
1 recipe (3 cups) Mexican Salsa Fresca (page 165)
1 recipe (2 ½ cups) Guacamole (page 166)

1. Arrange half the chips on a large ovenproof serving dish. Sprinkle with the beans and half the cheese. Top with the remaining chips and sprinkle with the rest of the cheese and the chiles.
2. Bake at 375°F until the cheese is bubbly—about 15 minutes.
3. Garnish with the cilantro and salsa. Top with the guacamole.

Variations

- Substitute 2 cups of finely chopped cooked chicken for the beans and a ½ cup of chopped green onion for the chiles.
- Substitute Papaya Salsa (see page xx) for Mexican Salsa.
- Substitute sour cream for the guacamole.
- Sprinkle mozzarella cheese, sliced black olives, and chopped sun-dried tomatoes (drained of oil) on top of chips. Garnish, after cheese is melted and bubbly, with fresh basil.

Potato Nachos

6 to 8 servings

2 large baking potatoes, cut in ⅛-inch thick slices
Olive oil
Salt and pepper
1 ½ cups grated cheddar or jack cheese
1 tomato, seeded and chopped
1 (4 oz.) can chopped green chiles
1 (4 oz.) can sliced black olives
1 small onion, finely chopped

Garnishes

Sour cream
Guacamole
Mexican Salsa
Chopped fresh cilantro

1. Line a baking sheet with foil. Place the potato slices in a single layer close together on the baking sheet. Brush the potatoes lightly with the olive oil (olive oil spray works even better). Season with salt and pepper.
2. Bake at 425°F for 10 minutes.
3. Top the potatoes with the remaining ingredients and bake until the potatoes are tender and the cheese is melted—about 8 to 10 minutes.
4. Serve with garnishes as desired.

Avocado and Bean Dip

Serves 4 to 6 people

1 tablespoon oil
1 onion, chopped
3 cloves garlic, minced
¼ pound ground beef
¼ pound ground pork
1 (16 oz.) can refried beans
1 (4 oz.) can Mexican salsa
4 ounces grated cheese
1 avocado, mashed and seasoned
1 cup chopped fresh tomatoes
Tortilla chips or warm tortillas

1. Heat the oil in a skillet and sauté the onion and garlic until tender.
2. Add the beef and pork and cook until done. Drain well. Combine the meat with the refried beans.
3. Place the meat and bean mixture in a serving dish and top with the salsa; sprinkle with the cheese. Mound the avocado in the center and garnish with the chopped tomatoes. Serve with chips or warmed tortillas.

Meatless Variation

Omit the first 5 ingredients. Layer the beans and then the salsa in a pie pan. Top with 1 cup of sour cream, 2 ½ cups of guacamole (see page 166), and the grated cheese. Top with some shredded lettuce, sliced black olives, chopped tomatoes, and chopped green onions.

Chile Relleño Wontons

12 egg rolls

1 medium onion, chopped
1 clove garlic, finely chopped
2 tablespoons olive oil
1 pound lean ground beef

½ teaspoon salt
½ teaspoon oregano
1 teaspoon cumin
2 cups shredded cheddar cheese
12 strips canned mild green chiles, deseeded
12 egg roll wrappers
1 egg white
Vegetable oil for deep-fat frying*
1 recipe Mexican Salsa Fresca (page 165)

1. Sauté the onion and garlic in the oil until tender. Add the beef, salt, oregano, and cumin; sauté until cooked and drain off fat. Allow the beef to cool, then stir in the cheese.
2. Place a chile strip diagonally on an egg roll wrapper. Top with 2 tablespoons of the meat mixture. Make the wonton by lifting the lower triangle flap over the chile and tucking the flap under the chile. Bring the left and right corners toward the center and roll, sealing the edges with a little egg white.
3. Deep-fry the wontons in 375°F oil until golden. Drain on paper towels. Serve immediately with a bowl of salsa for dipping.

**If you don't want to deep-fry, brush the outside of the wontons with warm oil and bake at 400° F until crisp and golden—about 20 minutes.*

Variation

Brown the meat and onion and stir in 1 package of Lawry's Taco Seasoning Mix, according to directions. Allow to cool before filling and sealing the wontons. Deep-fry as above until crisp. Serve with guacamole and salsa.

Spicy Corn Cakes with Cilantro and Avocado

16 servings

For the corn cakes

1 ½ cups dry pancake mix (page 32)
2 teaspoons Tabasco Sauce
2 eggs
¾ cup water
2 tablespoons butter, melted
1 (16 oz.) can corn, drained
Vegetable oil for frying
Cilantro leaves

Garnishes

Sour cream
Canned salsa
Sliced avocado

1. Combine the dry pancake mix with the Tabasco, eggs, water, and butter. Stir in the corn.
2. Heat a frying pan and add 1 tablespoon of oil. When the oil is hot, drop the batter by tablespoons into the pan. Press a leaf of cilantro into each corn cake. Lightly cook the corn cakes on both sides.
3. Serve hot with a dollop of sour cream and salsa, and a slice of avocado on top.

Do-Ahead Tip: Make the corn cakes 2 days in advance and store in the refrigerator. To reheat, wrap the corn cakes in foil and heat in a 325°F oven for 15 minutes.

Fried Mozzarella

12 cheese sticks

Mozzarella keeps for many months in a boat's refrigerator if it is tightly sealed. If you happen to be cruising in Latin America, you can substitute queso asadero or queso Chihuahua for the mozzarella. An old favorite of ours, this appetizer is surprisingly easy. The cheese must be thoroughly coated with the breading so it won't seep through when the appetizer is fried. Prechilling the breaded cheese sticks will also help keep the cheese from leaking out. If you wish, serve with Italian Tomato Sauce (see page 171).

6 ounces mozzarella cheese, cut into 3-inch lengths, each about ½-inch thick
½ cup flour
2 eggs, beaten
2 cups seasoned dry bread crumbs (if seasoned bread crumbs are not available, mix plain dry crumbs with ¼ teaspoon salt, ¼ teaspoon pepper, and 1 tablespoon dry parsley)
Vegetable oil for frying

Roll the cheese in the flour, then in the eggs, and finally in the bread crumbs. Be certain that each cheese stick is well coated and completely sealed before doing the next coating. Chill for 30 minutes. Heat ½ inch of oil to 375°F and fry until golden on all sides. Serve immediately.

Variations

- Grilled Mozzarella Kabobs—Cut squares of mozzarella and alternate them on skewers with pieces of sun-dried tomatoes and fresh basil leaves. Baste the ingredients with the olive oil from the jar of sun-dried tomatoes. Place the kabobs on foil on a barbecue; heat just until the cheese starts to melt. Serve with slices of crusty bread.
- Marinated Mozzarella—This works best with fresh mozzarella, which is even hard to find in the United States. Cube 1 pound of mozzarella. Marinate the cheese for a couple of hours in 3 tablespoons of olive

oil, 2 tablespoons of chopped fresh parsley, 1 teaspoon of chopped garlic, ¼ teaspoon of red pepper flakes, and salt and pepper to taste.

Cashew Brie Appetizer

1 ½ cups

This recipe is ideal to make if you have leftover Brie or Camembert cheese. (Once cheese has been hacked up at a party, it's difficult to make it look very neat again.) Instead, purée the cheese with the following ingredients and serve it as a spread. The coarser you chop the nuts, the more texture you will have in your spread.

¼ pound unsalted butter, at room temperature
¼ pound Brie, at room temperature, rind removed
¼ cup port or other dessert wine
½ cup cashews, lightly toasted if raw, and finely chopped

Purée together the butter, cheese, and wine until well combined. Stir in the nuts. Chill. Serve with crackers or celery.

Queso Fundido

6 to 8 servings

A Mexican-style cheese fondue, this is a delicious appetizer served with heated corn tortillas or homemade corn chips.

4 cups grated or sliced jack, Oaxaca, or Gruyère cheese
Your choice of seasoning (see list below)
Warm corn tortillas or chips (see following directions)
1 recipe Mexican Salsa Fresca (3 cups) (page 165)

1. Place the cheese in an ovenproof casserole and add your choice of seasoning. Broil or microwave until the cheese is melted.
2. If you're using warm tortillas, place a little melted cheese on the tortillas, add some salsa, and roll up to eat. If you're using chips, scoop up the cheese and seasoning with a chip and top with salsa.

Seasonings

- Cook ½ pound Mexican Chorizo sausage, casing removed, with 2 cloves of finely chopped garlic, breaking up the meat as it cooks. Drain well and mix the sausage with the cheese before heating.
- Mix 2 (4-oz.) cans of chopped green chiles with cheese before heating.
- Mix ¼ pound of bay shrimp with the cheese before heating.

To make warm corn tortillas, sprinkle tortillas lightly with water, wrap in foil, and heat in a 350° F oven for 15 minutes. Or, wrap the tortillas in paper towels and heat briefly—15 to 30 seconds—in microwave.

To make homemade corn chips, cut corn tortillas into quarters and fry in 2 inches of 375° F vegetable oil until crisp and golden. Drain.

Sourdough Bread Stuffed with Crab

This is an easily transportable appetizer, perfect to carry in your dinghy to another boat. When it's finished baking, remove the bread from the oven and wrap it in a towel or several layers of newspaper. Place the wrapped bread in an insulated container (a small cooler works well) and keep it covered until just before serving.

(**Note:** If sourdough bread is not available, use whatever round loaf of crusty bread you can find.)

The filling alone makes an excellent dip—either hot or cold.

1 large loaf sourdough bread, unsliced
One extra loaf of bread cut into chunks for dipping
8 ounces cream cheese, at room temperature
2 cups mayonnaise
2 cups Parmesan cheese
2 tablespoons fresh basil or 2 teaspoons dried
2 cloves garlic, finely chopped
8 ounces crab meat, real or imitation

1. Beat the cream cheese until smooth, gradually adding the mayonnaise. Stir in the Parmesan cheese, basil, garlic, and crab.
2. Cut a thick slice off the top of the bread and reserve it for a lid. Hollow out the bread, saving bread pieces for dipping. Fill with the crab mixture, cover with the bread lid, and wrap the filled bread in 2 layers of foil.
3. Bake at 300°F for 2 hours.

To serve: Remove the foil and lid. Dip the bread cubes into the crabmeat mixture and enjoy. Be sure to cut up the crust and serve it when most of the filling is gone. The crust, which is permeated with the flavors from the filling, is the best part!

Variations

- Substitute dill for basil and 3 (6 oz.) jars marinated artichoke hearts, drained and chopped, for crab.
- Substitute ¼ cup finely chopped sun-dried tomatoes for the crab.
- Add an additional 4 cloves finely chopped garlic.

Sourdough Bread Stuffed with Clams

16 ounces cream cheese, at room temperature
16 ounces chopped clams, drained, reserving ½ cup clam juice
2 tablespoons lemon juice
4 green onions, finely chopped
2 tablespoons finely chopped parsley
1 large loaf sourdough bread, unsliced
One extra loaf of bread cut into chunks for dipping

1. Beat the cream cheese until smooth. Stir in the clams, the reserved clam juice, lemon juice, onions, and parsley.
2. Continue with instructions as for the Sourdough Bread Stuffed with Crab, above.

Sourdough Bread Stuffed with Dry Beef and Chiles

16 ounces cream cheese, at room temperature
2 cloves garlic, finely chopped
2 tablespoons lemon juice
8 ounces canned green chiles, chopped
4 ounces dry beef, chopped
1 large loaf sourdough bread, unsliced
One extra loaf of bread cut into chunks for dipping

1. Beat the cream cheese until smooth. Stir in the remaining ingredients, *except* the bread.
2. Continue with instructions as for the Sourdough Bread Stuffed with Crab, above.

Caponata

8 servings

Capnoata is an eggplant-based appetizer that can be served on crackers, heated on pizza rounds, used as a pasta sauce, or served in scooped-out eggplant halves. It keeps for three weeks in the refrigerator.

¾ to 1 pound eggplant, cut into ½-inch cubes
1 bell pepper, chopped
1 large onion, chopped
2 cloves garlic, finely chopped
½ cup olive oil
1 (16 oz.) can tomatoes, undrained
2 tablespoons red wine vinegar
1 tablespoon sugar
1 tablespoon capers
1 tablespoon tomato paste
½ teaspoon *each* salt and freshly ground black pepper
¼ cup chopped parsley
1 (4 oz.) can sliced black olives
2 tablespoons chopped fresh basil or 2 teaspoons dried
½ cup pine nuts, roasted at 325°F until golden

1. In a heavy pan, sauté the eggplant, pepper, onion, and garlic in the olive oil until almost tender—about 15 minutes. Add the tomatoes and cook an additional 10 minutes.
2. Add the remaining ingredients *except* the basil and pine nuts. Cover and simmer 15 minutes. Stir in the basil.
3. Sprinkle with the pine nuts just before serving; serve warm or at room temperature.

Appetizer Tarts

18 tarts

This is one of the most popular appetizers with my cooking classes. The tarts can be prepared in advance and reheated, or they can be frozen. Miniature muffin pans with cups about 1½ inches in diameter are available at most cookware stores and are ideal for this recipe.

Pastry

3 ounces cream cheese, at room temperature
½ cup butter, at room temperature
1 cup flour

1. Make the dough by beating together the cream cheese and butter. Stir in the flour and chill for one hour.
2. Divide the chilled dough into 18 pieces. Press 1 piece of dough into each mini muffin cup so that it covers the bottom and sides.
3. Fill each cup with one of the following:

Shrimp Quiche Filling

2 teaspoons olive oil
¼ cup chopped onion
2 ounces drained bay shrimp
½ cup grated Jarlsberg or Swiss cheese
3 eggs, lightly beaten
¼ cup cream or milk
¼ teaspoon freshly grated nutmeg
Freshly ground pepper to taste

1. Sauté the onion in olive oil until tender.
2. Place a few shrimp, a small amount of cheese, and some of the onion in each tart.
3. Combine the remaining ingredients and pour into the shells.
4. Bake at 350° F for 30 minutes or until the filling is set. Allow to cool slightly before removing from pans. Serve warm.

Variation

Substitute chopped cooked bacon, crab, ham, or canned clams for the shrimp.

Chile Cheese Filling

⅓ cup sour cream
⅓ cup mayonnaise
1 cup grated jack cheese
4 ounces chopped, mild green canned chiles
Paprika

1. Combine the sour cream and mayonnaise.
2. Place a small amount of cheese in each tart and then top with the chiles and a dollop of the sour cream mixture. Sprinkle with paprika.
3. Bake at 350° F for 30 minutes. Allow to cool slightly before removing from pans. Serve warm.

Miniature Frittatas

2 dozen

8 medium shallots, peeled and chopped or 1 onion, chopped
1 small red pepper, chopped
2 medium zucchini, grated
1 cup fresh bread crumbs
½ cup freshly grated Parmesan cheese
2 cups ricotta cheese
1 teaspoon dried oregano
½ teaspoon black pepper
2 eggs, lightly beaten
24 very thin slices pepperoni

1. Stir all the ingredients together *except* the pepperoni.
2. Spray miniature muffin pans with nonstick coating. Place a slice of pepperoni in the bottom of each muffin cup and top with a spoonful of the egg mixture.

3. Bake at 375°F for 25 minutes. While the frittatas are still hot, remove them from the pans and allow to cool.
4. Serve warm or at room temperature.

Taco Tarts

16 appetizers

These tasty appetizers can be made in miniature muffin pans. They are easy to make and a great party treat. (This recipe can also be prepared in an 8-inch pie pan. Bake at 375°F for 30 minutes. Cool before serving.)

Crust

½ pound lean ground beef
1 tablespoon dehydrated taco seasoning mix
1 tablespoon spicy taco sauce

Filling

1 tablespoon spicy taco sauce
2 tablespoons chopped black olives
⅓ cup crushed nacho-flavored chips
½ cup sour cream
½ cup grated cheddar cheese

1. Combine the crust ingredients and press into muffin cups.
2. Combine the filling ingredients *except* the cheese. Divide the filling among the crust-lined cups and top with the cheese.
3. Bake at 425°F for 8 minutes. Allow to cool briefly. Gently loosen each tart with the tip of a knife and carefully remove.
4. Serve hot. Can be reheated in microwave.

Popcorn in the Pressure Cooker

This is the best way that I know of to make popcorn—and there are usually no dead soldiers lying in wait to break a tooth filling on an unsuspecting muncher.

2 tablespoons cooking oil
1 cup popping corn
One or more of the following seasonings: butter, cayenne pepper, grated Parmesan or cheddar cheese

1. Heat the oil in the pressure cooker. Add the popcorn, seal the pressure cooker, and set the pressure at the lowest setting.
2. Over high heat, pop the corn. As popping slows down, release the pressure, reduce the heat, and shake the pan vigorously.
3. When popping stops, turn off the heat and uncover.
4. Season as desired.

Ceviche

6 servings

Because Hal enjoys fishing and often catches more than I care to cook, inviting friends over to our boat for ceviche appetizers—raw fish marinated in lime juice—is a good way to use some of the excess fish.

A few words of caution about ceviche. Be sure that the fish you are using have been caught in unpolluted water. Since the fish will not be cooked, parasites might survive. Bottom-feeding fish tend to have more parasites than free-swimming fish, so avoid using bottom feeders such as halibut for ceviche. Hal and I have been eating ceviche for 30 years with no ill effects—but then, we don't eat fish caught in Santa Monica Bay!

Lots of lime juice is needed to "cook" fish for ceviche. Fresh lime gives the best flavor, but I have used bottled juice and/or vinegar in a pinch. The acid in the lime juice chemically cooks the fish, and the flesh turns an opaque color when it has finished marinating. A delicious chilled dish on a hot

summer day, ceviche can be served either as a main course salad for lunch, or as a crowd-pleasing appetizer.

1 ½ pounds fresh red snapper, mackerel, or firm white fish, cubed
1 ½ cups (or more) fresh lime juice
1 pound fresh tomatoes, peeled and chopped
1 ½ cups white onions, finely chopped
3 serrano (or other small, hot chiles) chiles, seeded and finely chopped
1 clove garlic, finely chopped
1 teaspoon oregano
¾ cup cilantro leaves
¼ cup olive oil
Salt and pepper to taste

Garnish

1 avocado, sliced
Lettuce leaves

1. Place the fish in a nonmetallic container and completely cover it with lime juice. Marinate the fish in the refrigerator for 5 hours, or until the flesh is opaque. Stir occasionally to evenly coat all of the fish. I marinate the fish in a Ziploc bag which fits easily into an already crowded refrigerator and saves on clean up.

2. Drain the fish and discard the liquid. Just before serving, combine the remaining ingredients and mix with the fish. Garnish with the avocado and serve on lettuce leaves.

Quick Fix: Substitute 8 ounces chunky Mexican salsa for the vegetables.

Stir-Fried Lobster with Cilantro

2 to 4 servings

We once anchored at Los Frailes in the Sea of Cortez for several days of diving and exploring. While there, we got to know some of the campers on the shore and, one evening, a camper named Suki invited us for an incredible meal around her campfire.

First, Suki placed her wok right in the campfire and stir-fried some freshly caught lobster. While we were enjoying this tasty treat, she soaked some corn husks in water (she had run out of foil) and placed seasoned chunks of fish inside the husks and cooked them right in the fire. Fabulous!

1 lobster tail
1 tablespoon olive oil
½ onion, chopped
2 cloves garlic
3 tablespoons cilantro

Cut the lobster tail through the shell into 1½-inch chunks. Heat the oil in a wok, add the onion, garlic, and lobster, and stir-fry until the lobster shell is pink and the meat is opaque. Garnish with cilantro and serve.

Mussels in Orange Sauce

4 servings

Gathering your own mussels on a rocky shore at low tide is a fun task. (Leather gloves will help protect your fingers.) Be sure to discard any mussels that do not open after you have steamed them.

Salt and freshly ground black pepper
6 ounces fresh orange juice, strained
4 tablespoons finely chopped fresh parsley
½ cup extra virgin olive oil
1 ½ cups white wine
24 large mussels, scrubbed clean and debearded*

**The beard, or byssus, of the mussel is a tuft of tough filament that mussels use to cling to rocks and other surfaces. To remove the beard, hold the shell in one hand and grasp the protuding "hair" firmly between your thumb and index finger of the other hand, pulling and wiggling the filament at the same time until it breaks free from the mussel.*

Combine the salt, pepper, orange juice, and parsley in a bowl. Whisk in the oil. In a large saucepan, heat the wine and add the mussels. Cover and allow to steam until the mussels are open. Place the cooked mussels on a serving plate and drizzle with the orange sauce.

Shrimp with Mango-Lime Sauce

8 servings

Through the generosity of Mexican shrimpers, I have had the opportunity of eating my share of fresh shrimp. Several years ago, Hal and I helped rescue a sailboat that had drifted ashore in Bahia Santa Maria on Mexico's Pacific Coast. The Mexican shrimp boat that eventually pulled *Gavotte* off the beach was generously paid and had no need to continue his shrimping trip. The skipper shared his catch with the yachties in the bay, and I eventually came up with this recipe.

1 pound shrimp, in shell and uncooked
1 cup white wine
1 recipe (1 ½ cups) Mango Lime Sauce (page 177)
Fresh cilantro leaves

Boil the shrimp in the wine for 5 minutes, or just until they start to turn pink. Drain. When cool enough to handle, shell and devein the shrimp. Serve chilled with Mango Lime Sauce and garnish with cilantro leaves.

Northern Thai Appetizer

6 to 8 servings

¼ cup uncooked rice
3 small dried red chile peppers, seeded
2 cups water
1 pound ground beef
¼ cup lime juice
2 tablespoons fish sauce or soy sauce
1 teaspoon sugar
¼ teaspoon salt
4 green onions, finely chopped
½ cup mint leaves, finely chopped
Butter lettuce for serving

1. In a *dry* saucepan, roast the rice and chiles over medium heat for about 5 minutes, shaking periodically. Remove from heat and grind to a powder in a food processor.
2. In the same pan, bring the water to a boil. Add the meat, stirring to break it up. Cook 30 seconds, or until the meat loses its pink color. Strain.
3. Mix the meat and rice with the remaining ingredients, *except* the lettuce. Serve while still warm, scooping up the meat mixture and eating it in a lettuce leaf. If done ahead, you can reheat the beef mixture. The contrast of cool lettuce and warm beef is irresistible.

Spicy Pecan Chicken Chunks

8 servings

Although this recipe is great as an appetizer, I have also coated boneless chicken breasts and fish fillets with the pecan coating and served them for a main course. Make up a large batch of the coating to have on hand.

1 egg, beaten
1 pound boneless, skinless chicken breasts, cut in bite-size pieces
Cooking oil

Breading

1 cup flour
1 cup chopped pecans
4 teaspoons ground cumin
2 teaspoons dried thyme
1 teaspoon cayenne pepper
Salt and pepper to taste

1. Combine all the breading ingredients; set aside.
2. Dip the chicken pieces in the egg and then roll in the breading.
3. Deep-fry the chicken in oil until done.

Sausage Stuffed Wontons

8 to 10 servings

This recipe has made me famous as a cook. When I show up with my bamboo steamers at a boaters' potluck supper, people go crazy. If you ever want a recipe that perks up your ego, this is the one. When pre-seasoned sausage is not available, make your own by seasoning well with soy, dried red pepper flakes, and even some minced water chestnuts. You can use pork, beef, chicken, or turkey sausage. Or, try the filling for Siu Mai (page 51).

The wontons can be steamed in advance and reheated just before serving.

Never throw away leftover wontons. Heat some oil

and deep fry them. For an appetizer, sprinkle them with cheese, herbs, and spices. (Lawry's Pinch of Herbs, some cayenne pepper, and grated cheese is my favorite.) Use wontons instead of chips with dips. For a simple dessert, sprinkle them with cinnamon and sugar.

1 (12 oz.) package spicy sausage (such as Jimmy Dean)
8 ounces wonton skins
Cabbage leaves for lining steamer
⅓ cup Spicy Soy Dipping Sauce (page 164)

1. Pinch off about 2 teaspoons of the sausage and place in the center of a wonton. Bring the edges of the wonton together and pinch to seal.
2. Line the bottom of a bamboo steamer with the cabbage leaves and steam in a wok over boiling water. When the cabbage is limp, arrange the stuffed wontons on top of the cabbage. Cover the steamer and steam for 15 to 20 minutes. Test for doneness by cutting one of the wontons in half. Pork is cooked when all traces of pink are gone.
3. Allow the wontons to cool slightly. Serve with Spicy Soy Dipping Sauce.

Siu Mai— Steamed Meat Dumplings

40 appetizers

Filling

1 pound lean ground pork
1 teaspoon salt
15 water chestnuts, finely chopped
6 scallions, finely chopped
5 dried mushrooms, reconstituted in warm water and minced (reserve liquid from mushrooms)
¼ cup finely chopped cilantro
2 teaspoons finely chopped ginger
1 tablespoon soy sauce
1 tablespoon sherry
2 tablespoons sugar
1 teaspoon sesame oil
¼ cup cornstarch
12 ounces wonton skins
Cabbage leaves for lining steamer

1. Mix all the filling ingredients together.
2. Trim off the corners of the wonton skins to form circles. Place 1 teaspoon of the mixture in the middle of a skin. Gather up the sides, letting the skin pleat naturally around the filling. Give the middle a light squeeze while tapping the bottom on a flat surface so the wonton will stand upright.
3. Follow the instructions on page 50 (Sausage-Stuffed Wontons) for steaming.
4. Serve with Spicy Soy Dipping Sauce (page 164).

Variation
Pot Stickers

Pot stickers are a delicious steamed dumpling with a crisp bottom. Rumor has it that the Chinese Emperor's chef allowed the water to evaporate from the wok when he was steaming dumplings and the bottoms of the dumplings almost burned. He rescued them in time, though—the bottoms were a delightful golden color with a nice crunch. The emperor was thrilled with this culinary invention.

1. Follow steps 1 and 2 for Steamed Meat Dumplings (below).
2. For each 2 dozen dumplings, heat 1 tablespoon of oil in a 10- to 11-inch nonstick skillet over medium heat. Set in the pot stickers (don't thaw if frozen). Cook, uncovered, until the bottoms are a deep golden brown—about 5 to 7 minutes.
3. Carefully pour in ¼ cup water; cover and reduce heat to low; steam for 10 minutes.
4. Remove from pan and serve with Spicy Soy Dipping Sauce (page 164).

Shrimp and Spinach Pot Stickers with Garlic-Lemon Sauce

30 pot stickers

Filling

10-ounce package frozen, chopped spinach, thawed and squeezed dry
½ pound shelled and deveined uncooked shrimp, chopped
6 water chestnuts, finely chopped
1 tablespoon finely chopped onion
1 egg white
1 tablespoon soy sauce
1 teaspoon chili paste with garlic
2 teaspoons finely chopped fresh ginger
1 tablespoon finely chopped lemon peel
30 wonton skins
2 tablespoons cooking oil

Combine all the filling ingredients; set aside.

Sauce

¼ cup lemon juice
2 tablespoons dry sherry
2 tablespoons soy sauce
¼ teaspoon chili paste with garlic
2 teaspoons finely chopped ginger
3 tablespoon sugar

Combine all the ingredients for the sauce; set aside.

1. Follow instructions for Steamed Dumplings (page 51), steps one and two.
2. Pour in the sauce, cover the pan, and steam for 10 minutes.
3. Spoon the sauce over dumplings before serving.

Cabbage-Wrapped Dumplings, Mexicana

18 rolls

18 pieces napa or other cabbage, cut into 4-inch × 2-inch pieces

Filling

1 pound ground beef or pork
1 teaspoon ground cumin
1 teaspoon dried oregano
½ cup chopped water chestnuts or jicama
2 tablespoons chopped mild green chile
1 stalk celery, chopped
¼ cup chopped onion
2 teaspoons cornstarch
1 egg

1. Heat 2 cups of water in the bottom of a wok. Place the cabbage in a bamboo steamer, cover, and steam until limp—about 5 minutes. Allow the cabbage to cool.
2. Combine the filling ingredients and place 1 tablespoon of the meat mixture in each cabbage leaf. Roll up and secure with a toothpick.
3. Place the cabbage bundles in the steamer, cover, and steam for 30 minutes. Test for doneness by cutting one roll in half. They are cooked when all traces of pink are gone.
4. Serve with Mexican Salsa (page 165) if desired.

Chinese Variation

Omit the cumin, oregano, and chile and substitute 2 teaspoons of Chinese five-spice powder (found in Oriental groceries; also made by Spice Island) and 1 teaspoon of cayenne powder. Serve with Spicy Soy Dipping Sauce (page 164).

Fresh Vietnamese Spring Rolls

8 servings

The Vietnamese use edible rice paper *(banh trang)* as the wrapping for their spring rolls. Available in Oriental markets, rice paper is sold dry and keeps indefinitely. To soften the papers and make them pliable, soak briefly in water. Wrap the softened rice paper around cooked shrimp and fresh vegetables for a refreshing appetizer.

8 (8-inch diameter) rounds edible rice paper
16 shrimp, cooked, peeled, deveined, and cut in half through center and chilled
8 pieces red lettuce
2 ounces bean threads, soaked in warm water until soft—about 20 minutes —drained and cut into 1-inch pieces.
1 large carrot, grated
1 cup fresh bean sprouts
¼ cup fresh mint leaves
¼ cup chopped green onion
¼ cup cilantro leaves
¼ cup finely chopped roasted peanuts

1. Moisten 2 rounds of rice paper at a time by lightly spraying them with warm water and rubbing with your hand. Allow the papers to sit on a sheet of aluminum foil until softened.
2. To assemble, place a lettuce leaf in the center of each rice paper and top with one-eighth of the above ingredients. Fold the sides over to cover the ingredients, then fold in the bottom and top, making a cylinder. Place seam side down on a plate while assembling remaining rolls.
3. Serve with Lime Dipping Sauce (page 165).

Deep-Fried Vietnamese Spring Rolls

16 rolls

16 (6-inch diameter) rounds edible rice paper, reconstituted (see Fresh Vietnamese Spring Rolls, this page)
1 egg, beaten
3 cups cooking oil
16 pieces red lettuce
¼ cup fresh cilantro leaves
¼ cup fresh mint leaves

Filling

1 tablespoon cooking oil
½ pound lean pork
4 reconstituted, drained, and chopped shitake mushrooms
½ pound chopped shrimp
2 tablespoons chopped green onions
2 teaspoons finely chopped garlic
1 carrot, grated
1 ounce bean threads, soaked in warm water until soft—about 20 minutes—drained, and cut into 1-inch pieces
1 tablespoon soy sauce
1 tablespoon sherry
½ teaspoon sugar
½ teaspoon pepper
1 egg

1. To make the filling, heat the oil in a wok and stir fry the pork until cooked. Add the remaining ingredients *except* the egg and stir fry until the liquid is absorbed. When cool, stir in the egg.
2. Place 2 tablespoons of the filling along the bottom third of 1 round of rice paper. Moisten the edges with the beaten egg and fold the sides over the filling; then roll the rice paper into a cylinder.
3. Heat the oil to 375° F and deep fry the spring rolls until golden.
4. Serve each spring roll wrapped in a lettuce leaf with the cilantro and mint leaves.
5. Serve with Lime Dipping Sauce (page 165).

Coffee Drinks and Entertaining

Boating's casual lifestyle lends itself to impromptu entertaining. Hal and I keep a variety of liqueurs on board and enjoy hosting a spur-of-the-moment coffee party on a cool evening.

You can make delicious drinks by adding any of the following liqueurs to steaming hot coffee:

- Kahlúa, Creme de Cocoa, and Grand Marnier
- Hazelnut liqueur, brandy, Creme de Cocoa, and rum
- Amaretto, Bailey's Irish Cream, and Kahlúa
- Brandy and Creme de Cocoa
- Irish whiskey and sugar (for Irish Coffee)

And of course, you can top off all these with a generous dollop of whipped cream.

Chilcotin's Coffee

This drink tasted fabulous when Hal and I visited with the cruising boat *Chilcotin* in Tonga. Their special concoction was made up of 2 parts of Kahlúa to 1 part Cointreau mixed with decaf coffee and a tablespoon of dry powdered milk. Delicious!

Iced Coffee

Make a very strong pot of coffee, sweeten to taste while it's still hot, and allow to cool. Serve each drink in a tall glass with ice cubes and cream. Or, purée the coffee, ice, and cream in a blender and add a shot of rum or brandy.

Agua de Jamaica (Hibiscus Flower Juice)

4 cups

In Mexico, *aguas*—refreshing ice cold drinks that are made with fresh fruits such as orange, lemon, and pineapple—are sold in stands throughout the country. One of my favorites is made with Jamaica, or hibiscus flowers. Popular all over Latin America and the Caribbean, it is the perfect pick-me-up on a hot summer day.

1 cup Jamaica flowers (available in Caribbean and Latin American markets in the U.S.)
3 ½ cups cold water
½ cup sugar (or more)*
¼ cup fresh lime juice*
Lime slices for garnish

1. Cover the Jamaica flowers with some of the water and bring to a boil. Continue boiling until the flowers lose their color—about 10 minutes. Stir in the sugar and dissolve. Strain.
2. Add the remaining water and the lime juice. Adjust sugar to taste.
3. Serve over ice, garnished with a lime slice.

**If available, you can substitute lime syrup (below) for the sugar and lime juice.*

NOTE: Hibiscus Flower Juice can be stored for several days, but because it is quite acidic, do not store it in aluminum, copper, or enamel containers. Instead, use glass, plastic, or stainless steel. The juice must be kept refrigerated or it will ferment. (Jamaica beer? Hmmm, not a bad idea either!)

Lime Syrup

Fresh limes are as essential to Mexican cooking as chile peppers. After boating for so many years in Mexico, I've become addicted to squeezing limes over our vegetables and meats, into salsa, and even into a cold bottle of beer. Consequently, I stock up on fresh limes whenever I can.

When limes are plentiful, make your own lime syrup which is the base for many cool and refreshing drinks.

2 cups sugar
3 cups water
2 cups fresh lime juice, seeds removed

In a saucepan, combine the sugar and water. Bring to a boil and then reduce to a simmer, stirring until the sugar dissolves. Allow to cool and then combine with lime juice.

For Limeade, dilute lime syrup with equal parts water. Add ice cubes and garnish each glass with a slice of fresh lime. For an even more refreshing drink, add soda water instead of tap water.

For Daiquiris, add equal parts rum to syrup. Blend with ice cubes or serve on the rocks. Strawberries, pineapples, bananas, or peaches can be blended with the lime syrup and rum for exquisite fruit daiquiris.

A Lime Sunburst is made with equal parts lime syrup, vodka, and orange liqueur. Add some lime peel and soda water to taste. (Use 1½ ounces of each ingredient for one drink.)

Santa Fe Margarita

5 cups, or about 8 to 10 drinks

12 ounces Gold Tequila
12 ounces frozen limeade or lime syrup
12 ounces beer
6 ounces Triple Sec
3 handfuls ice

Place all the ingredients in a blender and blend until frothy. Or, serve on the rocks.

For a ***Grand Gold Margarita,*** substitute Grand Marnier for the Triple Sec.

Melon Cooler

2 drinks

3 ounces tequila or vodka or rum
1 ounce orange liqueur
3 ounces pineapple juice
2 ounces lime juice
Soda water
Melon liqueur

Mix together the tequila, orange liquer, pineapple juice, and lime juice; divide into two tall glasses. Add ice and soda water to fill the glasses. Float melon liqueur on top.

Mint-Pineapple Tea

1 pot of mint tea, chilled
Equal amount of pineapple juice

Combine the tea and pineapple juice; pour over ice for a refreshing drink.

Coco Locos

4 drinks

Frozen limeade is the base for this drink, but if you can find powdered sweet and sour mix (in the liquor section of the market), it would also work well.

1 can frozen limeade or 6 ounces lime syrup
6 ounces vodka
1 to 2 cups water
2 tablespoons coconut powder
Ice

Mix all the ingredients in a shaker or blender.

Lime Wine Punch

12 servings

Don't use your best chardonnay for this recipe, because this is a great way to disguise cheap white wine. A bulk Chablis will do just fine.

1 cup lime juice (or substitute 1 cup lime syrup and eliminate fruit juice; you can also substitute frozen lime juice)
1 cup pineapple or orange juice
8 cups white wine
2 lemons, sliced
1 orange, sliced
2 cups club soda

Chill all ingredients and mix together.

Hot Buttered Rum Mix

¼ pound salted butter
½ cup powdered sugar
1 teaspoon nutmeg
1 tablespoon cinnamon

Combine the ingredients and store at room temperature.

To make a hot buttered rum, place 2 tablespoons of the mix in a cup, add 2 tablespoons of rum, and a ½ cup of boiling water. Stir well. Serve with a cinnamon stick, if desired. (**NOTE:** I've kept this mix on board, unrefrigerated, for months.)

Raspados and Raspberries

Driving down the Baja California highway several years ago, Hal and I passed through the wine growing region of the Santo Tomas valley. We decided to take a back road to see some of the countryside.

On a winding dirt road one block from the highway, in front of a well-maintained Mexican home, we saw a sign advertising *raspados.* Hal and I had the same reaction—were raspberries really growing in this agricultural valley? We approached the lady of the house who indicated, yes, indeed, she did have *raspados.* She removed a number of bottles from the refrigerator—*limon, fresa, piña*—and asked us what we wanted. We responded, smiling, *"raspado."*

We didn't want limes, strawberries, or pineapples. We were interested in raspberries. The lady of the house disappeared outside. Our mouths watered. She was gathering the succulent raspberries. When she came back inside we tried to maintain our smiles as she held out a glassful of shaved ice and asked us again: *limon, fresa, piña?*

We not only enjoyed a treat of thirst quenching, sweetened, fresh lime juice, but added a new word to our meager Spanish vocabulary—*raspado* (scraping)—which means "snow cone," *not* "raspberry."

Since then, Hal and I have tried to improve our Spanish. We spent a month in Antigua, Guatemala, living with a family and being privately tutored six hours daily. Although we are by no means fluent, we have noticed a decided improvement since our introduction to *raspados!*

To make your own *raspados,* add a ½ cup of lime syrup to 1 cup of shaved or crushed ice.

CHAPTER 5

Seafood

Seafood and Substitutions

Seafood lends itself to many different methods of cooking. It can be poached, broiled, baked, grilled, barbecued, and panfried. And many people enjoy it *au natural,* or fresh from the sea, with no cooking at all.

On board *SpiceSea* we enjoy fresh seafood whenever possible. Although I've suggested a specific type of seafood for many recipes in this chapter, the type of seafood, preparation methods, and the sauces often are interchangeable.

For example, if you don't have fresh salmon, you can prepare my recipes for Salmon with Green Chile Pesto or Salmon Fillets with Dill and Mandarin Orange Sauce by substituting bass, tuna, blue fish, croaker, rock cod, red snapper, shrimp, or scallops. There really isn't any type of fish that wouldn't be enhanced by these sauces and methods of preparation. The only adjustment that you have to make is to change the cooking time for larger or smaller fillets.

Fish Preparation

How to Fillet a Whole Fish

Insert the knife just behind the gills and side fin, cutting down until you reach the backbone. Holding the head with one hand, cut along the backbone toward the tail. Remove the fillet. Turn the fish over and repeat on the other side.

Lay the fillet skin side down. Starting near the tail, cut the fillet just through the meat. Slide the knife between the skin and the meat, holding on to the skin as you slide the knife along. Discard the skin.

If you want boneless fish, cut away the rib cage and any other bones that you are able to separate from the fillet.

Allow about ¼ to ⅓ pound of fish fillets per person.

Methods of Cooking Fish

Deciding how to cook fish depends on the thickness of the cut and how firm the fish is.

Broiling works best for small fish fillets. Season the fish with salt, pepper, and the herbs of your choice (cilantro, thyme, tarragon). Baste with a little fat—olive oil, butter, mayonnaise—to keep thin fillets from drying out. Broil for 2 to 3 minutes.

Fish is cooked when the flesh turns opaque, or when it reaches an internal temperature of about 120° F. If using a meat thermometer, check the temperature of the fish at its thickest part, but do not allow the thermometer to come in contact with the backbone. Allow about 12 minutes cooking time per inch of thickness. To test for doneness, cut a small slit in the center of a thick fillet, steak, or large whole fish.

Remove the fish from the heat source while the fish is still a little translucent—it will continue cooking due to residual heat.

Cooking in foil is the easiest way to prepare fish, especially on board a boat. There are no pans to wash and the fish can be cooked either in the oven or on the barbecue. (See page 153 for instructions on sealing the foil.) Fish with lean white meat—bass, pike, rock cod, snapper, porgies—are especially good when cooked in foil. I like to season foil-cooked fish with a little chopped onion, olive oil, and a fresh herb such as parsley, mint, dill, or basil. You can also add some tomatoes or a little white wine for extra juice. The fish can be served either in its own juice; drained and served with a warm seafood sauce; or chilled with mayonnaise or hollandaise.

In a preheated 400° F oven, bake foil-wrapped fish for 12 minutes per inch of thickness. On the barbecue, cook until the foil puffs up and is too hot to touch on top—then begin timing.

Barbecuing is a good method of cooking any firm fish such as mahimahi, salmon, yellowtail, or swordfish. Brushing the fish with an oil-based marinade or coating it with mayonnaise prevents it from drying out. (See pages 21 and 153 for barbecuing hints.) Always preheat the barbecue. To prevent thin fish from falling apart and disappearing into the coals, I line the barbecue with foil that has lots of holes punched in it. The fish cooks on top of the foil and the holes allow the barbecue flavor to permeate the meat.

Panfrying, the method I favor for fish such as rock cod and bass (cabrillo, striped, and kelp); bass is probably my favorite fish that Hal brings back to the boat. Nothing tastes better than fresh cabrillo breaded and fried in a little olive oil.

To panfry, pat the fish dry with a paper towel. Dip it in seasoned flour, then in a beaten egg, and finally coat it with bread crumbs. I prefer *panko,* the Japanese dried, unseasoned bread crumbs (readily available in West Coast grocery stores), because they make a very crispy crust. By seasoning the flour, egg, or bread crumbs you can vary the flavor in innumerable ways. One of my favorite combinations is lemon pepper seasoning in the flour, Italian herbs in the egg, and Cajun spices in the bread crumbs—the unusual mix provides a complex flavor that is surprisingly very good.

Another delicious coating for panfried fish is to first dredge the fillets in flour, then dip them in a mixture of 2 eggs that have been beaten with 2 tablespoons of Parmesan cheese and 1 tablespoon of chopped parsley. Sauté in olive oil.

Sole is a very thin fish that also panfries well. It cooks in just a few minutes and is best when prepared with a light flour coating to give it some color. Thicker flatfish such as flounder and halibut can be breaded before sautéeing them.

Deep-fried fish is wonderfully moist on the inside with a crispy coating outside. (See page 79 for deep-frying coatings and techniques.) This method, though, should be used only in calm anchorages because of the potential danger of spilling hot oil in the galley. I once was cooking fish tacos in my wok and not paying close attention to the pan when an errant wake knocked the pan off the burner. Four cups of hot oil spilled all over the galley. Yuck!

Poaching is a method I still use even though I gave up my fancy fish poacher when we moved aboard. I've been happily poaching fish in a frying pan with a tight fitting lid ever since. Halibut, salmon, sea bass, and thresher shark are all excellent fish for poaching. Sauté a little onion and garlic in olive oil and add a ½ cup of chicken broth or white wine. Bring the liquid to a boil and arrange the fish in a single layer in the pan. Cover and cook until the fish is opaque. For each half-inch thickness of fish, allow about 6 minutes of cooking time. Serve with a flavorful sauce.

Oven baking is good for any fish that can be barbecued, poached, fried, or cooked in foil. A favorite recipe of mine for oven-baked fish is Huachinango (red snapper) Veracruz with a flavorful tomato and olive caper sauce (see page 166). For baking fish without a sauce, allow 12 minutes per inch of thickness at 400° F.

Marinating uncooked fish in lime juice is another excellent way to prepare seafood. See page 48 for ceviche recipes and below for information about parasites and toxins in fish.

Finally, if you are faced with the delightful problem of having so much fresh fish aboard that you don't know what to do with it, try making ***Fish Jerky.***

Cut boneless fillets (albacore, wahoo, dorado, and bonito make especially good jerky) into quarter-inch thick slices and marinate overnight in a combination of soy sauce, teriyaki, and whatever spices you wish. Drain the fish well and dry on racks set over a baking sheet in the sunshine for two days or until dry. If it is damp at night, bring the fish inside each evening and put the fillets outside again when the sun is shining. Protect the fish with a cheesecloth tent if bugs and flies are a problem.

Store fish jerky in an airtight container. A great snack treat.

Parasites and Poisons

Ciguatera is a word that scares a lot of cruisers—and rightly so. It's no laughing matter to come down with a case of this toxic seafood poisoning that's common in both the Caribbean and South Pacific. Coral-eating fish are the chief carriers of ciguatera, and the toxin can be passed on to people who eat infected fish. One can also be infected with ciguatera by eating fish that have preyed on the coral eaters in the food chain. Ciguatera can affect 500 species of fish, including snapper, barracuda, sea bass, grouper, jack, perch, flounder, eel, and Spanish mackerel.

The dinoflagellate that causes the problem does not affect the fish. It can't be detected by color, odor, or flavor; it does, however, accumulate in the fish, especially internal organs, making older, larger fish more toxic. One rule of thumb states that if the whole fish won't fit on your plate, don't eat it.

Ciguatera is not affected by cooking, freezing, salting, marinating, or pickling. The few cases of cigautera poisoning that I have read about occurred when unsuspecting boaters ate at restaurants in the Caribbean. (Another reason to use this cookbook and learn to enjoy cooking on board!) Actually, statistically you're more likely to become ill eating chicken.

There is no cure for ciguatera. While this poisoning is normally not fatal, always ask local fishermen which fish are—and are not—safe. The U.S. Department of Agriculture hopes that there will soon be a simple test to check seafood for several toxins, including ciguatera.

Given how nervous some people are about eating cooked fish, it's not surprising that the idea of eating raw or marinated, uncooked seafood is less than appealing. By taking certain precautions and knowing where your fish came from, though, you should be able to enjoy uncooked seafood.

You should always fish in unpolluted water away from industrial and population runoff. When cruising in remote areas, be aware that pollution can be carried great distances to river mouths before being dumped into the ocean.

Fish are prey to a number of parasites, many of which do not affect humans. It's the parasites that can live in both humans and fish that are the problem. Many parasites can be killed by freezing the fish, but freezing does not get rid of toxins. You may be able to spot any parasites in the flesh of very thinly sliced fish by holding the fish up to a light.

Fin fish such as salmon that live in fresh water during any of their life cycle should not be eaten raw. Salmon should be served smoked, cured (as in lox), or cooked. Bottom-dwelling fish such as halibut and rock cod are more often infected with parasites than the more active pelagic fish such as yellowtail, bonito, albacore, and mackerel.

Shellfish

As much fun as it is to gather your own shellfish, you must exercise a certain amount of caution. Make sure that the filter-feeding bivalves you plan on eating—mussels, oysters, clams, and scallops—have not being gathered in polluted water. Filter feeders strain their food from the surrounding water and, if the water is polluted or toxic organisms are present, the shellfish might become contaminated. Although they may not be harmful to the shellfish, the toxin can become concentrated in a mollusk's intestinal tract, the syphons, and other organs.

Shellfish harvested in polluted water are particularly dangerous because we often eat the entire organism, including the digestive tract. Do not eat any shellfish from crowded harbors and anchorages, marinas, or river mouths that may have industrial or residential pollution runoff, nor from any areas where there aren't proper sewage systems.

Red tide outbreaks are also potentially dangerous to shellfish. In California, for example, there is a quarantine on bivalves from May to October due to the potential for a harmful plankton bloom. Many plankton blooms are caused by the rapid growth of harmless plankton and pose no threat. When water temperature, sunlight, and nutrients are in just the right combination, however, dinoflagellate micro algae such as *alexandrium catenellum* can start multiplying and become concentrated in the bivalves in toxic quantities. Paralytic Shellfish Poisoning is the human manifestation of this toxin.

In the United States and Canada there is always a lot of publicity about harmful plankton blooms, so ask the locals. Paralytic Shellfish Poisoning can be fatal; thirty-two deaths have been reported in California out of the 510 cases that have been documented. To be on the safe side, before cooking shellfish remove the stomach, intestines, and syphons where the poison accumulates. Since cooking does not kill this poison, stop eating if there is any sign of numbing or tingling. This is an accumulative poison, so it might be wise to eat only a few bivalves as a test.

Demoic Acid Toxicity, sometimes called Amnesic Shellfish Poisoning, is a relatively new threat. It is caused by a microscopic algae that is eaten by crabs, mollusks, anchovies, and other sea life, and then accumulates in the flesh—especially in the intestines of the shellfish. The acid is considered particularly dangerous in mussels because people eat them whole, intestines and all. Gastrointestinal problems, neurologic symptoms and, in extreme cases, loss of short-term memory have been documented. A few deaths have also been associated with this toxin.

When cruising in the United States, it's wise to contact governmental agencies to see what is safe to eat. In California the Department of Health Services maintains a toll-free hotline (1-800-553-4133) for information on bivalve quarantines. In New England, the local NOAA broadcasts during the summer include daily updates on the same. The United States Food and Drug Administration maintains a Shellfish Hotline which can also be helpful.

What does this mean to the cruising sailor? Should you forgo the pleasure of fresh shellfish? Hal and I say, "No!" You should, though, be cautious. We never eat shellfish the day they are harvested, for example; we prefer to allow them to purge their systems of all sand for twenty-four hours. Then we cook one or two of the shells and test them before we dive in and eat to our heart's content. Above all, when we're cruising in unfamiliar waters we always go right to the source for the most accurate, up-to-the-minute information on the state of shellfish—the locals. The people who work the waters and eat their own catches are the best sources of information on what is good and safe to eat.

Fish or Cut Bait

The expression "fish or cut bait" has recently taken on an entirely new meaning in my life. I've just returned from Italy where I attended cooking school in Amalfi, a Mediterranean seaside resort that supports a small fishing fleet. Daily, during the weeklong course, I observed the chef at the Hotel Luna prepare delicious appetizers, pasta sauces, and main course dishes from what normally passes for bait on our boat.

Until now, my only experience with anchovies had been buying a scoop of them at the bait barge or carefully picking them off of my pizza. During the cooking classes, however, I watched in fascination as the chef carefully beheaded fresh anchovies, gutted them, and removed the backbone from each little fish. He then marinated them in some white vinegar, fresh lemon juice, and salt. After a few hours he drained and blotted them dry and then covered them with a dressing of olive oil, chopped garlic, dried red hot chiles, and parsley. They were delicious. I decided that the next time I was out fishing with my husband, I'd save some of the live bait to make this delicious appetizer—Alicette Assurre del Golfo Marinate (Marinated Anchovies)—for a cockpit cocktail gathering.

Aboard *SpiceSea,* Hal and I frequently have gone out in the dinghy to gather mussels. Generally we are searching for bait, but occasionally we will decide to enjoy steamed mussels in seafood soup or as an appetizer. (See page 59 for information on collecting shellfish safely.)

While in Amalfi we enjoyed an incredible pasta sauce called Corallini alle Violette di Mare (Pasta with Mussels). You steam mussels, remove them from their shells, and then cook them with some fresh or canned tomatoes and garlic, olive oil, dried red hot chiles, and parsley. Serve this delicious sauce hot over tubes of pasta.

Squid (see page 61) is another highly valued bait aboard *SpiceSea.* I usually buy it at the supermarket when I am provisioning for a trip. As long as it is kept frozen or, if bought fresh, used within a couple of days, there is no reason why it can't be used for dinner rather than for baiting a hook. Calamari all'Amalfitana (see page 61) is a delicious way to serve squid and, once again, uses foolproof ingredients—tomatoes, olive oil, garlic, parsley, chiles, salt, and pepper.

I became so addicted to eating "bait" while in Italy that I found myself ordering fried calamari for dinner, Spaghetti con Vogole (clams and mussels), and pizza with anchovies as I continued my journey through the country. Back home where boating is an important part of my life, it has been fun to take advantage of readily available "bait" and create some new recipes in my galley.

Mackerel with Tomatoes and Peppers

4 servings

Mackerel is another live bait that makes great entrées. Try saving a few fresh mackerel for the cooking pot the next time you get skunked fishing.

2 teaspoons finely chopped garlic
1 onion, thinly sliced
3 tablespoons olive oil
1 bell pepper, sliced
4 Italian tomatoes, chopped
Salt and pepper to taste
4 (½-pound each) mackerel, cleaned, gills removed

1. Sauté the garlic and onion in the olive oil until limp. Add the bell pepper and cook an additional 3 minutes. Add the tomatoes and cook an additional 5 minutes. Season with salt and pepper.

2. In a baking dish just large enough for the mackerel, ladle in half of the sauce. Top with the fish and then the remaining sauce. Bake in a 400° F oven for 35 minutes.

Calamari all'Amalfitana

4 servings

1 ½ pounds squid, cleaned and cut into rings*
2 cloves garlic, peeled
⅓ cup olive oil
½ cup chopped fresh parsley
1 small hot dried chile pepper, seeded and finely chopped
¾ pound fresh tomatoes, peeled, seeded, and chopped (or use a 1-pound can of tomatoes, drained)
Salt and pepper to taste

Drain the squid well on paper towels. Brown the garlic in the olive oil in a frying pan. Add the squid, parsley, and chile pepper, and quickly sauté over a hot fire for about 5 minutes. Add the tomatoes and cook an additional 3 to 5 minutes.

**To clean squid, separate the head and tentacles from the body or mantle by gently pulling the squid apart—the pen, or backbone, will come out as you pull. Pull the mottled skin covering from the mantle with your fingers and discard. Turn the squid inside out and rinse away all internal material. Slice into ¼-inch rings and set aside.*

Cut the tentacles from the head and remove the beak from the center of the tentacles. Discard all but the tentacles and rings. (Most markets will clean the squid for you if you ask.)

Insalata di Mare al Limone

6 servings

While attending cooking school in Italy, I tasted this lavish seafood salad. When Hal and I returned to the cruising life, I realized that the salad was not such an extravagance after all. We often find our own mussels and clams and trade with shrimpers for some of their day's catch. It's great fun trying to catch squid at night, but it's just as much fun—almost—to stop in at a fish market and buy some that's already cleaned. Incorporate any leftovers into a great pasta sauce.

2 cloves garlic, finely chopped
1 pound shrimp, shells left on
½ cup olive oil
2 pounds mussels, purged in salt water overnight and shells scrubbed clean, debearded*
2 pounds small clams, purged in salt water overnight and shells scrubbed clean
1 pound squid, cleaned and cut into rings
5 tablespoons extra virgin olive oil
3 tablespoons lemon juice
4 tablespoons chopped parsley
Salt and white pepper to taste

1. In a wok, sauté the garlic and shrimp in 3 tablespoons of olive oil until the shrimp turn pink. Remove from pan and peel when cool enough to handle. Add the mussels and clams to the pan; cover and cook until opened, shaking the pan frequently while they cook. Shuck when cool enough to handle, holding the shells over a dish to catch the juice.

2. Strain the shellfish juice, discarding any sand left in the pan. Set the juice aside.

3. Bring a large saucepan filled with water to a boil; reduce the flame and add the squid. Simmer for 10 to 15 minutes. (If the squid are quite small, you may sauté them for 2 minutes in olive oil rather than boil them.)

4. Combine the strained seafood juices with the 5 tablespoons of olive oil, lemon juice, and parsley. Toss with the seafood and chill.

**See Chapter 4, page 49 for instructions on debearding.*

The Local Catch

Wherever I am anchored I enjoy scouting the availability of fresh seafood. Whether it is crab or shrimp in the San Juans, lobster or abalone on the West Coast of Baja, scallops or mussels at Santa Cruz Island, or a nice kelp bass off Catalina, I have my ingredients picked out for the next meal.

While cruising in the Sacramento Delta aboard *Spice-Sea,* Hal and I learned how to trap crayfish, which I steamed in wine with some herbs and spices. Delicious! On the same trip we dug clams out of the mud. We tried to eat them, but they tasted like mud. Then Hal thought of using them as bait. Bingo! Blackened catfish for dinner.

Aboard our friend Howard's boat in Washington's San Juan Islands we learned how to catch crabs. Bringing up the baited net filled with Dungeness crabs was a thrill even for us—the most jaded of anglers. I will long remember our lunch of boiled crab that was served chilled with a little lemon and mayonnaise.

Every summer we spend a couple of weeks at Santa Cruz Island in the Channel Islands off southern California. Two years ago we found a glory hole of rock scallops, which happen to be the skipper's all-time favorite meal. They are best when very lightly sautéed (too much cooking toughens the meat) in a little garlic-flavored olive oil.

Catalina Island, our favorite weekend getaway, still has a good fish population. Nothing is better for breakfast than a few freshly caught sand dabs, a flounder common in the Pacific, dredged in flour and pan fried.

The best seafood eating opportunities that I know of are in Baja California. Whether trading Snickers Bars for the local catch in Santa Maria Bay, or catching your own marlin or dorado in Cabo San Lucas, Baja is a seafood lover's paradise.

Diver's Cioppino

4 servings

Isla San Francisco in the Sea of Cortez is a favorite anchorage for West Coast cruisers. Hiking, swimming, fishing, diving, and shell collecting are just a few of the activities available. Once, when yet another excuse was found for a potluck supper, I offered to make a cioppino incorporating the seafood that the local divers had caught.

The ingredients for a dish of this type are extremely flexible. On this occasion I used lobster, clams, rock scallops, and some freshly caught yellowtail to make a delicious stew. But I have also made cioppino with only one type of seafood.

2 onions, sliced
6 cloves garlic, finely chopped
2 tablespoons olive oil
1 (28 oz.) can plum tomatoes, chopped
Grated peel from 1 orange
1 cup white wine
1 cup clam juice or chicken broth
2 teaspoons fennel seed
2 pounds seafood

1. Sauté the onion and garlic in the olive oil until tender. Add the tomatoes and orange peel, and simmer 10 minutes. Add the wine, clam juice or chicken broth, and fennel seed, and boil briefly. This can be done in advance and kept for a week in the refrigerator.

2. Ten minutes before serving, heat the soup and add the seafood, taking into account the different cooking times needed when using different types of seafood. Lobster and thick chunks of fish take the longest to cook; scallops need almost no cooking.

Note: I made this recipe recently and had a bowl of stew leftover. The next day I layered the leftovers with four instant lasagna noodles (see page 18), some ricotta cheese, and a little mozzarella. A great seafood lasagna!

Ratatouille Cioppino

4 to 6 servings

We had lots of vegies that needed to be used while anchored in Santa Maria Bay on the Pacific Coast of Baja California. I started making ratatouille, a vegetable stew, and then added a little Spanish chorizo. Then some Mexican *pescadors* dropped off a few lobsters, we found clams in the estuary, and Hal caught some halibut. Before I knew it, my vegetable stew had become a great cioppino.

2 onions, chopped
5 cloves garlic, finely chopped
1 eggplant, peeled and diced
3 carrots, chopped
4 tablespoons olive oil
1 (12 oz.) can tomato purée
⅓ pound Spanish chorizo or Italian pepperoni
2 cups white wine
2 lobsters tails, cut into 2-inch pieces
20 clams
½ pound halibut fillet, cut into 2-inch pieces

1. Cook the onions, garlic, eggplant, and carrots in the olive oil until tender. Add the tomato purée, sausage, and wine, and simmer for 30 minutes.
2. Add the lobster and clams and cook until done. Add the halibut and cook an additional 4 minutes.

Seafood Paella

6 servings

Having spent many vacations boating in Mexico, I have had lots of opportunity to experiment both with Hal's catch of the day, and with the catch of the Mexican *pescadors*. The most important ingredient in making any fish dish taste good is to use the very freshest fish available. Preparing seafood on board makes this a lot easier than if I were dependent on the fish markets ashore. If there is not an Izaak Walton on board your boat, make friends with the angler moored next to you. From my experience, the devoted angler is always looking for people to share in the catch.

Lobster, crab, abalone, clams, mussels, shrimp, and chunks of fish can all go into this dish.

2 tablespoons oil
2 medium white onions, peeled and chopped
4 cloves garlic, peeled and chopped
2 cups long grain white rice
1 (1 lb.) can chopped tomatoes
1 (4 oz.) can mild green chiles, diced
2 red bell peppers, seeded and chopped (if fresh are not available, use canned)
3 ½ cups chicken broth
2 teaspoons oregano
1 teaspoon cumin
1 teaspoon salt
1 pound clams, purged and scrubbed clean
2 lobster tails, cut into 1-inch pieces with the shell

Garnish

Chopped fresh cilantro
1 avocado, peeled, seeded, and cut into wedges

1. Heat the oil in a large deep sauté pan and sauté the onions and garlic until soft and translucent. Add the rice and cook until it just begins to color. Add the tomatoes, chiles, and bell peppers, and sauté briefly.
2. Add the broth, oregano, cumin, and salt to the rice; cover and bring to a boil. Reduce heat. After 5 minutes, add the shellfish and cook until the liquid is absorbed, the rice is tender, and the seafood is done—about 15 more minutes.
3. Garnish each serving with cilantro and avocado wedges.

Hazard's Cove Fish Stew

4 servings

I used a potpourri of ingredients for this delicious stew—invented to make use of ingredients I already had on board, including some shellfish we had caught while diving that day. I suggested to the skipper that we could really use a fish in the evening's stew, so Hal went trolling to catch the final ingredient, a nice-size kelp bass. What a guy!

2 onions, diced
2 cloves garlic, finely chopped
1 carrot, minced
3 tablespoons olive oil
1 (14 ½ oz.) can stewed tomatoes
1 (14 ½ oz.) can crushed strained tomatoes
1 cup white or red wine (I prefer red, but we had consumed it all by the time I first made this stew!)
1 tablespoon balsamic vinegar (If you use red wine, omit the balsamic vinegar.)
1 teaspoon crab boil
1 large kelp crab, legs and claws cracked
½-inch thick slice of dry Italian salami, diced
1 abalone, diced
1 pound fillet of any mild-flavored fish
2 rock scallops

1. Sauté the onions, garlic, and carrot in the olive oil until tender. Add the tomatoes, wine, vinegar (if using), and crab boil, and cook until boiling.
2. Add the crab legs and cook until done. Add the salami, abalone, and fish, and cook until done.
3. Just before serving, add the scallops—they will cook from the residual heat of the stew.

Stir-fried Lobster and Shrimp

2 servings

We had anchored in Bahia Chamela on the Mexican mainland and the shrimp boats were selling their catch. A little while later a *panga* (a small, open fishing boat) came by with some lobsters for sale. If you aren't lucky enough to have fresh shrimp and lobster on board, you can substitute chicken, pork, or beef.

2 tablespoons cooking oil
½ pound shelled shrimp and/or lobster
2 cloves garlic, finely chopped
2 serrano chiles, seeded and finely chopped
2 teaspoons fresh ginger, peeled and finely chopped
1 tablespoon cooking oil
1 onion, thinly sliced
1 zucchini, cubed
1 carrot, cubed
1 bell pepper, cubed

Marinade

1 tablespoon soy sauce
1 tablespoon dry sherry

Sauce

1 tablespoon soy sauce
1 tablespoon dry sherry
1 tablespoon cornstarch

1. Mix together the marinade ingredients and pour over the seafood. Allow to marinate at least 20 minutes.
2. Heat the oil in a wok and stir-fry the garlic, chiles, and ginger for 2 minutes. Add the marinated seafood and stir-fry until done. Remove from the wok.
3. In a clean wok, stir-fry the onion, zucchini, carrot, and bell pepper in 1 tablespoon of oil for 3 minutes. Add 3 tablespoons of water, cover, and steam until the vegetables are barely tender. Drain, add the seafood mixture, and reheat.
4. Combine the sauce ingredients. Make a well in the center of the seafood mixture, add the sauce, and stir-fry until the cornstarch is cooked. Serve over steamed rice.

Barbecued Lobster Tails Santa Rosalillita Style

2 servings

When we used to drive the Baja Highway, we always stopped in the little village of Santa Rosalillita where, over the years, we became friends with a local family. Our friends always saw that we left Santa Rosalillita with a few lobsters as we continued south. Hal and I would then find a good camping spot for the night, build a fire on the beach, and cook some of our lobster.

One of the easiest ways to cook lobster tails is to season them with garlic, butter, and a little white wine, wrap them in foil, and toss them in the fire. I frequently use the barbecue on the boat to prepare lobster tails the same way.

1 tablespoon freshly chopped garlic
4 tablespoons butter, at room temperature
2 lobster tails, split down the center and vein removed
4 tablespoons white wine

1. Make a paste of the garlic and butter and spread over the exposed meat of the lobster.
2. Carefully encase the tails in individual foil packets, dividing half of the white wine over each tail.
3. Place the packets on a grill over hot coals for 15 to 20 minutes—until the steam has puffed up the packets.
4. To serve, remove the meat from the shells and pour the drippings over the lobsters.

Sautéed Lobster Tails

2 servings

Simplicity is one of the keys to cooking aboard successfully and this recipe certainly qualifies. Besides being a simple dish for a family dinner, it will also impress your most discriminating guests.

2 tablespoons olive oil
2 lobster tails, split down the center and butterflied
2 cloves garlic, finely chopped
Lime wedges

1. In a wok, heat the oil and add the lobster tails. Sauté for a few minutes on each side. Add the garlic and continue sautéeing until the shells are bright pink and the meat begins to pull away from the shells.
2. Serve with pan juices and lime wedges.

East Coast Lobster

If you are lucky enough to have New England lobsters on board, you've got lots more to eat than just the tail. Cooking the entire shellfish is a must. To steam, place 1½ inches of water in a wok with a rack and a lid. Place lobsters on rack, cover, and cook until they are bright red.

Another way to cook lobsters is to place them in a large kettle of boiling water and cook until bright red. The wok method, though, certainly saves on water if that's a concern on your boat.

Save the lobster shells and make a delicious soup by tossing the following into a pot: a ½ cup of chopped onion, a ½ cup of chopped carrot, 6 cups of chicken broth, 1 cup of white wine, 1 cup of chopped tomatoes, a little tarragon, and the shells. Simmer for 1 hour and then strain. Adding chunks of fish or shellfish makes this an especially good soup.

Sautéed Shrimp with Feta Cheese

4 servings

1 teaspoon finely chopped garlic
2 tablespoons olive oil
1 pound shrimp, shelled and deveined
1 recipe Tomato, Garlic, and Wine Sauce (page 172)
½ pound feta cheese
½ cup toasted pine nuts

1. Make the Tomato, Garlic, and Wine Sauce. Sauté the shrimp in the garlic and olive oil until barely cooked.
2. Just before serving, stir the shrimp into the sauce to reheat.
3. Garnish with crumbled feta and toasted pine nuts.

Skewered Shrimp and Scallops

6 servings

⅓ cup olive oil
⅓ cup chopped parsley
3 cloves garlic, finely chopped
1 teaspoon grated lemon peel
½ cup dry unflavored bread crumbs
¼ teaspoon each salt and pepper
¾ pound medium shrimp, shelled and deveined
¾ pound medium scallops
Lemon wedges

1. Combine the olive oil, parsley, garlic, lemon peel, bread crumbs, salt, and pepper, and pour over the shrimp and scallops. Allow to stand for 1 hour.
2. Alternate the shrimp and scallops on 6 skewers. Baste with the marinade, pressing the bread crumbs into the seafood.
3. Broil 2 minutes per side, or until golden. Serve with lemon wedges.

Cold Marinated Shrimp with Cilantro and Garlic

4 to 6 servings

2 onions, thinly sliced
¼ cup olive oil
2 pounds shrimp, shelled and deveined
Salt and pepper to taste
1 recipe Cilantro Garlic Marinade (page 177)
2 tablespoons minced jalapeño en escabeche (pickled jalapeños)*

1. Sauté the onions in 2 tablespoons of the olive oil until soft. Add 2 more tablespoons of oil and sauté the shrimp until they're pink and barely cooked. Season with salt and pepper.
2. Pour the marinade over the cooked shrimp, stir to combine, and chill before serving.
3. To serve, garnish with jalapeños en escabeche.

**Or substitute fresh, chopped, seeded jalapeños.*

Variation

Marinate raw shrimp in Cilantro Garlic Marinade, grill on skewers, and serve with Tomatillo Sauce (page 166).

Shrimp Stuffed with Cheese and Wrapped In Bacon

I often order this delicious treat at my favorite La Paz beachfront *palapa* (a very casually constructed beach structure) restaurant, La Caleta. When I can find "grandes," I make this shrimp recipe myself: Peel and butterfly the shrimp until they are cut almost in half. Place a small wedge of cheese between the two shrimp halves, then tightly wrap a thin slice of bacon around the shrimp. Cook in a hot skillet and drain off the bacon fat.

For larger crowds, if stuffing and wrapping each shrimp seems like too much bother, try the following variation:

Variation

4 servings

¼ pound bacon, chopped
1 pound shrimp, peeled and deveined
½ pound jack cheese, grated
3 tablespoons fresh lime juice
3 tablespoons cilantro

1. Brown the bacon in a frying pan. Remove and set aside. Discard all but 1 tablespoon of fat.
2. Sauté the shrimp in 1 tablespoon of the bacon drippings. Add the bacon and lime juice. Top with the cheese and broil until the cheese is bubbly and golden.
3. Garnish with cilantro.
4. Serve with flour tortillas, salsa fresca, and fresh limes.

Hot and Sour Shrimp Soup

6 servings

A popular Thai recipe, this is an excellent dish to cook on board. It is spicy, light, and cooks in minutes. The flavor of the broth is enhanced by using the shrimp shells.

1 pound medium shrimp
1 tablespoon olive oil
6 cups chicken broth
Grated peel of 1 lime
Juice from 2 limes
2 hot chiles (serrano or jalapeño), seeded and finely chopped
1 tablespoon fish sauce (*Nam Pla*) or soy sauce
2 tablespoons cilantro leaves
3 green onions, finely chopped

1. Shell and devein the shrimp, saving the shells. In a large pan, heat the oil and sauté the shrimp shells for 3 minutes. Add the chicken broth and simmer for 15 minutes.
2. Strain the broth and return to the pan. Add the lime peel, lime juice, chiles, and fish or soy sauce, and bring to a boil. Add the shrimp and cook until barely pink.
3. Serve immediately, adding cilantro and onions to each bowl.

Thai Shrimp Salad

4 servings

3 tablespoons fish sauce
3 tablespoons lime juice
2 cloves garlic, finely chopped
½ teaspoon cayenne pepper
1 pound medium shrimp, cooked, peeled, and deveined
½ small red onion, thinly sliced
2 stalks lemon grass, soft part only, finely chopped
2 green onions, finely chopped
2 tablespoons cilantro leaves
¼ cup mint leaves
½ head cabbage, thinly sliced

1. Combine the fish sauce, lime juice, garlic, and cayenne pepper; pour over the shrimp and marinate for 30 minutes.
2. Toss the shrimp with the onion, lemon grass, green onions, cilantro and mint. Serve on a bed of cabbage.

Puerto Refugio Scallops

After a day of snorkling and diving on Isla Angel de Guardia in the Sea of Cortez, we had enough scallops for dinner. We marinated them in pepper, garlic, lemon juice, and oil. Using bamboo skewers that had been soaking in water, we threaded the scallops on the skewers intertwined with bacon and cooked them on the barbecue for 5 to 15 minutes until golden.

For large scallops, slice them about ¼-inch thick and pound them lightly. Dredge them in seasoned flour and sauté quickly in hot butter or olive oil.

Curried Rock Scallops

4 servings

1 clove garlic, finely chopped
2 onions, chopped
1 bell pepper, chopped
1 tablespoon olive oil
2 teaspoons curry powder
1 cup chicken broth
2 tablespoons flour
½ pound scallops
1 peach, peeled and sliced

1. Sauté the garlic, onions, and bell pepper in the olive oil until soft. Add the curry powder and cook 30 seconds.
2. Mix together the broth and flour; add to the pan and cook, stirring until the sauce boils and thickens.
3. Add the scallops and peach; heat thoroughly.
4. Serve over steamed rice.

Scallops in Spicy Black Bean Sauce

2 to 4 servings

1 tablespoon red wine vinegar
1 teaspoon cornstarch
2 tablespoons soy sauce
¼ teaspoon five-spice powder
1 tablespoon chili paste with garlic
2 tablespoons vegetable oil
1 tablespoon finely chopped ginger
1 teaspoon finely chopped garlic
1 serrano or other hot chile, seeded and finely chopped
2 tablespoons finely chopped green onion or shallot
2 bell peppers, seeded and cut in 1-inch cubes
1 pound scallops, sliced ¼-inch thick
2 tablespoons fermented black beans (soy beans)

1. Combine the red wine vinegar, cornstarch, soy sauce, five-spice power, and chili paste; set aside.
2. Add 1 tablespoon of oil to a hot wok. Stir-fry the ginger, garlic, chile, and onion for 30 seconds. Add the bell peppers and stir-fry an additional 30 seconds.
3. Add the scallops and stir-fry 30 seconds. Add the black beans and the sauce. Cook until the sauce bubbles and thickens slightly.
4. Serve over rice.

Scallops Baked in their Shells

4 servings

1 pound scallops
½ cup white wine
½ cup chicken broth
1 recipe Velouté Sauce (page 162), using ½ cup poaching liquid and ⅓ cup milk
¼ cup grated Swiss cheese

1. Poach the scallops in simmering wine and broth for 2 minutes. Remove and drain.
2. Reduce the poaching liquid to 1 cup and combine with the milk. Make the Velouté Sauce, using the reduced poaching liquid and milk.
3. Combine the drained scallops with the velouté sauce and spoon into scallop shells. Top with cheese.
4. Bake at 450°F until the cheese melts.

Octopus Los Frailes

4 servings

While tide-pooling at the breathtaking Los Frailes anchorage in the Sea of Cortez, Hal once caught a good-sized octopus in the rocks. We experimented with cooking it and then happily shared our find with friends anchored nearby.

(At low tide or when snorkeling, look under large rocks to spot octopi homes. They often stack telltale bits of leftover shells near the entrances to their lairs. To extract an octopus, grab one leg at a time until it comes loose. Eventually the octopus will cling to you rather than his home.)

1 medium octopus
1 onion, chopped
3 cloves garlic, finely chopped
3 tablespoons olive oil
1 (4 oz.) can Mexican salsa or 2 tomatoes
1 cup white wine

1. Blanch the octopus in boiling water (half fresh and half sea) for 10 minutes. Drain. When cool enough to handle, remove the skin from the hood and legs by scraping with a knife or rubbing with a stiff vegetable brush. Make a vertical cut up into the hood and remove the organs. Cut the tentacles into bite-sized pieces and slice the hood.
2. Sauté the onion, garlic, and sliced octopus in olive oil for 5 minutes. Add the salsa or tomatoes and wine. Cover and simmer until tender, about 30 minutes. Season to taste with pepper.
3. Serve as is, or over rice or pasta.

Note: After cleaning octopus you can tenderize it by pounding it lightly and marinating in lime juice. Octopus is also delicious cooked on the barbecue with a little garlic butter or deep-fat fried.

Cajun-Style Blackened Fish

4 servings

Cajun cooking is one of our passions and, since the skipper loves to fish, we often enjoy this classic dish on board. The blackened style of cooking requires cooking the meat quickly over a very hot fire to seal in the juices. It's an ideal method of cooking fish, but you must use a cast-iron skillet—it's the only kind that can withstand the high heat necessary in the blackening technique.

4 (½-inch thick) fish fillets
2 to 4 tablespoons cooking oil

Cajun Spice Mixture

1 tablespoon paprika
2 teaspoons garlic powder
1 teaspoon ground cayenne pepper
1 teaspoon ground black pepper
1 teaspoon ground white pepper
½ teaspoon salt
½ teaspoon dried oregano
½ teaspoon dried thyme

1. Combine all the ingredients for the Cajun Spice Mixture and set aside. (Premixed Cajun spices are available commercially but they are very salty.) The spices can be combined in advance and stored in a sealed container.
2. If using a propane barbecue, heat the skillet on the highest setting for 10 minutes. If using briquettes, allow the coals to burn down and place the skillet as close to coals as possible; allow to heat at least 10 minutes.
3. Coat each fillet with the spice mixture.
4. Pour the oil in the skillet and *carefully* place the fillets in the hot oil. Cook approximately 3 to 4 minutes before turning the fish. Add more oil if necessary. The object is to seal in the juices by searing the fish on a very hot fire and cooking until barely done.

Note: To adjust the spiciness of the Cajun Spice Mixture, add dry bread crumbs to suit your taste. For very thin fillets (⅛-inch thick), you can use half bread crumbs and half Cajun spice mixture.

Baked Red Snapper with Salsa Esmeralda

4 to 6 servings

½ teaspoon salt
¼ teaspoon pepper
4 cloves garlic, crushed
½ teaspoon oregano
¼ teaspoon cumin
⅓ cup fresh lime juice
¼ cup olive oil
2 pounds red snapper fillets or any mild fish
1 recipe Salsa Esmeralda (page 167)

1. Combine all the ingredients except the fish.
2. Butter a shallow baking dish and pour the marinade over the fish; marinate for 15 minutes.
3. Bake at 350° F for 12 minutes or until the fish is white and flaky inside. Serve with Salsa Esmeralda.

Huachinango Veracruz

6 servings

Huachinango is the Spanish word for red snapper, a firm-fleshed, mild-tasting fish. In this recipe, the snapper is served with a flavorful tomato sauce that hails from Mexico's state of Veracruz. You can gussy up this entrée by sprinkling cooked shrimp and crab over the baked fish and topping it with jack cheese before broiling. Yum!

6 (4 oz. each) red snapper fillets
2 tablespoons lime juice
Salt and freshly ground black pepper
1 recipe Veracruz Sauce (page 166)

1. Season the fish with the lime juice, salt, and pepper; set aside. 2. Make the Veracruz Sauce. Place the fish in a baking dish and pour the sauce over the fish. Bake at 375° F for 15 to 20 minutes.

Pesto Swordfish in Foil

4 servings

Cooking in individual foil-wrapped servings is a boon to the onboard chef. The cleanup is minimal and serving is easy. Homemade pesto is easy to make in the food processor, but you can substitute canned, which is available at many markets.

4 (6 oz. each) swordfish fillets or any firm-fleshed fish fillets
2 cloves garlic, finely chopped
2 shallots, finely chopped
¼ cup dry white wine
½ cup Basil Pesto Sauce (page 167)
Salt and freshly ground black pepper to taste
4 pieces heavy foil, each large enough to wrap 1 fillet
2 large tomatoes, cubed
1 teaspoon balsamic or red wine vinegar

1. Place the fillets in a Ziploc bag and marinate in the refrigerator with the garlic, shallots, and wine for 1 hour.
2. Preheat the oven and a baking sheet to 450° F.
3. Spread each side of the fish with 1 tablespoon of pesto sauce. Season with salt and pepper. Encase each fillet in a sheet of heavy foil and fold the edges tightly to seal.
4. Bake on the hot baking sheet for 12 minutes, or place on a hot barbecue.
5. While the fish is cooking, toss the tomato cubes with the vinegar; season with salt and pepper.
6. When the fish is done, open the foil and top each fillet with the tomatoes.

Salmon Fillets in Foil with Dill and Mandarin Orange Sauce

4 servings

When Hal and I were cruising in the Pacific Northwest on a friend's boat, Hal fished every day for salmon. And every day he assured us that "today is the day" for the big catch. We fantasized about how we were going to cook the succulent fresh salmon. After several days of rhapsodizing about this soon-to-be-caught delicious fish, we finally visited a fish market in the town of Friday Harbor and bought the elusive salmon!

4 large pieces aluminum foil
16 mandarin orange segments
4 salmon fillets (or sea bass), each about 1-inch thick and weighing about 6 ounces
Fresh dill sprigs or parsley for garnish

Sauce

3 tablespoons olive oil
3 tablespoons white wine vinegar
3 tablespoons chopped green onion
2 teaspoons chopped fresh dill or ½ teaspoon dried
2 teaspoons orange peel

1. Combine the sauce ingredients. Center 1 fillet on each piece of foil and spoon some sauce over it. Seal each fillet tightly in the foil.
2. Bake at 475° F for 7 to 10 minutes, or cook on a hot barbecue. To test for doneness, cut a tiny slit through the foil and gently probe the fillets with a fork. When the fish is no longer translucent, it's done.
3. Remove the fillets from the foil before serving. Garnish with dill or parsley (or something green). You can prepare the foil packets up to twenty-four hours in advance and store them in the refrigerator until ready to cook. If well chilled, add a few minutes extra to the cooking time.

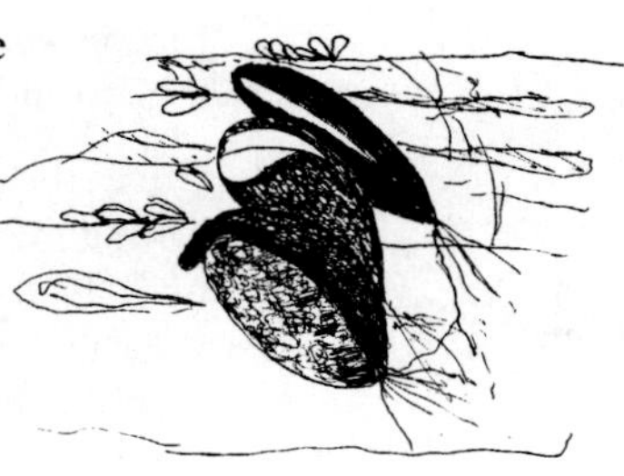

Grilled Salmon with Green Chile Pesto

4 servings

1 recipe Mexican Salsa Fresca (page 165)
1 cup diced papaya
4 salmon fillets with skin left on, descaled
1 cup Green Chile Pesto (page 168)

1. Combine the Mexican Salsa Fresca and papaya; set aside.
2. Broil the salmon about 2 minutes on each side, ending with the skin side down. Place ¼ cup of the pesto on each plate. Top with the salmon and garnish with the papaya salsa.

Bahia de los Puercos Pescado con Tomatoes

2 servings

While boating in the Sea of Cortez, Hal caught a Gulf grouper. Our favorite way to cook this firm-bodied fish is with a spicy tomato sauce and chopped clams. Stateside, we use halibut or any other firm-fleshed fish, and substitute canned clams when we can't get fresh.

1 pound fish fillets
2 ounces Spanish-style tomato sauce
12 clams, shucked and finely chopped

Place the fillets, tomato sauce, and clams in a foil packet and cook over medium hot coals for 5 to 7 minutes. Or, bake at 375° F for 15 minutes.

Steamed Fish, Chinese Style

2 servings

This is an excellent way to prepare fish that are too small to fillet.

2 small (total weight about 1 lb.) fish, gutted and scaled
½ teaspoon salt
2 tablespoons sherry
6 green onions, cut into 2-inch-long, very thin pieces
Several leaves of napa cabbage
3 tablespoons Spicy Soy Dipping Sauce (page 164)

1. Marinate the fish in the salt and sherry for 10 minutes.
2. Cover the bottom of a bamboo steamer (see page 20) with cabbage.
3. Place the fish in the steamer and scatter the onions on top. Sprinkle with 1 tablespoon of Spicy Soy Dipping Sauce over the fish. Steam over high heat in a wok with 1 cup of water for 6 to 10 minutes.
4. Pour the remaining dipping sauce over the fish just before serving.

Pescado con Achiote

2 servings

Achiote paste is a spice mixture whose primary ingredient is annanato seeds. It is available in Latin American markets, but you can also make your own (see page 176). The rich red color of the paste or marinade enhances most seafood.

4 teaspoons achiote paste
2 cloves garlic, finely chopped
¼ teaspoon freshly ground black pepper
2 tablespoons red wine vinegar
1 teaspoon oregano
4 small fillets of fish with skin left on, descaled

1. Combine the achiote paste, garlic, pepper, vinegar, and oregano, and spread over the skinless side of the fish at least 30 minutes before cooking.
2. Place the fish on a barbecue skin side down and cook until done. Remove the skin before serving.

Barbecued Parrot Fish

2 servings

Although parrot fish tend to be slightly tough, they can make an excellent meal when properly cooked. The fish tend to be large (or at least the large ones make attractive targets for the spear fisher) and they must be thoroughly cooked. Their connective tissue is coarse and needs to break down, so marinating parrot fish in citrus helps a lot.

On our many road trips south along the Baja peninsula, we always stop in the small town of San Bartolo, an attractive agricultural town with very friendly people. Roadside stands display string sacks full of juicy oranges and limes. We always buy more than we can eat, so I use a lot of fresh citrus juice in cooking. The citrus makes wonderful marinades for the fish caught along the Cortez.

1 (½-inch thick) fillet of parrot fish
1 onion, sliced
1 large tomato, sliced

Marinade

Juice of 1 orange
Juice of 2 limes
Juice of 1 lemon
1 tablespoon dried tarragon or oregano
2 teaspoons chopped fresh garlic
4 tablespoons olive oil

1. Combine the marinade ingredients and marinate the fish for at least 30 minutes.
2. In a disposable pan, distribute the sliced onion and tomato and top with the marinated fish.
3. Cover the pan with foil and barbecue over hot coals, basting frequently as the juices accumulate. Cook until the fish flakes—about 20 to 25 minutes. The vegetables in the foil are a great accompaniment to the fish.

Stir-Fried Curried Rockfish

4 servings

We had been cruising California's Channel Islands for two weeks and were almost completely depleted of fresh produce. Hal caught some rockfish and I created this recipe. We especially loved the unusual flavors of this recipe.

2 small onions, peeled and chopped
6 cloves garlic, finely chopped
2 tablespoons olive oil
1 ½ pounds rockfish fillets, cubed
1 tablespoon finely chopped fresh ginger
1 ounce dried mushrooms, soaked until soft, sliced
1 (15 oz.) can chopped tomatoes
2 tablespoons Green Chile Pesto (page 168)
2 tablespoons curry powder

Sauté the onions and garlic in the olive oil until tender. Add the fish and ginger and stir-fry until the fish is almost done. Add the mushrooms, tomatoes, pesto, and curry, bring to a boil, and cook 5 minutes. Serve over rice.

Bass with Pecan Cajun Coating

2 servings

At Catalina Harbor, Hal caught a couple of three-pound kelp bass. The fillets were a good size for panfrying, so I made a tasty coating of pecans and bread crumbs. I buy the Japanese bread crumbs called *panko,* which make a very crispy coating when fried. The crumbs are available at Oriental groceries and in some grocery stores with an Oriental section.

1 lime
1 pound kelp fish, rockfish, or sea bass fillets
Salt and pepper to taste
3 tablespoons finely chopped pecans
¼ cup dry, unseasoned bread crumbs
1 tablespoon Cajun Spice Mixture (page 69)
2 to 3 tablespoons olive oil

1. Squeeze the lime over the fillets and season with salt and pepper.
2. Combine the pecans, bread crumbs, and Cajun Spice Mixture; roll the fillets in the crumb mixture.
3. Heat a nonstick skillet with a small amount of olive oil and fry the fillets until golden.

Los Pelicanos Smoked Dorado

3 to 4 servings

In Bahia Navidad, just north of Manzanillo on the Mexican mainland, there is Los Pelicanos, a *palapa* on the beach that serves wonderful food. Philomena, the owner of Los Pelicanos, gave me her recipe for dorado. It is so simple and delicious I use it with almost any fish.

½ teaspoon Liquid Smoke
1 teaspoon soy sauce
3 tablespoons lime juice
2 to 3 tablespoons cooking oil
1 pound fish fillets
Salt and pepper

Combine the Liquid Smoke, soy sauce, and lime juice. Heat the oil in a skillet and sear the fish on one side. Turn the fish and drizzle in the lime juice mixture. Cook until barely done. Season with salt and pepper.

Pompano with Onions and Salsa

3 to 4 servings

While anchored near Manzanillo at Bahia Careyes, friends speared an eight-pound pompano and asked Hal to show them how to fillet it. Our reward was half of this delicious fish.

1 onion, sliced
1 tablespoon olive oil
1 pound pompano fillets (or halibut, red snapper, or any other firm-fleshed fish)
2 tablespoons canned or fresh Mexican salsa
Juice from ½ lime

Sauté the onion and fish fillets in the olive oil for 7 minutes, or until the fish is flaky and onion is tender. Add the salsa and lime juice and cook an additional minute.

Georgia's Marlin with Italian Mayonnaise Marinade

4 servings

One of the fishing-trophy winners in Catalina Island's Corsair Yacht Club brought in a prizewinning marlin on her way to the island. She generously shared her catch with those of us nearby and taught me this simple but delicious way to barbecue the fish.

⅓ cup mayonnaise
⅓ cup Italian bottled salad dressing
4 (1-inch thick) marlin steaks

1. Combine the mayonnaise and salad dressing. Marinate the marlin in a Ziploc bag with the mayonnaise mixture for at least 2 hours in the refrigerator.

2. Place the marlin on a preheated barbecue and cook until the fish is flaky. Baste occasionally with the marinade.

Halibut Breaded with Almonds with Mango-Basil Sauce

4 servings

Halibut are firm-fleshed, low-fat fish with a delicate flavor. They are prized as a food fish and can be sautéed, broiled, or baked. As with all fish, it is important not to overcook halibut. This recipe can be used for any firm-fleshed fish and can be served with or without the sauce.

¼ pound unsalted almonds, roasted and ground to a medium-fine texture
½ cup fine dry bread crumbs
4 (6 oz. each) halibut fillets (or salmon, walleye, or bass)
Salt and pepper to taste
3 to 4 tablespoons olive oil
Mango-Basil Sauce or Tomatillo Sauce (pages 178, 166)

1. Combine the almonds and bread crumbs. Season the halibut with salt and pepper and press the crumb mixture into both sides of the fish.

2. Heat the oil and cook the fish until it's lightly browned on both sides—be careful not to overcook.

3. Serve the fish surrounded by one of the sauces if desired.

Trigger Fish Salad

4 servings

Years ago when we were camping at the Bay of Los Angeles in the central Sea of Cortez, we had a little car-topper from which we could fish. This was our first encounter with triggerfish, which are buck-toothed crustacean eaters that can cut their way through any line. We ran out of toothy critter lures and made our own steel leaders out of wire. We finally got the hang of catching triggerfish and have been enjoying their mild taste and firm texture ever since.

1 pound triggerfish fillets

Poaching Liquid

1 cup white wine
1 cup chicken or vegetable broth
2 dry chiles, broken
8 peppercorns
2 cloves garlic, minced

Sauce

1 cup mayonnaise
2 tablespoons catsup
Juice of 1 lime
1 serrano chile, finely chopped
1 tablespoon capers, rinsed and drained
2 cloves garlic, finely chopped

Salad

1 cup jicama, cut in matchstick pieces
1 red bell pepper or 2 carrots, cut in matchstick pieces
1 cucumber, peeled, seeded, cut in half lengthwise and sliced
2 cups finely chopped cabbage

1. In a deep sauté pan, make the poaching liquid by combining the wine, broth, chiles, peppercorns, and garlic. Bring to a boil and lower the heat to simmer.
2. Add the fish and simmer until the flesh is opaque and flaky. Remove from the liquid and chill.
3. Make the sauce by combining the mayonnaise, catsup, lime juice, chile, capers, and garlic. Set aside.
4. Shred the chilled fish and combine with the sauce.
5. Arrange the jicama, pepper or carrots, cucumber, and cabbage on a platter and top with fish.

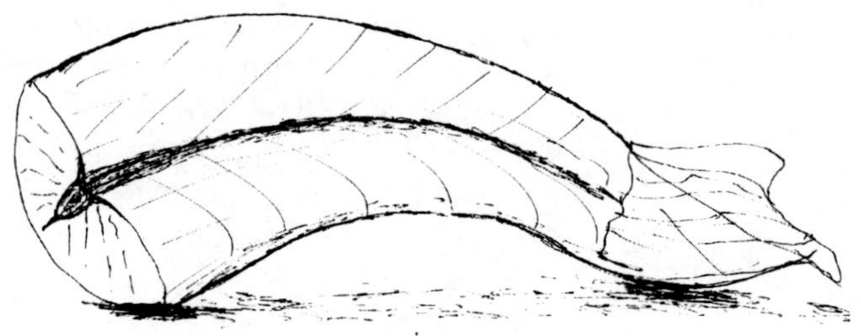

Tuna

Canned tuna, a dietary mainstay for many boaters, can be one of the most boring foods in the galley. Here are a few suggestions for perking up a can of tuna:

- Add some fresh herbs, such as cilantro or dill, to tuna salad.
- Add some chopped apple and walnuts or sliced marinated artichoke hearts and fresh basil to tuna salad.
- Go light on the mayonnaise or try substituting a creamy ranch dressing.
- Combine vinaigrette sauce with a can of white beans, a can of tuna, and some chopped tomatoes for a hearty dish.
- In a Salade Niçoise, tuna combines beautifully with boiled potatoes, black olives, and fresh string beans.

Since tuna lends itself to so many preparations, I always keep plenty of cans on board. Tapénade, an easy tuna-based dip, can be spread on crackers or used as a sauce on cold fish. Or, try this excellent tuna sauce with pasta. Leftovers are great served cold the next day.

Tagliatelle with Cold Tuna Sauce

4 servings

1 (6 oz.) can tuna, drained and shredded with a fork
Grated peel of 1 lemon
½ cup walnuts
2 tablespoons finely chopped parsley
1 pound flat noodles such as tagliatelle, cooked

Purée the tuna, lemon peel, walnuts, and parsley in a blender. Serve over hot pasta. This is also delicious as a cold leftover. Or, try the sauce over turkey or chicken.

Linguine with Tuna, Olives, and Capers

4 servings

2 cloves garlic, finely chopped
1 (2 ¼ oz.) can chopped black olives
2 tablespoons capers
1 hot red dried pepper, finely chopped
¼ cup olive oil
2 tablespoons finely chopped parsley
Salt and pepper to taste
1 (6 oz.) can tuna, drained and shredded with a fork
1 pound linguine, cooked

Sauté the garlic, olives, capers, and red pepper in the olive oil for 1 minute. Add 2 tablespoons of water, the parsley, and some freshly ground black pepper. Cook until heated through; season with salt and add the tuna. Serve over hot pasta.

Fresh Tuna Steaks with Olives and Capers

4 servings

2 tablespoons olive oil
4 fresh tuna steaks (about 6 oz. each)
1 tablespoon capers, rinsed and drained
¼ cup sliced green olives
1 (1 lb.) can Italian plum tomatoes, drained and chopped
Pinch of dried oregano
Salt and pepper
¼ cup chopped fresh basil

1. Heat the oil in a skillet and brown the tuna on each side for 2 to 3 minutes. Remove.
2. Add the capers, olives, tomatoes, oregano, salt, and pepper and simmer until the sauce is thick. Briefly reheat the tuna in the sauce before serving.
3. Garnish with basil.

Linguine with Tuna Sauce and Lemon

4 servings

2 cloves garlic, finely chopped
2 tablespoons finely chopped parsley
¼ cup olive oil
1 (6 oz.) can tuna, drained and shredded with a fork
Salt and pepper to taste
2 tablespoons lemon juice
½ cup Parmesan cheese
1 pound linguine, cooked

Sauté the garlic and parsley in the olive oil for 1 minute. Add the tuna and lemon juice. Cook for 2 minutes, just to heat. Toss with pasta and sprinkle with cheese. Serve over hot pasta.

For a spicier sauce, eliminate the Parmesan cheese and add ½ a can of anchovies and ¼ teaspoon of crushed red pepper when sautéeing the garlic and parsley.

Spaghetti with Tuna and Tomato Sauce

4 servings

1 medium onion, chopped
2 cloves garlic, finely chopped
1 (14 ½ oz.) can crushed tomatoes
1 (6 oz.) can tuna, drained and shredded with a fork
2 tablespoons capers
2 tablespoons finely chopped parsley
1 pound spaghetti, cooked

Sauté the onion and garlic until soft. Add the tomatoes and cook until the liquid evaporates. Add the tuna and capers and simmer 10 minutes. Add the parsley just before serving. Serve over hot pasta.

Fresh Tuna Steaks with 40 Cloves of Garlic

4 servings

Crossing the Sea of Cortez from mainland Mexico to Baja, we once encountered a school of hungry tuna. No sooner did we put a lure in the water than one of the football-shaped yellowfin tunas jumped on the line. I have never had such an exciting day fishing, nor as much challenge in figuring out different ways to serve the catch.

40 cloves garlic, peeled*
3 tablespoons olive oil
1 cup dry red wine
4 (4 oz. each) tuna steaks, each about ¾-inch thick
¼ cup Bruschetta Sauce (page 170)

1. In a large skillet, sauté the garlic in the olive oil until it just begins to color. Add the wine and cook 15 minutes, covered. Add the tuna and simmer an additional 10 minutes, or until the flesh is opaque and the garlic is soft.
2. Serve the tuna with the garlic and wine sauce. Top with a tablespoon of Bruschetta Sauce.

**To peel garlic, place the cloves in small pan of boiling water; boil for 3 minutes. Remove from the pan and allow to cool. The papery peeling should slip off easily.*

Variation

Cook the tuna as directed above, substituting Remoulade Sauce (see page 161) for the Bruschetta Sauce. Instead of using the 2 cloves of raw garlic called for in the remoulade recipe, substitute the 40 cloves of well-cooked garlic. Mash the garlic to a paste before combining with the remoulade ingredients.

Pacific Bonito

While motoring down Baja California's Pacific Coast, we usually trail a fishing line behind *SpiceSea*. We catch a lot of Pacific bonito and, when dressed immediately, the fish has an excellent, mild flavor. Bonito, like all fish in the tuna family, has strips of dark meat that give the fish a strong taste. If you trim away the dark meat the rest of the flesh, when cooked, is a nice flaky white color. The meat tends to be on the dry side, so be sure not to overcook.

Hal frequently barbecues bonito fillets with a marinade of white Worcestershire sauce. He leaves the skin on and cooks the skinless side first. He then flips the fillet over and cooks the side with the skin. Usually, the skin sticks to the barbecue and makes quite a mess, but if you leave the barbecue on for a while after removing the fish, the skin will burn off.

We usually cook more bonito than we can eat and the next day I make Tuna Bonito Salad. I finely chop whatever crisp vegetables are around (celery, carrots, napa cabbage, bell peppers), mix in shredded, cooked bonito, moisten with mayonnaise or Ranch Dressing, and add some chopped cilantro for color and great flavor.

We also enjoy bonito raw or sashimi style. Thinly slice the fillets on a diagonal, across the grain, and serve with wasabi (Japanese horseradish) and soy sauce.

Spinach Linguine with Bonito Sauce

4 servings

8 cloves garlic, finely chopped
¾ cup chopped onion
2 tablespoons olive oil
1 (28 oz.) can of drained, chopped tomatoes
2 teaspoons dried Italian herbs
2 to 3 cups 1-inch cubes of boneless bonito
1 (2 ¼ oz.) can sliced black olives
¼ cup red wine
Salt and pepper to taste
12 ounces spinach linguine, cooked

Sauté the garlic and onion in the olive oil until soft. Add the tomatoes and herbs and cook five minutes. Add the bonito, olives, and red wine, and cook just until the fish is opaque. Serve over pasta. (Any leftover sauce is great the next morning served on top of an omelette.)

Escabeche

6 servings

Escabeche is a popular Latin American method of pickling fish and is the perfect solution for the overzealous angler because it needs no refrigeration. The pickled fish can be served immediately but improves with aging. It has a shelf life of about three weeks but will last longer if stored in the refrigerator.

If you are going to pickle the fish and eat it within a week, eliminate the salt brine soak in the following recipe. Instead, add a couple of bell peppers to the vegetables in step 3 and, after sautéeing, add 2 cups of water and a ½ cup of cooking oil with the vinegar. Store in the refrigerator.

2 pounds red snapper, mackerel, tuna, or sea bass fillets, cut into individual portions
Brine solution of ¾ cup kosher salt dissolved in 1 quart water
6 tablespoons olive oil
2 cloves garlic, minced
2 bay leaves, crumbled
½ teaspoon crushed hot red pepper
4 medium-sized onions, peeled and cut into thin slices
2 large carrots, peeled and cut into thin rounds
1 teaspoon whole black pepper corns
¾ cup white vinegar

1. Wash and drain the skinned and boned fish. Soak the fillets in the brine solution for 30 minutes. Drain and pat dry.

2. Sauté the fish in the olive oil with the garlic, bay leaves, and red pepper until light brown—about 2 to 3 minutes per side. Remove from the pan and set aside.

3. Add the onions, carrots, and peppercorns to the oil in the frying pan and cook until the onions are translucent. Add the vinegar and cook slowly for about 15 minutes. Allow to cool.

4. When the fish are cold, place in sterilized jars and cover with the cooled vinegar solution. Cover tightly.

Ensenada Fish Tacos

8 tacos

For me, fish tacos are synonymous with Ensenada because that's where I tasted one for the first time. I was rather reluctant to try one—who had ever heard of a taco made with fish? But, I was on a shopping expedition with a girlfriend who kept insisting that we have fish tacos for lunch. I had been envisioning a gourmet meal of lobster and white wine but ended up standing at a taco stand scarfing down fish tacos. I have been addicted to them ever since.

The fish is tempura-fried while you wait, placed in a warm corn tortilla, and handed to you with a smile. Then the fun begins. Condiment bowls line the front of each taco stand (I always choose the stand that has the widest variety) and may include lime-flavored mayonnaise, soupy guacamole, shredded cabbage, red and green salsas, vinegared onions, marinated chiles, chopped fresh cilantro, and fresh limes. I pile my selections—usually a little of everything—on the fish and attempt to eat my taco before the tortilla falls apart.

Fish taco mania has finally spread to California, but somehow, they don't taste the same as they do in Ensenada. In part it's because the ambiance of roadside taco stands is gone when you sit in a restaurant. And, with our calorie-counting California consciousness, the restaurants don't dare to deep-fry the fish. Finally, although half the fun is choosing your toppings, it's not cost effective for a restaurant to serve eight different bowls of sauces and goodies with each order of tacos.

In desperation to have my fish taco fix stateside, I persuaded one of the women who made fish tacos in Ensenada to give me her recipe. Now I can have authentic Ensenada Fish Market Tacos whenever we're catching fish on the boat.

Tacos

8 ounces fresh fish (sea bass, halibut, shark), cut into 2 × 1-inch pieces
Oil for deep-fat frying
8 corn tortillas, warmed with a few drops of oil in a teflon skillet

Batter

2 cups flour thinned with 1 ¼ cups water or stale beer
Salt and pepper
Oregano
Pinch of baking powder

1. To make the tacos, heat the oil in wok to 375° F. Dry the fish with paper towels and then coat with the batter. Fry 2 or 3 pieces of fish at a time until golden.
2. Serve in warm tortillas with some or all of the suggested garnishes.

Garnishes

Red Salsa (Mexican Salsa Fresca, page 165)
Green Salsa (Salsa de Tomatillo, page 166)
Mayonnaise thinned with a little lime juice
Avocado puréed and thinned with a little juice from the salsa
Jalapeño chiles en escabeche (canned, marinated chiles)
Lime wedges
Chopped cilantro leaves
Chopped cabbage
Chopped white onions or pickled white onions (recipe follows)

Pickled White Onions

2 white onions, finely sliced into rings
½ cup white vinegar
1 teaspoon salt
½ teaspoon freshly ground black pepper
¼ teaspoon oregano

Blanch the onion rings in a ½ cup of boiling water for 20 seconds. Drain. Combine the vinegar, salt, and pepper, and pour over the onions. Allow to marinate at least 1 hour before serving. Keeps indefinitely in the refrigerator if covered with the marinade.

Abalone and Squid

The delicate abalone is becoming increasingly difficult to find and therefore expensive to buy. I recently toured a large abalone farm in San Luis Obispo County, California, where the raising of abalones has become a multimillion dollar business. If you can't find your own abalone or are unwilling to pay the high price charged by the abalone farms, try substituting squid or conch.

I once brought some black abalone to my Japanese cooking instructor, and he informed me that, in Japan, the abalone's intestinal sack is a delicacy. He removed the dark sack and cooked it very slowly for an hour in equal parts soy and mirin (sweetened sake). Once cooled and sliced, it had the texture of cooked liver.

I have also tasted abalone that's been cooked directly in a beach fire. Place the live abalone, shell and all, in hot coals and cook until the shell crumbles easily. Once it's cool, the meat is easy to extract and very tender. Slice and serve with teriyaki sauce.

To clean abalone and make it into steaks (you'll use the foot portion of the meat), remove the meat from the shell and cut away and discard the gut. Trim off the frilly edge of the meat and save it for chowders and fritters. Next, trim off and discard the tough skin next to where the muscle was attached to the shell. Cut away the dark tough meat of the foot and slice the remaining white muscle into ⅜-inch thick pieces. Pound until tender and cook, following directions for abalonetti (squid) on page 80.

The white abalone meat is excellent when thinly sliced and served with a little soy sauce.

Spaghettini with Abalone

4 to 6 servings

While gunkholing at Southern California's Santa Cruz Island one day, I got hungry for clam sauce. It happened that I found lots of abalone and very few clams, so I substituted one for the other and came up with this recipe.

1 teaspoon finely chopped garlic
1 small onion, chopped
4 tablespoons olive oil
½ cup sliced mushrooms
1 red bell pepper, diced
Meat of 3 abalone, ground
1 cup white wine
1 cup chicken broth
Chopped parsley
1 pound cooked thin spaghettini

Sauté the garlic and onion in the olive oil until tender. Add the mushrooms and red pepper and cook until tender. Add the abalone and stir-fry for 30 seconds. Stir in the wine and broth and heat thoroughly. Serve over hot spaghettini and sprinkle with parsley.

Variation

If you prefer a red sauce, substitute a 16-ounce jar of spaghetti sauce for the broth and wine.

Abalonetti (Calamari, Abalone-Style)

4 servings

Fisherman's Wharf in Monterery, California, features "abalonetti"—squid that's prepared abalone-style.

8 small squid
½ cup flour
Salt and pepper
2 eggs, beaten
Bread crumbs
Olive oil
½ cup toasted sliced almonds
Chopped fresh parsley
Sliced lemons

1. Clean the squid by gently pulling the tentacle section away from the body section. Cut the tentacles just above the beak and reserve for another use.* Slit the body section down the center, scraping the interior of the body with the flat of a knife. Pull off the skin. Rinse and pat dry.
2. Gently pound the inside and outside of the body. Dip the squid first in flour that has been seasoned with salt and pepper, then in the beaten eggs, and finally in the bread crumbs.
3. Heat a large skillet and add some olive oil. When the oil is very hot, add the breaded squid, being careful not to overcrowd the pan. Sauté until golden.
4. Serve garnished with almonds, parsley, and lemons.

**The tentacles are my favorite part. Quickly sauté in olive oil and garlic to eat as is or serve over pasta.*

Conch and Mussels

Conch (pronounced "konk") are found in tropical waters of the western North Atlantic from the Florida Keys and the Bahamas to the equator. The meat is full of protein but doesn't come out of its hard shell without a fight.

The easiest way to extract the meat is to take a hammer and crack the shell, but it seems a shame to break such a beautiful shell. Watching vendors prepare conch sold in Nassau made me realize the skill that goes into freeing this tenacious snail from its shell. The first time you try doing this yourself, have an empty shell in front of you to serve as your guide.

Knocking a hole in the precise spot is the secret. Although more laborious, you can extract the meat and leave the shell more-or-less intact by chiseling a small hole at the top of the shell where the third spiral starts. Carefully cut away the meat where it adheres to the shell, vigorously shake the shell, and the meat should come out. It take some practice, but that's part of the fun of catching and cooking live conch.

The foot is the edible portion of the meat. Cut it into ¼-inch thick pieces and pound until it's tender—it's then ready to sauté. For fritters and chowder, conch can be ground with a meat grinder or food processor. Abalone or giant squid meat can be substituted in any conch recipe.

Conch Salad

2 servings

In the Bahamas conch salad is the most popular way of eating this tasty snail.

2 conch, cleaned and finely chopped
1 small onion, finely chopped
2 tomatoes, coarsely chopped
2 small, fresh chiles. finely chopped (or 1 teaspoon dried chile)
juice of 1 orange
salt and pepper to taste

1. Combine conch and vegetables.
2. Just before serving, add orange juice and season with salt and pepper.

Conch Chowder

4 servings

¼ pound bacon, chopped, cooked and drained
1 pound conch meat, minced or ground
1 onion, chopped
1 clove garlic, finely chopped
1 (16 oz.) can chopped tomatoes
1 potato, peeled and cut into ½-inch cubes
2 cups water
½ cup evaporated milk

Combine all the ingredients *except* the milk and simmer for 1 hour. Add the milk and heat.

Conch Stew

2 servings

In Port Lucaya on Grand Bahama Island, I was told Billie Joe's beachfront stand in front of the Grand Bahama Hotel served the best conch in the islands. With his charcoal fire blazing and his mountain of shells attesting to his business success, the owner nonetheless had a simple method of preparing his most enjoyable conch stew.

1 conch, cleaned, lightly pounded, and chopped in chunks
1 large onion, thinly sliced
1 tomato, coarsely chopped
1 chile pepper, finely chopped
3 cloves garlic, finely chopped
1 green bell pepper, coarsely chopped
juice of ½ orange
salt and pepper to taste

Place ingredients in foil and tightly seal. Cook over hot charcaol fire for 15 minutes.

Conch Fritters

4 servings

1 pound raw conch meat, minced or ground
Salt and pepper to taste
Cooking oil for frying

Batter

1 cup flour
¼ teaspoon salt
1 egg
⅔ cup milk
1 onion, finely chopped
1 tomato, finely chopped
1 bell pepper, seeded and finely chopped

1. Mix all the batter ingredients together; set aside.
2. Pat the conch meat dry with a paper towel and season with salt and pepper. In a wok, heat 3 inches of oil to 375° F.
3. Coat the conch with the batter and *carefully* drop a heaping tablespoon of the conch in the hot oil. Fry until golden and drain on paper towels before serving. (**Note:** If you fry more than a few tablespoons of batter at a time, the oil will cool down and be absorbed into the food.)

When Hal and I were newlyweds, he introduced me to my first off-road camping experience by taking me to a beautiful and remote spot called Punta Cabras on the west coast of Baja California, about 75 miles south of Ensenada.

Twenty years later, we returned to Punta Cabras with friends. We reminisced about our first trip as we traveled into the back country and, although civilization had developed considerably in nearby Santo Tomás, the spectacular rocky promontory was exactly as it had been twenty years before. Our camping site for the next two nights gave us a 180-degree view of the ocean; a hillside behind us afforded complete privacy. (Our privacy was further secured because one has to traverse 150 yards of soft sand to reach "our" camping spot. Our friends got stuck in their two-wheel drive minivan, but with Hal's portable highway system—2 × 4s—we were soon comfortably set up for the night.)

We spent the weekend relaxing, walking on lovely Bahia Almejas, and eating the succulent mussels from the rocks below our campsite.

Mussels Punta Cabras

4 servings

2 strips of bacon, minced
1 onion, chopped
3 cups white wine
24 fresh mussels, rinsed and scrubbed in seawater and debearded*. (Gather the mussels in an area that is free from sand. If unable to do so, soak them for 24 hours in salt water so that they will purge the sand from their systems.)
3 tablespoons butter
2 cloves garlic, minced
1 lemon, cut into wedges
Tabasco sauce

1. Sauté the bacon and onion in a casserole until the onion is soft. Add the wine and allow to come to a boil. Add the mussels, cover, and steam until the shells open—about 5 minutes. Discard any mussels that do not open.
2. Meanwhile, melt the butter with the garlic.
3. To serve, remove the mussels from their shells. Dip the meat in the melted butter, squeeze with lemon, and season with hot sauce.

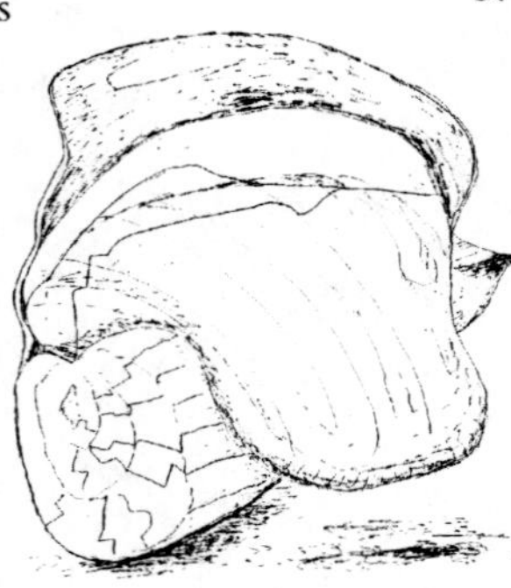

**To debeard a mussel, see page 49.*

Clams

A favorite pastime of ours while aboard *SpiceSea* is to anchor where clams are plentiful, get out our trusty hand rakes, assume the clamming position, and search for these delicious bivalves. To locate a good clamming spot, I start digging in areas where there are lots of empty shells. When walking on sand flats at low tide, watch for the telltale squirting of a clam as it closes up. When diving, I can usually spot the syphons of the clams winking at me under the sand.

We usually try to leave clams in salt water for at least a day before eating them so they clams can purge the sand out of their intestines. Clams will keep for several days in a mesh bag hanging in the water. (Don't do this, of course, if you are anchored in water that may be polluted.) We were once able to keep clams this way for up to two weeks while cruising the islands adjacent to La Paz.

If you scrub clam shells well before using them you should eliminate the grit. We once motored for a day with clams hanging over the side and found that they had purged themselves with fresh, sand-free seawater, and the friction of the shells rubbing on each other loosened any remaining sand. Grit-free clams and no work!

As with all seafood, be very careful about where you gather your catch. (See page 59.)

Stuffed Clams

Chocolates (clams) are shiny, brown-shelled clams that are plentiful in the Sea of Cortez. Diving for them in about six to eight feet of water, you look for their two syphons just visible in the sand. When they sense movement they quickly withdraw the syphons and are impossible to spot.

Lightly steam the clams to open the shells and extract the meat. Finely chop the clam meat, season with a little chopped onion, lime juice, Worcestershire sauce, and Tabasco. Stir in an egg and enough bread crumbs so the mixture holds its shape. Stuff the mixture back into the shell, top with grated cheddar cheese and a small square of bacon, and grill on the barbecue until the bacon is cooked.

Wedge Shells

Wedge shells are tiny, colorful smooth bivalves that can be dug up just below the surf line of many beaches. When I search for wedge shells I sit in the sand and feel for them with my fingers. You can also place a strainer in the water, scoop up a few handfuls of sand, and rinse until the sand drains out.

Because of their insignificant size, many people overlook wedge shells, but they are very plentiful and lots of fun to find. For a different appetizer, steam 8 cups of sand-free wedge shells in 1 cup of white wine and 1 cup of bottled salsa. Allow to cool and serve as finger food. Guests will enjoy sucking out the delicate morsels and tossing the shells overboard.

You can also steam wedge shells in water (2 cups of water per 8 cups of shells). Strain and use the broth for soup.

Clam Sauce with Porcinis and Pesto

6 servings

1 gallon butter clams
1 cup white wine
1 tablespoon chopped parsley
1 onion, chopped
2 cloves garlic, finely chopped
2 tablespoons olive oil
1 red bell pepper, chopped
1 green bell pepper, chopped
2 ounces porcini mushrooms, soaked in water for 30 minutes
1 (2 oz.) jar pesto
1 pound cooked pasta

1. Steam the clams in the wine and parsley until the shells open. Strain the steaming liquid and reserve 1 cup. When cool enough to handle, shuck the clams over a bowl, catching their juice.
2. Sauté the onion and garlic in the olive oil until tender. Strain the soaked mushrooms, reserving the liquid. Add the peppers, mushrooms, and 1 cup of the strained soaking liquid from the mushrooms. Boil this mixture until reduced to about 3 tablespoons.

3. Add 1 cup of the reserved clam steaming juice and the pesto sauce.
4. Add the clams with their juice and serve over pasta.

Clam Chowder San Ignacio

3 to 4 servings

On one of our many camping trips down the Baja peninsula, Hal and I took a side trip to a whale-watching lagoon. After many trials and tribulations, we finally reached Bahia San Ignacio, a bay on the Pacific side of Baja California where the whales go to spawn. This was many years before whale-watching became popular and the road out of the town of San Ignacio seemed to be somewhat of a secret to the unfamiliar tourist. We were fortunate, though, to meet a man who was willing to show us the way, but he couldn't believe that we really wanted to go on such a rocky and rough road.

At the local fish camp at La Fridera we watched as villagers shucked mountains of scallops *(almejas catarina)* that sit on top of this shallow sandy bay at low tide. We were lucky to hit especially low tides while we were there and walked for miles collecting clams and scallops. In an hour and a half, we had filled buckets, pockets, and anything in sight with *hachas* (a large form of scallop), *catarinas*, (a small, free-swimming scallop), *chocolates,* and butter clams. Shellfish heaven!

One of the recipes that I made on that cold winter trip was this hot clam chowder, which I have made many times since.

2 tablespoons butter
1 onion, chopped
1 teaspoon finely chopped garlic
1 large carrot, diced
1 potato, diced
2 cups chopped clams
1 package dehydrated cream of mushroom soup mix*
1 cup reconstituted milk
1 cup white wine
2 cups water
Hot sauce, to taste
Lime juice, to taste

Melt the butter in a deep skillet and sauté the onion, garlic, carrot, and potato until tender. Add all of the remaining ingredients and heat thoroughly.

**If not available, soak some dried mushrooms and drain. Make a white sauce (2 tablespoons butter, 2 tablespoons flour, and 1 cup milk) and flavor with the soaked mushrooms.*

Linguine with Clam Sauce

4 servings

I will always associate Linguine with Clam Sauce with the day Hal and I moved aboard *SpiceSea*. It had sounded like such a simple plan but, in reality, the stress was almost overwhelming. We sold everything—furniture, appliances, cookware, china, tools—the works. Our plan was to go cruising again, not for a season or two, but for several years. We wanted to spend at least another season in Mexico and experience the charms of Costa Rica, Panama, Venezuela, and the Caribbean. We envisioned cruising the Intracostal Waterway and then drifting down the mighty Mississippi River.

For a trip of this duration we felt it wasn't practical to store our possessions, so we systematically got rid of twenty-five years of collecting. In many ways, doing so was cathartic. Once we unloaded the "stuff," we realized that we were free to do anything and go anywhere. At times, though, the experience was very painful.

When we were finally within days of moving aboard *SpiceSea* and literally camping out in our own home, too exhausted to run down to the local takeout, I rummaged through the bags of food that were destined for the boat and tried to come up with a meal that would not only be delicious, but would boost our sagging spirits and energy.

I found a package of pasta, two cans of chopped clams, and kept on digging until I found the rest of the ingredients for one of our favorite dinners—Linguine with Clam Sauce. As I prepared dinner in my skeleton kitchen I realized that anyone cruising on the most simply outfitted boat could enjoy this recipe.

Simplicity is one of the keys to cooking aboard and this dish certainly qualifies. Add some heated Boboli bread or toasted garlic bread and a tossed salad, and you have a delicious dinner that's simple enough for the family yet impressive for even your most discriminating guests.

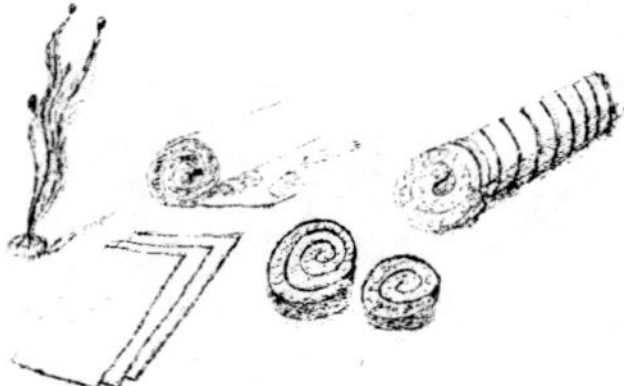

3 small dried red chiles, crumbled
4 to 6 cloves garlic, chopped
4 tablespoons olive oil
2 (6½ oz.) cans chopped clams*, drained, reserving ¼ cup of the clam juice**
2 tablespoons dried parsley or ½ cup chopped fresh
1 pound linguine or spaghetti or other pasta

Sauté the chiles and garlic in the olive oil for 30 seconds. Add the clams, reserved clam juice, and parsley, and heat. Pour over the cooked and drained pasta and toss well to coat.

Variation

1 tablespoon vegetable oil
1 minced serrano chile
2 tablespoons fresh chopped ginger
2 tablespoons chopped fresh garlic
4 tablespoons grated orange peel
2 tablespoons dry sherry
2 tablespoons soy sauce
2 (6 ½ oz.) cans chopped clams, drained
1 pound linguine, spaghetti, or other pasta

Follow the directions for Linguine with Clam Sauce (above), making the substitutions and additions as indicated.

**Substitute 3 pounds of fresh clams if available. If you can get small fresh clams (littlenecks), wash them several times in fresh water and scrub the shells well. Steam them with a little water until their shells open. When cool enough to handle, shuck. Strain the broth and pour into the olive oil mixture. Add the clams and spoon over pasta.*

***Save any of the unused clam juice as a base for a seafood soup. I keep a container in the freezer and just keep adding the leftover clam juice. Once I fill a four-cup container, it's time to make Easy Seafood Soup.*

Easy Seafood Soup

4 servings

On our first night on *SpiceSea* after moving aboard, I made a fish soup using leftover clam juice from the dinner I'd made the night before. (See Linguine with Clam Sauce, above.) Generally I coordinate this soup with whatever Hal has caught that day but, since Hal was still stowing gear, I stopped by the local seafood market and picked out what looked good.

1 onion, chopped
4 cloves garlic, chopped
1 bell pepper, chopped
2 tablespoons olive oil
4 cups clam juice
1 chicken bouillon cube, diluted with ½ cup water
1 (8 oz.) can chopped tomatoes
1 teaspoon dried thyme
1 dried hot red chile pepper, crumbled
Grated peel from 1 orange
1 pound red snapper fillets, cut in bite-size pieces
½ pound peeled, deveined, uncooked shrimp
½ pound scallops
2 to 4 tablespoons chopped parsley

1. In a deep sauté pan, sauté the onion, garlic, and bell pepper in the olive oil for 3 minutes. Add the clam juice, bouillon, and the tomatoes with their juice; bring to a boil.

2. Add the thyme, dried chile pepper, orange peel, and fish. Cook 2 minutes before adding the shrimp. Just as the shrimp start to turn pink, turn off the heat and add scallops. (Scallops toughen very easily—adding them after the heat is turned off will prevent overcooking.)

3. Toss in a handful of parsley just before serving to give the soup some color.

Beach Party Barbecued Clams

While hiking in Santa Maria Bay on Baja's Pacific Coast, we came across a treasure trove of butter clams. We announced on the radio that there would be a potluck and clam feast that evening, and seventeen boats showed up in the anchorage for a memorable party.

Santa Maria Bay, which is just north of Bahia Magdalena, is one of my favorite anchorages on Baja's Pacific Coast. White sandy beaches, friendly lobstermen, an intriguing estuary to navigate by dink, and miles of beachcombing are a few of its charms. The fishing is good, too. Hal caught all of the halibut in the surf line that we could eat and I caught one while I was walking along the shore of the estuary dragging a lure.

1 stick butter
6 cloves garlic, finely chopped
Lots of clams
1 to 2 cups white wine
1 onion, chopped
2 tablespoons dried parsley
1 large disposable roasting pan
Aluminum foil

1. Build a fire on the beach and allow to cook down.
2. Heat the butter and garlic together, being careful not to let it burn.
3. Place the clams, wine, onion, and parsley in the disposable roasting pan and cover tightly with foil.
4. Place the pan on a rack in coals (we used the rack from our barbecue) and cook until the clams steam open. With a long pair of tongs, lift out the clams and "serve"—each person fills an empty clam shell with hot garlic butter and dips the clams in butter.

Easy Clambake

4 servings

2 (36-×18-inch) pieces extra heavy aluminum foil
1 pound seaweed or kale
2 leg/thigh portions chicken
Paprika
2 lobster tails
1 pound linguiça sausage, cut in chunks
12 steamer clams
2 ears of corn, husked and broken in half
2 small onions, peeled and quartered
2 potatoes, cut in eighths
Salt and pepper
½ cup white wine
Melted butter

1. On each piece of foil, line the area to be covered with food with half the seaweed, leaving the edges of the foil unlined so that it can be folded into packets (see page 153).
2. Sprinkle the chicken with paprika. On each piece of seaweed-lined foil, place half of the chicken, lobster, sausage, clams, corn, onions, and potatoes. Season with salt and pepper. Add ½ a cup of wine to each packet.
3. Seal the packets very well, following the directions on page 153.
4. Cook in a covered barbecue over medium-hot heat for 35 minutes. Open the packet and check the chicken for doneness.
5. Serve with melted butter.

New England Clambake

Dig a large shallow pit about 8 inches deep in the sand and line it with rocks. On the morning of the clambake, make a large bonfire in the pit. Allow it to cook down to hot coals.

In the meantime, soak unhusked corn, seafood, a heavy cotton tarp, and seaweed in saltwater for several hours. Make food sacks from dampened cheesecloth and bundle separate sacks of onions, sausage, chicken, and potatoes.

Place seaweed on hot rocks. Top with corn, potato bundles and whole lobsters. Place clams around edge of pit. Top with seaweed and wrung out tarp. Weight down tarp with rocks and sand.

After an hour, carefully remove tarp and serve.

Sturgeon

The dense rich flesh of sturgeon tastes best with marinades made with olive oil and robust herbs and spices. Garlic, basil, and rosemary can be combined with a little olive oil and brushed on sturgeon fillets before grilling on the barbecue. Skin the fish before cooking since the skin shrinks as it cooks and misshapens the fillets.

Caviar

If you are lucky enough to catch a sturgeon full of roe, you can make your own caviar. In Europe, only sturgeon roe can be sold as caviar, but in the United States the roe of any fish (whitefish, lumpfish, salmon), can be called caviar. For the best caviar, the eggs should be tender and flavorful. Test one of the eggs by crushing it with your tongue against the roof of your mouth. It should pop easily and have no fishy flavor.

To make your own caviar, open the egg sac and scrape the eggs away from the membrane into a fine mesh strainer. Rinse with cold water until the water is clear. Place the drained roe in a stainless steel (not aluminum or other reactive metal) container with a lukewarm brine (2 ounces of salt dissolved in 1 quart of water) solution for 15 minutes. Pack in jars and store in the refrigerator for up to a month.

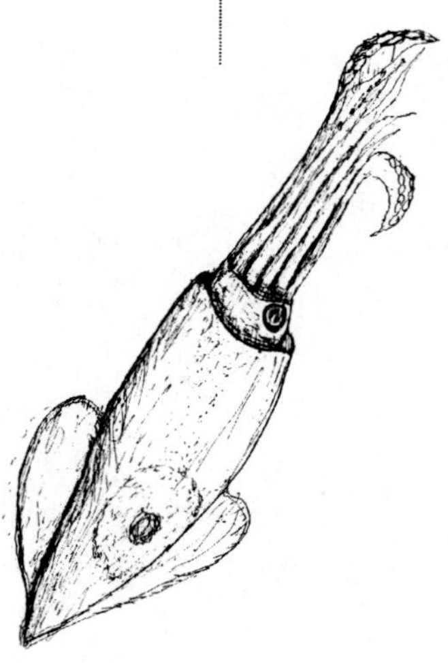

Sushi and Sashimi

Sushi refers to a number of rice-based delicacies made with short grain rice that's tossed with a sweetened rice wine vinegar mixture. *Nigiri* sushi looks like a delicate fish sandwich with the seafood perched attractively on top of a rectangle of hand pressed rice. *Maki* sushi uses a sheet of nori, a type of dried seaweed, that is spread with a layer of rice and then filled with layers of colorful vegetables and seafood before being rolled into a cylinder and sliced.

Sashimi is the easiest of seafood dishes. All you need is very fresh fish, cut into bite-sized pieces, soy sauce, and wasabi (very pungent Japanese horseradish) for dipping. Wasabi in its powdered form should be dissolved in a little water or dry sherry to form a paste. You can also purchase tubes of premade wasabi paste.

Basic Vinegared Rice

6 tablespoons rice vinegar
4 tablespoons sugar
2 teaspoons salt
3 cups short grain white rice, washed several times
3 cups water

1. Combine the rice vinegar, sugar, and salt. Heat, stirring until dissolved.
2. Soak the rice in water for 1 hour. Bring to a boil, cover the pan, reduce the heat, and simmer for 15 minutes. Turn off heat and allow to stand for 10 additional minutes before removing lid.
3. Transfer the rice to a large bowl and fluff it with a fork. Pour in the vinegar mixture, tossing to coat the grains of rice.
4. Do not refrigerate the rice. To keep it from drying out, cover with a dampened towel after it has cooled.
5. Serve with soy sauce and wasabi (for dipping) and sliced preserved ginger.

Maki Sushi California-Style

32 slices

Many types of seafood and vegetables can be used in maki sushi. Cooked shrimp, raw tuna, or bonito are all great. Strips of cooked carrots, omelettes, and soaked shitake mushroom slices are tasty alternatives.

4 sheets dried nori
2 cups cooked vinegared rice (this page)
2 teaspoons wasabi dissolved in 2 teaspoons water
1 small avocado, peeled and cut into strips
½ seedless cucumber, thinly sliced lengthwise (skin intact)
2 teaspoons toasted sesame seeds
¼ pound crab meat

1. If nori is not pretoasted, do so by passing the shiny side over a high flame. The color will change from brownish black to dark green. Without toasting, the nori will be gummy, hard to chew, and lacking in flavor.
2. Lay out one sheet of nori with the narrow side at the bottom. Spread rice in a ⅜-inch layer over the nori except for a 2-inch edge at the top. Press the rice in place with your fingers that have first been moistened with rice vinegar.
3. Spread a ½ teaspoon of wasabi mixture across the rice.
4. Arrange ¼ of the avocado and cucumber slices across the center of the rice. Sprinkle with a ½ teaspoon of sesame seeds. Place some of the crab on top of the cucumber and roll the nori up tightly.
5. Cut in 1-inch slices and garnish with ginger. Serve with dipping sauces.

Make-Your-Own Sushi Party

Arrange a platter of cooked carrot sticks, steamed spinach leaves, raw cucumber strips, strips of rehydrated shitake mushrooms, salmon caviar, crab legs, raw tuna, cooked shrimp, and smoked salmon. Serve with a bowl of vinegared rice and a dish of toasted nori. Provide small bowls of soy sauce for each person and a container of wasabi that guests can mix into the soy sauce according to their palates.

Each guest takes a piece of nori and adds rice and selections from the platter. The nori is folded over the filling (like a taco) and dipped into soy.

Nigiri Sushi

30 pieces

1 recipe vinegared rice (page 88)
1 tablespoon powdered wasabi mixed into a paste with water
30 pieces small slices raw fresh tuna or sea bass*
Rice vinegar for moistening your hands

1. Moisten your hands with some of the vinegar. Pick up about 1 ½ tablespoons of the prepared rice and shape into an egg-shaped oval (1 ½ inches × ¾ inch).
2. Gently, but firmly, squeeze the rice in the palm of your hand. Smear a dab of wasabi in the center of a slice of fish and press the fish and rice oval together. The fish should cover the top of the rice.

**You can also use cooked shrimp. Peel, devein, and place a toothpick along the underside of each shrimp to prevent it from curling up while it cooks. Boil briefly and butterfly when cool.*

CHAPTER 6

Meat and Poultry

Many of the recipes included in this chapter use the quick, stir-fry method of cooking, others are one-pot meals that cook slowly while you attend to other tasks, and still others are some of my favorite main course recipes for the pressure cooker.

Chicken or Veal Picatta

6 servings

I love this recipe. It uses basic ingredients, it's quick to prepare, and has a delightfully pungent flavor. Besides chicken and veal, I have also used abalone, squid, and turkey breast. My favorite? All of them!

3 whole chicken breasts, halved, skinned, and boned, or 1 pound other meat (see suggestions above)
1/3 cup flour
1/4 teaspoon salt
1/4 teaspoon freshly ground black pepper
2 tablespoons olive oil
1/4 cup dry white wine
2 tablespoons fresh lemon juice
2 teaspoons freshly grated lemon peel
1/4 cup rinsed and drained capers
1/4 cup minced fresh parsley
Lemon slices

1. Place the meat of your choice between sheets of waxed paper and pound them until thin. Combine the flour, salt, and pepper in a Ziploc and shake with the meat to lightly coat. Shake off excess flour.
2. In a large skillet, heat the olive oil and sauté the meat 2 to 3 minutes per side. Drain on paper towels and cover to keep warm.
3. Pour off most of the fat and deglaze the pan with the wine. Add the lemon juice and peel. Return the meat to the pan to reheat.
4. Sprinkle each serving with capers and parsley. Garnish with lemon slices.

Yucatecan-Style Chicken

2 servings

Marinate 2 boneless chicken breasts in Achiote Paste (see page 176), wrap the chicken in banana leaves (if available), and then in foil. Steam until done—about 30 minutes. This dish can be marinated for up to three days in the refrigerator, or it can be frozen. I often cook the chicken in a bamboo steamer basket in the wok. You can also bake it in the oven or on the barbecue.

Baked Herbed Chicken

6 servings

3 whole boneless, skinless chicken breasts

Coating

3 tablespoons Dijon-style mustard
1 tablespoon lemon juice
1 tablespoon chopped parsley
1/4 teaspoon dried basil leaves
1/4 teaspoon dried tarragon
1/8 teaspoon dried thyme leaves
1/8 teaspoon freshly ground black pepper
1/4 cup dry bread crumbs
2 tablespoons olive oil

Mix together all the coating ingredients and coat the chicken. Roll the coated chicken in the bread crumbs and drizzle with the olive oil. Bake at 375°F on a rack set in a pan for 25 minutes.

Serve hot or cold.

Chicken with Curry Mayonnaise

4 to 6 servings

3 boneless breasts, split in half, skinned
2 to 3 tablespoons olive oil
Salt and pepper to taste

Sauce

1 ½ cups homemade mayonnaise (page 160)
1 tablespoon olive oil
1 small onion, finely chopped
2 teaspoons curry powder
¼ cup tomato juice
¼ cup red wine
1 tablespoon apricot jam

1. Sauté the chicken in the olive oil until just done. Season with salt and pepper and chill.
2. Make the mayonnaise; set aside.
3. Heat the olive oil in a small skillet and sauté the onion until soft, but not browned. Stir in the curry powder and cook for 60 seconds. Stir in the tomato juice and wine. Bring to a boil and reduce liquid in half. Stir in the jam. Cool and strain.
3. Stir the cooled curry mixture into the mayonnaise to complete the sauce. Serve with chicken or seafood.

Foil-Wrapped Chicken with Salsa

4 servings

In most countries, chicken is not mass produced like it is in the United States—it's often one of the more expensive meats at foreign markets. Hal and I found great chicken at the public market in San Jose del Cabo (just north of Cabo San Luca) and bought a whole chicken—it was delicious.

1 whole chicken, cut into serving pieces
1 teaspoon chopped garlic
1 (4 oz.) can chunky Mexican Salsa
1 onion, chopped
1 cup chopped celery

1. Place the chicken pieces on a large piece of heavy foil and cover with the garlic, salsa, onion, and celery. Wrap tightly and marinate for 30 minutes.
2. Bake over hot coals for 35 to 45 minutes. Serve warm, using the juices from the foil as a sauce. If there is any leftover chicken, make Chilaquiles (page 32) for breakfast the next day.

Helen's Chicken

4 servings

The most difficult part of this easy and delicious recipe is to find paper bags that are not made of recycled paper.

1 4- to 5-pound chicken
1 onion, coarsely chopped
10 cloves garlic
1 lemon
2 sprigs fresh rosemary
Paprika
Salt and pepper
1 paper bag made of nonrecycled paper

1. Stuff the chicken with the onion, garlic cloves, and lemon. Place a sprig of rosemary under each wing. Sprinkle the outside with the paprika, salt, and pepper.
2. Place the chicken on a rack inside the paper bag and place the bag in another pan in case there is any leakage. Bake for 1 hour at 450° F; reduce oven temperature to 350° F and bake another 45 minutes.

Chicken With 40 Cloves of Garlic

4 servings

This simple recipe has always been popular with my cooking classes. Aboard *SpiceSea,* I use my deep sauté pan for baking the chicken in the oven.

3 ½- to 4-pound chicken
Salt and pepper
½ teaspoon Italian seasoning
¼ cup olive oil
40 cloves of garlic, separated but unpeeled
8 croûtons made from 4 slices of firm white bread with crusts removed, sliced in half diagonally into triangles and browned in olive oil or toasted

1. Season the inside of the chicken with salt, pepper, and Italian seasoning.
2. In an ovenproof casserole, brown the chicken in the olive oil. Add the garlic, cover the casserole tightly with foil, and weight the foil down with a lid.
3. Bake at 350° F for 1½ hours.
4. Remove the foil just before serving—a delicious aroma of garlic will be released and the chicken will be tender and fragrant. The cooked garlic has a mild, nutty flavor with the texture of butter.
5. Serve with the croûtons.

Note: To release the garlic from its skin, gently squeeze the root end of the clove and spread the cooked garlic thickly on the croûtons.

Sautéed Chicken Breasts with Provençal Herbs

6 servings

3 whole chicken breasts, boned, skinned, and cut in half
3 tablespoons olive oil
Salt and pepper
¾ cup dry white wine
3 large tomatoes, peeled, seeded, and coarsely chopped
2 cloves garlic, finely chopped
1 teaspoon anchovy paste
Pinch of dried savory
Pinch of dried marjoram
¼ cup chopped fresh basil or 1 tablespoon dried
1 bay leaf
1 (4 oz.) can sliced black olives

1. Sauté the chicken breasts in the olive oil until barely cooked. Season with salt and pepper and set aside. Pour off excess oil.
2. Add the wine, tomatoes, garlic, anchovy paste, savory, marjoram, basil, and bay leaf and simmer for 10 minutes. Add the olives and return the chicken to pan to reheat.
3. Serve with brown rice or Italian orzo.

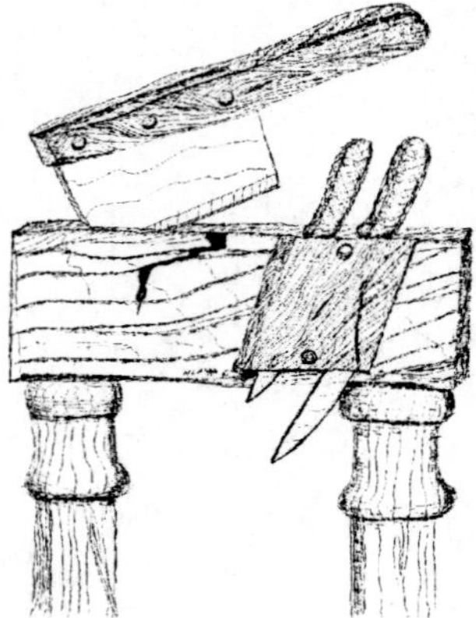

Chicken with Tomato and Feta Cheese

4 servings

2 tablespoons olive oil
4 half boneless, skinless chicken breasts
1 onion, chopped
2 cloves garlic, minced
1 (28 oz.) can Italian-style plum tomatoes, drained and chopped
½ cup white wine
2 teaspoons dried oregano
4 ounces crumbled feta cheese
2 tablespoon chopped fresh mint, if available

1. Sauté the chicken in the olive oil until golden. Remove from pan. Add the onion and garlic and sauté briefly. Add the tomatoes, wine, and oregano, and simmer until the sauce is thick.
2. Return the chicken to the pan to finish cooking; sprinkle with the feta cheese and mint and heat an additional minute.
3. Serve with rice.

Basque-Style Chicken and Sausage

4 servings

1 tablespoon minced garlic
2 or more tablespoons olive oil
4 half chicken breasts, skinned and boned, cut into ½-inch cubes
Salt and freshly ground black pepper
1 tablespoon dried red pepper flakes (optional)
2 zucchini, cut in ¼-inch wide slices
1 red bell pepper, cut into 1-inch cubes
1 yellow bell pepper, cut into 1-inch cubes
½ pound hot Italian sausage, sliced
1 cup dry white wine
2 tablespoons finely chopped parsley

1. In a nonstick skillet or wok, sauté the garlic in 1 tablespoon of oil. Do not allow to brown. Season the chicken with salt and pepper and sauté with the garlic until barely cooked. Remove from the pan and set aside.
2. Sprinkle the zucchini and bell peppers with the red pepper flakes and sauté in the remaining tablespoon of oil until barely tender. Remove and set aside.
3. Sauté the sausage until cooked. Drain off any fat and add the wine. Combine the chicken, sausage, and vegetables and stir while reheating.
4. Garnish with chopped parsley and serve over rice.

Chicken Breasts with Chili Hollandaise

6 servings

3 whole boneless chicken breasts
1 recipe Chili Hollandaise Sauce (page 159)

Marinade

2 cloves garlic, finely chopped
2 tablespoons finely chopped fresh ginger
½ cup dry sherry
¼ cup soy sauce
1 tablespoon chili powder
3 tablespoons chicken broth

Combine the marinade ingredients; marinate the chicken in a Ziploc bag for at least 2 hours in the refrigerator. Bake at 350° F for 25 minutes, skin side up, or until cooked. Serve with Chili Hollandaise Sauce.

Chicken with Chunky Thai Peanut Sauce

4 servings

2 whole boneless chicken breasts, barbecued and sliced

Sauce

2 tablespoons chunky peanut butter
3 tablespoons soy sauce
3 tablespoons fresh lime juice
1 tablespoon Oriental sesame oil
1 teaspoon sugar
1 tablespoon finely chopped garlic
1 tablespoon finely chopped ginger
1 teaspoon dried red pepper flakes
2 green onions, finely chopped

Garnish

2 tablespoons chopped cilantro
2 tablespoons chopped roasted peanuts
1 cucumber, peeled, cut in half lengthwise, seeded, and cut into strips

Gently heat all the sauce ingredients and serve over the chicken with the garnishes. This delicious peanut sauce can also be used as a vegetable dip or as a sauce with broiled beef.

Tea Smoking

4 to 6 servings

Tea smoking, a Chinese cooking technique, lends a wonderful flavor and golden color to chicken, duck, turkey, and even seafood. I have a Burton Stove Top Smoker (see "Essential Galley Equipment," page xx) that is ideally suited to this technique, but a disposable foil pan will also work.

4 pounds poultry or seafood
Salt and pepper to taste

Smoking Mixture

⅓ cup black tea leaves
¼ cup uncooked rice
¼ cup brown sugar
1 tablespoon cinnamon
1 tablespoon orange peel

1. Season the meat with salt and pepper.
2. Mix the smoking ingredients together and place on the bottom of a disposable roasting pan. Spray a roasting rack with nonstick coating and place it in the pan.
3. Place the meat on the rack, skin side up. Tent the roasting pan with foil by wrapping the foil under the pan and joining at the top, being careful that the foil does not touch the poultry. Seal the foil tent with a tight fold.
4. Place on a preheated covered barbecue and cook on high for 20 minutes. Turn heat to medium and cook until done—about 30 to 40 additional minutes.

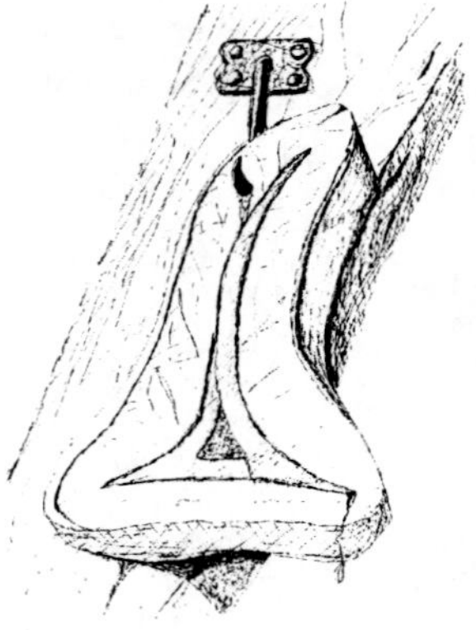

Stir-Frying

Stir-frying is a perfect method for cooking on a boat. You need only one pan and one burner, so it's fuel efficient, easy to clean up, and quick. And, since a little bit of meat goes a long way, it's also economical.

Stir-frying techniques are simple—most recipes consist of a meat marinade and a seasoning sauce. The marinade tenderizes the meat and gives it a special flavor, while the seasoning sauce unifies the flavor of the recipe.

To ensure that all the ingredients in a stir-fry recipe will be properly cooked, cut them into uniform pieces. If cornstarch is added at the end of the recipe, make a well in the center of the food in the wok and pour the cornstarch mixture into the well. Allow it to heat and begin to thicken before stirring it into the rest of the food.

When stir-frying, always preheat the wok before adding the oil. (The oil disperses faster in a hot pan and you use less.) Be sure that the oil is hot before adding any food—if you stir-fry in cold oil, the food will absorb the oil.

Stir-frying works well for tougher cuts of beef, especially if you first cut the meat into thin slices and marinate it. Flank or round steak, partially frozen and cut into thin slices, across the grain, stir-fry very well. You can also substitute chicken, pork, or seafood for many cuts of beef.

Serve stir-fried dishes with steamed rice.

Kung Pao Chicken (Spicy Chicken with Peanuts)

I keep a container of the marinade (omitting the egg white) and premixed seasoning sauce on board to make preparing this recipe easier. Don't be intimidated by the long list of ingredients—the recipe goes together very fast. There are lots of substitutions that are possible for the chicken, including pork, scallops, beef, fish. Fresh ginger root stores well in a jar of sherry at room temperature. The pea pods are a garnish and are not necessary to the finished dish.

Marinade

2 teaspoons cornstarch
1 egg white
1 tablespoon soy sauce
1 teaspoon salt
1 tablespoon sugar
½ teaspoon garlic powder
1 tablespoon sherry

Combine all the marinade ingredients. (If making in advance, omit the egg white until just before using.)

6 tablespoons vegetable oil
1 pound boned, skinned chicken breasts and thighs, cut into 1-inch pieces
1 cup snow peas, ends trimmed, strings removed, or whatever fresh vegetable is available
Pinch of sugar
Salt
4 dried red chile peppers, cut into ½-inch pieces
1 medium onion, diced
1 clove garlic, minced
2 slices ginger root, peeled and minced
10 dried black mushrooms, soaked in warm water for 1 hour, stems removed, sliced
1 can water chestnuts, thinly sliced
½ cup bamboo shoots
1 tablespoon cornstarch dissolved in 3 tablespoons cold water
4 green onions cut into 3-inch long slivers
½ cup dry roasted peanuts

Seasoning Sauce

2 tablespoons cider vinegar or other vinegar
2 tablespoons dark soy sauce
1 tablespoon sherry
1 tablespoon brown sugar
1 tablespoon water

Combine all the ingredients for the sauce; set aside. (Can be made in advance.)

1. Marinate the chicken for 20 minutes at room temperature.
2. Heat 2 tablespoons of the vegetable oil in a wok and stir-fry the chicken until barely done. Remove the chicken and allow to drain.

3. Clean and dry the wok. Heat 2 tablespoons of the vegetable oil in the wok and stir-fry the pea pods (or other vegetables) until they glisten. Season with a pinch of sugar and salt and place 2 tablespoons of water in the wok. Cover and allow to steam until the pea pods are bright green. Remove the pea pods to serving platter.

4. Dry the wok with a paper towel and pour in the remaining 2 tablespoons of oil. Heat and add the chiles. (Be very careful not to inhale the fumes from chiles.) Cook until the chiles begin to blacken.

5. Add the garlic and ginger and stir-fry for a few seconds. Add the mushrooms, water chestnuts, and bamboo shoots. Add the seasoning sauce and bring to a boil. Add the chicken and reheat. Make a well in the center of the wok and pour in the cornstarch. As the sauce begins to thicken, stir to combine.

6. Serve the chicken garnished with peanuts and raw green onions surrounded by pea pods.

Cashew Chicken

4 servings

1 egg white
1 teaspoon cornstarch
1 tablespoon soy sauce
¾ pound boneless, skinned chicken breasts, cut into 1-inch cubes
½ cup peanut oil
3 green onions, cut into long, thin slivers
1 green bell pepper, cut into cubes
1 red bell pepper, cut into cubes
2 teaspoons finely chopped ginger root
3 tablespoons roasted cashews

Seasoning Sauce

2 tablespoons soy sauce
1 tablespoon dry sherry
1 tablespoon cider vinegar
2 teaspoons cornstarch
½ teaspoon salt
1 teaspoon sugar
¼ teaspoon cayenne pepper

1. Make a marinade by combining the egg white, cornstarch, and soy sauce; marinate the chicken for 20 minutes.

2. Heat the peanut oil in a wok to 350° F and deep-fat fry the chicken for 2 minutes. Remove the chicken and pour out all but 1 tablespoon of oil. Drain the chicken in a strainer set over a bowl.

3. Stir-fry the onions, peppers, and ginger root until they are crisp-tender. Add the chicken to the pan and pour in the seasoning sauce. Stir-fry until thickened. Sprinkle with cashews and serve with steamed rice.

Stir-Fried Thai Chicken in Coconut Sauce

4 servings

3 cloves garlic, finely chopped
1-inch piece of ginger, finely chopped
¼ cup coconut milk
2 whole chicken breasts, skinned, boned, and cut into 2-inch pieces
1 pound broccoli, chopped
1 tablespoon vegetable oil
1 onion, chopped

Seasoning Sauce

1 teaspoon cayenne pepper
3 tablespoons chunky peanut butter
1 tablespoon sugar
2 teaspoons fish sauce or soy sauce
¾ cup coconut milk

1. Make a marinade by combining the garlic, ginger, and coconut milk. Marinate the chicken for 30 minutes.

2. Boil or steam the broccoli until crisp-tender; set aside.

3. Heat the oil in a wok and stir-fry the onion until soft. Add the chicken with the marinade and stir-fry until barely cooked. Add the seasoning sauce and heat. Stir in the broccoli.

Spicy Stir-Fried Chicken with Pine Nuts Wrapped in Lettuce Leaves

6 to 8 appetizer servings or 3 to 4 entrees

4 half chicken breasts, skinned and boned, cut into ¼-inch cubes
3 tablespoons white wine Worcestershire sauce
½ cup pine nuts
2 tablespoons olive oil
1 red bell pepper, cut in thin strips
3 cloves garlic, minced
1 tablespoon minced fresh ginger root
3 serrano chiles, minced
2 teaspoons cornstarch dissolved in 1 tablespoon cold water
12 to 16 small butter lettuce leaves, cleaned and dried

1. Marinate the chicken in the Worcestershire sauce for 10 minutes at room temperature.
2. Heat a wok over high heat for 30 seconds. Toast the pine nuts until golden by tossing frequently in the wok to prevent burning. Remove from the wok and set aside.
3. Pour in 1 tablespoon of oil and swirl it around until it is thoroughly heated. Add the bell pepper and stir-fry for a minute. Remove with slotted spoon to a dish.
4. Put the remaining tablespoon of oil in the wok and allow it to heat. Add the garlic, ginger, and chiles and stir-fry 1 minute. Add the chicken, stir-frying over moderate heat until the chicken is opaque—about 2 minutes. Stir in the cooked red pepper.
5. Make a well in the center of the chicken and add the cornstarch mixture. Stir constantly, until all the ingredients are coated with a light glaze.
6. Immediately transfer the contents to a heated platter and sprinkle with the pine nuts. Serve the lettuce on a separate plate.
7. To eat, each guest picks up a lettuce leaf in one hand and places 2 tablespoons of the chicken mixture in the center of the leaf. The leaf is then eaten like a taco.

Spicy Orange Chicken Szechuan-Style

4 servings

Marinade

1 egg
2 tablespoons cornstarch
½ teaspoon salt
2 teaspoons peanut oil

Combine the marinade ingredients and mix until smooth; set aside.

2 whole chicken breasts, skinned, boned, cut into ½-inch cubes
6 tablespoons peanut oil
Outer peel from 1 orange
2 tablespoons minced garlic
1 tablespoon fresh minced ginger
1 green bell pepper, cut into 1-inch cubes
1 red bell pepper, cut into 1-inch cubes

Sauce

½ teaspoon chile paste with garlic
4 tablespoons soy sauce
2 tablespoons sugar
4 tablespoons dry sherry
4 tablespoons water

Combine all the sauce ingredients; set aside.

2 teaspoons cornstarch, dissolved in 2 tablespoons cold water
1 teaspoon dark sesame oil

1. Marinate the chicken for 30 minutes at room temperature.
2. In a heated wok, add ¼ cup of peanut oil. When the oil is hot, add the chicken and stir-fry. Remove from the wok and place in a strainer; set over a bowl to drain.
3. Clean the wok and heat. Add 2 tablespoons of oil. Stir-fry the orange peel for 30 seconds. Add the garlic and ginger and stir-fry briefly.

4. Add the peppers and stir-fry 1 minute.
5. Add the sauce and stir until it comes to a boil. Return the chicken to the wok and stir 1 minute until reheated. Add the cornstarch and stir until thickened—about 1 minute.
6. Remove from heat and stir in the sesame oil. Serve immediately with steamed rice.

New Mexican Green Chile Enchiladas

4 servings

Enchiladas are traditionally made by lightly frying tortillas in oil to make them flexible, then filled and rolled into cylindrical shapes before baking. In New Mexico, flat enchiladas are popular—the tortillas are layered open-faced with the filling and sauce and cut into wedges after baking. You can use this technique with any enchilada recipe and save some calories and time.

¾ cup chicken broth
1 (8 oz.) can chopped tomatoes
1 small onion, chopped
2 tablespoons flour
2 tablespoons cold water
1 (4 oz.) can chopped mild green chiles
1 ½ cups chopped cooked chicken or ground or shredded beef
8 corn tortillas
12 to 16 ounces jack cheese, shredded
Sour cream
Guacamole (page 166)

1. In a saucepan, heat the chicken broth, tomatoes, and onion. Cook until the sauce begins to thicken and the onion is tender.
2. In a separate bowl, mix together the flour and water until smooth; add to the broth. Stir until the sauce comes to a boil and thickens. Stir in the chilies and meat.
3. Place one tortilla in an ovenproof casserole, top with some of the sauce, and sprinkle with some of the cheese. Repeat layers until all the tortillas are used. Top with any remaining sauce and cheese.
4. Bake at 350° F for 15 minutes or until the cheese is melted and bubbly.
5. To serve, cut into wedges and top with sour cream and guacamole.

Variations

- Substitute 1 ½ cups tomatillos for the tomatoes.
- Substitute 1 (10 oz.) can red enchilada sauce for the broth, tomatoes, flour, and water.

Turkey Mexicana with Cherry Tomatoes

4 servings

1 pound ground turkey
2 tablespoons of cumin, oregano, or chili powder
4 cloves garlic, finely chopped
2 potatoes, chopped
2 medium onions, chopped
2 bell peppers, chopped
¼ cup white wine
3 tablespoons chopped cilantro
Cherry tomatoes
3 tablespoons Mexican salsa (page 165)

Combine all the ingredients *except* the tomatoes and salsa on a large piece of foil; seal the edges well. Place on a preheated barbecue for 25 minutes or until the top is hot and puffy. Serve with a bowl of cherry tomatoes mixed with salsa.

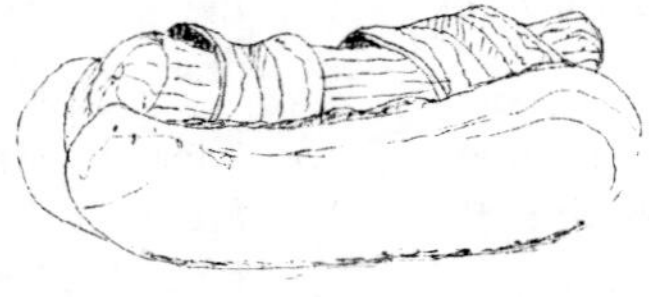

Turkey Breast with Curried Papaya Salsa

8 servings

2 tablespoons grated orange peel
Juice from 1 orange
2 tablespoons olive oil
1 tablespoon dried red pepper flakes
1 tablespoon chili powder

1 boneless turkey breast (about 3 pounds)
1 recipe Curried Papaya Salsa or Orange Chile Salsa (pages 166)

Combine the orange peel, orange juice, oil, red pepper flakes, and chili powder. Place the turkey on a rack in a pan and brush generously with the marinade. Roast at 350° F for 45 minutes (160° F on a meat thermometer), basting with the marinade every 10 minutes. Slice and serve with either of the suggested salsas.

Fillet of Beef with Sun-Dried Tomato Aioli Sauce

6 servings

This is a recipe for a really special occasion. If good quality beef is not available, you can substitute pork tenderloin.

1 recipe Marinade for Red Meat (page 176)
1 tablespoon olive oil
1 2-pound beef fillet, center cut
1 recipe Sun-Dried Tomato Aioli (page 161)

Marinate the beef overnight in the refrigerator. In a frying pan, brown the drained meat in the olive oil. Bake on a rack in a roasting pan in a 350° F oven—about 20 minutes for medium-rare (125° F; 160° F for pork). Allow to stand before slicing. Serve with aioli sauce.

Barbecued Bistec

4 servings

1 pound thinly sliced beef
1 teaspoon Adolf's Meat Tenderizer
3 tablespoons achiote paste (page 176)
½ cup red wine
2 tablespoons red wine vinegar
1 tablespoon minced garlic

1. Sprinkle the meat with the tenderizer and marinate for 30 minutes in a Ziploc bag.
2. Combine the achiote paste, wine, vinegar, and garlic and add to the Ziploc bag, making sure that all the meat is well coated. Allow to marinate at least 1 hour in the refrigerator.
3. Grill quickly over hot coals and serve with tortillas, guacamole, and salsa. If the steak is still not tender, chop it into bite-sized pieces and roll it up taco-style in the tortillas. Prepared this way, meat always has a good flavor, no matter how tough it is.

Enchiladas Oaxaceñas

8 servings

Sometimes referred to as Enchiladas Suisse, this recipe is always a hit. When I don't have sour cream on board, I use Nestle's Crema flavored with a little lime juice.

Thick white sauce (béchamel), using 2 cups milk (page 162)
2 cups sour cream
1 cup Salsa de Tomatillo (page 166)
16 ounces cooked chicken meat
8 ounces chopped onion
1 ¼ pounds jack, Jarlsberg, or Chihuahua Cheese, grated
8 medium corn tortillas, sautéed briefly in a little oil (to soften)

1. Make the white sauce, stir in the sour cream, and set aside.
2. Dip the sautéed tortillas in the white sauce. Place 2 ounces of chicken, 1 ounce of onion, 2 ounces of cheese, and 2 tablespoons of salsa inside each tortilla.

3. Place the tortillas in a baking dish, seam side down. Pour the remaining sauce on top, sprinkle with the remaining 4 ounces of cheese, and bake in a 350°F oven until heated through—about 15 to 20 minutes. If you have a broiler, place briefly under flame to brown the top.

BEEF FAJITAS

4 servings

Marinade

2 tablespoons soy sauce
2 tablespoons red wine vinegar
2 tablespoons olive oil
2 tablespoons fresh lime juice
2 cloves garlic, finely chopped
¼ teaspoon freshly ground black pepper
¼ teaspoon cumin
1 teaspoon chili powder
3 tablespoons canned, sliced, Jalapeños en Escabeche

1 pound flank, skirt, or round steak, or 1 pound chicken
Lime wedges
1 or 2 onions, sliced
2 bell peppers, sliced (red and yellow if available)
Salt and pepper to taste
1 recipe Guacamole (page 166)
1 recipe Mexican Salsa (page 165)
Warm flour tortillas

1. Combine all the marinade ingredients; set aside.
2. Place the beef or chicken and marinade in a Ziploc bag and marinate in the refrigerator for at least 1 hour.
3. Remove the beef from the marinade when ready to barbecue, reserving the marinade and sliced jalapeños. Barbecue the beef about 3 to 5 minutes per side. Season with salt and lime juice and slice in ½-inch wide strips.
4. In a wok, stir-fry the onion and bell peppers in the marinade until cooked al dente; stir in the beef to reheat. Drain. Serve by wrapping some of the beef and vegetables in the warm tortillas. Pass the guacamole and salsa.

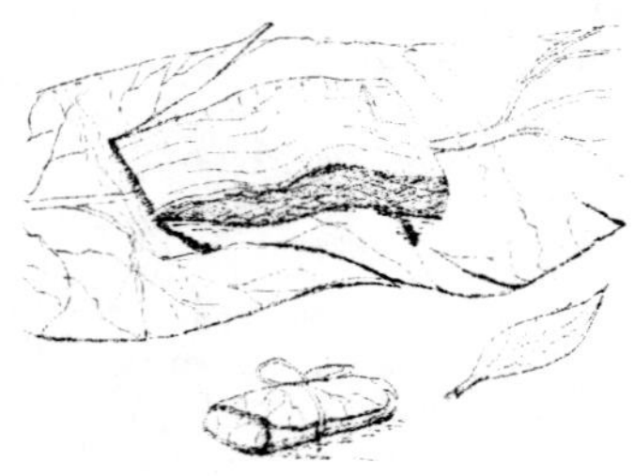

Holiday Survival Guide

Every year, newspapers and magazines run articles about how stressful the holidays have become. The shopping, decorating, party-giving and party-attending often turn a supposedly joyous time of the year into a panic-stricken ordeal.

I have discovered a perfect way to survive the holidays and reduce my stress level. When the social calendar seems to be taking over my life and I need to find some peace and quiet, I escape to *SpiceSea*. She provides a peaceful environment during the winter that allows me to curl up with a book and read for a few hours free of guilt.

Large parties no longer have the appeal they once had for me, perhaps because of all the months I have spent contentedly living aboard *SpiceSea* with only the company of my husband. Or perhaps it is just a natural part of the aging process. I find I prefer a quiet get-together with one or two couples with whom I can have more meaningful contact. There is no better place for an intimate get-together than on a boat—especially during the winter when there is an innate coziness aboard. What better setting for sharing a dinner and being with friends.

I also find there is less stress when entertaining on the boat. Our friends dress more casually on board and so are more relaxed. I don't feel the pressure of having to have everything just perfect, either. Disposable plates and glasses seem expected, so there's no washing dishes at midnight after guests have departed.

Steaming bowls of soup make a great wintertime shipboard dinner. The soup can be prepared at home and reheated on board. (I hosted such a dinner party on my first boat—which had no galley. I brought the soup in individual wide-mouth thermoses and the guests held their own containers. I still remember, twenty years later, what fun the evening was.)

Whether you are planning a boat parade party, a New Year's Eve gathering, or just a holiday gathering, think small, intimate, and simple. Think boat!

Cocido (Hearty Vegetable-Beef Soup)

6 servings

Cocido is a hearty vegetable-beef soup that's perfect for a winter night aboard. It can be made in advance and transported easily to the boat, or you can make it on board.

The first time I tasted Cocido was on Christmas day at a small rancho in Baja California. The family had slaughtered the "fatted calf" the night before and, by the time my husband and I arrived, the soup had been simmering for several hours. We were served huge bowls with large chunks of vegetables and tender morsels of meat swimming in a thin, but flavorful, broth. Bowls of garnishes were passed around the table and diners customized their own soups with rice that had been flavored with tomato sauce, fresh salsa, chopped white onions, and minced cilantro—all topped with freshly squeezed lime juice. It was a simple and satisfying meal.

For the broth

3 pounds beef shanks
2 quarts water
3 cloves garlic
1 onion, sliced
6 peppercorns
1 teaspoon salt

For the soup

2 large carrots, cut in thick slices
1 large potato, peeled and cubed
2 zucchini, cut in thick slices
1 stalk celery, thinly sliced
2 ears of corn, cut in three pieces each
Salt and pepper to taste

Garnishes

1 white onion, chopped
1 bunch cilantro, finely chopped
2 limes, cut in wedges
1 can (8 oz.) Mexican Salsa or 1 recipe Salsa Fresca (page 165)
1 recipe Red Rice (page 129)

1. Make the broth by covering the beef with cold water. Add the garlic onion, peppercorns, and salt and bring to a boil. Reduce the heat and cover loosely. Simmer until the meat is tender—about 3 hours. Strain the broth, cool, and remove and discard fat. When cool enough to handle, remove the meat from the bones and discard the bones. Cut the meat into large chunks.

2. Reheat the broth and add the carrots and potato. Simmer, covered, for 30 minutes. Add the zucchini, celery, corn, and meat, and cook an additional 15 minutes. Season to taste with salt and pepper.

3. Ladle the soup into bowls and top each serving with ¼ cup of red rice.

4. Pass the garnishes at the table and allow guests to help themselves. Serve cocida with large napkins, because the corn is eaten with your fingers.

Playa Maria Beef Stew

4 servings

Hal and I were once motoring toward Mexico's Turtle Bay when the Santa Ana winds began to pick up. We decided to change course for Bahia Playa Maria, a two-and-a-half-mile-long beach that would offer us fair protection and, we hoped, a good night's sleep. The wind howled all night; in the morning the anemometer registered gusts of 32 knots. It was a good day to experiment in the galley.

We had provisioned 10 days earlier in San Diego and many of the vegetables were getting a little tired. The turnips were getting soft, the tomatoes were getting spots, and the cilantro was getting soggy. It was definitely time to make stew!

To make clean-up simple, I put all the ingredients in an oven cooking pouch and baked it. The stew was delicious and a cinch to clean up. And, the warmth of the oven was very welcome. (This is also a good recipe for the pressure cooker when the weather is warm and you don't want the oven on.)

1 ½ pounds stewing beef, cubed
2 tablespoons flour
3 tablespoons oil
3 large carrots, sliced
3 small red potatoes, cubed
2 onions, diced
2 turnips, cubed
1 bell pepper, diced
4 tomatoes, cubed
2 tablespoons Mexican spices (such as cumin or chili powder)
1 package Lipton onion soup mix
2 tablespoons canned chipotle chiles (smoked jalepeños), chopped (Optional—this very hot chile is available in Mexican markets.)
3 cups liquid (red wine and water)
1 bunch cilantro, chopped

1. Dredge the meat in flour and brown it in the oil in a heavy skillet. Place the carrots, potatoes, onions, turnips, bell pepper, and tomatoes in an oven cooking bag with the meat and sprinkle with the Mexican spices and onion soup mix.

2. Heat the optional chiles, wine, and water in the pan you browned the meat in. Bring to a boil and scrape up all the browned bits that have stuck to the bottom of the pan. Pour this over the vegetables and meat, seal the bag, and place in an ovenproof dish.

3. Bake at 350° F for 2 hours or until the meat is tender.

4. Sprinkle with cilantro and serve.

Kay's Dynamite Chili

8 servings

This is a tasty do-ahead, one-pot meal that is ideal for easy entertaining. It came about when our Corsair Yacht Club had a chili cook-off. My recipe didn't win—but I still think it was the best!

By the way—if you're making soups, stews, or chili at home to take to your boat, freeze them in half-gallon milk containers that you can dispose of when they are empty.

2 onions, coarsely chopped
6 cloves garlic, finely chopped
2 tablespoons olive oil or other cooking oil
1 green bell pepper, cubed
2 stalks celery, thinly sliced
1 ½ pounds stew beef, cut into bite-size pieces
Flour for coating beef
1 tablespoon seasoned salt
3 to 4 tablespoons cooking oil
1 pound Italian sausage or breakfast sausage
2 (1 lb. cans) sliced tomatoes, undrained

1 can beer
5 tablespoons chili powder
1 tablespoon ground black pepper
1 teaspoon salt (or to taste)
3 tablespoons Old Bay seasoning

Garnishes

1 (16 oz.) can black beans, drained
1 avocado, peeled and diced
6 ounces grated cheddar cheese
1 (4 oz.) can sliced black olives
1 (8 oz. or larger) jar of salsa
1 onion, coarsely chopped

1. In a deep sauté pan or wok, sauté the onions and garlic in the olive oil for 2 to 3 minutes. Add the bell pepper and celery and sauté until soft. Remove the vegetables from the pan and set aside.
2. Pat the beef dry with paper towels. Combine the flour and seasoned salt and sprinkle on the meat. Cook in just enough oil to keep it from sticking; remove it from the pan as it browns. Cook the sausage and drain well. Set aside.
3. Clean the pan. Return the drained meat and sautéed vegetables back to the pan and add the undrained tomatoes, beer, chili powder, salt, and pepper. Mix 1 tablespoon of flour with ¼ cup of water and add to the pan. Simmer, covered, about 1 ½ hours. Adjust the seasoning, serve in bowls, and pass garnishes.

Meatballs with Tomatillo Sauce

6 servings

For the meatballs

½ pounds ground meat (half pork and half beef)
1 onion, finely chopped
2 cloves garlic, finely chopped
¾ cup bread crumbs
½ teaspoon salt
¼ teaspoon thyme
¼ teaspoon pepper
2 eggs, lightly beaten

For the sauce

1 recipe Salsa de Tomatillo (page 166)
1 to 2 canned chipotle chiles (smoked jalapeños), minced
1 ½ cups beef broth

1. Make the meatballs by combining all the meatball ingredients and then forming 30 small balls.
2. Make the sauce by combining all the sauce ingredients and bringing to a boil in a large pan.
3. Add the meatballs, a few at a time, to the sauce. Simmer until done—about ½ hour.
4. Remove the meat from the sauce and boil the sauce until it begins to thicken. Serve the sauce over the meatballs accompanied with steamed rice.

Easy Beef Burgundy

2 servings

Using an oven cooking pouch for this old favorite makes the clean-up a cinch. If you don't have any of the cooking bags, wrap everything in a foil packet and seal well before baking.

1 pound beef chuck steak, about 1-inch thick
1 potato, quartered
2 carrots, quartered
1 envelope instant onion soup mix (single serving size)
⅓ cup burgundy wine
¼ cup water
Salt and pepper to taste
1 bay leaf

Marinate all the ingredients overnight in the refrigerator in an ovenproof pouch placed in a baking pan large enough for the meat to lie flat. Make several slits in the top of bag. Bake at 350° F for 1 hour or until tender.

Pork Tenderloin

Pork tenderloins are ideal food on a boat. They come vacuum sealed and therefore have a long shelf life in the refrigerator, or they can be easily frozen. They are virtually fat free and have fewer calories than a boneless skinless chicken breast.

If tenderloins are not available, try using pork chops or other cuts of pork. Beef, chicken, or turkey breasts can also be substituted.

PORK TENDERLOIN PASILLA

6 servings

2 (8 oz.) pork tenderloins, sliced in ½-inch thick slices
½ recipe Pasilla Marinade (page 176)
½ cup dry red wine

Garnish

Shredded red cabbage
Sour cream
Salsa de Tomatillo (page 166)

1. Spread the marinade on both sides of the pork slices. Reassemble the tenderloin and hold it together with a long skewer. Marinate for at least an hour.
2. Place the wine in a baking pan, add the pork, and bake for 25 minutes at 400° F.
3. To serve, place the roast on a bed of cabbage. Pass the sour cream and salsa. Serve with Green Rice (page 129).

STUFFED PORK TENDERLOIN WITH ORANGE SAUCE

6 servings

3 tablespoons Dijon mustard
3 cloves garlic, finely chopped
1 teaspoon freshly ground black pepper
2 (8 oz. each) pork tenderloins
4 tablespoons orange marmalade
2 (8 oz. each) pork tenderloins
½ cup white wine
3 tablespoons orange marmalade
⅓ cup chicken broth

1. Combine the mustard, garlic, and pepper; set aside.
2. Slit the tenderloins three-quarters of the way down the centers and spread with the mustard mixture; tie up. Coat the tenderloins with 4 tablespoons of marmalade.
3. Place the wine in a baking pan, add the tenderloins, and bake for 25 minutes at 400° F.
4. Heat the 3 tablespoons of marmalade and chicken broth; serve as a sauce with the tenderloins.

Variation

Omit the marmalade and coat the pork with mustard.

PORK CHOPS WITH APPLE-YOGURT SAUCE

4 servings

4 pork chops
2 tablespoons olive oil
¾ pound peeled and sliced cooking apples
½ onion, finely chopped
1 cup apple juice
½ cup white wine
1 tablespoon flour mixed with 1 tablespoon cold water
½ cup yogurt
2 tablespoons Dijon mustard
¼ teaspoon thyme
Salt and pepper to taste

1. In a medium-sized skillet, brown the pork chops in the olive oil and remove from the skillet. Sauté the apples and onion in pan drippings. Set aside.
2. In a saucepan, boil the apple juice and white wine until reduced in half—about 5 minutes. Add the flour and cook until the mixture begins to thicken. Remove from heat and stir in the yogurt, mustard, thyme, salt, and pepper.
3. Add the apple and onion mixture and pork chops back to the skillet. Stir in the sauce.

PORK CHOPS WITH PORCINI MUSHROOM SAUCE

2 servings

2 boneless pork chops
2 tablespoons olive oil
1 onion, sliced
2 cloves garlic, finely chopped
½ cup dried porcini mushrooms, reconstituted in water and rinsed
½ cup dry red or white wine
Salt and pepper to taste

1. Brown the chops in the olive oil and remove from the pan. Sauté the onion and garlic in the pan drippings. Add the drained mushrooms and sauté briefly.
2. Strain the liquid that the mushrooms soaked in and add to the onion, garlic, and mushrooms. Add the wine. Cook until the liquid is reduced to a ½ cup.
3. Place the chops on top of the sauce, cover the pan, and simmer until the pork is cooked. Season to taste with salt and pepper.

PORK CHOPS WITH CRISPY POTATO CRUST

4 servings

4 pork chops or boneless, skinless chicken breasts
Salt and pepper to taste
½ teaspoon dried thyme
Flour
2 eggs, beaten
2 large potatoes, peeled and grated
¼ cup fresh bread crumbs
2 tablespoons olive oil

Season the pork chops with salt, pepper, and thyme. Roll in the flour, then in egg. Combine the grated potatoes and bread crumbs and press the mixture into the pork chops. Pan fry in olive oil until golden brown.

PORK CHOPS WITH OLIVES AND FENNEL

4 servings

2 tablespoons olive oil
4 pork chops, lamb chops, or chicken breasts
Salt and pepper to taste
1 tablespoon fennel seeds
4 cloves garlic, finely chopped
1 pound tomatoes, chopped
1 (4 oz.) can sliced black olives

Heat the olive oil in a large frying pan. Season the pork chops with salt and pepper and brown on both sides. Add the fennel, garlic, tomatoes, and olives and cook for 10 minutes or until the pork is done.

HOT GARLIC EGGPLANT WITH PORK

2 servings

⅓ cup ground pork
2 teaspoons soy sauce
2 tablespoons cooking oil
10 garlic cloves, finely minced
1 tablespoon chili paste with garlic
½ teaspoon finely minced ginger
1 ½ pounds Japanese eggplant, trimmed, quartered and cut into ½-inch cubes
1 large onion, chopped

Seasoning Sauce

¼ cup dry sherry
3 tablespoons oyster sauce
1 tablespoon soy sauce
2 teaspoons Oriental sesame oil
1 teaspoon sugar

1. Mix the pork with the soy sauce; set aside.
2. Combine all the seasoning sauce ingredients; set aside.
3. Heat a wok and add the oil. Stir-fry the garlic, chili paste, and ginger for several seconds, being careful that it does not brown.

4. Add the pork mixture and stir-fry until the meat loses its pink color.
5. Add the eggplant, onion, and seasoning sauce. Cover and cook for 3 minutes or until the eggplant softens and no longer tastes raw. Continue cooking until most of the sauce evaporates. Adjust seasonings.

BARBECUED BABY PORK RIBS

4 servings

At the public market in San José del Cabo, I stood in line next to a Mexican woman who seemed to be a very knowledgeable shopper. By listening to her conversation with the butcher and observing what she bought, I was able to make some good selections. The *costillas* (baby pork ribs) that I ordered were cut into 1 ½-inch lengths. We enjoyed them cooked over an open fire.

1 onion, chopped
1 tablespoon minced garlic
3 tablespoons red wine vinegar
3 tablespoons soy sauce
¼ cup white wine
⅓ cup adobo sauce, barbecue sauce, or hot sauce
2 pounds baby pork ribs cut into 1 ½-inch lengths

1. In a Ziploc bag, mix together the onion, garlic, vinegar, soy sauce, wine, and adobo sauce. Add the ribs and marinate for 2 hours, turning occasionally.
2. Carefully place the ribs on a sheet of extra heavy foil, making sure they don't puncture the foil. Wrap securely so the marinade will not leak and so that the ribs will steam.
3. Place over hot coals for 30 minutes, until the meat is nearly falling off the bones. (Much of the fat is rendered out in the cooking process while the meat becomes tender.)
4. Carefully remove the ribs from the foil and place them on a grill. (A hot dog cooker works well for this. We carry one aboard *SpiceSea* for beach fires. They're great for grilling anything that needs to be hand held over a fire.) Baste the ribs with the marinade and barbecue until golden.

ITALIAN SAUSAGE

1 pound

When you can't find good Italian sausage, it's easy to make your own.

1 pound ground lean pork
1 teaspoon salt
1 teaspoon fennel seeds
½ teaspoon freshly ground black pepper
½ teaspoon dried pepper flakes (for hot sausage)
2 cloves garlic, finely chopped

Mix all the ingredients together. Chill before using. Keeps for 4 days.

CHORIZO

1 pound

Easy to make and delicious, the Mexican sausage known as chorizo is a spicy mixture that goes well with eggs, Queso Fundido (page 45), and Pizza Margherita (page 189).

1 pound ground lean pork
1 teaspoon salt
3 tablespoons chili powder
2 cloves garlic, finely chopped
2 teaspoons oregano
1 teaspoon coriander or cumin
3 tablespoons vinegar

Mix all the ingredients together. Chill before using. Keeps for 4 days.

CURRIED GOAT

4 servings

Young goat, which is a popular meat in third world countries, has a mild flavor (see page 14).

2 pounds goat meat, cubed, with fat removed
4 tablespoons cooking oil
2 cups chopped onions
2 tablespoons curry powder
2 teaspoons chopped green chiles
1 teaspoon salt
Freshly ground black pepper
¾ cup canned, unsweetened coconut milk (or make your own—see page 8)
¾ cup chicken broth
1 bay leaf
2 tablespoons fresh lime juice

1. Brown the goat meat in 2 tablespoons of the cooking oil and set aside.
2. In the same pan, sauté the onions in the remaining oil until soft. Add the curry powder and chiles and simmer 2 to 3 minutes, stirring constantly.
3. Return the meat to the pan. Season with salt and pepper and add the coconut milk, broth, bay leaf, and lime juice. Cover and simmer until the meat is tender—about 1½ hours.

BRATWURST ENCHILADAS

4 servings

I created this recipe while camping in Mexico. On our last day before breaking camp, all we had left were a few cans of salsa, some tortillas, and two bratwursts.

4 corn tortillas
1 teaspoon vegetable oil
2 bratwursts (precooked), cut in half lengthwise
1 onion, finely chopped
12 ounces Salsa de Tomatillo (page 166), or use canned
⅓ pound grated cheese
¼ cup chopped fresh cilantro

1. In a frying pan, soften the tortillas in the oil. Fill each tortilla with ½ of a bratwurst, ¼ of the onion, and some of the salsa. Place in a baking dish, seam side down.
2. Top the tortillas with the remaining salsa; sprinkle with the cheese and bake at 350°F for 15 minutes.
3. Serve garnished with cilantro.

EXQUISITOS

Near Marina de La Paz, Baja California Sur, on the west coast of Mexico, there is a hot dog stand that sells the most incredible tasting hot dogs in the world. Whenever Hal and I were anywhere near La Paz, our mouths would water in anticipation of getting an Exquisito Fix.

We were once cruising in the Sea of Cortez for more than a month without reprovisioning when some friends joined us at Partida Island. They not only had some fresh produce on board, but they had learned the secret to making Exquisitos and invited us over for dinner!

Hot dogs
Bacon
Hot dog buns
Mustard
Mayonnaise thinned with a little lime juice
Chopped tomato
Salsa de Tomatillo (page 166)
Chopped onion

Wrap the bacon around the hot dogs and sauté in a frying pan until the bacon is nearly crisp. Smear the buns with mustard and mayonnaise; add the hot dogs and top with tomato, salsa, and onion. Exquisito!

ENDLESS SOUP IN THE PRESSURE COOKER

If you think of your pressure cooker as a giant canning jar, you can make a large quantity of soup or stew, heat the cooker up to pressure each night, turn off the heat, and let it cool, never releasing the lid. If reheated each day and stored in this manner, you don't need to store the contents in the refrigerator. Boaters who cruise without refrigeration report that they have had very good luck with this method of preservation. I would not recommend doing this for more than four or five days with the same pot of food, however.

I used my pressure cooker to make the following soup recipe and we enjoyed it (and its variations) for several days. The soup marathon started when I bought a tough chicken in Mexico. The best way to get the meat off the bones was to boil the carcass. Then, since I had all those lovely chicken bones, I decided to make soup.

Chicken Stock

2 quarts

1 chicken
2 carrots, chopped
1 onion, chopped
2 ribs celery, chopped
2 bay leaves

1. In the pressure cooker, combine the chicken, carrots, onion, celery, bay leaves, and 2 quarts water. Secure the lid. Over high heat, bring to high pressure. Reduce heat to medium and cook 10 minutes. Allow the pressure to reduce slowly with the heat off. When the chicken is cool enough to handle, remove the meat from bones. Reserve the meat for the following recipe or for another use. Place the bones back in the cooker.
2. Over high heat, bring back to high pressure. Reduce heat to medium and cook the stock 30 minutes. Allow the pressure to reduce slowly with the heat off. Strain and discard the solids. Reserve the stock.

White Bean Soup

8 servings

1 pound dry white beans
4 carrots, chopped
2 onions, chopped
3 ribs celery, chopped
6 cloves garlic, finely chopped
2 pounds plum tomatoes, chopped, or 1 (28 oz.) can tomatoes
2 quarts chicken stock
1 teaspoon dried oregano
½ teaspoon dried red chile
Freshly ground black pepper
1 cube chicken bouillon

In the pressure cooker, combine all the ingredients. Secure the lid. Over high heat, bring to high pressure. Reduce heat to medium and cook 20 minutes. Allow the pressure to reduce slowly with heat off.

Meal 1— White Bean Chicken Soup

Place ¼ cup of cooked chicken meat in each bowl. Pour the soup over the chicken and sprinkle with some fresh parsley.

Meal 2— Tortilla Soup

Slice 2 tortillas and sauté in a little oil until crisp. Drain and arrange in 2 soup bowls. Sprinkle the tortillas with ¼ cup shredded jack cheese (or mozzarella or Chihuahua). Ladle just the broth and vegetables (no beans) over the tortillas. Garnish with sliced avocado. Serve with Salsa Fresca (page 165) and fresh limes.

Meal 3— Italian Bean Soup with Fresh Chard

We had just provisioned and had a bunch of chard that was taking up space in the refrigerator. So I diced the chard and reheated the soup. It tasted great served with a little fresh lemon juice and Italian Bruschetta Sauce (page 170). You can substitute a package of frozen chopped spinach for the chard.

Meal 4— Bean soup with Sausage

On the final night for this soup, I added some smoked sausage. Ham or Italian Sausage would also be excellent.

LAMB SHANKS WITH ORZO in the Pressure Cooker… And Some Thoughts about Substitutions

4 servings

Recently I purchased some lamb shanks and was looking for a recipe that would cook them quickly and yet make them tender. Since the pressure cooker is the perfect method for quickly cooking less tender cuts of meat, I turned to *The Joys of Pressure Cooking* by Toula Patsalis for inspiration. There, I found a Greek-style recipe for lamb shanks. Although there were several ingredients listed that I didn't have on board, there were several ingredients on board that were about to expire.

The recipe called for parsley; I used a large head of fennel. Instead of beef broth, I used chicken. I also had some bell peppers that were crying to be used and a couple of carrots that were starting to sprout new tops. Although the recipe I ended up cooking bore little resemblance to the original, I still was able to use the cooking techniques and some of the quantities that were suggested.

3 tablespoons olive oil
4 lamb shanks (or substitute veal)
Freshly ground black pepper
2 large onions, chopped
1 cup chopped fennel root (or ½ cup chopped parsley)
3 carrots, chopped
6 cloves garlic, finely chopped
2 cubes Knorr's chicken or beef broth (enough bouillon for 4 cups water)
4 cups water
1 (16 oz.) can chopped tomatoes with juice (or fresh tomatoes)
½ teaspoon dried red pepper flakes
2 teaspoons oregano
2 yellow or green bell peppers, cubed
1 red bell pepper, cubed
1 ½ cups orzo

1. In an uncovered pressure cooker, heat the olive oil and brown the lamb shanks. Season the lamb with freshly ground black pepper; remove from pot and set aside.
2. In the same cooker, sauté the onions, fennel, carrots, and garlic for 5 minutes. Add the bouillon, water, tomatoes, pepper flakes, and oregano. Place the shanks and accumulated juices back into the pressure cooker and seal.
3. Over high heat, bring to high pressure. Reduce heat and cook on high pressure for 10 minutes. Turn off the heat and allow the pressure cooker to cool until you can safely open the lid—about 10 minutes. With the lid off, bring to a boil, add the peppers and orzo, and stir to distribute. Boil until the orzo is cooked al dente—about 8 minutes.

POSOLE: HOMINY AND PORK STEW IN THE PRESSURE COOKER

8 to 10 servings

10 cups chicken broth
2 medium onions, chopped
2 tablespoons fresh mint or 2 teaspoons dried
2 tablespoons fresh oregano or 2 teaspoons dried
6 dried California or New Mexican chiles (see page 140), stems and seeds removed, cut into 1-inch pieces
3 pound pork shoulder roast, with bone
1 (28 oz.) can canned hominy, drained and rinsed
Salt to taste

Garnishes

Shredded lettuce or cabbage
Thinly sliced green onions
Chopped radishes
Chopped avocado
Lime wedges
Shredded jack cheese
Chopped jalapeño chiles

1. Place the broth, onion, mint, oregano, chiles, and pork in a pressure cooker. Cover and bring to high

pressure. Reduce heat and cook on high pressure for 1 hour. Turn off heat and allow pressure cooker to cool until you can safely open the lid—about 10 minutes.

2. Remove and shred the meat. Return to pressure cooker.
3. Add the hominy to the cooker and simmer an additional 30 minutes. Season with salt. Serve posole in large bowls and pass the garnishes.

Cocinita Pibil: Yucatecan Steamed Pork in Banana Leaves

8 to 10 servings of 2 tortillas each

This is a fun dish to make, especially if you're boating in southern latitudes where banana palms are prolific and the leaves are free for the taking. (Banana leaves can also be purchased in Latin American markets.)

1 large banana leaf, washed and trimmed to make a 12- × 20-inch rectangle
1 boned pork butt, approximately 4 pounds
1 recipe Achiote Paste (page 176)
Hot corn tortillas
Salsa Fresca (page 165)
Pickled Onions (page 79)

Banana Leaf

Remove the stalk and center vein from a well-washed leaf. (Save the vein for tying up the packet if you wish.) If you've had to buy the leaf from a market, it may be dry and inflexible. If necessary, place the leaf in boiling water for 10 seconds to increase its flexibility.

The Pork

Score the fat side of the pork in a diamond pattern with ½-inch deep cuts. Place the meat in the center of the prepared banana leaf. Spread achiote paste all over the roast and rub into the cuts. Fold the leaf around the roast like an envelope; tie with a string to secure. Marinate overnight in the refrigerator.

To Cook

Place a rack in the bottom of a pressure cooker and pour in 1½ cups of water. Set the wrapped roast on the rack, cover, and bring to high pressure. Reduce heat and cook on high pressure for 1 hour. Turn off the heat and allow the pressure cooker to cool until you can safely open the lid—about 10 minutes. Remove the meat and set aside. Remove the fat from the juices in the cooker and boil the broth to thicken.

Presentation

Place the roast on a platter or carving board. Slit the packet open lengthwise on top and peel back the leaf. Pour the pan juices over the meat. Diners pull off pieces of pork, pile them on fresh hot tortillas, and top with salsa and pickled onions.

Corn Tortillas

Stack 16 to 20 tortillas together, sprinkle with a little water, and wrap in foil. Heat in a 350°F oven until warm—about 20 minutes.

Shredded Beef in the Pressure Cooker

6 cups

Mexican beef is notoriously tough, but it can be boiled with spices and then shredded to make a very tasty taco or sandwich filling called either *machaca* or *ropa vieja*. This recipe freezes well, too. You can substitute ground beef for the stew meat and cook it in a frying pan, omitting the water—but it won't have the excellent texture and flavor of the pressure cooked beef.

2 pounds boneless beef stew meat (or chuck or flank steak)
1 cup water
1 (14 oz.) can tomatoes

1 onion, chopped
2 cloves garlic, chopped
2 teaspoons chili powder
1 teaspoon ground cumin
1 teaspoon salt

1. Place the meat, water, tomatoes, onion, garlic, chili powder, cumin, and salt in a pressure cooker. Cover and bring to high pressure. Reduce the heat and cook on high pressure for 30 minutes. Turn off the heat and allow the pressure cooker to cool until you can safely open the lid—about 10 minutes. Shred the meat using two forks to pull the meat apart.
2. Cook the meat, uncovered, stirring frequently, until most of the liquid has evaporated.

For Enchiladas

12 servings

12 tortillas
4 tablespoons oil
3 cups shredded beef
1 recipe Green Chile Enchilada Sauce (page 98)
3 cups shredded jack cheese (12 oz.)

Soften the tortillas in oil for 5 seconds per side; drain on paper towels. Spoon ⅓ cup of Green Chile Enchilada Sauce, ¼ cup of beef, and 2 tablespoons of cheese in the center of each tortilla. Roll to enclose and place seam side down in baking dish. Top with any remaining sauce and cheese and bake at 350° F for 15 to 20 minutes.

For Tacos

Serve with warm tortillas garnished with guacamole, shredded lettuce, or cabbage and Mexican salsa.

Carnitas in the Pressure Cooker

4 to 5 pounds pork shoulder roast
2 teaspoons salt
½ teaspoon oregano
1 teaspoon cumin
½ teaspoon coriander
2 onions, chopped
2 cloves garlic, chopped

1. Place a rack in the bottom of a pressure cooker and pour in 1½ cups of water. Set the roast on the rack, season with the salt, oregano, cumin, and coriander, and sprinkle with the onion and garlic.
2. Cover the cooker and bring to high pressure. Reduce the heat and cook on high pressure for 1 hour. Turn off the heat and allow the pressure cooker to cool until you can safely open the lid—about 10 minutes.

Carnitas Tacos

Hot corn tortillas
Chopped cilantro
Chopped onions
Sliced avocados
Shredded carnitas
Chopped tomatoes
1 recipe Mexican Salsa (page 165)

Each person assembles tacos from the above selections.

Carnitas Salad

Fried tortilla strips
Shredded carnitas
Lettuce
Chopped green onion
Chopped cilantro
Chopped tomato
Sliced black olives
Oil and vinegar dressing (2 parts oil to 1 part vinegar)

Combine all the above ingredients.

Cornish Game Hens in the Pressure Cooker

4 to 8 servings

4 Cornish game hens
1 recipe Wild Rice Stuffing (page 127)
1 recipe glaze (see below)
½ cup white wine

1. Thaw the game hens if frozen. Make the stuffing and spoon ¼ of it into the cavity of each hen. Make the glaze and brush the hens. Place a steamer rack or trivet in a pressure cooker, add the wine, and place the hens on rack, neck end down, in a circle.
2. Cover the cooker and cook at lowest pressure for 15 minutes, following the manufacturer's instructions for relieving pressure.
3. Brush the hens with any remaining glaze and serve.

Soy Glaze for Game Hens

1 tablespoon soy sauce
1 tablespoon brown sugar
3 tablespoons melted butter
2 tablespoons white wine
1 tablespoon orange juice

Mix together all ingredients.

CHAPTER 7

Pasta, Grains, and Beans

Dried Beans and Lentils

Beans and other legumes are a great source of protein and ideal food for cruising. The only drawback to dried beans is that they use a lot of water and take a long time to cook.

It is generally a good idea to soak beans overnight in enough water to measure one inch above the level of the beans. Remove any beans that float because they might be moldy. The next day, drain and rinse the beans. If you forget to presoak the beans, bring them and the water to a boil and boil for 3 minutes. Cool, tightly covered for 1 hour, then drain and rinse the beans.

One cup of dried beans or lentils yields about 2 to 2½ cups when cooked.

To cook beans, add fresh water (at least 3 cups of water for every cup of beans or legumes), bring to a boil, and reduce to a simmer. Cook until tender, about 1½ to 3 hours, depending on the age and type of bean.

Since there are dozens of types of beans and lentils available in the world, and since you have no way of knowing the age of the legumes, you have to experiment with the cooking times. Check the legumes periodically while they are cooking to see if they are soft. White beans, for example, usually cook in about 3 hours; on the other hand, lima beans take only about 30 minutes.

If you use a **PRESSURE COOKER** you can greatly reduce the cooking time and the amount of water needed. Presoak the beans overnight as directed above, or pressure-soak the beans with water by securing the lid on the pressure cooker, bringing to high pressure, and cooking 2 minutes. Allow the pressure to reduce naturally at the end of the cooking cycle. Drain.

Once the beans have soaked, they take about 10 to 15 minutes to cook on high pressure. Use 3 cups of liquid for each cup of soaked beans. Add 1 tablespoon of oil to prevent foaming and allow the steam to reduce slowly at the end of the cooking time.

PASTA E FAGIOLI

8 servings

Pasta and beans are a classic Italian combination. This soup has an infinite number of variations—red beans, white beans, cranberry beans, butterfly pasta, spaghetti, fusilli—almost whatever you have on hand.

1 pound cannellini beans (Great Northern), soaked overnight and drained
3 stalks celery, chopped
2 carrots, chopped
1 onion, chopped
1 clove garlic, chopped
1 cup crushed plum tomatoes
½ cup olive oil
1 dried red chile pepper, crumbled
½ cup chopped fresh parsley
¼ cup chopped fresh basil
Salt and pepper to taste
1 pound pasta, cooked

1. Combine the beans, celery, carrots, onion, garlic, and tomatoes and cover with water, 3 inches above the beans. Simmer for 2 hours.
2. When almost tender, add the oil, chile pepper, parsley, basil, salt, and pepper. Continue cooking until the beans are tender.
3. Place a serving of pasta in each bowl and top with the bean soup. **NOTE:** If you add the pasta to the beans in the cooking pot, all the liquid will be absorbed and, if there are any leftovers, you won't have any broth for soup. So, I add the pasta to each person's soup bowl and store the leftovers separately.

Variation

Add 1 pound of cooked Italian sausage and 2 cups of chopped fresh spinach or Swiss chard to step 2. Use fusilli pasta and serve with freshly grated Parmesan cheese.

White Beans with Sausage and Tomatoes

8 servings

2 tablespoons olive oil
2 pounds sliced Italian sausage
8 cloves garlic, finely chopped
2 onions, coarsely chopped
2 stalks celery, coarsely chopped
2 carrots, coarsely chopped
1 (28 oz.) can tomatoes, chopped
1 pound white beans, soaked overnight and drained
2 ½ cups chicken broth
Salt and pepper to taste

Garnish

½ cup chopped fresh parsley
½ cup chopped fresh basil (or 1 tablespoon dried)
½ cup freshly grated Parmesan cheese

1. Sauté the sausage in a deep sauté pan in 1 tablespoon of olive oil until cooked. Drain and set aside.
2. Sauté the onion and garlic in the remaining oil. Add the celery and carrots. Cook until soft. Add the tomatoes with their juice and the drained beans. Cover with enough broth and water so that the beans are submerged in liquid. Bring to a boil and simmer until the beans are tender—about 2½ hours (or 15 minutes on high pressure in pressure cooker.
3. Add the cooked sausage and simmer an additional 10 minutes. Season with salt and pepper.
4. Sprinkle each serving with fresh herbs and Parmesan.

Hal's SpiceSea Beans

4 servings

Hal loves beans, and one day made up a pot of beans that received rave reviews from this cook. Luckily, he recorded the recipe.

1 pound pinto beans, soaked overnight and drained
2 large onions, chopped
4 cloves garlic, finely chopped
2 stalks celery, chopped
2 carrots, chopped
8 ounces tomato sauce
8 ounces Mexican salsa
3 ounces tomato paste
2 tablespoons olive oil
2 teaspoons chili powder
2 teaspoons Lawry's Lemon Pepper
1 teaspoon oregano

Mix all the ingredients together in a large soup pot and add enough water to cover. Bring to a boil and simmer 2 hours or until beans are tender.

Easy Black Bean Gazpacho

4 servings

1 can black beans
1 cup chicken broth

Purée beans with broth and heat. Serve hot or cold. Pass bowls of garnishes.

Garnishes

Chopped cilantro
Cucumber
Tomato
Green onion
Bell pepper

Cajun Red Beans and Rice in Pressure Cooker

6 servings

1 pound dry red kidney beans, soaked overnight and drained
4 cups cooked long grain white rice
2 cups finely chopped celery
2 cups finely chopped onions
2 cups finely chopped green bell peppers
4 cloves garlic, finely chopped
1 bay leaf
2 teaspoons white pepper
2 teaspoons dried thyme

1 teaspoon cayenne pepper
½ teaspoon black pepper
1 tablespoon Tabasco sauce
1 pound smoked sausage, thinly sliced

1. Place the drained beans in a pressure cooker with all the ingredients except the sausage. Cover with 8 cups of water, secure the lid, and bring to high pressure. Cook for 10 minutes on high and then allow the pressure to reduce naturally.
2. Add the sausage and heat briefly.
3. Place a mound of rice in the center of each plate and surround with the red beans.

White Chili

6 servings

2 tablespoons olive oil or other cooking oil
2 cloves garlic, finely chopped
2 onions, chopped
1 pound white beans, soaked overnight and drained
1 teaspoon dried oregano
1 teaspoon ground cumin
¼ cup lime juice
1 cup white wine
2 cups chicken broth
2 (4 oz.) cans chopped green chiles
2 pounds boneless, skinless cooked chicken

Garnish

1 cup shredded jack cheese
¼ cup chopped fresh cilantro leaves
1 cup chopped fresh tomatoes
½ cup sliced black olives

1. Sauté the garlic and onions in oil. Add the beans and enough water to cover. Cook until tender.
2. Add the remaining ingredients and heat thoroughly.
3. Serve with garnishes as desired.

Cooking Italian

If I had to limit my cooking to only one country's cuisine, Italian would be my choice. Can you imagine life without pasta, Parmesan, or pepperoncini?

Since many of the basic ingredients for delicious Italian recipes—tomatoes, pasta, garlic, onions, olive oil, and cheese—don't need refrigeration, cooking Italian on board not only makes great sense but makes great food.

Tomatoes are one of the few vegetables that often taste better canned than fresh, and dried pasta keeps for months on board. I actually prefer it to fresh—there is more texture to the dried variety.

Many other Italian foods—capers, black olives, and anchovies—have at least a two-year shelf life. Olive oil, if it's not exposed to sunlight and excessive heat, will survive for years. Even many of the Italian cured meats will keep for several months without refrigeration. Pepperoni and dry salami kept well aboard *SpiceSea* while we were cruising in tropical Mexican waters.

We all know that Kraft Parmesan cheese keeps without refrigeration, but I find that it has little flavor compared with its fresh counterpart. I keep Food Saver bags of vacuum-sealed fresh Parmesan (preferably the rich, nutty-flavored imported variety) and find that the slow aging that occurs makes the fresh cheese even tastier than when I first bought it. I store it in a cool place and have had good results even after a year of storage. If sealed Parmesan gets too warm, some of the oil will separate; just blot it up with a paper towel when you open the package.

Tuscan-Style White Beans

4 first course or side dish servings

1 (16 oz.) can white beans, drained
1 teaspoon dried sage
2 cloves minced fresh garlic
Freshly ground black pepper
2 tablespoons olive oil

Gently mix the beans and sage, garlic, and pepper. Drizzle with the olive oil and serve at room temperature.

Variation

- Substitute 2 tablespoons of chopped fresh parsley for the sage and add 4 anchovy fillets and 2 tablespoons of red wine vinegar to the beans, garlic, black pepper, and oil.

- Substitute 3 tablespoons of chopped parsley for the sage and add 3 tablespoons of chopped green onion, 3 tablespoons of chopped pepperoncini, 3 tablespoons of chopped dry salami, and 1 tablespoon of red wine vinegar to the beans.

Pasta

When stored in a cool dry place, dried pasta will last almost indefinitely. At one point while cruising I had a terrible weevil infestation; the critters came aboard in some imported Italian linguine and ate their way out of the box and into everything on board. To prevent that from ever happening again, I now microwave (for a few seconds) any dried pasta I bring on board to kill any bugs and their eggs.

Pasta should be cooked in plenty of water—3 to 4 quarts of boiling water for each pound of dried pasta. If you are not on a salt-restricted diet, add 1 to 2 tablespoons salt to the water. Or, you can use $\frac{1}{3}$ part salt water to $\frac{2}{3}$ parts fresh water. In a covered pot, bring the water to a rolling boil and add the pasta gradually so that the water continues to boil. Stir occasionally to prevent sticking. Always cook pasta uncovered at a fast boil.

Do not overcook pasta. It is done when it is tender but firm to the bite (al dente). If you're using the pasta in a recipe that requires further cooking, such as lasagna or stuffed shells, reduce the cooking time by about a third. Drain pasta to stop the cooking action, but do not rinse it unless you are preparing a pasta salad.

One pound of pasta feeds Hal and me for two or three meals. I put a little olive oil in with the leftover pasta and keep it refrigerated for up to four days.

Select the shape of pasta that goes best with the sauce you are making. Delicate angel hair or vermicelli is ideal for thin tomato sauces; thicker strands stand up to more robust creamy sauces. The crevices in fancy shapes such as shells and fusilli are perfect for trapping bits of meat and seafood.

Cooking on board is always made easier, of course, if you plan ahead. Cooking dried pasta every night uses a lot of water and cooking fuel and heats up the cabin. Hal looks askance at me if I want to cook pasta too often during the week. I have solved this problem by doubling the pasta that I need for a meal and then using it the next day as a cold pasta salad, or reheating it briefly in the microwave or in a nonstick pan when I want to serve the leftovers.

Sometimes, I find myself working up to a pasta dinner. On the first night, we might make barbecued chicken breasts, and Hal will cook a couple of extra for another meal. I'll steam some asparagus or broccoli to go with the chicken and put some aside. On the second night, we might have some barbecued turkey sausage and marinated bell peppers (see page 151), some of which I put aside. Then, on the third night, I'll chop up all the leftovers, cook a pound of pasta, add some of my favorite Bruschetta Sauce (see page 170), and we'll enjoy an incredible pasta dinner. The next day, I serve the pasta cold— and never once do we feel like we're eating leftovers.

Tasty Pasta Combinations

- Angel hair pasta with fresh tomatoes, garlic, basil, and olive oil. Add cooked shrimp or steamed mussels if desired.

- Fusilli pasta with corn, mushrooms, red and yellow peppers, jicama, and red onion in Green Chile Pesto Sauce (page 168). Add some marinated cooked chicken, toasted pine nuts, and sun-dried tomatoes if desired.

- Penne pasta tossed with garlic, olive oil, roasted eggplant, black olives, sun-dried tomatoes, broccoli, peppers, and Parmesan cheese.

- Pasta with mozzarella, Parmesan, Romano, and fresh basil in Italian Tomato Sauce (page 171).

- Ziti pasta with garlic, olive oil, fresh mint, and sautéed mushrooms.

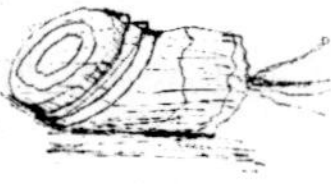

- Pappardella with calamata olives, olive oil, lemon and orange peel, dried red pepper flakes, parsley, and thyme.
- Spaghetti with Italian Tomato Sauce (page 171) and lots of chopped, sun-dried tomatoes.
- Pasta with toasted walnuts, butter, and Parmesan cheese.

Garlic and Oil Pasta

4 servings

The simplest ingredients sometimes make the best pasta. My friend Toni aboard *Sun Happi* introduced me to this wonderful dish and it has become one of our favorites.

1 cup olive oil
1 ½ tablespoons ground black pepper
1 large head garlic (12 to 14 cloves), peeled and coarsely chopped
Salt
1 pound linguine, cooked

1. In a saucepan over very low heat, cook the black pepper in the oil for 4 to 5 minutes. The pepper should cook long enough so that it does not have a raw taste. As it cooks, the flavor mellows.
2. Add the garlic and cook an additional 7 to 10 minutes; do not allow the garlic to brown—it should be a pale golden color.
3. Combine the sauce with the pasta and season with salt.

Variations

- Add broccoli or cauliflower to the pasta water and cook until tender but still crisp. Remove and set aside before cooking the pasta. Add the vegetables to the olive oil sauce just before serving and reheat; combine with the pasta.
- Clean some squid, cut into rings, and add to the sauce. Sauté briefly (2 to 3 minutes) after the black pepper and garlic have cooked.

Angel Hair Pasta Primavera

4 servings

1 ½ cups chopped fresh tomatoes
½ cup shredded carrots
¼ cup chopped fresh basil
4 tablespoons olive oil
2 tablespoon lemon juice
½ cup small cubes of fresh Parmesan cheese
1 cup broccoli florets, cut into bite-size pieces
1 cup cauliflower florets, cut into bite-size pieces
½ pound cappellini (angel hair) pasta, broken up
Salt and pepper to taste

1. In a large bowl combine the tomatoes, carrots, basil, olive oil, lemon juice, and Parmesan cheese.
2. Bring 4 quarts of salted water to a boil. Add the broccoli, cauliflower, and pasta and cook 3 minutes. Drain and add to the other ingredients in a large bowl. Season with salt and pepper.

Eggplant and Tomato Pasta

4 servings

1 medium eggplant, peeled and sliced in ½-inch thick slices
Olive oil
1 cup white sauce (or a 10 ½ oz. can)*
⅓ cup Parmesan cheese
1 (8 oz.) jar spaghetti sauce
8 ounces cooked fusilli pasta mixed with ½ cup Anchovy Herb Sauce (page 168)

1. Salt the eggplant and allow to sit for a ½ hour. Rinse off the salt and pat dry with paper towels. Brush both sides of the eggplant with olive oil and bake on a baking sheet in a 350° F oven until soft—about 20 minutes.
2. In an 8- to 9-inch square dish, layer some of the spaghetti sauce, the pasta with Anchovy Herb Sauce,

white sauce, sliced eggplant, and Parmesan cheese. Repeat the layering; top with spaghetti sauce and Parmesan cheese. Bake at 350° F for 30 minutes.

**If using canned white sauce, thin with a little milk.*

Peppery Artichoke Tomato Pasta

6 servings

1 cup coarsely chopped onions
3 cloves garlic, finely chopped
3 tablespoons olive oil
1 teaspoon dried oregano
1 small dried chile pepper, finely chopped
1 tablespoon coarsely ground black pepper
2 teaspoons white pepper
1 (28 oz.) can Italian-style plum tomatoes
1 jar (6 oz.) marinated artichoke hearts (reserve the marinade)
¼ cup chopped fresh parsley
⅓ cup chopped fresh basil
¼ cup freshly grated Parmesan cheese
1 pound spaghetti or fusilli, cooked

1. Sauté the onions and garlic in the olive oil until tender. Add the oregano, chile pepper, black pepper, white pepper, tomatoes and artichokes with their marinade. Cook until the sauce thickens.
2. Add the parsley and basil and simmer an additional 2 minutes.
3. Serve over pasta; pass the Parmesan cheese.

Pasta Shells Filled with Three Cheeses

6 servings

1 recipe Italian Tomato Sauce (page 171)
12 ounces jumbo pasta shells, cooked until barely tender

Cheese Filling

16 ounces ricotta cheese
14 ounces feta cheese, crumbled
16 ounces grated mozzarella cheese
1 teaspoon dried oregano
1 cup finely chopped fresh basil
2 green onions, finely chopped
2 eggs

1. Combine the ingredients for the cheese filling and stuff into the cooked shell pasta.
2. Place the pasta on a bed of tomato sauce in a 9×13-inch baking dish. Top with remaining sauce and bake at 350° F until the cheese is melted and the sauce is hot—about 15 minutes.

Pasta with Bacon and Avocado

4 servings

When fishing and diving conditions are not good, I often make up impromptu recipes with whatever ingredients are on hand. This pasta dish was so popular with the captain that I have made it many times since.

½ pound diced bacon
½ cup chopped onion
½ pound sliced mushrooms
1 red bell pepper
1 avocado, diced
2 tablespoons butter
2 eggs
½ pound cooked pasta
Parmesan cheese

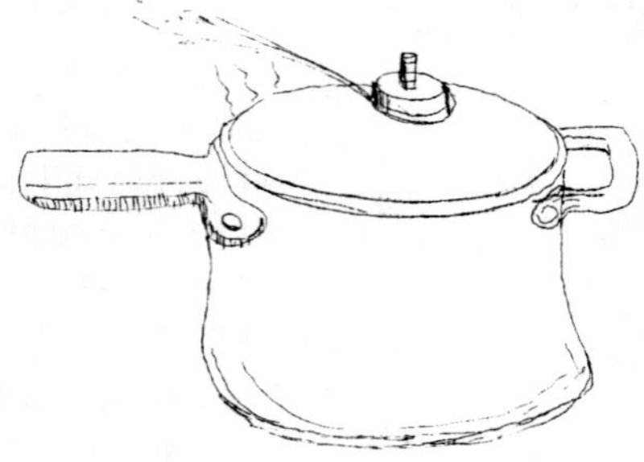

1. Cook the bacon and drain off all fat. Add the onion, mushrooms, and bell pepper and cook until tender. Add the avocado, carefully mix, and set aside.
2. In a separate pan, melt the butter until hot. Add the eggs and stir until barely cooked. Add the cooked pasta and stir until heated through.
3. Mix in the avocado/bacon sauce and sprinkle with Parmesan cheese.

Bucatini alla Puttanesca

6 servings

This classic southern Italian pasta dish actually translates as "Whore's Sauce." Certainly sounds better in Italian!

5 cloves garlic, coarsely chopped
½ cup olive oil
1 cup capers, rinsed
3 dried small red chile peppers, finely chopped
1 (28 oz.) can Italian plum tomatoes with purée
4 teaspoons oregano
1 cup chopped fresh basil
1 cup green olives, sliced
1 cup black olives, sliced
16 ounces cooked bucatini or penne

Sauté the garlic in the olive oil for 2 minutes. Add the capers, chile pepper, and tomatoes and cook for 10 minutes. Add the oregano, basil, and olives; cook an additional 10 minutes. Pour the sauce over hot pasta.

Hazard's Cove Spaghetti

4 servings

After seven days away from any provisioning opportunity, with no freezer and very limited refrigeration, I prepared this gastronomic wonder—or so it seemed to 4 hungry divers. This sauce will keep for five to six days in the refrigerator.

1 pound Italian sausage, sliced
2 onions, chopped
1 teaspoon finely chopped garlic
1 green bell pepper
1 cup dried button mushrooms
1 (28 oz.) can Italian tomatoes
1 pound cooked pasta

1. Sauté the sausage until it's almost cooked; drain off excess fat. Add the onions and garlic and sauté until the onions are tender and transparent.
2. Add the bell pepper, mushrooms, and tomatoes, and cook until the mushrooms are soft.
3. Serve over hot pasta.

Sun-Dried Tomatoes and Basil Pasta Sauce

4 servings

8 ounces sun-dried tomatoes packed in oil
1 (4 oz.) can sliced black olives
1 cup fresh basil or 2 tablespoons dried
3 tablespoons grated fresh lemon peel
3 cloves garlic, minced
1 ½ teaspoons freshly grated black pepper
4 ounces slivered fresh Parmesan cheese
¼ cup olive oil
1 pound cooked penne or linguine pasta

1. Drain and chop the tomatoes, reserving oil. (I chop the tomatoes on a paper plate which makes cleanup easier and catches the oil that drains off.)

2. Combine the olives, basil, lemon peel, garlic, pepper, cheese, and oil and set aside. This can be done early in the day or even the night before. Sitting at room temperature for several hours allows the sauce ingredients to marinate.

3. Serve over hot pasta.

Acini di Pepe Stracciatella Soup

4 to 6 servings

Acini di pepe (seed of the pepper) is a small round ball of pasta. Any small pasta can be substituted.

2 quarts chicken broth
½ cup acini di pepe or other small pasta
3 eggs
½ cup chopped Italian parsley
½ cup freshly grated Parmesan cheese
Salt and pepper

1. Heat all but 1 cup of the broth and bring to a boil. Add the pasta and cook 5 minutes (al dente).

2. Beat together the reserved cup of broth with the eggs, parsley, and cheese. Pour into the hot broth and, stirring constantly, simmer for 2 to 3 minutes. Salt and pepper to taste.

Green Peas and Angel Hair Pasta Soup

4 to 6 servings

1 small onion, finely chopped
2 cloves finely chopped garlic
2 tablespoons olive oil
2 cups small frozen peas, thawed
2 quarts chicken broth
2 cups angel hair pasta, broken up
Salt and freshly ground black pepper
1 cup freshly grated Parmesan cheese
3 slices pancetta or bacon, chopped, cooked, and drained

Sauté the onion and garlic until soft. Add the peas and broth and bring to a boil. Add the pasta and cook 30 seconds (al dente). Season to taste with salt and pepper. Serve topped with the cheese and pancetta.

Bell Peppers Stuffed with Orzo

6 servings

When I have lots of bell peppers (my favorites are the sweet red and yellow bells that are so easy to find in the markets these days), I double the Orzo with Sun-Dried Tomato recipe and use half of it to stuff the peppers.

Any small pasta will work in this recipe. Try *acini di pepe* (seed of the pepper) in place of orzo. You can even use chopped up leftover spaghetti to stuff the peppers.

8 ounces small pasta, cooked and seasoned as directed in Orzo with Sun-Dried Tomatoes (below)
6 bell peppers
Salt and pepper
1 clove garlic, finely chopped
4 anchovy fillets, finely chopped
1 tablespoon capers, rinsed and drained
1 (4 oz.) can black olives, chopped
¼ cup chopped parsley
8 ounces mozzarella cheese, shredded

Cut the tops off the peppers and remove the seeds. Season the insides with salt and pepper. Combine the remaining ingredients in a large bowl and fill the peppers with the pasta mixture. Bake at 350° F for 30 minutes.

Orzo with Sun-Dried Tomatoes

4 servings

I love the texture and taste of orzo. Many people mistake it for rice because of the similarity in shape and size. Orzo makes a great side dish for meat, poultry, and fish main courses.

1 cup small pasta such as orzo
1 teaspoon salt
2 tablespoons olive oil
¼ cup sun-dried tomato seasoning (page 167)

Bring two quarts of water to a boil. Add the orzo and salt boil until tender—about 10 to 12 minutes. Drain well. Season the pasta with the olive oil and sun-dried tomato seasoning.

Crab Linguine

4 servings

If you haven't had any luck catching fresh crab, try this sauce with imitation crab. It's great.

2 tablespoons olive oil
2 teaspoons chopped garlic
½ onion, chopped
2 tablespoons pine nuts
1 tablespoon pesto sauce
½ pound crab meat
¼ cup Parmesan cheese
½ pound cooked linguine

Heat the oil in a skillet and sauté the garlic, onion, and pine nuts. Combine with the pesto, crab, and cheese. Toss with hot pasta.

Pennette with Zucchini

4 servings

1 onion, chopped
1 pound zucchini, cut in half lengthwise and cut in ¼-inch thick slices
3 tablespoons olive oil
½ cup cream
12 ounces cooked pennette (small pen-shaped pasta)
½ cup freshly grated Parmesan cheese

Sauté the onion and zucchini in the olive oil in a wok until tender. Add the cream and cooked pasta and heat gently while mixing together. Stir in the cheese and serve.

Acini di Pepe and Sausage Soup

2 to 4 servings

The weekend that we moved aboard *SpiceSea,* I concocted this soup from leftover salad ingredients, some chicken bouillon, a small can of marinara sauce, and some seed pasta. Voilà!—a great tasting soup that warmed the cockles of our hearts on that cold January day.

¾ pound Italian sausage, crumbled, cooked, and drained
4 cloves garlic
1 cup each Savoy cabbage and Swiss chard, chopped
6 cups chicken broth
½ cup Italian tomato sauce
¾ cup acini di pepe or orzo
Freshly grated Parmesan cheese

Combine all the ingredients *except* the pasta and cheese and heat well. Add the pasta and cook until done. Pass the cheese.

Lasagna

I love lasagna, but I hate to make it. Cooking the noodles and handling them while they are hot just seems to be too much trouble. Occasionally I go to the effort at home, but on the boat I don't have the space to deal with all of those noodles.

That is, I didn't until the advent of instant pasta. This new type of pasta requires no boiling—no waiting for the water to come to a boil, no hot noodles to handle, no extra pot to wash and, best of all, it makes my husband happy because there is no wasted water.

Needless to say, I was a bit skeptical about this wonder pasta. How could you put hard sheets of pasta in a pan with sauce and get al dente-cooked lasagna? Much to my surprise, however, I got perfect lasagna the first time I used "NoBoil"—and in less than half the usual preparation time.

Now, making lasagna is quick and fun. Just make sure that when you layer the noodles you leave about an inch around the edges of the pan to allow for expansion as they absorb moisture from the sauce and the other wet ingredients.

If you want to make cannelloni or manicotti, soak the pasta in a little hot tap water for 5 to 8 minutes or until softened. Spread with desired vegetable, cheese, and sauce, and roll up. Place seam side down in a baking dish, top with additional sauce, cover and bake.

The Del Verde Company of Italy distributes one of the new pasta products in some Italian delis. It's called Lasagna Instanti and comes with 3 disposable aluminum foil pans and a ½ kilo of pasta, which is enough to make 3 pans of lasagna.

In this country, Shade Pasta Inc. (P.O. Box 645, Fremont, NE 68026) has secured the right to make instant pasta. Their product is Pasta DeFino NoBoil Lasagna. It's packaged in 8-ounce boxes, (there are 15 noodles in each box; 9 noodles fill a 9×13-inch pan in 3 layers) and is available in grocery stores throughout the United States. You can order NoBoil Lasagna (1-800-N0-BOIL-1) using your Visa or MasterCard.

These instant noodles are made from 100 percent enriched durum semolina wheat flour and water. The pasta is first extruded into a continuous sheet, then passed through boiling water to cook and wash away the surface starch. Finally the pasta is dried, cut, and packaged.

I like to keep some staples on *SpiceSea* for impromptu entertaining and for times when provisioning is difficult. With a 32-ounce jar of spaghetti sauce, 8 ounces of NoBoil noodles, and some cheese, I have everything I need to make lasagna at a moment's notice. With the addition of leftover meat (chicken, seafood, sausage), vegetables, cream soups, sun-dried tomatoes, or black olives, I can receive kudos for very little effort.

Easy Lasagna

8 to 10 servings

32 ounces low-fat ricotta or cottage cheese
2 eggs (optional)
2 teaspoons Italian seasoning
2 (4 oz.) cans sliced black olives (optional)
2 cups chopped zucchini (optional)
28 to 32 ounce jar spaghetti sauce
9 sheets dry DeFino NoBoil lasagna noodles
12 ounces grated mozzarella cheese
¼ cup grated Parmesan (optional)

1. In a small bowl, combine the ricotta cheese, eggs, Italian seasoning, and black olives and zucchini if using.
2. For 3 layers of pasta, spread 1 cup of spaghetti sauce in a greased 9×13-inch pan. Cover with 3 dry NoBoil noodles placed side by side. Cover the noodles with 1 cup of spaghetti sauce. Layer ⅓ of the ricotta mixture and ⅓ of the mozzarella cheese on top of the sauce. Repeat the layers twice more, ending with mozzarella on top. Sprinkle with Parmesan.
3. Cover with foil and bake at 350° F for 30 to 40 minutes. Uncover the dish during the last 10 to 15 minutes to brown the cheese. Allow the lasagna to stand 5 minutes before cutting. If cooking in a microwave, cover the dish with plastic wrap and cook on high power 17 to 19 minutes, turning the dish twice.

Variation

4 ½ cups diced raw vegetables
1 ¾ cups grated cheese

1. Make a thick white sauce using 6 tablespoons butter, 6 tablespoons flour, and 3 cups milk (see page 162). Add 1 ¼ cups of the grated cheese.

2. Follow the directions for Easy Lasagna, placing a cup of the cheese sauce on the bottom of the baking dish and layering the noodles, then the cheese sauce, and then the vegetables in 3 layers. Sprinkle a ½ cup of grated cheese over the top. Cook following directions for Easy Lasagna (page 122).

Seafood Manicotti

6 servings

6 NoBoil Lasagna noodles
1 12-ounce package light cream cheese
1 cup cottage cheese
1 ½ cups cooked shrimp, crab, or other seafood
½ cup sliced green onion
1 (10 ¾ oz.) can cream of celery soup
¾ cup evaporated skim milk
1 tablespoon mustard
1 tablespoon White Wine Worcestershire sauce
¼ cup grated Parmesan cheese
2 tablespoons parsley

1. Soak the lasagna noodles in hot tap water for 5 to 8 minutes or until softened, taking care that they don't stick together.
2. In a large bowl, combine the light cream cheese, cottage cheese, seafood, and onion.
3. Cut each softened noodle in half, making two 4-inch squares. Spray a 9×13-inch baking dish with nonstick cooking spray. Divide the seafood mixture equally among the softened noodles (⅓ cup each) and roll up. Place seam side down in baking dish.
4. Combine the soup, milk, mustard, and Worcestershire sauce. Pour over the rolled noodles and sprinkle with the Parmesan cheese and parsley.
5. Cover with foil and bake at 400° F for 15 minutes. Uncover and bake 20 to 25 minutes longer. For cooking in a microwave, cover the dish with plastic wrap and cook on high power 15 to 18 minutes, turning the dish twice.

Variation

6 NoBoil lasagna noodles
1 cup ricotta cheese
2 eggs
1 ½ cups finely shredded zucchini
1 cup finely shredded carrots
⅓ cup finely chopped green onions
24-ounce jar spaghetti sauce
¾ pound shredded Mozzarella cheese

1. Soak the lasagna noodles as directed for Seafood Manicotti (this page), then cut in half as directed in step 3 of Seafood Manicotti.
2. In a medium-sized bowl, combine the ricotta and eggs. Set aside.
3. In a separate bowl, combine the zucchini, carrots, onions, and spaghetti sauce.
4. Spread the noodles with the ricotta mixture and some of the sauce, as in step 3 of the recipe for Seafood Manicotti.
5. Cover the bottom of a 9×13-inch baking dish with sauce, top with the manicotti, and pour the remaining tomato sauce over noodles. Cover the pan with foil and bake for 15 minutes at 400° F. Uncover, sprinkle with mozzarella cheese, and bake an additional 20 to 25 minutes until hot and bubbly.

Bean Threads

Bean threads, transparent noodles made from mung bean flour, are a great boat store. They conserve energy since they don't need cooking and will keep in their dehydrated state indefinitely. Soak in water for 30 minutes to reconstitute.

Pork with Bean Threads

2 servings

3 ounces bean threads
½ pound ground lean pork
2 tablespoons soy sauce
2 teaspoons sugar
1 teaspoon cornstarch
2 teaspoons chili paste with garlic
1 teaspoon finely chopped ginger
2 tablespoons vegetable oil
⅓ cup chopped onion
½ cup chicken broth
Green onion or cilantro for garnish

1. Soak the bean threads in water for about 30 minutes and cut into 2-inch pieces with scissors. Combine the pork, soy, sugar, cornstarch, chili paste, and ginger and allow to marinate for 15 minutes.
2. Heat the oil in a wok and stir-fry the onion for a few seconds. Add the meat and stir-fry 2 minutes. Add the broth and drained noodles to the pan and cook until the liquid evaporates.
3. Serve hot, garnished with chopped green onion or cilantro.

Bean Threads with Chicken Wrapped in Lettuce Leaves

2 main course or 8 to 10 appetizer servings

The simple ingredients and exciting taste of Thai cooking make it popular fare aboard *SpiceSea*.

5 to 6 ounces bean thread noodles
1 tablespoon vegetable oil
¾ pound finely chopped chicken
2 cloves garlic, finely chopped
½ cup thinly sliced green onion or 1 onion, chopped
1 recipe Lime Dressing
2 small heads red or green leaf lettuce, cleaned and dry
Lime wedges
Sprigs of cilantro

1. Soak the bean threads in water for about 30 minutes and cut into 2-inch pieces with scissors.
2. Heat the oil in a wok. Add the chicken and cook over high heat until done—about 2 minutes. Stir in the noodles, onion, and lime dressing.
3. Place the filling on a serving platter and surround with lettuce leaves, lime wedges, and cilantro.
4. To eat, spoon some of the noodle mixture onto a lettuce leaf and top with a squeeze of lime and a sprig of cilantro.

Lime Dressing

½ cup fresh lime juice
¼ cup sugar
3 tablespoons *nam pla* (Oriental fish sauce) or soy sauce
½ to ¾ teaspoons crushed dried hot red chile pepper

Combine all the ingredients.

Chinese Noodles with Spicy Peanut Sauce

4 servings

1 ½ cups thinly sliced carrots
8 ounces Chinese egg noodles (fresh or dried)
2 teaspoons dark sesame oil
½ cup cilantro leaves

Spicy Peanut Sauce

½ cup chunky peanut butter
½ cup soy sauce
1 ½ tablespoons chili oil

1 teaspoon dry sherry
2 tablespoons finely chopped garlic
3 tablespoons finely chopped cilantro leaves

1. Bring 2 quarts of water to a boil. Add the carrots and blanch for 5 seconds. Remove with a slotted spoon and drain.
2. Add the noodles and cook 1 to 3 minutes (if fresh) or 7 to 9 minutes (if dried). Drain and rinse under warm water. Drain well and season with the sesame oil. Add the carrots and ½ a cup of cilantro leaves.
3. Combine peanut sauce ingredients.
4. Toss the sauce with the noodle mixture.

Chinese Noodles with Garlic Sauce

4 servings

½ pound Chinese egg noodles (fresh or dried)
1 tablespoon cooking oil
½ pound ground pork
2 teaspoons Chinese bean sauce

Garlic Sauce

1 teaspoon chili paste with garlic
2 tablespoons chopped green onion
½ teaspoon finely chopped fresh ginger
1 teaspoon dark sesame oil
¼ cup chicken broth
1 teaspoon dry sherry

1. Cook the noodles as directed in Chinese Noodles with Spicy Peanut Sauce (see above).
2. Cook the pork in oil and season with the bean sauce.
3. Combine all the garlic sauce ingredients; toss with noodles.

Wonton Raviolis

Making homemade raviolis is not something I enjoy doing on the boat. Actually, it's not something I enjoy doing at home! Wontons to the rescue. Wontons are Oriental egg roll wrappers that are made with flour, eggs, and oil and are very similar to pasta. They keep many weeks under refrigeration and also freeze well. Wontons are readily available in the United States and also in countries that have a sizable Oriental population. I take several packages with me aboard *SpiceSea* so I can make my favorite hors d'oeuvre (see page 50) and an occasional batch of raviolis.

Wontons are cut into quarters; gyoza wrappers or dumpling skins are cut into circles and may be a little thicker than wontons. If you can't find the round wrappers for the raviolis, you can cut wontons in circles with a pastry cutter after assembling.

Chicken Raviolis with Green Chile Pesto

4 dozen large raviolis

1 pound boneless, skinless chicken, cubed
2 tablespoons green chile pesto
1 egg yolk
2 teaspoons cornstarch
Salt and pepper
1 ½ pounds wonton or dumpling skins
1 egg white
1 recipe Green Chile Pesto (page 168)

1. In a food processor, combine the chicken, pesto, egg yolk, cornstarch, salt, and pepper. Purée to a smooth paste.
2. Place one tablespoon of the filling in the center of a wonton skin. Brush the edges with the egg white. Cover with another skin and press the edges well to seal.
3. If not cooking the raviolis immediately, you may either place them in a single layer on a platter that's lined with plastic wrap and then cover them with more plastic wrap and chill for up to 4 hours, or freeze them until they're solid and then transfer them to freezer containers to store.

4. To Cook: Bring 4 quarts of water to a boil in a large pan. Add about half of the raviolis. Boil gently, uncovered, over medium heat until just tender—about 5 minutes (6 minutes if frozen). With a large slotted spoon, lift out ravioli and drain.

5. Serve with Green Chile Pesto Sauce.

Shrimp Raviolis with Tomatillo Sauce

4 dozen large raviolis

½ cup jicama, cubed
1 pound shrimp, cleaned, deveined, and cooked
1 tablespoon tomatillo sauce
1 egg yolk
1 tablespoon cornstarch
Salt and pepper
1 ½ pounds wonton or dumpling skins
1 egg white
1 recipe Salsa de Tomatillo (page 166)

1. In a food processor, finely chop the jicama and remove.

2. In a medium-sized bowl, combine the shrimp, tomatillo sauce, egg yolk, cornstarch, salt, and pepper. Stir in the jicama.

3. Fill and cook (or store) raviolis as directed for Chicken Raviolis with Green Chile Pesto (see page 125).

Tabbouleh

4 servings

Caleta Santa Maria is a small cove located about 3½ miles northeast of Cabo San Lucas, with room for four boats if they cooperate and anchor bow and stern. Colorful reef fish and beautiful rock formations abound in crystal-clear water. But the real treasure that Hal and I once found there was ashore—fresh limes and mint growing wild. Margaritas and mint juleps were definitely in order!

I also made tabbouleh, a refreshing salad of Lebanese origin that keeps well and uses both limes and fresh mint. If romaine or butter lettuce is available, you can serve tabbouleh as a tasty hors d'oeuvre, passing the lettuce and allowing your guests to fill the leaves with the tabbouleh and eat the salad like you would a taco.

½ cup cracked wheat* (bulgur wheat)
½ cup water
2 tomatoes, diced
1 cucumber, peeled, seeded, and diced (or 1 cup diced Jicama or water chestnuts)
1 small onion, finely chopped
1 teaspoon minced garlic
½ cup finely chopped fresh parsley (use dry if you don't have fresh)
½ cup fresh chopped mint (use dry if you don't have fresh)
4 tablespoons lemon or lime juice
4 tablespoons olive oil
Salt and pepper to taste

1. Combine the wheat and water in a large bowl or Ziploc until the wheat softens and absorbs the water—about 30 minutes.

2. Toss with the remaining ingredients and allow to marinate for at least 30 minutes to combine flavors.

**Cracked wheat is a delicious grain made by boiling, grinding, and drying whole wheat. It is available in U.S. markets and Middle Eastern groceries.*

I once tasted a very creative nontraditional tabbouleh that a boater made for a potluck. The cook aboard *Chelsea* had used bulgur wheat, onions, tomatoes, parsley, and oil in true Middle Eastern tradition, but then added a can of chickpeas, sunflower seeds, and raisins. Further, vinegar was substituted for lemon juice.

This unique salad illustrates perfectly my feeling about following recipes; that is, use them as basic guides and never be afraid to substitute.

Wild Rice

Wild rice is the seed of a grass that grows in the northern United States. It is delicious when cooked and mixed with white rice or it can be served by itself. One cup of wild rice equals about 3 cups of cooked.

Cook 1 cup of wild rice in 3½ cups of boiling water seasoned with a ½ teaspoon of salt for about 40 minutes or until tender.

To cook wild rice in a pressure cooker, place 3 cups of water or bouillon in the cooker with the rice. Cook at high pressure for 22 minutes.

BARLEY AND WILD RICE

4 to 6 servings

1 onion, chopped
2 cloves garlic, finely chopped
1 cup pearl barley
½ cup wild rice
1 tablespoon olive oil
4 cups water
2 teaspoons salt

1. Sauté the onion, garlic, barley, and rice in the oil until the onion is soft.
2. Add the water and salt and bring to a boil. Cover and simmer until the grains are tender and the water is absorbed—about 1 hour.

WILD RICE STUFFING

Enough to generously stuff 4 Cornish gamehens or 1 large chicken

1 cup wild rice, cooked
½ cup fresh bread crumbs
½ cup raisins
½ cup toasted pine nuts
1 apple, coarsely chopped
2 tablespoons orange juice
2 tablespoons melted butter
Salt to taste

Combine all the ingredients.

Barley

ROASTED BARLEY AND PINE NUTS

4 to 6 servings

The chewy texture of the roasted barley, coupled with the roasted pine nuts, always brings rave reviews.

2 tablespoons olive oil
1 cup pearl barley
1 onion, chopped
1¼ cups chicken broth
Salt and pepper
½ to ¾ cup pine nuts
1 cup parsley, chopped

1. Grease a 2½-quart casserole.
2. Heat the olive oil and add the barley and onion; cook until the barley is lightly colored and the onions are soft. Add the broth, season with salt and pepper, and bring to a boil.
3. Turn into the prepared casserole and bake at 375°F, uncovered, for 45 minutes or until all the liquid is evaporated and the barley is tender.
4. Brown the pine nuts on a baking sheet in the oven for 5 to 7 minutes.
5. Stir in the pine nuts and parsley just before serving.

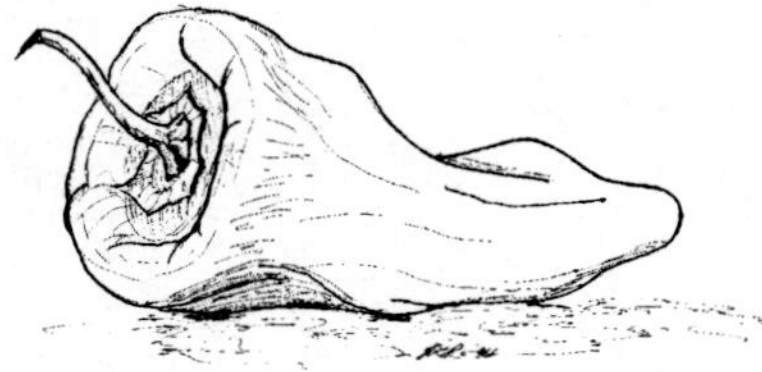

Rice

To cook each cup of white or brown rice, you need 2 cups of liquid in the form of water, broth, or bouillon. Bring the liquid to a boil, add 1 tablespoon of fat (butter or oil), a ½ teaspoon of salt, and the rice. Bring back to a boil, lower the heat to simmer, and cook covered for 25 to 30 minutes for white rice, 40 to 50 minutes for brown rice. Fluff with a fork and add more water if necessary. One cup of raw rice equals about three cups of cooked.

Rice cooks perfectly in the **PRESSURE COOKER.** To do so, though, you need to find a pot or pan that fits inside your pressure cooker. (I use a 2-quart Charlotte pan.) For ease in removing the baking pan from the pressure cooker, you need to make two aluminum foil straps that go under the baking pan and that are long enough to fold over the top of the pan (see page 25).

For each cup of rice, use 2¼ cups liquid and 1 tablespoon of oil. Cook on medium pressure for 7 minutes for white rice and on high for 15 minutes for brown or arborio rice. Allow the pressure to reduce naturally when the cooking time has finished.

Whether you cook rice the conventional method or in a pressure cooker, adding chopped vegetables such as onions, carrots, or celery to the liquid will add flavor and texture. Or, try some of the special rice recipes that follow.

Jambalaya

6 to 8 servings

1 recipe Creole Sauce (page 171)
1 cup water
1½ cups long grain rice
1 pound hot sausage, sliced and cooked
1 pound uncooked shrimp, cleaned and peeled

Bring the Creole Sauce and water to a boil. Add the rice and sausage; cover and simmer 15 minutes. Add the shrimp and stir well. Simmer an additional 5 to 10 minutes until the rice and shrimp are cooked.

Risotto in the Pressure Cooker

4 to 6 servings

I don't think I would make this recipe without a pressure cooker. Creamy Italian risotto normally takes a lot of attention and stirring. In the pressure cooker, however, it is easy.

½ cup finely chopped onion
2 tablespoons olive oil
1 cup arborio rice
3¼ cups chicken broth
1 tablespoon lemon juice
¼ teaspoon white pepper
½ teaspoon salt
1 cup freshly grated Parmesan cheese

1. In a pressure cooker, sauté the onion in the olive oil for 2 minutes. Stir in the rice and cook for 1 minute, making sure that all the grains of rice are coated with oil.
2. Add the broth, lemon juice, white pepper, and salt.
3. Secure the lid and bring the pressure to high. Cook on high pressure for 12 minutes. Allow the steam to reduce naturally. Stir in cheese.

Pecan Pilaf

6 to 8 servings

1 cup chopped pecans
3 tablespoons olive oil
⅓ cup chopped onion
1½ cups long grain white rice
2½ cups chicken broth
½ teaspoon salt
½ teaspoon freshly ground black pepper
¼ teaspoon thyme
¼ cup chopped parsley

1. In a saucepan, sauté the pecans in 2 tablespoons of the olive oil. When lightly brown, remove from pan and reserve.
2. Add the remaining oil and sauté the onion and rice until all the grains of rice are coated with a little oil.

3. Add the broth, salt, pepper, and thyme and bring to a boil. Reduce heat, cover, and simmer for 20 to 25 minutes until the rice is tender. Stir in the parsley and pecans.

Green Rice

6 to 8 servings

2 medium green bell peppers, chopped
1 onion, chopped
1 clove garlic, finely chopped
2 tablespoons olive oil
1 ½ cups long grain white rice
2 ½ cups chicken broth
½ teaspoon salt
¼ teaspoon Tabasco sauce
¾ cup chopped cilantro

1. In a saucepan, sauté the bell peppers, onion, and garlic in the olive oil until tender. Stir in the rice and sauté 3 to 5 minutes longer, stirring until all the grains of rice are coated with a little oil.
2. Add the broth, salt, and Tabasco sauce and bring to a boil. Reduce heat, cover, and simmer for 20 to 25 minutes until the rice is tender. Stir in the cilantro and serve.

Red Rice

6 to 8 servings

Traditionally served with Cocido (see page 101), this is an excellent rice dish to accompany any Mexican meal.

1 small onion, chopped
1 clove garlic, minced
2 tablespoons olive oil
1 ½ cups long grain white rice
2 cups beef broth
½ teaspoon salt
1 cup (8 oz.) tomato sauce

1. In a saucepan, sauté the onion and garlic in the olive oil until tender. Stir in the rice and sauté 3 to 5 minutes longer, stirring until all the grains of rice are coated with a little oil.
2. Add the broth, salt, and tomato sauce and bring to a boil. Reduce heat, cover, and simmer for 20 to 25 minutes until the rice is tender.

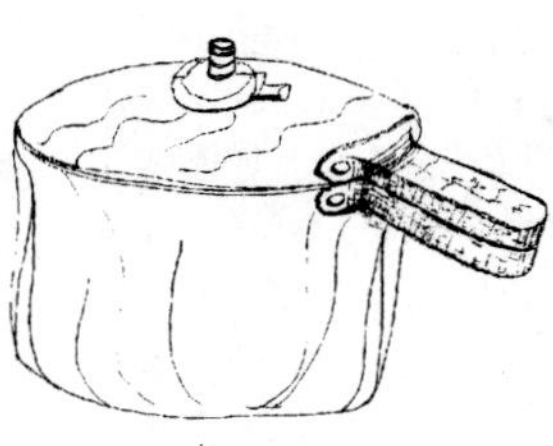

Lemon Caper Rice

6 to 8 servings

This is one of my favorite rice dishes and a great accompaniment to fish or chicken. For a change of texture you can substitute one of the small pastas such as orzo for the rice.

2 tablespoons olive oil
1 ½ cups long grain white rice
2 ⅓ cups chicken broth
2 ½ tablespoons lemon juice
½ teaspoon salt
½ teaspoon freshly ground black pepper
2 tablespoons capers, rinsed and drained
¼ cup chopped parsley

1. In a saucepan, sauté the rice until all the grains are coated with a little oil.
2. Add the broth, lemon juice, salt, and pepper and bring to a boil. Reduce heat, cover, and simmer for 15 to 20 minutes until the rice is tender. Stir in the capers and parsley.

Chinese Fried Rice with Egg Pancake

4 to 6 servings

The secret of fried rice is to use cold, leftover rice. Any bits of meat or fish can be added to make this a main course.

2 to 4 tablespoons peanut oil
½ cup chopped onion
½ cup sliced celery
3 cups cold cooked rice
1 cup bean sprouts
3 tablespoons soy sauce
2 eggs, beaten

Garnishes

Egg pancake
2 green onions, chopped

1. Heat a wok, add 2 tablespoons of oil, and heat. Add the onion and celery and cook until crisp-tender. Add the rice, breaking up with a spoon, and stir-fry until all the grains glisten with a little oil. Add a little more oil if necessary. Add the bean sprouts and soy sauce and cook until heated through.
2. Make a well in the center of the rice and pour in the beaten egg; allow to set briefly and then scramble with chopsticks before stirring into rice.
3. Serve on a platter garnished with egg pancakes and chopped green onion.

Egg Pancake

1 egg
1 tablespoon water
⅛ teaspoon salt
½ tablespoon peanut oil

In a small bowl, combine the egg, water, and salt. Heat the oil in a nonstick skillet, add the egg mixture, and cook like a pancake until set. Allow to cool, then roll up tightly and slice into slivers.

CHAPTER 8

Fruits and Vegetables

Leaving Southern California's produce markets and their year-round supply of nearly all the fresh fruits and vegetables I could ever want, to shop in often-limited Third-World markets, was one of the most difficult adjustments I had to make in cruising. Even when I could find fresh artichokes, pea pods, peaches, or plums, there wasn't enough room in my small refrigerator to keep them.

I had to learn how to preserve fresh produce at room temperature and became quite skilled at wrapping carrots in newspaper and making do with fresh cabbage because lettuce was too fragile and had too short of a shelf life. I also learned that I enjoy watching tomatoes ripen in a basket—I'll never refrigerate tomatoes again!

Hal and I are big salad eaters and I experimented with combinations that helped to keep our salads interesting: coleslaw with lemon and olives, crystallized ginger and raisins, chiles and pineapple; a Greek salad that uses lots of marinated artichoke hearts and bell peppers, topped off with feta cheese; a Thai salad with a cabbage base, but with interesting flavors provided by roasted peanuts, cilantro, and lots of garlic and chile.

We ate lots of carrots because they keep well and are available in most parts of the world. I prepared them with a simple honey glaze, some mint and garlic, or Chinese-style with ginger, chile, fermented black beans, and soy sauce, all of which kept our taste buds happy.

In this chapter I've included directions for roasting and stuffing peppers; chopping a medley of vegetables and sealing them in foil before cooking on the barbecue; pickling produce to extend its shelf life; and making use of both green and ripe papaya.

I've also included some recipes using foods you'll encounter when cruising in foreign ports: Breadfruit Vinaigrette, Cactus Leaf Salad, and Shrimp Stuffed Chayote Squash will help you make use of local produce.

Many of my recipes lend themselves well to substitutions—and improvising and experimenting with substitutes is an important part of learning to cook on board a boat. Try substituting zucchini for broccoli in the recipe for Broccoli with Anchovies and Garlic, or using broccoli instead of cauliflower in Cauliflower with Garlic and Chile. There is a simple Chinese Vegetable Stir-Fry recipe that relies on canned ingredients and any fresh green that you can find. Be creative! In Curried Cauliflower, omit the cauliflower and use just potatoes.

Finally, I suggest that you read Chapter 1 (Philosophy, Provisioning and Preserving) carefully to learn how to best shop for and store produce, including some that might not be too familiar. That chapter also includes information about growing sprouts to augment your fresh produce and suggestions for some excellent canned produce items that will enhance your salads on board.

Broccoli

Broccoli does not have a long shelf life and should be stored in the refrigerator whenever possible. When the weather is cold, it lasts a few days without refrigeration, but even under ideal conditions this vegetable starts deteriorating after a week.

Stir-Fried Broccoli Stems with Oyster Sauce

4 servings

½ pound broccoli stems, washed, peeled, cut into ¼-inch diagonal slices (can substitute cauliflower or asparagus)
2 tablespoons cooking oil
1 clove garlic, finely chopped
1 teaspoon salt
1 tablespoon chicken broth

Sauce

1 tablespoon oyster sauce
1 tablespoon soy sauce
1 teaspoon sugar
1 tablespoon chicken broth
1 tablespoon sherry

1. Combine the sauce ingredients and set aside.
2. Heat the oil in a wok and add the broccoli, garlic, and salt. Stir-fry until the broccoli is evenly coated with oil, then add the chicken broth. Lower the heat, cover, and cook for about 30 seconds.
3. Remove the cover, add the sauce mixture, and stir-fry several times.

Broccoli with Anchovies and Garlic

4 servings

1 ½ pounds broccoli
2 tablespoons olive oil
4 garlic cloves, finely chopped
3 anchovy fillets, mashed
Salt and pepper
3 tablespoons chopped parsley

1. Cut off the tough bottoms from the broccoli and peel the outer skin. Cut into chunks.
2. Bring 4 quarts of salted water to a boil and add the broccoli. Reduce heat and simmer 5 minutes or until the stalks are tender. Drain well.
3. Just before serving, heat the oil in a large skillet. Stir in the garlic and anchovies. Add the drained broccoli and season with salt, pepper, and parsley. Turn the broccoli gently and cook until reheated.
4. Serve hot with the pan drippings spooned over the broccoli.

Broccoli with Red Wine and Olives

4 servings

1 ½ pounds broccoli
1 tablespoon olive oil
1 onion, chopped
¼ cup sliced black olives
3 anchovy fillets, chopped
¾ cup red wine

1. Cut the broccoli tops into florets. Peel the stems, trim off any tough ends, and cut into thin slices.
2. Sauté the onion in the olive oil until soft. Add the olives, anchovies, and wine. Bring to a boil and cover tightly.
3. Lower the heat and simmer until tender—about 25 minutes.

Cauliflower with Garlic and Chile

2 to 4 servings

2 tablespoons olive oil
1 pound cauliflower, cut into florets
2 cloves garlic, finely chopped
1 dried red chile pepper
Salt and pepper to taste

Heat the oil in a wok and stir-fry the cauliflower with the garlic and chile pepper. Add 2 tablespoons of water, cover, and allow to steam until tender.

Chinese Vegetable Stir-Fry

4 servings

Stir-fry this recipe while grilling chicken breasts on the barbecue. Use two canned vegetables (bamboo shoots and water chestnuts), supplemented by any fresh green vegetable that you have on board.

1 tablespoon vegetable oil
1 clove garlic, minced
½ pound fresh vegetables cut in uniform pieces: Chinese pea pods, broccoli, asparagus, bell pepper
1 (5 oz.) can water chestnuts, thinly sliced
1 (5 oz.) can bamboo shoots, thinly sliced
2 teaspoons soy sauce
¼ cup chicken broth
1 teaspoon cornstarch dissolved in 1 tablespoon water

1. Heat a wok, add the oil, and swirl it around the pan to distribute. Add the garlic and cook for a few seconds. Add the vegetables and cook over high heat for 1 minute, stirring frequently.
2. Add the soy sauce and broth. Cover and cook 2 minutes. Stir in the cornstarch and cook until a light glaze forms.

Cauliflower with Garlic Crust

4 servings

1 pound cauliflower, cut into florets and boiled until tender
Salt and pepper to taste
¾ cup dry bread crumbs
4 cloves garlic, finely chopped
4 tablespoons olive oil

Place the cooked cauliflower in a baking dish, flower side up. Mix the remaining ingredients together and spread on top of the cauliflower. Bake at 375°F for 20 minutes or until golden.

Curried Cauliflower

4 servings

2 tablespoons chopped fresh ginger
1 onion, chopped
2 teaspoons curry powder
2 tablespoons cooking oil
1 pound cauliflower, cut into 1½-inch pieces
2 potatoes, finely chopped
½ teaspoon salt
¼ cup water

Sauté the ginger, onion, and curry powder in the oil for 3 minutes. Add the cauliflower, potatoes, salt, and water, cover the pan, and cook until the vegetables are soft—about 20 minutes. Add more water if the vegetables start to stick to the pan.

Cabbage

When all other produce has faded, good old dependable cabbage seems to still hold up. The longer we cruise aboard *SpiceSea,* the more I rely on cabbage. In addition to coleslaw, which can be spruced up with unusual ingredients to give it some zip, try combining red and green cabbage for an eye appealing salad or stir-frying cabbage for a great vegetable dish.

Jalapeño Pineapple Coleslaw

4 to 6 servings

½ large head cabbage, shredded
2 cups pineapple chunks, fresh or canned
½ cup chopped green onion

Marinade

½ cup mayonnaise
½ cup plain yogurt
4 pickled jalapeño chiles (chiles en escabeche)
1½ teaspoons Dijon mustard
1 tablespoon sugar
1 tablespoon lime juice
¼ teaspoon salt

Combine all the marinade ingredients and mix with the cabbage and pineapple. Marinate for at least a ½ hour. Sprinkle with the green onions just before serving.

Raisin-Ginger Coleslaw

4 servings

½ large head cabbage, shredded
½ cup golden raisins or 1 apple, diced
2 ounces crystallized ginger, minced
¼ cup mayonnaise
¼ cup rice wine vinegar

Combine all the ingredients and marinate for at least a ½ hour. Add a ½ cup of roasted macadamia nuts or salted peanuts if desired.

Stir-Fried Spicy Cabbage

4 servings

2 tablespoons sugar
2 tablespoon rice wine vinegar
1 tablespoon soy sauce
1 teaspoon salt
¼ teaspoon cayenne pepper
1 tablespoon cooking oil
¾ pound napa cabbage, cut into 1-inch squares

Make a sauce by combining the sugar, wine vinegar, soy sauce, salt, and cayenne pepper; set aside. Heat a wok, add the oil, and heat. Add the cabbage and stir-fry for 2 minutes, making sure that all the cabbage has a thin coating of oil. Remove the wok from the heat and stir in the sauce. Serve warm or cold.

Lemon-Olive Coleslaw

4 to 6 servings

1 small head cabbage, grated
1 small onion, finely chopped
½ cup sliced olives
½ cup chopped celery
½ cup yogurt cheese (page xx)
2 tablespoons lemon juice
½ teaspoon dry mustard

Combine the cabbage, onion, and olives. In a separate bowl, combine the remaining ingredients; mix with cabbage. Chill and serve

Salad 16 Days Out

4 servings

The name of this recipe says it all! I created this salad from what was left on the boat after 16 days away from a grocery store. (When produce is stored at room temperature, it can get very dehydrated. This is a great way to rejuvenate tired greens.)

4 leaves napa cabbage, chopped
½ cup chopped red cabbage
1 seedless cucumber, peeled and chopped
½ yellow bell pepper, chopped
½ red bell pepper, chopped
1 carrot, chopped
1 cup assorted sprouts: clover, sunflower, mung bean

Clean and cut up all the ingredients, sprinkle with cold water, and toss into a Ziploc bag. Store for a minimum of 20 minutes in the refrigerator to crisp. Serve with your favorite dressing.

Greek Salad

8 servings

We had been cruising with the same group of boats for several days, going ashore most nights for a potluck. As the provisions got sparser, it became more of a challenge to fix something different each night. When it was my turn to make a salad I found I still had a package of feta cheese in the refrigerator, so I made this version of a Greek salad.

2 cups each napa, purple, and green cabbage, chopped
3 carrots, chopped
6 sliced Roma tomatoes
1 (4 oz.) can sliced black olives
1 (6 oz.) jar marinated artichoke hearts
1 (8 oz.) jar red bell peppers
3 ounces feta cheese

1. Sprinkle the cabbage and carrots with water and chill in a Ziploc bag until crisp.
2. For the nicest presentation of this salad, use a dish with a large circumference. (I have a 9×13-inch covered, unbreakable casserole that I use to take food ashore.) Place the cabbage and carrots in the dish and arrange the tomatoes, olives, artichoke hearts, and bell peppers over the top. Sprinkle with crumbled feta cheese.
3. For a dressing, use the marinade from the artichoke hearts or try the Lemon Garlic Dressing (page 174).

Puerto Gato Salad with Raisins and Cheese

4 to 6 servings

We were going ashore for a trash-burning ceremony when we noticed that another boat had anchored in Puerto Gato. The folks on board had flown down from the States, picked up their boat in La Paz, and were cruising for a few weeks in the Sea of Cortez. We decided to join forces for dinner and Pat made the following salad, which had an interesting combination of ingredients—including some stateside lettuce!

½ head iceberg lettuce
½ cup grated cheddar cheese
¼ cup raisins
2 tomatoes
1 can kidney beans, drained and rinsed
1 recipe Dijon Vinaigrette Dressing (page 174)

Combine all the ingredients and toss with the dressing.

Cabbage and Mint Salad

4 servings

Hal and I once found fresh mint growing in a cove near Cabo San Lucas and, after enjoying mint juleps, I saved the rest for salads. Two weeks after our last provisioning stop, I was out of most fresh veggies, but the mint was still surviving. This simple salad, with the addition of the fresh mint, became a memorable dish. I've made it often since.

2 cups chopped napa cabbage
1 cup chopped purple cabbage
3 Roma tomatoes, diced
½ small white onion, minced
½ cup fresh mint leaves, minced

If the cabbage is limp, sprinkle it with water and crisp it in the refrigerator in a Ziploc bag for 20 minutes. Combine the remaining ingredients and serve with a little squeeze of fresh lime juice or some seasoned rice vinegar.

Cucumber Salad with Mint-Yogurt Dressing

6 servings

2 hothouse cucumbers*
¼ cup chopped fresh mint or 2 tablespoons dried mint, crumbled
¼ cup unflavored yogurt

Thinly slice the unpeeled cucumbers. Combine the mint with the yogurt and mix with the cucumbers. Allow to marinate for 30 minutes before serving.

**I use hothouse cucumbers when I can get them because they are sweeter tasting and the skin is more tender than other varieties of cucumbers. I also like the fact that they are seedless—some people refer to them as burpless cucumbers.*

Oriental Cucumber Salad

4 servings

This is a refreshing salad that can accompany a stir-fried main course. For a special treat, add a can of bay shrimp or crab meat.

2 medium cucumbers, peeled, cut lengthwise, seeds removed
2 tablespoons rice wine vinegar
2 tablespoons soy sauce
1 teaspoon sugar
⅛ teaspoon ground white pepper
1 tablespoon sesame oil

Slice the cucumbers in ¼-inch thick slices. Combine the remaining ingredients and chill for 1 hour or less.

Orange, Jicama, and Cilantro Salad

4 to 6 servings

1 small red onion, finely chopped
1 small jicama, peeled and finely chopped
¾ cup cilantro leaves
6 oranges, peeled and thinly sliced
⅛ teaspoon cayenne pepper

Sprinkle the onion, jicama, and cilantro evenly over the sliced oranges. Season with cayenne pepper.

Chinese Chicken Salad

6 servings

Dressing

1 tablespoon sugar
2 teaspoons finely chopped ginger*
3 tablespoons rice vinegar
2 tablespoons Oriental sesame oil
¼ cup vegetable oil
1 teaspoon salt
⅛ teaspoon white pepper

2 whole chicken breasts
⅔ cup fresh ginger*
½ onion
Oil for deep frying (approximately 4 cups)
2 ounces rice sticks (or substitute 2 cups chow mein noodles)
½ cup slivered almonds
¼ cup sesame seeds
1 medium head napa cabbage, chopped (or half napa and half purple cabbage)
6 green onions, thinly sliced
2 carrots, cut into thin strips

1. Combine the dressing ingredients and set aside.
2. Cook the chicken in 2 cups of simmering water flavored with the ginger and onion for about 30 minutes. When cool enough to handle, debone, discard skin, and cut into strips.
3. Heat the oil in a wok (375° F). Break up the rice sticks into small pieces and cook in the hot oil in small batches until the rice sticks puff up. Drain and set aside.
4. Toast the almonds and sesame seeds on a baking sheet at 300° F until golden—approximately 20 minutes.
5. Assemble the salad in a large salad bowl by combining the cabbage, nuts, green onions, carrots, and chicken. Toss with the dressing and mix well. Scatter the rice sticks on top just before serving.

**Fresh ginger keeps for up to one year without refrigeration in a container of dry sherry. I peel and slice the ginger before storing so it is convenient to use. Use the leftover sherry in marinades.*

Do-Ahead Tip

The rice sticks and nuts can be prepared up to a week in advance and stored in airtight containers.

Spicy Thai Salad with Roasted Peanuts and Cilantro

4 servings

Dressing

5 large garlic cloves
1 seeded red chile pepper
¼ cup fresh lime juice
1 tablespoon sugar
1 tablespoon *nam pla* (Oriental fish sauce) or soy sauce
¼ cup chopped cilantro

1 head napa cabbage, chopped
1 large cucumber, peeled, seeded, and cut into ½-inch cubes
1 cup mung bean sprouts
¼ cup finely ground roasted peanuts
1 sliced hard cooked egg
¼ teaspoon cayenne pepper

1. Make the dressing by finely chopping the garlic and chile pepper. Combine with the lime juice, sugar, fish sauce, and cilantro.
2. Pour the dressing over the cabbage and cucumber and toss gently. Sprinkle the sprouts and peanuts on top.
3. Garnish with the sliced egg and a sprinkling of cayenne pepper.

BLACK BEAN SALAD WITH GARLIC SOY DRESSING

6 to 8 servings

Marinated bean salads are healthy and easy to fix. This recipe, though, is a delightful change of pace from that run-of-the-mill three bean salad that's so popular at potlucks.

Keeping fresh bell peppers on board for any length of time can be a problem, so I always try to keep several jars of marinated peppers on hand for backup use. I also like to keep several varieties of mustard on board (forget that bright yellow stuff!). By the way—I've never refrigerated mustard in my life and it has never gone bad, despite what the labels say. Just don't put a dirty spoon in the container or you'll contaminate the contents.

If you don't have all the garnish ingredients listed for this recipe, leave them out or improvise. No problema!

3 (15 oz. each) cans black beans, rinsed and drained
1 red bell pepper, chopped
1 yellow bell pepper, chopped
⅔ cup chopped red or green onions
1 recipe Garlic Soy Dressing (page 174)

Garnish

Minced jalapeño peppers
Chopped cilantro
Halved cherry tomatoes

Pour the dressing over the beans, bell peppers, and onions. Allow to marinate for at least an hour. Serve slightly chilled or at room temperature. Garnish if desired.

CORN, RED PEPPER, BLACK BEAN, AND FETA CHEESE SALAD

6 to 8 servings

This is a great salad to make when all of your fresh produce is gone. The dressing is made with ingredients you probably have on board. Use two tablespoons more vinegar if you don't have a lime; if you don't have any fresh cilantro, double the amount of dried tarragon.

1 (8 oz.) can garbanzo beans, drained and rinsed
1 (8 oz.) can pinto or black beans, drained and rinsed
2 (8 oz. each) cans corn, drained and rinsed
1 (8 oz.) jar roasted red peppers, drained and chopped
¼ cup crumbled feta cheese
1 recipe Tarragon Cilantro Dressing (page 174)

Combine the beans, corn, and red pepper in a salad bowl and toss with the dressing. Sprinkle with cheese.

Carrots

Carrots are the ideal boat vegetable. They keep for weeks without refrigeration, add color to a plate, can be served either cooked or raw, and provide many nutritional benefits. If they are somewhat limp, clean, cut, and place them in the refrigerator in a Ziploc bag with a little water for 1 hour.

Honey Glazed Carrots

2 to 4 servings

½ pound carrots, cleaned and sliced
2 tablespoons butter
1 tablespoon honey or 2 tablespoons brown sugar
Salt and pepper

Steam the carrots in a small amount of liquid until tender. Drain well. Add the butter and honey or sugar, season with salt and pepper, and cook until the sugar dissolves.

Variation
Carrots with Marsala Wine

Substitute a ½ cup of Marsala wine for the honey. Sauté the carrots in the butter, add the wine, salt, and pepper. Cover and allow to steam until tender.

Carrots with Mint

2 to 4 servings

Seasoning Sauce

2 tablespoons red wine vinegar
1 teaspoon finely chopped garlic
3 tablespoons chopped fresh mint or 1 tablespoon dried
Salt and pepper to taste
½ pound carrots, cleaned and sliced
1 tablespoon olive oil
¼ cup chicken broth

1. Combine all the seasoning sauce ingredients; set aside.
2. Stir-fry the carrots in the oil for 4 minutes. Add the chicken broth to the pan, cover, and simmer until the carrots are tender—about 10 to 15 minutes. Drain well and mix with the seasoning sauce.

Variation
Ginger Carrots

Stir-fry 1 tablespoon of chopped fresh ginger with the carrots. Substitute 3 tablespoons of orange juice, 2 teaspoons of sherry, and 1 tablespoon of soy sauce for the chicken broth.

Carrots Chinese-Style

2 to 4 servings

1 pound carrots, cleaned and sliced
2 teaspoons finely chopped garlic
2 teaspoons finely chopped ginger
½ teaspoon dried red pepper flakes
1 tablespoon fermented black beans, mashed
1 tablespoon vegetable oil
⅓ cup chicken broth plus 2 tablespoons
1 tablespoon soy sauce
1 tablespoon rice wine vinegar
2 teaspoons cornstarch

1. Sauté the carrots, garlic, ginger, red pepper, and black beans in the oil for 2 minutes.
2. Add ⅓ cup of chicken broth, the soy sauce and vinegar. Cover and simmer for 5 minutes.
3. Combine the remaining chicken broth and the cornstarch and add to pan. Cook until the sauce thickens slightly.

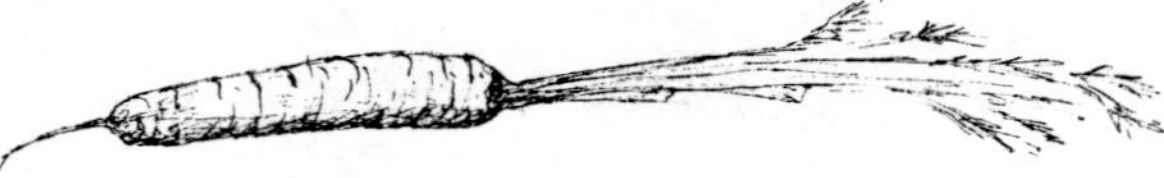

Peppers and Chiles

I love peppers—from mild red and yellow to the incendiary chiles found in New Mexican and some Latin cuisines. The jalapeño chile is the logo for my boat *Spice-Sea,* which should be testimony in itself to my fondness for the more fiery types of peppers. Peppers keep fairly well on board without refrigeration for several days, and their shelf life can be further extended by roasting them and storing them in the refrigerator.

A favorite hors d'oeuvre of mine is roasted and peeled bell peppers that have been sliced and sprinkled with chopped garlic and olive oil. One of my favorite dinners is Chile Relleños—roasted, mild chiles that are stuffed with seafood, cheese, or chopped meat. The addition of a couple of roasted hot chiles to a Mexican salsa changes its flavor from the mundane to the magnificent.

To roast peppers

Most boat ovens don't have good broilers, but if yours is the exception, lay the peppers on a baking sheet and, turning frequently, broil 3 to 4 inches from the heat source until they are blistered on all sides.

You can also place the peppers on a wire rack over your stove burner. Turn the peppers frequently until they are blistered and charred on all sides. This is my preferred method when I need just a couple of chiles for a salsa recipe. Doing many peppers in this fashion, though, takes a lot of time and really heats up the galley.

When you have lots of peppers to be peeled, place them on a baking sheet uncovered in a 450°F oven for about 25 minutes, turning them several times until the skins are brown and blistered.

My favorite method for roasting peppers takes some advance planning, but is definitely the easiest. The night before I need the peppers, I instruct Hal that he'll be barbecuing our dinner. Before he starts to cook, I hand him the peppers and he roasts them outside on the barbecue while sipping a glass of wine and enjoying the sunset.

To peel a pepper

No matter which method of roasting you choose, the peppers should be placed in a brown paper bag, a plastic bag, or a covered bowl to steam for 15 minutes after they've been roasted. The skin will loosen and it's easy to remove the peel with the tip of your knife or your fingers.

To seed a pepper

If the peppers are to be stuffed, carefully slit open one side and remove the seeds. If they are to be diced or used in strips, cut in half and scrape out any seeds. Pat dry with a paper towel.

Chiles

A member of the capsicum family, chiles add flavor and heat to many of the world's cuisines. While often referred to as peppers, chile peppers bear no resemblance to the bell pepper in flavor. The heat from a chile comes from its fleshy white interior veins—not from the seeds. You can reduce the amount of a chile's heat by removing its veins. Most people find that the more chiles they consume, the more addicted to spicy food they become.

Uncooked sauces (salsas) call for fresh chiles, while cooked sauces often make use of dried. When you cannot find fresh chiles, and need some spice for a recipe, substitute crushed dried red chiles, cayenne pepper, or Tabasco sauce.

If your palette cannot tolerate a lot of spiciness, try substituting green bell peppers for half the amount of chiles. For example, if a recipe calls for 6 diced serrano chiles, try using 3 chiles and ¼ cup of chopped bell pepper.

How to handle chiles

It's a good idea to wear rubber gloves to protect your hands when handling chiles. It's not at all uncommon for people with sensitive skin to break out in a rash after coming in contact

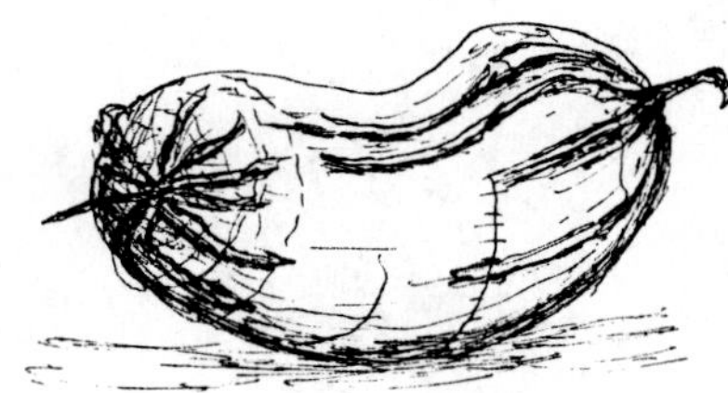

with capsaicin, the colorless irritant found in chiles. Never rub your face or touch your eyes after handling chiles, and avoid inhaling their aroma while grinding or frying them—the fumes from a fresh chile can get into your lungs and make it difficult to breathe.

Types of chiles

- Mild Green Chiles (Anaheims) are very often sold in cans and are usually toasted and peeled before eating due to their tough outer skin. Anaheim chiles are long (6 to 8 inches) and narrow. They are ideal for chile relleños, although in Mexico a poblano chile is used. When dried, Anaheim chiles are called "California." They are not to be confused with their cousin, the New Mexican chile, which is much hotter.
- Poblanos are mild green chiles found in Latin markets. They are almost triangular in shape—a cross between a bell pepper and an Anaheim in appearance—and measure about 3 to 5 inches in length. They are usually toasted and peeled before eating because of their tough outer skin. When dried, poblanos are called "ancho" or, mistakenly, "pasilla," and often you will see them mislabeled in the produce market.
- Serranos are thin hot chiles 2 to 3 inches long that are common in Thai and Mexican cuisines. They are usually sold when they are green; they turn a bright red when ripe. You can substitute jalapeños for serranos, if necessary.
- Jalapeños are glossy green chiles that are slightly milder than serranos and have more pulp. They are usually about 3 inches long and much bigger in diameter. They are often served pickled *(escabeche)* or smoked and dried *(chipolte)*. They are usually sold when they are green; they turn a bright red when ripe. Chipotle chiles are often canned in adobo (tomato-based) sauce and add a wonderfully rich, smoky flavor to foods. Use them sparingly—they are very hot.
- Habanero or Scotch Bonnets are fiery chiles common in the Caribbean and Yucatan. They look like small green bell peppers, vary in color from orangish red to green, and are hot! hot! hot! You can substitute serranos or jalapeños.
- Dried Red Chile Peppers are sold whole, crushed (flakes), or powdered (cayenne pepper). These small red chiles are common in Italian and Chinese cooking and store indefinitely.
- Chili Powder, like curry powder, is a blend of several spices. Although the primary ingredient is powdered red chiles, cumin, oregano, garlic, and salt are usually added. It is relatively mild compared with its unadulterated counterpart.

Roasted Pepper and Mozzarella Salad

4 servings

4 roasted, peeled, and seeded bell peppers (red and yellow)
½ recipe Anchovy Sauce (page 142), omitting the anchovies
½ cup grated mozzarella cheese
Salt and pepper to taste

Mix all the ingredients together; marinate for at least 30 minutes before serving.

Chile Relleños

Chile peppers can be filled with many different stuffings and baked, fried, or served cold. The mild poblano chile (sometimes called chile ancho) that is available in Latin American markets is a good size for stuffing. The Anaheim (California) chile can be substituted, as can a bell pepper.

Try stuffing roasted, peeled peppers with tuna fish salad and serving them chilled with a tomatillo sauce. Poblano chiles stuffed with guacamole make a lovely presentation and can be served with a light vinaigrette sauce. For a spicy appetizer, try using jalapeños. For a delicious main course, chiles can be stuffed with a flavorful mixture of ground meat and baked in a tomato sauce.

Cheese-Stuffed Chile Relleños

4 servings

4 poblano or Anaheim chiles, roasted, peeled, and seeded (or 4 whole canned chiles)
4 ounces jack or Chihuahua cheese, cut into 1-ounce strips
2 eggs, separated
⅓ cup flour
½ cup cooking oil
1 recipe Spanish Tomato Sauce (page 171)

1. Place a strip of cheese inside each chile and close the opening with a toothpick. If the chiles are particularly large you may want to use more cheese. You can also grate the cheese and add 2 minced tomatillos and 2 chopped green onions to the cheese.
2. Beat the egg whites until stiff. Fold in the yolks.
3. Roll each chile in flour and then dip in egg mixture.
4. Carefully lower the chiles into hot (375° F) oil and fry until the egg mixture is golden.
5. Place warm tomato sauce on each plate and top with a chile.

Crab-Stuffed Chile Relleños with Curried Papaya Salsa

4 servings

1 cup crab meat (imitation crab works great)
1 cup shredded jack cheese
½ cup mayonnaise
2 teaspoons lime juice
¼ teaspoon Tabasco
Salt and pepper to taste
4 poblano or Anaheim chiles, roasted, peeled, and seeded (or 4 whole canned chiles)
2 eggs, separated
⅓ cup flour
½ cup cooking oil
1 recipe Curried Papaya Salsa (page 166)

1. Combine the crab, cheese, mayonnaise, lime juice, hot sauce, salt, and pepper. Stuff the chiles and secure the opening with toothpicks if necessary.
2. Beat the egg whites until stiff. Fold in the yolks.
3. Roll each chile in flour and then dip in egg mixture.
4. Carefully lower the chiles into hot (375° F) oil and fry until the egg mixture is golden.
5. Serve with Curried Papaya Salsa.

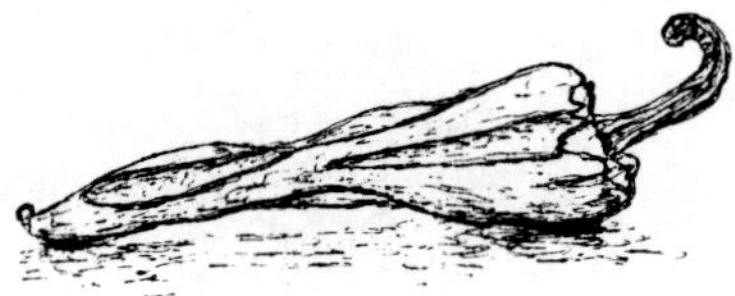

Eggplant

When I have been lucky enough to find really fresh eggplant, I've been able to keep it as long as three weeks without refrigeration if it's kept wrapped in paper to prevent bruising.

In the States we see mainly large eggplants that often tend to be watery. Small Japanese eggplants are great on the barbecue, and the tiny pea-sized Thai eggplant are good in curries.

Baked Eggplant

2 to 4 servings

1 medium eggplant, cut into ¼-inch slices
Salt
½ cup fresh basil packed in olive oil (page 170)
1 teaspoon finely chopped garlic
1 cup tomato purée
¼ teaspoon crushed red pepper
Salt and pepper to taste
Parmesan cheese

1. Salt the eggplant and allow to drain in a colander for 45 minutes. Rinse and dry. Using the olive oil that covered the basil, brush both sides of the eggplant and place on a baking sheet. Bake at 375° F for 30 minutes or until tender, turning once.
2. Make the tomato sauce by simmering the garlic, tomato purée, and red pepper until thick. Stir in the basil and season with salt and pepper. (Or substitute some leftover Italian Tomato Sauce—see page 171.)
3. Spread the tomato sauce on the cooled eggplant and sprinkle with Parmesan cheese.

Variation
Eggplant with Anchovy Sauce

2 to 4 servings

1 medium eggplant, cut into ¼-inch slices
Salt
1 teaspoon finely chopped garlic
¼ cup olive oil
1 can anchovies, mashed
2 tablespoons chopped fresh parsley
2 tablespoons red wine vinegar

Prepare the eggplant as directed in step 1 for Baked Eggplant. Sauté the garlic in the olive oil, add the anchovies, and turn off the heat. Add the parsley and vinegar. Sprinkle this mixture evenly over the eggplant and marinate at room temperature for 30 minutes before serving.

Eggplant Caviar

1 medium eggplant, steamed until soft—about 30 minutes
2 teaspoons garlic, finely chopped
Salt and pepper to taste
2 tablespoons lemon juice
3 tablespoons olive oil

To determine when the eggplant is done, stick a skewer into the inside. When cool enough to handle, cut it in half and scoop out the flesh. Discard the seeds. Mash the eggplant with the garlic, salt, and pepper. Season with the lemon juice and olive oil. Use as a spread on crackers or as a sauce on pizza.

Garlic

"Double the garlic" is one of my favorite instructions when teaching a cooking class. As far as I'm concerned, there is no such thing as too much garlic. These recipes will attest to this philosophy. A word of caution, though. Be sure everyone on your boat is partaking of these wonderful garlic-laden dishes!

Always try to buy fresh, firm heads of garlic—they'll keep for two to three months, so there is no reason not to have a large supply on hand.

One of the things I enjoy about cooking and cruising is talking with other boat cooks who are anxious to share dishes that work well for them on their boats. I recently spent some time talking with my friend Toni about some of her favorite boat recipes. She is Italian and has an ingrained sense of good cooking—probably passed down through generations of southern Italian cooks. Toni spends many weeks each year living on her boat at Catalina Island and shared with me some of her easier dishes that have the kind of robust flavor that boaters seem to appreciate.

Toni's Roasted Red Peppers with Garlic and Tomatoes

4 servings as a side dish or appetizer

1 (15 oz.) jar seasoned roasted red peppers
5 ripe Roma tomatoes, coarsely chopped
6 cloves garlic, minced
2 tablespoons good quality olive oil
Crackers or crusty bread

Arrange the peppers with their juices in a dish. Top with the tomatoes and sprinkle with garlic. Dress with the olive oil. Serve at room temperature with crackers or bread. Messy, but delicious.

Toni's Garlic Soup

4 servings

The first time I tasted this soul warming soup was in the rain at a yacht club function at Catalina. We set up tarps over the barbecue area and Toni passed out bowls of this soup to warm our chilled bodies. Toni says her mother always made this soup when someone in the family was coming down with a cold. It certainly beats aspirin!

4 cups water
1 large head garlic (14 to 16 cloves), cloves smashed and peeled
⅓ cup olive oil
1 can (14 ½ oz.) Italian plum tomatoes (crushed)
1 tablespoon ground black pepper
1 cup small pasta such as acini di pepe (seed shaped), orzo (rice-shaped), or angel hair (broken in small pieces)

Bring the water to a boil and add the garlic and olive oil. Bring back to a boil and add the tomatoes and black pepper. Boil the soup vigorously for about 15 minutes—until it has slightly reduced in volume and begins to thicken. Add the pasta and cook until tender. Serve immediately.

Roasted Garlic

4 servings as an appetizer or side dish

A whole head of garlic per person? Yes! When cooked for an hour, the garlic becomes delightfully mild and nutty.

4 heads garlic
Salt and pepper
½ teaspoon thyme
2 tablespoons olive oil
½ cup white wine

1. Remove any loose papery skin from the garlic heads and trim across the top, exposing a little of the garlic. Place the whole heads in a baking dish and sprinkle the top with the salt, pepper, and thyme; drizzle with the olive oil. Pour in the wine.
2. Tightly seal the top of dish with foil and bake at 350° F for 1 hour or until the garlic is very soft. (You can also eliminate the dish, wrap the garlic in foil, and bake in the oven or on the barbecue.)
3. Serve each person a head of garlic with some crusty bread. Squeeze the garlic on the bread and enjoy.

Note: If you want to make a luscious, but easy, sauce, purée the whole heads of garlic (including the skin) with the pan juices and some chicken broth. Strain and heat. Great served over chicken, beef, or pork.

Onions

Onions are the mainstay of many recipes but are often overlooked as vegetable dishes by themselves. Try placing unpeeled onions, root ends down, in a foil lined baking dish. Bake at 400° F for one hour or until soft. Cut open the tops of the onions and drizzle with garlic flavored olive oil.

When our yacht club has a potluck, one of the members always throws a couple of dozen onions onto the coals. We peel away the skins and enjoy the smoky flavor of perfectly cooked onions.

Onions can be hollowed out and stuffed with many great combinations. My Spanish teacher in Guatemala suggested cooking a mixture of ground pork flavored with chopped almonds, olives, chopped onion, and a little tomato paste. Make a stuffing by mixing together some grated mozzarella, Parmesan, and enough bread crumbs until the stuffing holds its shape. Fill the onions with the mixture and bake at 350° F for 45 minutes.

Potatoes, Sweet Potatoes, and Yams

I use potatoes frequently on the boat and often cook more than I need for dinner so that I have leftovers to fry with onions in a little olive oil for breakfast, or to use in potato salad.

A medium-sized potato takes about an hour to bake in the oven or about 20 minutes (for two) in a microwave. (Wrap them in microwave-proof plastic.)

Yams and sweet potatoes are wonderfully nutritious and keep well on a boat. Our friends on *Nordic* mash the pulp of yams and mix with some fresh orange juice for an outstanding and tasty vegetable.

Italian Potato Salad

4 servings

Small red potatoes are my favorites to use for potato salad; they should be cooked in boiling salted water until tender—about 20 minutes.

1 pound cooked potatoes, thinly sliced
2 tablespoons capers
6 anchovy fillets, chopped
½ cup chopped bell pepper, preferably yellow or red
½ cup chopped celery
3 tablespoons chopped red onion

Dressing

3 tablespoons olive oil
1 tablespoon white wine vinegar
¼ teaspoon dried oregano
Salt and pepper to taste

Combine the potatoes, capers, anchovies, bell pepper, celery, and red onion; set aside. Combine the dressing ingredients and toss with the potatoes. Serve at room temperature.

Variation

Combine the potatoes with ⅓ cup of chopped green onions, 3 tablespoons of olive oil, and freshly ground black pepper. Be sure to leave the red peel on the potatoes.

Delicious Scalloped Potatoes

6 to 8 servings

Scalloped potatoes are an easy and inexpensive dish for potluck suppers. Use nonfat or regular milk, half and half, or cream, depending on your caloric desire.

3 cups sliced onion
2 tablespoons olive oil
3 pounds boiling potatoes (white, rose or red skinned), peeled and sliced
1 ½ cups milk
1 clove garlic, finely chopped
¼ teaspoon Italian herbs
Salt and pepper

Sauté the onions in the olive oil until soft. In a 9 × 13-inch oiled baking dish, layer the potatoes and onions. Cover with the milk, garlic, herbs, salt, and pepper. Bake at 400° F for 40 minutes.

Variation
Cheesy Potatoes

Substitute chicken broth for the milk and add 2 cups of grated Jarlsberg cheese to the layers of onions and potatoes. Sprinkle some remaining cheese on top.

Breadfruit and Plantains

Breadfruit are large green fruits that hang lantern-like from trees. The cooking time for breadfruit (they can't be eaten raw) depends on their size and ripeness. They taste like potatoes and can be substituted in any potato recipe. Try breadfruit scalloped, stuffed, fried, or in salads.

FRIED BREADFRUIT

4 servings

1 slightly underripe breadfruit, boiled in salted water for 15 minutes
Cooking oil for frying
Salt and pepper to taste

Peel and core the parboiled breadfruit. Slice in ¼-inch thick slices. Heat 2 inches of oil in a wok to 375° F and fry the slices until golden. Season with salt and pepper.

BREADFRUIT VINAIGRETTE

4 servings

1 ripe breadfruit, boiled in salted water for 40 minutes or until tender
4 slices chopped bacon
1 onion, chopped
¼ cup vinegar
¼ cup olive oil
Salt and pepper to taste

Peel and slice the cooked breadfruit. Fry the bacon and onion together. Drain well and mix with the vinegar and oil. Pour the mixture over warm breadfruit, season with salt and pepper, and serve.

CURRIED PLANTAINS

4 servings

1 tablespoon curry powder
2 tablespoons butter
4 plantains, peeled and sliced
½ teaspoon salt
½ teaspoon pepper
1 ½ cups coconut milk

Cook the curry powder in the butter for 2 minutes. Add the plantains and sauté until golden. Season with salt and pepper and add the coconut milk. Simmer on low for 30 minutes.

MASHED PLANTAINS

4 servings

4 plantains, peeled and quartered
½ cup wine vinegar
½ cup lime juice
2 tablespoons butter
¼ teaspoon cinnamon
Pinch of nutmeg
Pinch of cayenne pepper
Salt and pepper to taste

Simmer the plantains with the vinegar and lime juice, covered, on low heat, until tender—about 30 minutes. Mash with a fork and add the butter, cinnamon, nutmeg, cayenne, salt, and pepper.

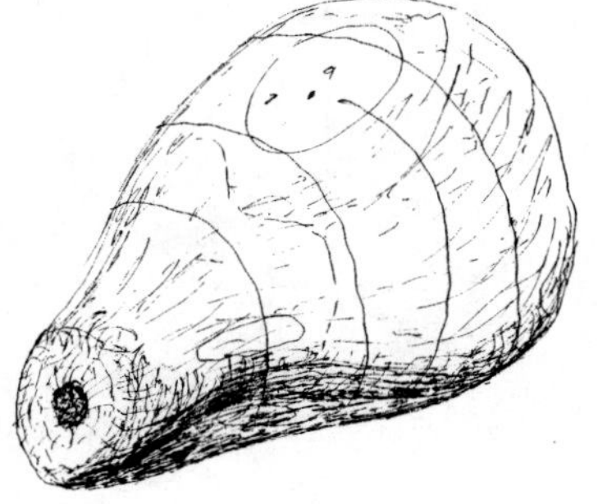

Papaya

I love the taste of a sweet, ripe papaya (*pawpaw* in some parts of the world). Served with a little fresh lime juice squeezed over the flesh, it's my favorite fruit.

Unripened papaya makes a delicious cooked vegetable and tastes quite different from the ripened fruit. I first experimented with using papaya as a vegetable after dropping one of the large Mexican varieties and smashing in one of the sides. I knew that the damaged papaya could never ripen, so I peeled it, removed the seeds, (they're delicious when ground up and added to a salad dressing), and diced the undamaged flesh into cubes before cooking it.

Even papayas that are green on the outside have a nice orange meat on the inside, which retains the color when cooked. My friend Diane aboard the vessel *Sorcery* says that her husband, Clyde, likes the flavor of cooked papaya better than carrots. She usually sautés some finely chopped onion and garlic, adds a little hot sauce and whatever meat is leftover from the previous night's dinner, tosses everything with some diced and peeled papaya, covers the pan, and cooks the ingredients for about 10 minutes. Served over rice, it's a great way to use up leftovers.

Sautéed Green Papaya

6 servings

1 cup chopped onions
3 tablespoons cooking oil
3 cups peeled and diced green papaya
1 (24 oz.) can chopped tomatoes, drained
¼ teaspoon ground cumin
Salt and freshly ground black pepper

Sauté the onions in the oil until translucent. Add all the remaining ingredients, reduce the heat, and cover. Cook over moderate heat until the papaya is tender. Uncover the pan and, stirring frequently, cook until most of the liquid has evaporated.

Variation
Stuffed Green Papaya

4 servings

2 (1 lb. each) papayas, boiled for 30 minutes
1 cup chopped onions
1 (24 oz.) can chopped tomatoes, drained
¼ ounce ground cumin
Salt and freshly ground black pepper
Bread crumbs
Melted butter

Cut the papayas in half (reserve the shells), remove the seeds, and scoop out the pulp. Sauté the pulp with the onions, tomatoes, cumin, salt, and pepper. Pile the stuffing back in the empty papaya shells, sprinkle with dry bread crumbs, and drizzle with a little melted butter. Bake at 375° F for 20 minutes. (Chopped, cooked meat can also be added to the stuffing.)

Papaya and Avocado Salad

6 servings

4 cups finely slivered purple cabbage
1 large ripe avocado, peeled and sliced into 18 slices
18 slices peeled papaya
1 recipe Papaya Seed Dressing (page 175)

Arrange the fruit slices over the cabbage and spoon on the dressing.

Variation
Papaya Slaw
6 servings

2 cups chopped cabbage
1 cup diced papaya
2 chopped tomatoes
5 grated carrots
½ recipe Papaya Seed Dressing (page 175)

Combine all the ingredients and mix with the dressing.

Sorcery's Papaya Chutney
6 cups

1 tablespoon finely chopped fresh ginger
1 tablespoon finely chopped garlic
1 tablespoon finely chopped citrus peel
1 cup vinegar
1 ½ cups sugar
1 tablespoon hot sauce, or to taste
½ teaspoon cloves
½ teaspoon cinnamon
4 cups firm papaya, peeled and coarsely chopped

1. Combine the ginger, garlic, citrus peel, vinegar, and sugar in a saucepan and bring to a boil.
2. Add the hot sauce, cloves, cinnamon, and papaya and simmer until the sauce thickens.
3. Serve on the side with rice as an accompaniment to seafood, meat, or poultry. This keeps without refrigeration for several months.

Green Papaya Salad
4 servings

This intriguing salad is from Thailand and is perfect when you despair of your papayas ever ripening. The Thais make this salad in a deep mortar, but you could use a salad bowl, crushing the ingredients together with a pestle.

½ cup shredded green papaya
1 tablespoon tamarind pulp, dissolved with 2 tablespoons lime juice
4 red serrano chiles, seeded and chopped
2 cloves garlic
2 long beans, cut into 2-inch pieces
¼ cup dried shrimp
1 tablespoon brown sugar
2 tablespoons dry roasted unsalted peanuts
2 tomatoes, diced
2 tablespoons fish sauce
¼ teaspoon salt

Gradually add to the mortar the ingredients in the order listed, crushing and stirring until they reach the desired consistency.

Variation

This variation also uses green papayas, some more familiar ingredients, and doesn't need to be pounded with a pestle.

4 very green papayas, peeled and shredded

½ pound jicama, peeled and shredded
4 green onions, thinly sliced

Dressing

1 tablespoon vegetable oil
3 tablespoons lime juice
2 cloves garlic, finely chopped
2 tablespoons fish sauce or soy sauce
2 tablespoons brown sugar
3 tablespoons chunky peanut butter
¼ teaspoon black pepper
½ teaspoon red chile flakes

Gently heat all the dressing ingredients so that the sugar melts and the peanut butter is well combined. Allow to cool before pouring over the salad ingredients.

GAZPACHO

6 cups

In small-capacity boat refrigerators, gazpacho is an ideal way to store fresh vegetables. Once they are pureed they take up less space and are not subject to bruising or dehydration. If you add a couple of tablespoons of vinegar to gazpacho, it will keep in the refrigerator for about three weeks. When I'm short on space, I purée the vegetables and add everything but the tomato juice. Just before serving I open a can of chilled juice and add it to the vegetables.

1 clove garlic, finely chopped
3 pounds tomatoes, peeled and cut in chunks
1 small onion, peeled and quartered
½ bell pepper, seeded and quartered
1 cucumber, peeled, cut in half lengthwise, seeded, and cut in chunks
½ teaspoon ground cumin
1 teaspoon salt or to taste
Freshly ground black pepper
½ cup olive oil
½ cup white wine vinegar
2 cups tomato or V-8 juice

Garnishes
(use some or all the following)

½ cup finely chopped green onion
½ cup finely chopped bell pepper
½ cup finely chopped cucumber
Garlic croûtons (made from crustless white bread cubes sautéed in garlic and olive oil until golden)

Finely chop the vegetables. Add the remaining ingredients. Pass the garnishes.

WHITE GAZPACHO WITH SUNFLOWER SEEDS

6 to 8 servings

This is a deliciously refreshing summertime soup that should keep for about three weeks depending on the expiration dates for the yogurt and sour cream.

1 clove garlic
3 medium cucumbers, peeled, seeded, and cut into eighths
1 cup sour cream
1 cup low fat yogurt
1 ½ cups chicken broth
1 tablespoon white vinegar
½ teaspoon salt
1 teaspoon white pepper

Garnishes
(use some or all the following)

¼ cup toasted sunflower seeds
1 cup diced tomatoes
½ cup chopped scallions
¼ cup chopped parsley or cilantro

1. Mince the garlic in a food processor or blender. Add the cucumbers and process until smooth. Combine with the sour cream, yogurt, broth, vinegar, salt, and pepper. When using a small capacity food processor, combine the ingredients in small batches.
2. Refrigerate the soup until it's thoroughly chilled. Serve in small bowls and pass the garnishes.

MEDITERRANEAN VEGETABLE SOUP

6 servings

1 onion, chopped
3 cloves garlic, minced
2 tablespoons olive oil
1 (28 oz.) can Italian-style plum tomatoes, cut up
1 (15 oz.) can tomato sauce
1 ½ cups beef broth
1 (10 oz.) package frozen chopped spinach, thawed
1 (9 oz.) package frozen cut green beans, thawed
1 large carrot, sliced
1 teaspoon oregano
6 ounces feta cheese

1. In a Dutch oven, sauté the onions and garlic in the olive oil for about 3 minutes. Add all the remaining ingredients *except* the cheese and bring to a boil. Reduce the heat and simmer for 20 minutes.
2. Top each serving with feta cheese.

Spinach and Callaloo

I frequently bring a couple of containers of frozen chopped spinach to the boat. They store easily and are good additions to omelettes and soufflés. (We also like creamed spinach.) Even if you don't have a freezer, boxes of frozen spinach will keep in the refrigerator for a couple of days—just be sure to store them in something that will catch the water as it drains out. If you are short on space, thaw the spinach, squeeze it dry, and store it in a Ziploc bag. It will keep for a week in the refrigerator.

If you are fortunate to be cruising in the Caribbean or the South Pacific, you can substitute callaloo, the fresh green leaves of the taro plant, for spinach. Although fresh spinach can cook in its own water, callaloo is much drier. Add 1 cup of water for each cup of callaloo leaves that you substitute for spinach.

Spinach Rockefeller

6 servings

1 onion, finely chopped
3 tablespoons olive oil
2 (10 oz. each) packages frozen chopped spinach, thawed and drained
2 teaspoons thyme
½ teaspoon cayenne pepper
Salt and pepper
4 eggs
½ cup Parmesan cheese
¾ cup bread crumbs
3 large tomatoes, peeled and cut in half

1. Sauté the onion in the olive oil. Add the spinach, thyme, cayenne, salt, and pepper. Cook until the spinach is tender and all the liquid has evaporated.
2. Remove the pan from the heat and stir in the eggs, cheese, and bread crumbs.
3. Place the tomatoes in a baking dish and divide the spinach mixture over top.
4. Bake at 350°F for 20 minutes.

Variation
Oysters Rockefeller

In Los Frailes Bay in Baja, California, we once found giant rock oysters while snorkeling. Hal dived down and sliced the meat out of the shells that were attached to the rocks, bringing up oysters on the half shell. When we tired of eating the oysters raw with a squeeze of lime and Tabasco, I spooned some of the above spinach mixture over the oysters and baked them in their shells.

Variation
Callaloo Rockefeller

16 to 18 callaloo leaves
3 cups water

Wash the callaloo and remove and discard the center vein from each leaf. Finely chop the stems and leaves. Bring water to a boil and add the callaloo. Cook until tender—about 30 minutes. Drain and squeeze dry. Follow the directions for Spinach Rockefeller (above).

Cactus Leaf Salad

4 servings

Leaves from the *nopales* (prickly pear cactus) are common in Latin American markets. While returning from cooking school in Mexico, one of my students stopped by the side of the road along a California highway and carefully cut the leaves from a cactus plant and took them home to prepare. She later told me that she'd never do it again. It was a difficult process at best because the thorns must be removed before the leaves can be diced. In most Latin American markets you can find the fresh leaves already peeled and diced. Then, all you need to do is boil the leaves until they're tender. Rinse them well to remove the slimy liquid that exudes from the cactus.

You can also buy canned *nopales* (sometimes called *nopalitos)* in most Latin American markets. Be sure to rinse them thoroughly before marinating.

1 pound diced and cooked nopales, rinsed well
1 white onion, peeled and cut into thin strips

Marinade

2 cloves garlic, finely chopped
1 hot green chile, seeded and finely chopped
2 tablespoons vinegar
3 tablespoons olive oil

Garnishes

1 avocado, sliced
1 large tomato, chopped
½ cup cilantro leaves
1 cup farmers or feta cheese, crumbled

Marinate the cactus leaves and onion for at least 30 minutes. Garnish with any or all the suggestions.

Chayote

Chayote in California, *mirliton* in New Orleans, and *christophene* in the Caribbean—this easy-to-grow vegetable is nearly tasteless. While attending language school in Guatemala, Hal and I were served chayote squash almost daily. They often weighed as much as five pounds—a lot more than the half-pound squashes that I was used to in the States. The *chayote* were boiled and barely seasoned and we quickly became bored with them. They need a lot of seasoning but are a great vegetable to stuff since their mild flavor goes well with many other foods.

Chayote with Corn

Although canned foods are an essential part of boating, I dislike them—so I'm always on the lookout for recipes that disguise their bland and boring taste. This is a good way to enhance canned corn.

2 tablespoons oil
3 cloves garlic, finely chopped
1 onion, diced
1 pound chayote squash, peeled and sliced
2 (16 oz. each) cans corn, drained
1 (4 oz.) can diced green chiles
1 (16 oz.) can undrained, chopped tomatoes
1 teaspoon oregano
Salt and freshly ground black pepper
¼ cup chopped cilantro

Sauté the garlic and onion in the oil until soft. Add the squash and sauté until crisp-tender. Add all the remaining ingredients and cook an additional 5 to 10 minutes. Sprinkle with cilantro just before serving. (You can also sprinkle the top with grated jack cheese and broil until golden.)

SHRIMP STUFFED CHAYOTE

8 servings

If you have a food processor on board, the chopping can be done in just a few seconds. Otherwise get out a sharp knife and go for it!

4 (8 oz. each) chayote squash
3 tablespoons olive oil
½ pound shrimp, shelled, deveined and finely chopped
1 onion, finely chopped
2 teaspoons finely chopped garlic
¼ cup finely chopped parsley
¼ teaspoon thyme
½ teaspoon cayenne pepper
½ teaspoon salt
1 cup fresh soft bread crumbs
2 tablespoons butter

1. In a large pot of boiling salted water, boil the squash for 25 minutes. When the squash is cool enough to handle, slice it in half lengthwise and discard the seeds. Scoop out the shells to make containers about ¼-inch thick.
2. Finely chop the pulp from the squash and sauté it in a dry skillet until all the juices have evaporated. Add the olive oil, the shrimp, onion, garlic, parsley, thyme, cayenne, and salt and sauté until cooked. Set aside.
3. Spoon the shrimp filling into the squash, mounding the filling slightly. Sprinkle the bread crumbs on top and dot with butter.
4. Place the stuffed squash in a baking dish and bake in the middle of a 400° F oven for 20 minutes or until the tops are brown.

Variation
Meat Stuffing

Substitute a ½ pound of ground beef for the shrimp and 1 cup of grated cheese for the bread crumbs and butter.

Pickled Vegetables

One tasty way to preserve your produce is to pickle it. When cruising for any length of time, keep plenty of wine vinegar on board and a few glass jars for storing your pickled vegetables. For a weekend away, bring your pickled vegetables to the boat.

PICKLED PEPPERS

1 quart

I am a sucker for red and yellow bell peppers and often purchase more than I can use. I get back to the boat and wonder how we'll be able to eat all of them before they start to deteriorate. Pickling is the answer! You can preserve their beauty and know that you'll have bell peppers for salads and snacking. Pickled peppers will keep for several months in the refrigerator.

2 cups white wine vinegar
1 teaspoon salt
3 cloves garlic, peeled and coarsely chopped
1 teaspoon dried oregano
2 pounds bell peppers, cored, seeded, cut in 1-inch strips

1. Bring the vinegar to a boil and add the salt, stirring to dissolve. Remove from heat and add the garlic and oregano.
2. Place the peppers in a storage container (I use 2 pint-sized canning jars) and cover with the cooled vinegar and enough water to completely cover the peppers. Cover and store in refrigerator.
3. To serve, drain and drizzle with olive oil; season with freshly ground black pepper. Add some additional chopped garlic if desired.

Marinated Mushrooms

2 ½ cups

Fresh mushrooms have a very short shelf life, even if you can store them in the refrigerator. They'll keep an additional week if you slice and sauté them in olive oil or butter and lots of garlic. When prepared as directed below, they'll keep up to three weeks.

¾ cup white wine vinegar
1 ½ cups water
½ teaspoon salt
1 pound button mushrooms, cleaned, stems trimmed
2 cloves garlic coarsely chopped
1 sprig fresh rosemary or 1 tablespoon dried
¼ teaspoon crushed red pepper flakes
Olive oil

1. Bring the vinegar, water, and salt to a boil. Reduce the heat, add the mushrooms, and simmer until tender—about 5 minutes. Drain.
2. Mix the mushrooms with the garlic, rosemary, and pepper flakes. Place in a small container completely covered with olive oil.
3. Store in the refrigerator, but serve at room temperature. Drain off the olive oil and reserve for use in salads.

Dilled Spicy Green Beans

6 pints

Fresh green beans have a short shelf life, especially if they can't be kept in the refrigerator. To extend their use, try pickling them. These beans make great cocktail food and also work well as a garnish in Bloody Marys.

4 pounds green beans, cleaned and cut into 4-inch lengths
6 (1-pint size each) canning jars
½ teaspoon dill seed
½ teaspoon mustard seed
3 peppercorns
1 dried red chile pepper
1 clove garlic
4 tablespoons salt

3 cups white vinegar
3 cups water

1. Pack the beans in the hot, sterilized canning jars. Add the dill seed, mustard seed, peppercorns, chile pepper, and garlic.
2. Bring the salt, vinegar, and water to a boil; pour the boiling liquid over the beans.
3. Process in a boiling water bath (make sure that the jars are covered with boiling water) for 20 minutes.
4. For shorter term storage, eliminate the water bath and store in the refrigerator.

Cooking in Foil

During my first year of boating in a 16-foot converted ski boat, aluminum foil became my backup for all the pots and pans I didn't have room for. If our one-burner hand-held stove wasn't able to cope with the cooking job, I wrapped the dinner in foil and Hal built a fire on shore. Once the fire had burned down to coals, dinner either sizzled on a grill over the hot coals or was plopped directly on the coals. There were no pots to wash and the food tasted fantastic.

I have a bigger boat now, with a well-equipped galley, but still enjoy cooking in foil, which is basically a method of steaming food. All the moisture is retained within the foil packet (although the foil must be well sealed), so it's a great way to cook if dinner stands a chance of being late.

Foil cooking is fun for guests. You can make individual foil packets for each guest, bring the hot foil packets to the table, and bask in the compliments as the diners puncture the seals on their packets and inhale the luscious clouds of fragrant hot steam that are suddenly released.

Following are a few tips to make foil cooking easy and successful:

- The packets can be prepared in advance and refrigerated until just before cooking.
- It is important to cut similar foods the same size for evenness of cooking. The hardest vegetables, such as potatoes and carrots, should be cut the smallest. Softer vegetables, such as onions and bell peppers, can be left in larger chunks.
- Be sure there is plenty of liquid in each packet. Add some wine or broth to any recipe that doesn't call for it.
- I buy extra-heavy-duty aluminum foil so the packets won't puncture when they're put onto the grill or in the fire. Regular strength foil just isn't sturdy enough for this type of use.
- A disposable foil pan works well for food that doesn't need to be turned. Seal the top of the pan by crimping the foil along the edge.
- When cooking with foil on a barbecue, cook at a medium heat. On a campfire, be sure the fire has burned down to coals. Setting the foil on a roaring fire can melt the foil or burn the food.
- To test for doneness, carefully touch the top of the foil packet. When it feels very hot, start timing. Cook an additional 5 minutes for a vegetable pack and 10 to 15 minutes more for meats. (When the packets begin to get puffy, that's another sign that you're ready to begin timing.)

The method of folding the foil for cooking packets is called the drugstore wrap. Place the food you are going to cook in the center of a rectangular piece of foil that is large enough to allow for folding at the top and ends. Bring two sides together above the food; fold down in a series of l-inch folds and flatten. Fold the ends toward the center in tight folds to seal the package.

Suggested Uses for Foil Wraps

- Sprinkle fish fillets with garlic, chopped scallions, soy sauce, and a few drops of sesame oil; seal in foil and cook for an easy main course.
- Chop a variety of vegetables, season with herbs, and add a little liquid (such as white wine) before sealing.
- Ribs—and other fatty foods—work especially well in foil. Place the ribs and a marinade in foil; allow to steam until tender. This method of cooking renders out the fat from the ribs and, since they are sealed in the foil, there won't be any flare-ups. When done, remove the ribs from foil, brush with barbecue sauce, and place over the grill for 10 to 20 minutes.

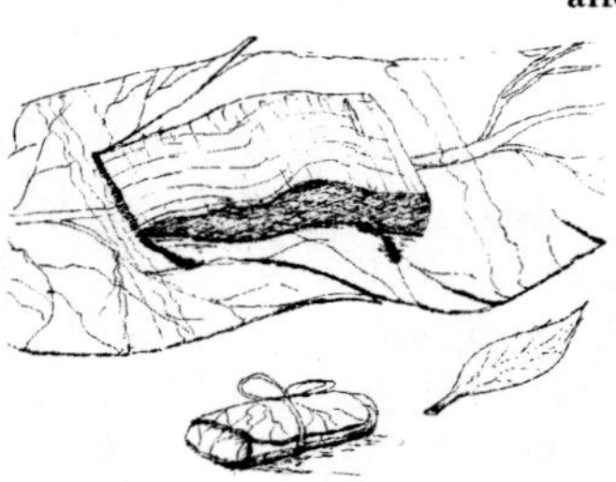

Foil-Wrapped Veggie Pack

2 servings

You can put virtually anything in a foil vegetable pack. Carrots, onions, and potatoes keep for long periods without refrigeration, so they often form the basis of my vegetable pack. I vary the taste with different herbs and spices and any other fresh vegetables that I have on hand. For a main course, I frequently add chopped Italian sausage, ground beef, or ground turkey.

1 tomato, chopped
2 carrots, chopped
1 potato, chopped
1 onion, peeled and chopped
2 cloves garlic, finely chopped
2 tablespoons fresh or canned pesto sauce
3 tablespoons white wine

1. Place the vegetables in foil and sprinkle with the garlic, pesto sauce, and white wine.
2. Wrap the packet as directed above on page 153 and place on a preheated barbecue. Cook until the package puffs up and is hot on top—about 30 minutes.

Garlic Potatoes

2 servings

While cruising off the coast of Manzanillo, Mexico, the beautiful produce store La Verudra Loca in nearby Santiago was selling tiny new potatoes for a few cents a pound—the same "gourmet" potatoes that go for a dollar a pound in the States. I dredged them in olive oil and chili powder before roasting in foil. Below is another tasty way to prepare foil potatoes.

4 red skinned potatoes, thinly sliced
8 cloves garlic, finely chopped
2 teaspoons Lawry's Lemon Pepper Seasoning
3 tablespoons olive oil

Dip each potato slice in olive oil and sprinkle with the lemon pepper and garlic. Spread on a piece of heavy foil and seal the foil. Cook on the barbecue about 10 to 15 minutes or until the foil is hot to the touch on top and you can hear the oil sizzling inside. If you like crispier potatoes, open the foil for the last five minutes of cooking.

Yam Veggie Pack Los Frailes

2 servings

We once built a campfire on the beautiful white sand beach at Los Frailes in Baja California and cooked our foil wrapped dinner in the coals. I was very pleased with the way this slightly spicy veggie pack turned out. Hal had caught a fish that morning, which we barbecued with the veggie pack. Delicious!

1 large yam or sweet potato, about a pound, peeled and diced
1 purple onion, finely chopped
2 tablespoons butter or olive oil
3 ounces Mexican Salsa
1 cup Port wine

Make a foil packet, mixing the ingredients together before sealing. Barbecue 20 to 25 minutes, until the packet is puffy and the top is very hot.

Zucchini with Green Chile Pesto in Foil

4 servings

4 small zucchini, sliced in half lengthwise
½ cup Green Chile Pesto (page 168)

Spread the pesto on the cut side of the zucchini and place 2 halves together. Wrap each zucchini in foil. Bake until tender—about 20 to 25 minutes at 350° F.

Foil-Wrapped Ratatouille

1 serving

1 slice eggplant
1 slice tomato
1 slice onion
4 slices mushrooms
½ teaspoon finely chopped garlic
Salt and pepper to taste
⅛ teaspoon basil
1 tablespoon olive oil

Stack all the ingredients in the center of a piece of foil. Seal well and cook on a barbecue for 30 minutes.

Grilled Vegetables on the Barbecue

Grilling vegetables on the barbecue brings out their flavor and the veggies make great accompaniments to meat and fish. Preheat the barbecue before cooking.

GRILLED TOMATOES

2 to 4 servings

4 Roma tomatoes
2 tablespoons olive oil
½ teaspoon dried basil
½ teaspoon thyme leaves
¼ teaspoon salt
¼ teaspoon freshly ground black pepper

1. Ripen the tomatoes for several days at room temperature.
2. Cut each tomato in half lengthwise and marinate in a Ziploc bag with the olive oil, basil, thyme, salt, and pepper for at least 15 minutes.
3. Grill the tomatoes until the skin begins to char.

GRILLED ARTICHOKES

2 to 4 servings

4 artichokes, boiled until tender enough to strip leaves—about 30 minutes
3 tablespoon lemon juice
2 cloves garlic, finely chopped
3 tablespoon olive oil
Freshly ground black pepper

1. Remove the leaves and chokes from the artichokes, saving only the hearts.
2. Marinate the hearts in a Ziploc bag with the lemon juice, garlic, olive oil, and pepper for at least 15 minutes.
3. Skewer the hearts and grill until golden.

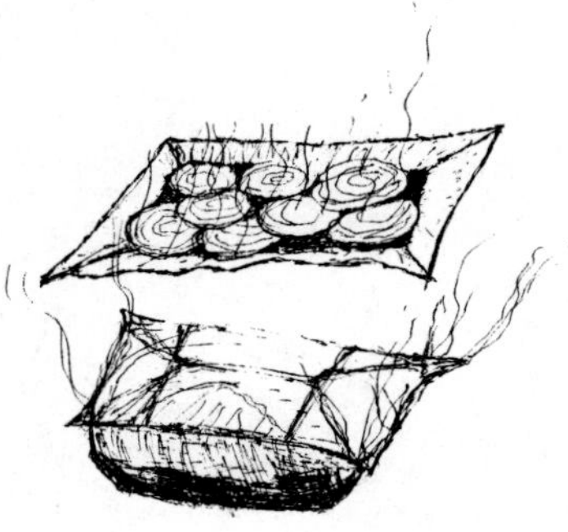

GRILLED CARROTS WITH VINAIGRETTE

2 to 4 servings

4 large carrots, cleaned, cut into ¼-inch thick slices, and steamed until crisp-tender
2 tablespoons red wine vinegar
1 clove garlic, finely chopped
1 tablespoon fresh tarragon, chopped
4 tablespoons olive oil

1. Place the carrots in a Ziploc bag with the vinegar, garlic, tarragon, and olive oil. Marinate for at least 15 minutes.
2. Thread the carrots on skewers and grill until golden.

GRILLED ORIENTAL EGGPLANT

2 to 4 servings

4 long Oriental eggplants
3 tablespoons soy sauce
3 tablespoon dry sherry
2 tablespoons Oriental sesame oil
3 cloves garlic, finely minced

1. Split the eggplants in half lengthwise, combine the soy sauce, sherry, sesame oil, and garlic, and marinate in a Ziploc bag for at least 15 minutes.
2. Grill until tender and golden.

Mixed Grilled Vegetables with Rosemary

2 to 4 servings

1 yellow bell pepper, seeded and cut in quarters
1 eggplant, cut in lengthwise strips
4 Roma tomatoes
2 zucchini cut in lengthwise strips
2 cloves garlic, finely chopped
2 tablespoons rosemary
¼ cup olive oil

1. Marinate the bell pepper, eggplant, tomatoes, and zucchini with the garlic, rosemary, and olive oil in a Ziploc bag for at least 15 minutes.
2. Grill until tender.

CHAPTER 9

Sauces and Marinades

Sauces and Marinades

A good sauce can turn a mundane dinner into a memorable meal. It can transform canned chicken or beef into a gourmet treat. And marinades can transform a tough cut of meat into a tasty main course.

Instead of serving a broiled chicken breast *au natural,* accompany the meat with Curried Papaya Salsa or Tomato, Garlic, and Wine Sauce. Transform leftover chicken into a remarkable alfresco luncheon served by adding a garlic-flavored Aioli Mayonnaise. Try the Sun-Dried Tomato Aioli Sauce with grilled beef and Salsa Esmeralda with your favorite fish. Before opening a jar of ordinary spaghetti sauce for pasta, take a look at the recipe for Artichoke-Walnut Pesto Sauce or Mushrooms with Chipotle Chile Sauce.

Some of the sauces are quick to make (Mustard Sauce or Citrus Vinaigrette for Seafood), while some take more preparation time but can be made in quantity and stored for months (Chimichurri Sauce or African Sauce). Most of the marinades are simple and will greatly enhance whatever meat you are fixing (Marinade Dijon or Cilantro Garlic Marinade). Salad dressings such as Walnut Blue Cheese or Lemon Garlic will transform the cruiser's tired cabbage and carrot salad into a favorite side dish.

There is a thorough discussion about basic sauces such as hollandaise, béchamel (white sauce), and mayonnaise. Some of these sauces harbor a few pitfalls, so I've included some helpful hints and step-by-step instructions where needed.

Read this chapter and start using these recipes. Your cooking will never taste so good.

Egg-Based Sauces

There are two types of egg-based sauces that I find useful: egg yolk and butter-based sauces, in which hollandaise serves as the mother sauce; and egg yolk and oil-based sauces, in which mayonnaise serves as the mother sauce.

In each sauce an emulsion must be formed so that the sauce hangs together. Using a blender or food processor greatly simplifies making these sauces.

Hollandaise-Based Sauces

Hollandaise is a cooked, emulsified sauce consisting of an acid (lemon juice), egg yolks, and butter. To emulsify hollandaise sauce, the yolks must absorb the butter. Adding an acid to the egg loosens the bond of the protein in the egg and makes it able to bind to the butter in the sauce. Without the acid, this emulsion would not take place and the butter could not be absorbed.

Hollandaise sauce is made of warmed egg yolks flavored with lemon juice, into which butter is gradually incorporated to make the sauce thick and creamy. It is probably the most well known of the classic sauces. It is also one of the most feared of sauces because the egg yolks can easily curdle and ruin the sauce. If you have a food processor, though, your hollandaise will be delicious and absolutely foolproof (see Blender Hollandaise Sauce, page 158).

Although hollandaise is traditionally served on eggs benedict, try it on delicate fish fillets, roasted chicken, sautéed mushrooms, or steamed asparagus.

Tips for making hollandaise-based sauces

- The egg yolks must be heated slowly and gradually. They will become granular if they're heated too quickly, and overcooking scrambles them. You may beat them over hot water (in a double boiler) or over very low heat directly in the pan; it makes no difference so long as the process is slow and gentle.

- Egg yolks will absorb a certain quantity of butter when it is fed to them gradually. When too much is added too soon, particularly at first, the sauce will not thicken. And if the total amount of butter is more than the yolks can absorb, the sauce will curdle. Three ounces of butter is usually the maximum amount a large yolk can absorb. To be on the safe side, however, use 2 ounces (¼ cup) for the best results.

Traditional Hollandaise Sauce

1 to 1½ cups

3 egg yolks
1 tablespoon cold water
6 to 8 ounces melted butter
1 to 2 tablespoons lemon juice
Salt and freshly ground white pepper
1 tablespoon grated lemon peel (optional)

1. In a small saucepan, whisk together the egg yolks and water until frothy. Place over low heat and whisk briskly until the yolks thicken.

2. Gradually add the butter, whisking briskly. As the mixture thickens, add the lemon juice and season to taste. Add the lemon peel, if desired, remove from the heat, and keep in a warm place (a heated thermos works well) until ready to serve. **Note:** Never let hollandaise sauce sit at room temperature; salmonella might develop.

Problem Solving

1. If the sauce is too thick, add a little hot water, milk, or cream.

2. To hold the sauce for a long period, beat in a teaspoon of cornstarch to the yolks at the beginning.

3. If the sauce doesn't thicken (usually caused by adding the butter too quickly), place 1 teaspoon of lemon juice and one tablespoon of the sauce in a warm, clean, dry bowl. Beat with a whisk for a moment until the sauce emulsifies and thickens. Then beat in the rest of the sauce, a half tablespoon at a time, beating until each addition has thickened before adding the next.

4. If the sauce curdles or separates, add an ice cube and whisk vigorously. This should draw it together. If not, begin with another egg yolk in a clean bowl and slowly add the separated sauce while whisking.

5. Leftover hollandaise can be kept for several days in the refrigerator or it can be frozen. Use leftover sauce to enrich veloutés or béchamels (see page 162) by beating it into the hot sauce a tablespoon at a time, just before serving. Or, stir leftover sauce vigorously and spread on cold meats or seafood. It's also great as a dip for vegetables.

6. To reheat hollandaise, beat 2 tablespoons of the sauce in a saucepan over very low heat or over hot water. Gradually beat in the rest of the sauce by spoonfuls.

Blender Hollandaise Sauce

1½ cups

2 tablespoons fresh lemon juice
1 teaspoon Dijon mustard
3 egg yolks
Salt and white pepper to taste
½ pound hot melted butter

Note: Use room temperature eggs and lemon juice, and very hot butter. In order to thicken, the yolks must be over 140°F—but at 180°F, they scramble! If the sauce doesn't thicken, place it very briefly over some heat and stir.

In a food processor or blender, combine the lemon juice, mustard, yolks, salt and pepper, and blend. With the processor or blender running and the butter extremely hot, gradually add the butter to the sauce. If the butter is not hot enough it will not bind with the egg yolks and an emulsion will not form. Serve immediately.

Microwave Hollandaise

¾ cup

Follow the directions for Blender Hollandaise Sauce (page 158), but use only ¼ cup of butter and add ¼ cup of half and half. Melt the butter in a microwave safe container, add the lemon juice, mustard, yolks, salt, and pepper, and cook on high power for 1 minute. Stir well and cook another 45 seconds or until the sauce reaches 150°F. Whisk again and serve immediately.

Orange Hollandaise

Follow the directions for Blender Hollandaise Sauce (page 158), substituting 2 cups of orange juice that has been reduced to ⅓ cup liquid for the lemon juice, eliminating the Dijon mustard, and adding 1 tablespoon of grated orange peel. Serve on seafood, steamed asparagus, or eggs.

Chili Hollandaise

Follow the directions for Blender Hollandaise Sauce (page 158), substituting lime juice for the lemon juice. Dissolve 1 tablespoon of chili powder and 1 teaspoon of cumin powder in 2 tablespoons of hot water; add to the egg mixture. Stir in 1 tablespoon of finely chopped cilantro to the emulsified sauce. This is a slightly spicy sauce that's excellent on chicken or fish.

Béarnaise Sauce

Follow the directions for Blender Hollandaise Sauce (page 158), substituting tarragon vinegar for the lemon juice and 1 tablespoon of fresh tarragon for the Dijon mustard. Just before serving, add 2 tablespoons of finely chopped fresh tarragon or parsley. Optional: Add 1 tablespoon of tomato paste. This is an excellent sauce for beef.

Mayonnaise-Based Sauces

Mayonnaise is a cold emulsified sauce made of egg yolk and oil with an acid (lemon or vinegar), which makes it possible for the egg to absorb the fat. It may have other flavorings, such as herbs, chopped cornichons (pickles), garlic, or tomatoes. It may also be lightened to a mousseline sauce with whipping cream.

Mayonnaise can be made by hand or in a food processor. (It's foolproof when made in a processor.)

Tips for making mayonnaise-based sauces

1. All of the ingredients should be at room temperature.
2. Always beat the egg yolks for a minute or two before adding anything to them. As soon as they are thick they are ready to absorb the oil.
3. The oil must be added very slowly at first, until the emulsion process begins and the sauce thickens into a heavy cream. After this, the oil may be incorporated more rapidly.
4. The maximum amount of oil that one large egg yolk will absorb is ¾ of a cup. When this maximum is exceeded the binding properties of the yolk breaks down and the sauce thins or curdles. To be on the safe side, use only a ½ cup of oil per yolk.
5. Although commercial mayonnaise keeps unrefrigerated (a plus on a boat), the homemade variety must be kept cold and has a shelf life of only a couple of weeks.

Traditional Mayonnaise

½ cup

3 egg yolks
1 tablespoon vinegar or lemon juice
½ teaspoon salt
¼ teaspoon dry mustard
¾ cup mild flavored olive oil
¾ cup vegetable oil

1. Place the egg yolks in a warm bowl and whisk for 1 to 2 minutes.
2. Add the vinegar, salt, and dry mustard.
3. Whisk in the oil, drop by drop. Once you start, do not stop beating. You may switch hands or directions, however. Check to be certain that the oil is in suspension. After ⅓ to ½ cup of the oil has been added, you may rest your arm (finally!). Beat in the rest of the oil by adding 2 tablespoons at a time.

How to correct curdled or separated mayonnaise

Warm a mixing bowl in hot water. Dry it. Add 1 teaspoon of prepared mustard and 1 tablespoon of the curdled or separated mayonnaise. Beat with a wire whisk for several seconds until they cream and thicken together. Beat in the rest of the sauce by teaspoons, thickening each addition before adding the next. This always works. Just be sure that you add the separated sauce a little bit at a time, particularly at first.

Blender Mayonnaise

1 cup

Homemade mayonnaise is easy to make with a blender or food processor. Have all the ingredients at room temperature to be certain that an emulsion will form.

1 egg
1 ½ teaspoons Dijon mustard
1 ½ teaspoons fresh lemon juice
¼ cup olive oil
½ cup vegetable oil
Salt and freshly ground white pepper

1. In a food processor or blender, blend the egg, mustard, and lemon juice.
2. With the machine running, gradually add the oil in a slow, steady stream. Blend until smooth and thick. Season with salt and pepper.

Variations

- Substitute a flavored vinegar such as tarragon, raspberry, or red wine for the lemon juice. Excellent with cold meat, seafood, or chicken.
- Add chopped fresh dill or tarragon to the mayonnaise. Excellent with fish.

Aioli Sauce

Aioli is a garlicky variation of traditional mayonnaise and a personal favorite. Make Blender Mayonnaise, adding 1 to 2 tablespoons of finely chopped garlic to the egg mixture before adding the oil.

Ailoi is delicious on fish, boiled potatoes, green beans, and hard-cooked eggs.

Sun-Dried Tomato Aioli Sauce

Chop ¼ cup of drained, oil-packed, sun-dried tomatoes. Add 1 cup of aioli sauce and combine. Excellent with beef, chicken, or cold vegetables.

Remoulade Sauce

1 ½ cups

1 recipe Blender Mayonnaise (page 160), using only 1 tablespoon Dijon mustard
2 tablespoons capers, drained
2 tablespoons finely chopped pickles, drained
1 teaspoon finely chopped garlic
2 ounces canned roasted red peppers, chopped
1 tablespoon chopped fresh parsley
1 tablespoon chopped fresh tarragon

Combine all the ingredients and blend. Delicious with seafood, vegetables, or chicken. Use as you would a tartar sauce.

Starch-Based Sauces

For centuries, the roux has been the basic thickener for sauces. It is a paste of melted butter and flour that is cooked until frothy (for white sauces) or until a rich golden brown (for brown sauces).

All of the many variations of the starch-based sauces are based on three mother sauces: **White Sauce** or **Béchamel**, which is made of milk that is thickened with a white roux; **Velouté**, which is made of white stock (veal or chicken) that is thickened with a white roux; and **Brown Sauce** or **Espagñole**, which is made of brown stock (beef) that is thickened with a brown roux.

The roux, once made, is thinned with a broth to the desired consistency. There are many good-quality instant or concentrated stocks or broths on the market. Knorr and Maggi are two of my favorites, and they can be stored without refrigeration.

There is an easy way to know which sauce goes best with which meat: the lighter the meat, the paler the sauce.

Sauces that are based on basic white sauce can be kept in the refrigerator for up to three days; brown sauces can be kept for up to a week. Brown and velouté sauces freeze well, so they can be made in large amounts. White sauces that contain egg yolks separate when defrosted, and all sauces that contain cream tend to thin when thawed.

Tips for making starch-based sauces

1. Use a heavy pan—thin pans will allow the sauce to scorch.
2. Cook the roux thoroughly to avoid any raw flour taste.
3. Stir the roux constantly to prevent burning. Do not allow it to brown when making velouté and béchamel sauces.
4. To prevent the roux from being lumpy, allow it to cool slightly before adding a hot liquid. Add the hot liquid in a steady stream, whisking constantly. (Adding a hot liquid will cut down on the amount of time that you have to stir.)

5. Whisk constantly as the sauce comes to a boil. If lumps form, remove from heat and whisk. Avoid cooking the lumps. If necessary, strain the sauce.

6. If prepared in advance, rub the surface of the sauce with butter or press a piece of wax paper on the top to prevent a skin from forming.

Basic White Sauce or Béchamel

1 cup

1 cup milk
Salt
Freshly ground pepper
Nutmeg

- For a thin roux (for cream soups):
  1 tablespoon butter
  1 tablespoon flour
- For a medium roux (for eggs, vegetables, pasta):
  1 ½ tablespoons butter
  1 ½ tablespoons flour
- For a thick roux (for binding soufflé mixtures):
  2 tablespoons butter
  2 tablespoons flour

1. Heat the milk.
2. In a heavy-bottomed saucepan melt the butter, whisk in the flour, and cook until the roux is foaming but not browned—1 to 2 minutes.
3. Strain the hot milk. Allow the roux to cool slightly and then whisk in the milk in a steady stream. Bring the sauce to a boil, whisking constantly, and add salt, pepper, and nutmeg to taste. Reduce the heat and simmer for 5 minutes.
4. If you aren't using the sauce immediately, seal the surface with butter or wax paper.

Mornay Sauce

1 cup

1 recipe Basic White Sauce or Béchamel (above)
1 egg yolk (optional)
1 teaspoon Dijon mustard (optional)
¼ cup grated cheese (Gruyère or Parmesan)
1 tablespoon butter
Salt
White pepper

Prepare white sauce as directed in master recipe (above). Then, remove sauce from heat and stir in the above ingredients. Mornay sauce is served with eggs, fish, white meats, and vegetables, and is an important ingredient in most gratinés.

Velouté Sauce

1 cup

1 ½ tablespoons butter
1 ½ tablespoons flour
1 cup fish, chicken, or white veal stock, heated
Salt and pepper

1. In a heavy-bottomed saucepan, melt the butter, whisk in the flour, and cook until the roux is foaming but not browned—about 1 to 2 minutes.
2. Whisk in the stock in a steady stream. Bring the sauce to a boil, whisking constantly. Add just a little salt and pepper. Reduce the heat and simmer for 15 to 30 minutes, skimming occasionally.
3. If you aren't using the sauce immediately, seal the surface with butter or wax paper.

Note: Velouté sauce is usually enriched with an egg yolk, cream, or butter just before serving. It can accompany eggs, fish, poultry, light meats, and vegetables.

Variation
Brown Sauce or Espagñole Sauce

Follow the directions for Velouté Sauce, but use a beef stock.

Dry Mushrooms

Dry mushrooms come in many textures and varieties. Hal says they are the ideal boat food because they weigh little, store well, take up little space, and have excellent flavor. They are also low in calories, cholesterol, and fat free. Oriental shitakes, Italian porcinis, French morels, and common button mushrooms can all be found aboard *SpiceSea*.

You should always presoak and rinse morels and porcinis since they usually contain a lot of dirt. The strained soaking liquid from porcinis is extremely flavorful and can be boiled down and used in place of broth in many recipes. Shitakes also should be presoaked until soft and their stems cut off completely because they never get tender.

Button mushrooms don't need to be reconstituted when you're adding them to foods that contain liquid and that require 20 minutes or more cooking time. To reconstitute as fresh or use as toppings on entrées that don't have much moisture, soak one part mushrooms in three parts water until soft—about 1 hour. Drain and handle the mushrooms like fresh. To sauté, drain after 30 minutes.

Dry mushrooms can be used in sauces, marinades, gravies, chowders, soups, stews, casseroles, salad dressings, omelettes, salads, and as pizza toppings. One-half cup of dried mushrooms equals about ½ pound of fresh.

Mushroom Sauce

1 cup

Try this delicious sauce on chicken breasts or a tender fillet.

1 cup sliced dried button mushrooms, soaked in 3 cups water for 20 minutes
2 cloves garlic, chopped
2 tablespoons butter
1 teaspoon dried thyme
Salt and pepper to taste
½ cup chicken or beef broth
1 cup white or red wine
½ cup chopped fresh parsley, if available

Sauté the mushrooms and garlic in the butter for 5 minutes. Season with the thyme, salt, and pepper. Add the broth and wine and bring to a boil. Cook until the volume is reduced in half. Sprinkle with parsley and serve.

Variations

Cream Sauce—Add 1 cup Nestle's Crema, evaporated milk, or cream to mushroom sauce and boil until thick.

Cheese Sauce—Add a ½ cup of blue cheese to cream sauce and stir until dissolved.

Green Peppercorn Sauce—Add 3 tablespoons of green peppercorns to cheese sauce and simmer 5 minutes.

Mushrooms with Chipotle Chile Sauce

1 cup sauce

Chipotle chiles are smoked jalapeño chiles and can be found either dried or canned. Serve this sauce over beef or chicken or try it as an appetizer with toast.

2 tomatoes, peeled, seeded, and chopped
1 canned chipotle chile
1 tablespoon tomato paste
¾ cup chicken broth
2 tablespoons lime juice
1 small onion, finely chopped
2 cloves garlic, finely chopped
3 tablespoons olive oil
1 ½ pounds fresh mushrooms, preferably oyster mushrooms, cleaned and sliced
Salt and pepper to taste

1. Purée the tomatoes, chile, tomato paste, chicken broth, and lime juice. Place in a saucepan and boil until reduced to ⅓ cup.

2. In a skillet, sauté the onion and garlic in the olive oil until soft. Add the mushrooms and cook until tender. Add the purée, season with salt and pepper, and heat thoroughly.

African Sauce

1 cup

I first tasted this sauce in a southern California seafood restaurant. After pleading for the recipe, the waitress gave me a list of the ingredients—but it was up to me to figure out the proportions. I came up with this flavorful concoction after a lot of trial and error. African Sauce is excellent on many kinds of meat and seafood and also makes a good marinade—but it can overwhelm delicate fish or veal. It keeps for months without refrigeration, so I make up a large batch when time permits.

1 teaspoon dry mustard
1 tablespoon sugar
1 teaspoon black pepper
¼ teaspoon cayenne pepper
⅛ teaspoon allspice
⅛ teaspoon cinnamon
¼ cup tomato paste
¼ cup olive oil
½ teaspoon Tabasco Sauce
2 tablespoons lime juice
2 tablespoons Worcestershire Sauce or Jamaican Sauce
2 tablespoons balsamic vinegar or red wine vinegar
1 tablespoon finely chopped fresh garlic
1 tablespoon finely chopped fresh ginger

Mix all the ingredients together.

Oriental Sauce Mix

3 cups

Oriental stir-fry cooking is an ideal way to prepare food on a boat. You can cut and chop the ingredients early in the day and need only a few minutes of cooking time just before serving. Most vegetables and meats lend themselves to stir-frying—even tough cuts of beef can be stir-fried successfully if they are sliced very thin.

I have included some of my favorite stir-fry recipes in the "Meat and Poultry" chapter (Chapter 6, pages 95–98). No one always has the time or inclination to make the marinade and seasoning sauces called for in a particular recipe, so I'm including this universal sauce mix that can be made in large quantities and used whenever you want to stir-fry.

¼ cup cornstarch
2 tablespoons sugar
¼ cup rice wine vinegar
¼ cup dry sherry
½ cup soy sauce
1½ cups chicken broth (2 teaspoons chicken base and water)
2 tablespoons chopped garlic
2 tablespoons chopped ginger root

Dissolve the cornstarch and sugar in the vinegar. Add the remaining ingredients and store in a wide-mouthed jar. Stir well just before using. Spoon the sauce out from the bottom to help prevent the cornstarch, ginger, and garlic from settling.

1. Marinate a ½ pound of pork, chicken, fish, or beef in 2 tablespoons of the sauce for a ½ hour.
2. Stir-fry the meat in 1 tablespoon of oil until cooked; remove from wok and clean the wok.
3. Stir-fry your choice of vegetables in 1 tablespoon oil (add a little water if the vegetable needs steaming). Add ½ to ¾ cup of the sauce mix with the cooked meat and stir until the sauce thickens.

Spicy Soy Dipping Sauce

¾ cup

6 tablespoons soy sauce
6 tablespoons rice vinegar
1 teaspoon dark sesame oil
1 teaspoon chile oil

Combine the soy sauce, rice vinegar, sesame oil, and chile oil and store at room temperature. Just before serving, sprinkle with chopped cilantro or green onion, if available. Great with steamed dumplings.

Lime Dipping Sauce

¾ cup

2 cloves garlic, finely chopped
1 hot red fresh chile, seeded and finely chopped
1 tablespoon sugar
2 tablespoons lime juice
¼ cup fish sauce or soy sauce
¼ cup rice vinegar

Combine all the ingredients. Serve with Vietnamese spring rolls or steamed dumplings.

Chimichurri Sauce

4 cups

I first tasted this garlicky herb sauce in Costa Rica where I had been asked to conduct a series of cooking classes for hotel chefs. Costa Rican cooking is notoriously bland, and if it hadn't been for this sauce which Hal and I ladled on everything, we would have found the cuisine much too mundane for our palates.

I can keep this sauce for several weeks without refrigeration. Serve chimichurri over grilled meats and vegetables or use as a marinade.

12 cloves chopped garlic
2 cups chopped parsley
1 cup chopped cilantro
1 tablespoon dried oregano
1 tablespoon dried thyme
1 teaspoon freshly ground black peppercorns
1 teaspoon dried crushed red pepper flakes
½ teaspoon salt
¾ cup red wine vinegar
1 cup olive oil

Combine all the ingredients.

Mexican Salsa Fresca

3 cups

We love Mexican salsa and I usually have the ingredients to make it on board. I serve salsa over eggs, in tortillas with melted cheese, as an essential part of guacamole, as a dip with chips, and any time we cook anything that has a Mexican theme.

Years ago when we traveled the Baja Peninsula by camper, even the simplest restaurant had a delicious bowl of salsa fresca on the table. Now I often find the restaurants serving canned and bottled sauces. *¡Que lastima!* (What a pity!)

3 tomatoes chopped (2 cups)
½ cup chopped white onion
2 cloves finely chopped garlic
2 serrano chiles, seeded and finely chopped (or to taste)
⅓ cup cilantro leaves, chopped
½ teaspoon dried oregano
Salt and pepper to taste
2 tablespoons lime juice

Mix all the ingredients together and allow the flavor to mellow for at least 15 minutes before serving.

Cilantro, Garlic, and Chile Purée for Salsa

1 ⅓ cups

When I know that I'll be cruising for a few weeks without a chance to reprovision, I make this purée that preserves the cilantro flavor and keeps for three weeks in the refrigerator.

12 cloves garlic
12 serrano chiles, stemmed
1 tablespoon dry oregano
2 cups cilantro leaves
Olive oil

In a food processor, chop the garlic and chiles. Add the oregano and cilantro. Place in a small container and cover with olive oil.

Uses

- Use with tomatoes and onions when making Salsa Fresca.
- Add to chopped avocado for a simple guacamole.
- Use sparingly with pasta.
- Use as a marinade with lime juice for meats and seafood.

Guacamole

2 ½ cups

2 avocados, peeled, seeded and diced
1 tablespoon fresh lime juice
1 cup salsa fresca or 1 cup canned Mexican salsa and 3 tablespoons chopped fresh cilantro

Mix all of the ingredients together until combined. The sauce should be very chunky.

Salsa de Tomatillo (Green Tomato Sauce)

2 ½ cups

1 pound fresh tomatillos, husked and chopped
1 onion finely chopped
4 to 6 serrano chiles, finely chopped
Juice of 1 lime
3 cloves garlic, finely chopped
½ teaspoon salt
¼ cup chopped cilantro

Combine all the ingredients *except* the cilantro and simmer in a saucepan until tender. Allow to cool before adding the cilantro. (If you have a food processor or blender you can chop all the ingredients in the processor and combine, eliminating the hand chopping.

Curried Papaya Salsa

3 cups

2 tablespoons finely chopped onion
1 tablespoon finely chopped ginger root
1 teaspoon curry powder
1 tablespoon oil
2 tomatoes, chopped
1 small papaya, peeled, seeded and chopped
Salt and pepper
Juice of 1 lime
2 tablespoons chopped cilantro leaves

Sauté the onion, ginger, and curry in the oil in a small skillet for about 5 minutes—be careful not to let the onion brown. Allow the mixture to cool before combining with the tomatoes, papaya, salt and pepper, lime juice, and cilantro.

Veracruz Sauce

1½ cups

This savory sauce comes from the east coast of Mexico. Although it is typically used on seafood—shrimp, sea bass, halibut—it's also terrific over pasta or chicken.

3 tablespoons olive oil
2 cloves garlic, finely chopped
2 bell peppers, chopped
1 medium onion, finely chopped
5 tomatoes (1 ½ pounds), peeled and chopped
3 tablespoons finely chopped cilantro
10 Spanish-style stuffed green olives, sliced
2 chiles jalapeños en escabeche, cut into thin strips
2 tablespoons sherry
2 tablespoons capers
½ teaspoon oregano
¼ teaspoon white pepper

Heat the olive oil in a large skillet and sauté the garlic, onion, and bell peppers until the onions are translucent. Add the tomatoes, cilantro, olives, chiles, sherry, capers, oregano, and white pepper and simmer for 10 minutes.

Orange Chile Salsa

2 cups

2 tomatoes, chopped
1 orange, peeled, seeded and chopped
1 (4 oz.) can chopped mild green chiles
½ cup finely chopped green onions
¼ cup cilantro leaves
2 tablespoons finely chopped ginger

Combine all the ingredients.

Salsa Esmeralda (Green Sauce)

2 cups

I have a small food processor on board that allows me to make this garlic-almond sauce in minutes. It is a tasty accompaniment to any seafood or roasted chicken, and is also good with sliced tomatoes or as a spread with crackers. It keeps for about two weeks in the refrigerator.

½ cup almonds, toasted at 350° F for 10 to 15 minutes
3 cloves garlic, crushed
2 tablespoons chopped capers, rinsed and drained
4 hard-boiled eggs, mashed
¼ cup chopped parsley
½ cup olive oil
¼ cup white wine vinegar
Salt and pepper to taste

1. Finely chop the almonds in a food processor. Add the garlic, capers, eggs, and parsley; purée.
2. Slowly drizzle in the olive oil while the food processor is going. Add the vinegar, salt, and pepper.
3. Store in the refrigerator. Remove from refrigerator at least 15 minutes before serving.

Sun-Dried Tomato Seasoning

3 cups

2 cups ground sun-dried tomatoes (do not use the tomatoes packed in oil)
½ cup dehydrated parsley
½ cup Lawry's Lemon Pepper Seasoning
½ cup Italian herbs

Mix all the ingredients together and store in an airtight container for up to one year. I store this seasoning in a canning jar, using the Foodsaver to seal the lid, and keep a ½ cup or so in a spice jar in the galley for immediate use, replenishing as needed.

Uses

- For pasta, either cold or hot, add 1 tablespoon of chopped fresh garlic and 3 tablespoons of olive oil. Toss to coat and sprinkle with the sun-dried herb mixture to taste (¼ to ⅓ cup or more).
- Sprinkle on top of cooked vegetables—it really perks up cauliflower and broccoli.
- Combine with cream cheese as a spread for crackers.
- Sprinkle over your favorite cheese as a topping for pizza.
- See Orzo with Sun-Dried Tomatoes (page 120).

Basil Pesto Sauce

2 cups

Pesto is one of my favorite pasta sauces. It is also delicious on vegetables and in vegetable soup. Making pesto sauce is also a way to preserve the flavor of fresh basil since it keeps for many weeks in the refrigerator and can be frozen.

2 cups fresh basil leaves, firmly packed
½ cup olive oil
2 tablespoons pine nuts
2 cloves garlic, peeled
¼ teaspoon salt
⅔ cup freshly grated Parmesan cheese

Purée all the ingredients together in a food processor.

Green Chile Pesto

1½ cups

This pungent sauce is great served over grilled seafood, steak, or pork tenderloin. It also makes a very robust pasta sauce with just enough spiciness to wake up the taste buds.

1 (4 oz.) can mild green chiles, rinsed and seeded, or 4 fresh poblano or Anaheim chiles, roasted, peeled, seeded
4 cloves garlic, finely chopped
¼ cup grated Parmesan cheese
2 cups chopped cilantro leaves
2 cups chopped parsley leaves
¼ cup walnuts
2 tablespoons lime juice
½ cup olive oil
Salt and pepper to taste

Combine all the ingredients in a food processor and purée. If a food processor is not available, mince the chiles, garlic, cilantro, and walnuts as finely as possible and combine with the cheese, parsley, lime juice, olive oil, and salt and pepper. The pesto keeps for several weeks in the refrigerator.

Artichoke-Walnut Pesto

4 cups

8 cloves garlic, finely chopped
1 cup chopped parsley
½ cup chopped walnuts
2 (6 oz.) jars marinated artichoke hearts
1 cup freshly grated Parmesan Cheese
2 teaspoons freshly ground black pepper
6 ounces chopped green olives
6 ounces chopped black olives
2 tablespoons lemon juice
1 cup olive oil

Combine all the ingredients and store in the refrigerator for two to three weeks.

Uses

- As a pasta sauce.
- As a topping for vegetables or meats.
- Drain off the olive oil and use as a spread on crackers.
- Drain off the olive oil and serve over cream cheese as a spread for crackers.
- As a topping for pizza.

Anchovy-Herb Sauce

1 cup

We were once enjoying the anchorage at the San Benitos Islands, about 500 miles into Mexican waters. I had purchased some beautiful red and yellow bell peppers before leaving San Diego and they were starting to shrivel. I baked the peppers and dressed them with a tasty sauce of oregano, garlic, capers, anchovies, and olive oil. The Anchovy-Herb Sauce turned out to be an excellent sauce for pasta; it tasted great on top of cooked vegetables; and I found that it kept for several months in the refrigerator.

One night I cooked a pound of fusilli pasta and dressed it with some of the herb sauce. I stored the leftover pasta in a Ziploc bag in the refrigerator and, a couple of days later, made another meal with it, using an eggplant that was threatening to spoil. (See page 142.) Looking back, it seems that a key ingredient to most of our cruising menus were foods that were about to spoil!

1 tablespoon dried oregano
8 cloves garlic, chopped
4 tablespoons capers, rinsed
1 can anchovies
½ cup olive oil

Combine all the ingredients.

To use as a pasta sauce

Cook the pasta according to package directions, drain well, and toss with the desired amount of herb sauce. Sprinkle with Parmesan cheese if desired.

To use as a sauce with roasted bell peppers

Cut the peppers (preferably red and yellow) into quarters and bake in a 350° F oven for 20 minutes or until tender. (You can also roast them on the barbecue.) Place on a serving dish, concave side facing up, and put a teaspoon of the fresh herb sauce in each pepper quarter, while the peppers are still hot. Serve at room temperature as an appetizer, or as a side dish with grilled meats.

Variation

4 Roma tomatoes, chopped
¼ cup chopped black olives
½ teaspoon black pepper

Add the above ingredients to Anchovy-Herb Sauce and serve as above in bell peppers or as a pasta sauce.

Piperade (Bell Pepper Sauce)

2 cups

We love sweet bell peppers but never have space for them in our boat's refrigerator. When the peppers aren't bruised and the weather is cool they keep quite nicely at room temperature; as soon as the weather gets hot, though, they start to shrivel. And, they start rotting very quickly if they've been bruised.

If the peppers cannot stay another day at room temperature, I make this mild pepper sauce. It stores in relatively little space in the refrigerator or freezer. Reheat it and serve over chicken, seafood, or steamed vegetables or eat it as is. Try it on pizza or over eggs. Add a few chopped chiles and use the sauce with fajitas. Add a can of tomatoes and serve over pasta.

6 cloves garlic, finely chopped
1 onion, chopped
2 tablespoons olive oil
6 red, yellow, and green bell peppers, cored, seeded, and chopped
Salt and pepper

Sauté the garlic and onion in the olive oil until tender. Add the peppers, cover the pan, and simmer until tender. Serve as noted above, or purée the mixture for a smooth sauce.

Bruschetta

Bruschetta, an Italian delicacy, is a thickly sliced piece of country bread that's toasted over a fire, rubbed with fresh garlic, and drizzled with fruity virgin olive oil. Chopped tomatoes, fresh basil, and capers are usually added as toppings.

Leaving out the bread, I frequently make what I call a "bruschetta sauce" with plum tomatoes as the basic ingredient. They are available year-round and keep for two to three weeks if carefully selected. If allowed to ripen at room temperature in a sunny location, they develop excellent flavor and a good, firm texture; they can sit for days on the counter. I use them just before I think they are going to start to shrivel.

The other important ingredients in my bruschetta sauce are the garlic (always fresh, no other substitutes), the capers (sold in jars), and the olive oil (the best you can afford), all of which keep well on the boat.

Fresh basil is the only tricky part to fixing this recipe on board. The herb will keep for about a week in the refrigerator, but only if you are careful not to bruise it. (Unfortunately, the chances of my not bruising the basil are next to impossible in my overcrowded refrigerator.)

I have solved this problem by prechopping fresh basil covering it with olive oil, and storing it in the refrigerator. The oil prevents air from hitting the basil and causing it to mold. I have successfully kept fresh basil in this manner for six months.

For me, bruschetta sauce is as versatile in Italian food as salsa is in Mexican. I seem to always be discovering new ways to use this delightful sauce. Once, while cruising in the Sacramento Delta, friends stopped by and, before we knew it, it was cocktail time. I found an over-ripe avocado and some of my trusty bruschetta sauce in the galley. Why not? I mashed the avocado, mixed in the sauce, and presto! Italian guacamole! It was delicious.

Bruschetta Sauce

Serves 4 to 6 with bread as an appetizer

5 cloves garlic, peeled and minced
2 pounds room temperature Roma tomatoes, coarsely chopped
1 cup fresh basil
2 teaspoons dried oregano
1 teaspoon crushed dried red pepper
2 tablespoons capers
Salt and pepper to taste
3 to 4 tablespoons olive oil

Combine all the ingredients. If made in advance, you can keep the sauce in the refrigerator, but always serve at room temperature. Leftovers will keep for a week or more if you add a couple of tablespoons of wine vinegar.

Uses for bruschetta sauce

- Combine all the bruschetta sauce ingredients *except* the tomatoes and use as a sauce for pasta, seafood, chicken, or vegetables.
- The complete bruschetta recipe makes a flavorful and versatile Italian sauce. In addition to the traditional presentation of bruschetta as an appetizer served on crackers or toasted bread, I like it over pasta, either lightly heated or served at room temperature.
- I sometimes toss in a bit of bruschetta for salad dressing
- Steamed vegetables have more zip with bruschetta sauce ladled over them. Cauliflower looks particularly enticing when accompanied by bright red tomatoes and emerald green basil.
- We love to grill vegetables on the barbecue. Try lightly brushing sliced eggplant, red bell peppers, and zucchini with olive oil and sprinkling them with rosemary before grilling; serve them topped with a little bruschetta sauce.
- Sprinkle pizza rounds with some cheese (mozzarella or smoked Gruyère), top with drained bruschetta sauce, and bake long enough to melt the cheese.
- As a variation to my foil-wrapped vegie pack recipe (see page 153), I often add bruschetta sauce for flavor and moisture.
- I mix two cups of bruschetta sauce with a can (16 oz.) of white beans for a flavorful salad.
- The sauce is great on baked chicken or fish or served as an accompaniment to grilled meat.

Tomato-Mushroom Sauce

4 cups

This is a good sauce for pizza and, with the addition of a pound of Italian sausage, it makes a robust meat sauce to serve over pasta.

2 cloves garlic, finely chopped
1 onion, chopped
1 cup sliced mushrooms
2 tablespoons olive oil
1 (28 oz.) can tomatoes, chopped
1 (8 oz.) can tomato paste (see note on this page)
1 cup chicken broth
Salt and pepper to taste
1/8 teaspoon allspice
1 teaspoon sugar
1/4 teaspoon sage
1/4 teaspoon thyme
1/2 teaspoon grated lemon peel
3/4 cup dry sherry

1. Sauté the garlic, onion, and mushrooms in the olive oil until limp.
2. Add the tomatoes, tomato paste, and chicken both and bring to a boil. Reduce heat and simmer, uncovered, for 1 1/2 hours.
3. Add all the remaining ingredients the last 30 minutes of cooking time.

Spanish Tomato Sauce

3 cups

1 1/2 pounds tomatoes or 1 (16 oz.) can chopped tomatoes
1 medium white onion, chopped
2 cloves garlic, finely chopped
3 dashes Tabasco sauce
1/2 cup chicken broth
Salt and pepper
1/4 teaspoon oregano

Combine all the ingredients in a blender or food processor and purée. Simmer in a medium saucepan for about 15 minutes or until thick. Serve over omelettes or chile relleños.

Italian Tomato Sauce

2 1/2 cups

This is an excellent sauce for pasta or pizza and the leftovers are great with the morning eggs. It keeps in the refrigerator for up to a week and freezes well.

Note: Purchasing tomato paste in a tube is a very convenient and spacing-saving item for a boat. You simply squeeze out the amount you need when you need it. Best of all, the leftover paste doesn't get moldy. If you do use canned tomato paste, transfer the unused portion to a small container and cover the paste with cooking oil to help preserve it.

1 medium onion, finely chopped
2 tablespoons olive oil
2 teaspoons dried basil, crumbled
1 teaspoon dried oregano, crumbled
2 tablespoons tomato paste
1 (28 oz.) can crushed tomatoes
Salt and pepper to taste

Sauté the onion in the olive oil until soft. Add all the remaining ingredients and simmer until the sauce is very thick—about 30 minutes.

Creole Sauce

2 1/2 cups

This is terrific when served with chicken, seafood, omelettes, or over your favorite pasta.

3/4 cup chopped onions
3/4 cup chopped celery
3/4 cup chopped green bell peppers
3 cloves garlic, finely chopped
2 tablespoons olive oil
1 cup chicken broth
1 (8 oz.) can tomato sauce
1 (16 oz.) can tomatoes, chopped
2 bay leaves
3/4 teaspoon oregano
1 teaspoon cayenne
1/2 teaspoon thyme
1/2 teaspoon basil
Salt and pepper to taste
1 teaspoon sugar
1/2 teaspoon Tabasco sauce

Sauté the onions, celery, bell peppers, and garlic in the olive oil until soft. Stir in all the remaining ingredients and bring to a boil. Reduce the heat and simmer about 20 minutes. Remove bay leaves before serving.

Tomato, Garlic, and Wine Sauce

3½ cups

This delicate sauce goes well with Shrimp with Feta Cheese (page 66), with chicken, or over pasta. It keeps well in the refrigerator and can also be frozen.

¼ cup olive oil
2 teaspoons finely chopped garlic
½ cup chopped onion
1 (16 oz.) can Italian-style plum tomatoes, drained
1 cup dry white wine
½ cup finely chopped fresh parsley
½ cup finely chopped celery
1 bay leaf
½ teaspoon cumin
Salt and pepper to taste

1. Heat the olive oil in a large skillet and sautè the garlic and onions until soft.
2. Add the tomatoes and bring to a boil. Add the wine, parsley, celery, bay leaf, and cumin. Simmer covered about 30 minutes. Season with salt and pepper.

Seafood Sauces

I keep a variety of sauces on board to vary the taste of the seafood that Hal catches. Many of these store for several weeks.

Mustard Sauce

1 cup

Try this mustard sauce for poached, steamed, or grilled fish fillets. It is especially good on salmon and halibut. For small fillets of less fatty fish, coat the fish well and broil.

½ cup sour cream
½ cup plain yogurt
4 teaspoons Dijon mustard
1 tablespoon, finely chopped fresh dill or 1 teaspoon dried
⅛ teaspoon Tabasco sauce

Mix all the ingredients together. The sauce keeps about two weeks in the refrigerator.

Lime-Chili Butter

⅓ cup

Flavored butter is a popular topping for broiled or barbecued fish fillets and this recipe stores for weeks in the refrigerator. Restaurants usually form the butter into a roll, chill it, slice it, and place on hot seafood just before serving. I keep the mixture in a small container and use a teaspoon or so for each serving.

½ cup salted butter, at room temperature
1 tablespoon grated orange peel
1 tablespoon grated lime peel
2 teaspoons chili powder
½ teaspoon cayenne pepper

Combine all the ingredients.

Yogurt Glaze

1¼ cups

This is a low-calorie coating for delicate fish fillets such as sole or rockfish and it will keep in the refrigerator for a couple of weeks.

½ cup nonfat plain yogurt
1 tablespoon prepared horseradish
1 tablespoon dry mustard
¼ cup grated Parmesan cheese
2 tablespoons lemon juice
2 tablespoons chopped fresh dill or 2 teaspoons dried
3 tablespoons capers, rinsed and drained

Mix together all the ingredients and coat both sides of the fish fillets. Bake fillets at 350° F until just done.

Citrus Vinaigrette

¾ cup

2 tablespoons Dijon mustard
1 shallot, finely chopped
1 clove garlic, finely chopped
2 tablespoons lime juice
2 tablespoons orange juice
¼ cup olive oil

Combine all the ingredients. Serve with cooked fish or chicken. If used as a marinade, marinate no more than 30 minutes before cooking. Excellent served over cold seafood.

Cilantro-Lemon Sauce

½ cup

3 tablespoons finely chopped green onion
2 tablespoons butter
2 tablespoons finely chopped cilantro leaves
1 tablespoon lemon juice
1 tablespoon soy sauce

Sauté the onion in the butter until soft. Add the remaining ingredients and heat. Serve over cooked seafood or chicken.

Caper-Mayonnaise Sauce

1¼ cups

Hal and I once caught land crabs when we were hiking on Mexico's Socorro Island. We removed one pincer from each crab so it could still feed (and we knew that the missing limb would regenerate). We steamed the claws, cracked them, and dipped the meat into this simple sauce.

1 cup mayonnaise
1 tablespoon freshly ground black pepper
1 tablespoon capers, rinsed and drained
Juice from ½ lime

Mix all the ingredients together. This tangy sauce is excellent served on cold seafood or as a sauce for shrimp.

Lemon-Caper Sauce

½ cup

Try this sauce on mild-flavored fish such as sole, sand dabs, or sheep's head.

1 lemon
2 tablespoons capers, rinsed and drained
2 tablespoons chopped fresh parsley
3 tablespoons butter

1. Finely grate the lemon peel and set aside. Scoop out the lemon pulp, discard the seeds, and chop.
2. Combine the pulp with the capers and parsley.
3. Brown the butter until just golden, add the lemon mixture, and pour over broiled, sautéed, or grilled fish fillets.

Salad Dressings

These tasty salad dressings can double as meat marinades. Simply combine all the ingredients for each recipe in a small jar; shake the dressing before using it. These dressings keep for weeks without refrigeration.

Dijon Vinaigrette

1 tablespoon Dijon mustard
1 tablespoon minced red onion
3 tablespoons wine vinegar
Salt and pepper
½ cup olive oil

Walnut and Blue Cheese Dressing

3 tablespoons wine vinegar
2 tablespoons chopped walnuts
2 tablespoons crumbled blue cheese
Salt and pepper
½ cup olive oil

Garlic-Soy Dressing

1 teaspoon ground cumin
2 tablespoons fresh lime juice
2 tablespoons soy sauce
1 tablespoon Dijon mustard
1 tablespoon minced garlic
⅓ cup olive oil

Lemon-Garlic Dressing

2 cloves garlic, chopped
Juice of 1 lemon
Salt and pepper
½ cup olive oil

Caper Vinaigrette Marinade

1 tablespoon Dijon mustard
2 tablespoons red wine vinegar
1 tablespoon finely chopped shallot or onion
2 cloves garlic, finely chopped
2 tablespoons chopped fresh parsley
2 tablespoons capers, rinsed and drained
Salt and pepper
½ cup olive oil

Tarragon-Cilantro Dressing

¼ cup rice vinegar
Juice of 1 lime
½ teaspoon dried tarragon
3 tablespoons chopped cilantro (if available)
2 teaspoons cinnamon
¼ teaspoon coriander
¼ teaspoon cayenne pepper
½ cup olive oil

Papaya Seed Dressing

⅓ cup wine vinegar
1 tablespoon lime juice
¼ teaspoon dried tarragon
1 tablespoon finely chopped onion
2 tablespoons papaya seeds, coarsely ground
3 tablespoons sugar
Salt and pepper
½ teaspoon dry mustard
½ cup olive oil

Tomato Vinaigrette

2 cloves finely chopped garlic
3 tablespoons balsamic vinegar
½ cup tomato juice
1 tablespoon fresh lemon juice
1 teaspoon basil
1 tablespoon finely chopped sun-dried tomatoes
Salt and pepper to taste
¼ cup olive oil

Basil-Parsley Vinaigrette

2 tablespoons white wine vinegar
¾ teaspoon Dijon mustard
1 tablespoon finely chopped fresh basil
1 tablespoon finely chopped fresh parsley
Salt and pepper
⅓ cup olive oil

Oriental Vinaigrette

½ teaspoon dry mustard
½ teaspoon sugar
½ tablespoon finely chopped g inger
1 teaspoon finely chopped garlic
1 tablespoon finely chopped s hallots or green onion
2 tablespoons rice vinegar
1 tablespoon soy sauce
1 tablespoon olive oil
1 tablespoon Oriental sesame oil

Marinades

A marinade consists of an acid (lemon, lime juice, wine, or vinegar), spices, herbs, and often some oil. The food is soaked in the marinade so that it absorbs the flavor of the marinade and, in the case of meat, to help tenderize. Foods that are marinated at room temperature absorb the flavor faster than if refrigerated. To prevent bacterial growth, however, meat, poultry, and seafood should be refrigerated if they will be marinated longer than 15 minutes.

Never reuse a marinade. Meat juices will contaminate the marinade and harmful bacterial growth can occur. Also, the acid in marinades is neutralized during the marinating process. I use a Ziploc bag to marinate foods and then discard the bag. If you marinate foods in a dish, wash it with hot soapy water before reusing to prevent contaminating the cooked product with any harmful bacteria that could have been present in the raw meat.

Marinade Dijon

In the south of France, I ate a delicious rabbit that had been slathered with Dijon mustard and rosemary, wrapped in foil, and marinated for 30 minutes before being cooked on the barbecue. I have used this Dijon and rosemary marinade with chicken and it is equally as delicious.

Mustard-Soy Marinade

1¼ cups

This marinade can be made in large batches and kept for months without refrigeration. Try it on fish, beef, chicken, or pork.

12 cloves garlic, finely chopped
¼ cup Dijon mustard
½ cup soy sauce
½ cup olive oil
1 tablespoon Worcestershire Sauce
¼ teaspoon Tabasco Sauce

Marinade Tomas

Marinade for 2 pounds of meat

Boating friends are always a source of good ideas when it comes to cooking on board. Our friend Tom on the vessel *Limerick* introduced me to a delicious marinade that can be used on chicken, fish, or pork. It is delightfully spicy and enhanced by the flavors of garlic and lemon.

To further improve the flavor of foods on the barbecue, Tom uses mesquite or hickory chips. He makes a small dish out of heavy foil, fills the "dish" with wood chips that have been presoaked in water for at least an hour, and places the foil directly on the coals. Once the wood starts smoking, Tom adds the marinated meat. The smoke from the wood permeates the flesh and imparts a delicious flavor.

¼ cup fresh lemon or lime juice
2 tablespoons olive or peanut oil
2 tablespoons Cajun spice
2 tablespoons chopped fresh garlic

Combine all the ingredients together in a Ziploc bag. Allow the meat to marinate for at least an hour. Drain before grilling.

Lemon-Worcestershire Marinade

Marinade for 4 pounds of chicken or fish

1 cup lemon juice
½ cup olive oil
¼ cup Worcestershire sauce
1 teaspoon salt
2 teaspoons thyme
4 cloves garlic, finely chopped
2 teaspoons paprika

Combine all the marinade ingredients.

Red Wine Marinade

Marinade for 2 pounds of meat.

¾ olive oil
¾ cup dry red wine
1 teaspoon dried thyme
1 tablespoon minced garlic
1 tablespoon minced fresh parsley
1 teaspoon freshly ground pepper

Mix together all the marinade ingredients. This is a good marinade for any red meat.

Achiote Paste

¾ cup

This flavorful marinade is popular in southern Mexico on the Yucatán Peninsula. It keeps for months without refrigeration and is excellent on beef, pork, chicken, and fish. When cruising in Mexico, Achiote Adobo is readily available. Look for annatto seeds in Latin American markets when north of the border.

110-gram package Achiote Adobo (or substitute 2 tablespoons softened and ground annatto seeds)
2 teaspoons ground cumin
1 teaspoon freshly ground black pepper
2 teaspoons ground allspice
2 tablespoons chopped garlic
1 teaspoon ground red pepper
2 tablespoons orange juice
2 tablespoons wine vinegar

Mix all the ingredients together.

Chile Pasilla Marinade

Marinade for 2 pounds of meat.

The *pasilla* chile is a dried *poblano* (the pepper used in making chile relleños). This mild-to-medium-hot chile is about 6 inches long and almost black in color when dried. (Chile *ancho* can be substituted.) Try this flavorful marinade on pork, beef, or chicken. It lasts for months with no refrigeration.

6 dried, medium-hot pasilla chiles
½ cup white vinegar
2 teaspoons salt
6 cloves garlic, minced
½ teaspoon cumin
½ teaspoon oregano
½ teaspoon thyme

1. Toast the chiles on a griddle, turning often so they don't burn. Slit open, remove, and discard seeds.
2. Cover with hot water and soak for 20 minutes; drain and purée. Pour the purée into a strainer and, using

the back of a spoon, force as much of the chiles through the strainer as possible. Discard the pulp.

3. Combine the strained purée with the remaining marinade ingredients.

Jim Babb's Caribbean Jerk Marinade

Marinade for 2 pounds of meat.

While working on this book, one of my editors, Jim Babb, whose love for spicy food rivals that of my own, sent me his special recipe for jerk. Jerk has long been popular in the Caribbean and is finding its way into U.S. grocery stores. The marinade is rubbed into beef, chicken, goat, pork, or fish and allowed to marinate in the refrigerator for at least three hours or as long as overnight before cooking it on a hot grill.

Typically *habañero*—or Scotch Bonnets as they are sometimes called—are used in jerk marinades. They are some of the hottest chiles around; you may substitute serrano chiles or cayenne pepper.

4 habañero chiles, finely chopped, or 4 teaspoons cayenne pepper
1 onion, finely chopped
8 cloves garlic, finely chopped
2 teaspoons cinnamon
2 teaspoons allspice
2 teaspoons nutmeg
2 teaspoons thyme
2 tablespoons soy sauce

Grind all the ingredients together in a food processor or mash together with a fork.

Teriyaki Sauce

1/3 cup

1/4 cup soy sauce
2 tablespoons brown sugar
1 tablespoon finely chopped ginger

Combine all the ingredients. Use as a marinade or sauce.

Mango-Lime Sauce

1 1/4 cups

We love mangoes and eat them right off the tree in Mexico. The small variety has a tender skin and can be eaten unpeeled. When stateside, I resort to using the canned variety. If the mangoes are packed in syrup, be sure to rinse them before using.

1 cup mango pulp
2 tablespoons lime juice
1 tablespoon white wine vinegar
Grated peel of 1 lime
1/4 teaspoon cayenne pepper
Salt and pepper to taste
3 tablespoons olive oil

Purée all the ingredients together. Serve cold with seafood or chicken.

Cilantro-Garlic Marinade

Marinade for 1 to 2 pounds of seafood.

The flavor of the cilantro is preserved for several weeks in this tasty marinade.

3 tablespoons lime juice
3 tablespoons white wine vinegar
5 cloves garlic, finely chopped
4 tablespoons cilantro, finely chopped
1 teaspoon Dijon mustard
1/4 cup olive oil

Combine all the ingredients.

Mango-Basil Sauce

2 ½ cups

When served warm, this sauce goes well with fish, chicken, or pork. It can be prepared in advance and reheated (it keeps in the refrigerator for seven to 10 days), or it can be frozen.

3 large ripe mangoes, peeled, seeded, and chopped
2 tablespoons grated fresh ginger
3 cups chicken stock
Juice of 1 lime or to taste
1 bunch basil leaves, finely chopped
Salt to taste

Purée the mangoes, ginger, and chicken stock; cook until the volume is reduced by half. Add the remaining ingredients just before serving.

Cranberry, Pine Nut, and Chile Relish

3 cups

Heading south out of San Diego one fall, we anchored at San Jeronimo Island on Thanksgiving Day. In keeping with the traditions of the holiday, I served the following relish as a delicious accompaniment to our main course—Sautéed Lobster with Garlic (see page 65).

2 cups fresh cranberries, chopped
2 tart green apples, cored and chopped
1 serrano chile, stemmed, seeded and minced
Juice from 3 limes
3 tablespoons sugar
1 tablespoon chili powder
3 tablespoons pine nuts
Salt to taste

Mix all the ingredients together.

Whiskey Sauce

½ cup butter
1 ½ cups powdered sugar
1 egg yolk
½ cup bourbon or your favorite liqueur

1. In a saucepan, cream the butter and sugar together over medium heat until all the butter is absorbed. Remove from heat and blend in the egg yolk.
2. Gradually pour in the bourbon, stirring constantly—the sauce will thicken as it cools. Serve warm over bread pudding.

Orange-Butter Sauce

1¾ cups

8 ounces butter, at room temperature
½ cup sugar
Peel of 1 orange
Peel of 1 lemon
2 tablespoons orange juice
2 tablespoons orange liqueur

Beat the butter until soft and fluffy; gradually add the remaining ingredients.

Hints on Using Orange-Butter Sauce

- The liqueur helps to preserve the butter; if you use salted butter, the sauce keeps for several weeks at room temperature.
- For Crêpes Suzette, melt 2 to 4 tablespoons of the sauce in a skillet and add a cooked crêpe. Cook until the butter begins to sizzle. Fold the crêpe into quarters and serve drizzled with sauce.

Maple-Flavored Syrup

1½ cups

1 cup sugar
¾ cup hot water
⅓ teaspoon maple flavoring
⅓ teaspoon vanilla

Dissolve the sugar in hot water. Add the maple flavoring and vanilla.

CHAPTER 10

Breadmaking

Before we left the docks, I fantasized that I would have mornings free to experiment in the galley. I knew there would be many hours I could fill with experimenting with new recipes, making fresh bread every day, hours of unplanned activity. In reality passagemaking became my time for making bread. When at anchor there was always too much exploring to do, with places to go and people to meet.

When you have the time, experiment with making No Knead Yeast Bread, Garlicky Dinner Rolls, or sinfully rich Schnecken. Take the time to make your own sourdough starter and fix Sourdough Pancakes for breakfast. Make your own pizza dough and experiment with various toppings. But when the clock is ticking and you have to get dinner on in a hurry, there is nothing like a quick Beer Bread, a batch of flour tortillas, or New Mexican Sopapillas.

Yeast Breads

There is nothing more satisfying than the odor of freshly baked bread wafting out of your boat's oven. Having some basic knowledge about the ingredients used in making bread will help make your bread baking go smoothly.

Flour

Unbleached all-purpose flour is a blend of hard and soft wheat flours and has the necessary gluten needed for bread baking. Gluten provides the elasticity in the dough which holds the gases produced by the yeast during baking.

Breads made with whole wheat flour don't have to be kneaded, although a coarser textured bread is the result. Whole wheat breads can be mixed and allowed to rise once in the pan. The flour tends to turn rancid rather quickly, so it's best to store it in the refrigerator or freezer. Some boaters carry the whole grains on board and grind it in small quantities.

Nonwheat flours such as rye, graham, corn, and oat do not have the necessary gluten for successful bread baking. They should be combined with wheat flour when baking bread.

Yeast

Yeast is a living plant that thrives on sugar in the dough, produces carbon dioxide that makes the dough rise, and makes the delicious flavor and aroma characteristic of bread. Yeast is very sensitive to temperature variations. If you add it to liquid that's too cold, the yeast just sits there. If the liquid is too hot, the yeast is killed. Active dry yeast does best when combined with tepid liquids between 90° F and 115° F. Compressed yeast should be dissolved in liquid at 85° F. (If you don't have a thermometer, test the liquid on the inside of your wrist—it should not feel too hot or too cold.)

Compressed yeast and dry yeast can be used interchangeably. One package of dry yeast equals 2½ teaspoons and is equivalent to a 0.6 ounce cake of compressed yeast, which is enough to leaven 2 to 3 cups of flour.

Yeast will stay active until the expiration date on the package or indefinitely if frozen. If you are uncertain about your dry yeast, you can proof it by dissolving it in ¼ cup of tepid (100° F to 115° F) water with a pinch of sugar. If the yeast bubbles and foams, it's ready to use. (Reduce the amount of liquid in the bread recipe by ¼ cup if you have proofed the yeast.) Active cake yeast should be firm, a light grayish tan color, and smell fresh.

Liquids

Use room temperature liquids and tepid water to dissolve and activate yeast. Tepid liquids are at least 90° F. Hot liquids are 120° F to 130° F. Water makes bread crusty and milk keeps bread fresher longer and makes a softer crust. Many people like to use the water that is leftover from cooking potatoes—it gives the bread a coarser, moister texture and also keeps the bread fresher longer.

To make a soft but workable dough, use 1⅓ cups of liquid to 3½ to 4 cups of flour. Don't forget that shortening, eggs, sugar, and honey count as liquids.

If you use clean seawater in place of fresh water in bread recipes, remember that one cup of seawater contains about 2 teaspoons salt.

Tips and Techniques

Batter dough is the simplest of all breads to make and the bread only needs one rising. Strong beating (with an electric mixer) develops the gluten and takes the place of kneading—but you have to beat the dough until it comes away from the sides of the bowl. The texture is usually more porous for this type of bread. Most batter-type breads can be successfully cooked in a microwave oven.

Conventional dough breads must be kneaded. In a large bowl, stir half the flour into the dissolved yeast, the lukewarm liquids, and the shortening; beat for about one minute. Mix in the remaining flour by hand. When the dough starts to leave the sides of the bowl, dump it out onto a floured counter and knead.

Kneading. When a recipe gives a range for the amount of flour, start with the smaller amount. Using more flour than necessary makes the dough stiff and less manageable, producing heavier bread. On humid days, the dough will take more flour; on dry days, it will take less.

Kneading develops the gluten into long thin strands. As the yeast grows it gives off carbon dioxide which is trapped in the strands of gluten. This stretches the gluten, giving the bread its high, light texture and its small uniform holes.

You should always knead on a board or countertop that has a little flour on it. Rub some flour on your hands, too. Form the dough into a round ball and fold it toward you. Using the heels of your hands, push the dough away with a rolling motion. Turn the dough one-quarter and repeat until the dough is smooth and elastic—about 8 to 10 minutes. Knead until the dough develops a life of its own. If the dough becomes sticky, sprinkle the board with more flour and rub more flour onto your hands.

Rising. It's best to let bread rise where there is an even temperature of about 75° F to 85° F. A "cold" oven is often the best place to let bread rise. (If the galley is cold, preheat the oven for 60 seconds, turn it off, and place the bread in to rise.) Place the dough in a well-oiled bowl and cover with a clean dry towel.

The first time the dough rises it should double in bulk in about one to two hours. Press the tips of two fingers lightly and quickly a ½-inch into the dough. If the dents remain when you remove your fingers, the dough has doubled. The next step is to punch the dough down by pushing your fist into the center of the dough, pulling the edges to the center, and turning the dough over.

A brief kneading at this stage will give a finer grained texture to the bread. Let the dough rise again until it's almost doubled in bulk.

Shaping and Baking. Punch the dough down once again and divide it into the number of pieces specified in the recipe. Follow recipe directions for rolls or unusual shapes. To make loaves, roll the piece into a rectangle. Beginning with the upper, short side, roll it toward you and seal it with your thumbs or the heel of your hand. Seal the ends and fold them under. Be careful not to tear the dough. Place the dough seam side down in a greased pan. Use a round cake pan or pie pan for round loaves or encircle each loaf loosely with a one-inch band of aluminum foil.

Cover the pan with a clean dry cloth and allow the dough to rise until almost double. Bake in a preheated

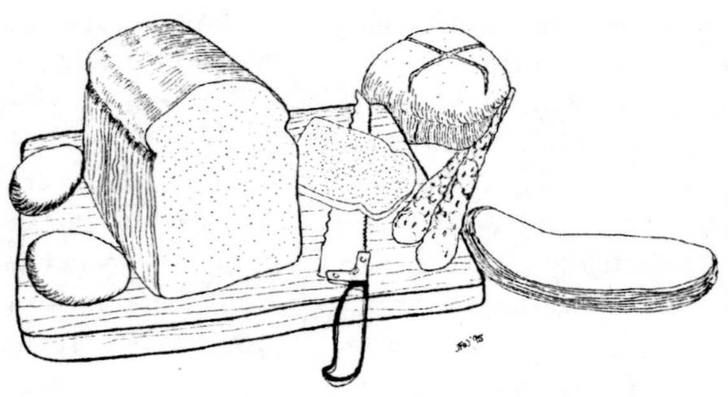

oven. To test for doneness, tap the bottom or sides of the bread; it's done when it sounds hollow. Allow the bread to cool out of the pan on a wire rack so that crust doesn't become soggy.

Storage. Wrap cooled bread in foil or plastic wrap. Although refrigerating helps prevent mold from growing, it also causes the bread to turn stale. Freezing is the best way to store an excess of bread. If you have a problem with bread getting moldy, spray the uncut loaves with white vinegar and allow them to dry before wrapping. You will not taste the vinegar, and most types of bread will last one week, even in the tropics.

No-Knead Yeast Bread

2 loaves

Cruising friends on *Panacea* gave me the following bread recipe and the recipe for Cheese Rolls (below), which were always a big hit at our potlucks. When I learned that no kneading was necessary in either recipe, I couldn't wait to try them.

1 envelope yeast
2 cups tepid water
1 tablespoon sugar
1 ½ teaspoons salt
4 cups unbleached white flour

1. Proof the yeast in a small amount of tepid water with a pinch of sugar. When it begins to foam, combine it in a bowl with the remaining water, sugar, and salt. Stir in the flour. The mixture will be very runny.
2. Cover the bowl and allow the dough to rise in a warm place until it's doubled in size. Punch it down and allow to rise again. Shape into two loaves and allow to rise once again. (This process takes three or four hours.)
3. Bake at 350°F until done—about 45 minutes.

Variations

The flavor of No-Knead Bread can be easily changed by adding the following:

- Brush the top of the bread with an egg wash (1 egg yolk and 1 tablespoon milk) and sprinkle on sesame or poppy seeds.
- When making the bread, stir in 1 to 2 tablespoons of your favorite herbs and spices: Italian spices, Cajun or Mexican seasonings, garlic powder, or chili powder are some possibilities. If you have any fresh herbs on board, chop them and mix them into the dough. You can also chop an onion and add it to the dough.
- You can also add nuts—walnuts, pine nuts, pecans or others—to the dough.
- For Black Olive Bread, add 1 cup of chopped black olives and 1 cup of chopped onions that have been sautéed in olive oil to the No-Knead Bread.

Cheese Rolls

16 to 24 rolls

These are rich, buttery rolls.

1 cup grated cheese
1 tablespoon of your favorite blend of spices
½ cup soft butter or margarine
1 recipe No-Knead Bread (above)
Egg wash
Sesame seeds

1. Mix the cheese and spices together; set aside.
2. Coat the work surface and your hands with the butter. After the second rising, spread half of the dough onto the prepared work surface. Cut into 6 to 8 rectangles and sprinkle with the cheese mixture. Fold the rectangles to enclose the filling and place seam side down on a buttered baking sheet. Repeat with remaining dough.
3. Allow to rise for 1 ½ hours. Brush the tops with an egg wash and sprinkle with sesame seeds.
4. Bake at 400°F for 25 to 30 minutes.

Variation
Rosemary Bread with Smoked Gruyère Cheese

2 loaves

1 recipe No-Knead Yeast Bread (page 181) (Use 1 cup of whole wheat flour and 3 cups of white flour; 2 teaspoons of chopped, dried rosemary.)
1 recipe Cheese Rolls (page 181)
1 tablespoon dried Italian herbs
1 cup smoked Gruyère

Follow the directions for making No-Knead Yeast Bread on page 181.

Rosemary Bread Pizza Rolls with Pepperoni

16 to 24 rolls

We took these rolls on many of our hikes. They travel well and are the envy of the bologna and cheese sandwich crowd! They also make great appetizers when sliced.

Follow the recipe for Rosemary Bread (above). After the second rising, roll out small balls of dough, spread with some pizza sauce, chopped pepperoni, and grated mozzarella cheese. Roll into cylinders, allow to rise, and bake until done.

Easy Oatmeal-Wheat Germ Bread

1 loaf

½ cup oatmeal, ground fine in blender or food processor
½ cup wheat germ
3 cups all-purpose flour
1 ½ teaspoons salt
1 teaspoon yeast
1 ½ cups tepid water

Mix together all the ingredients, knead until smooth, and place in a greased bowl, covered with a damp towel. Allow to rise—as long as overnight. Follow steps 3 and 4 for Easy White Bread (page 183). Bake the bread for 40 minutes.

Garlicky Dinner Rolls

40 mini rolls

1 package active dry yeast
¼ cup tepid water
1 teaspoon sugar
½ cup milk
½ cup olive oil
1 egg
½ cup water
1 ½ teaspoons salt
4 cups flour
½ cup butter
2 teaspoons finely chopped fresh garlic

1. Proof the yeast with the water and sugar.
2. Combine the yeast mixture with the milk, olive oil, egg, remaining water, salt, and 2 cups of the flour. Beat with an electric mixer until well blended. Add most of the remaining flour and knead on a floured surface until the dough is smooth and elastic.
3. Place the dough in a greased bowl, turning the dough to grease top. Allow to rise, covered with a clean, dry towel, in a draft-free area until it has doubled in bulk.
4. Punch the dough down and allow to rise again until almost doubled in bulk.
5. Punch the dough down. Heat the butter and garlic.
6. On a lightly floured board, roll the dough into a 12×15-inch rectangle. Cut lengthwise into 16 strips, each about ¾-inch wide. Stack 4 strips together, brushing each strip with garlic butter. Cut each stack into ¾-inch pieces.
7. Place on end in greased mini-muffin pans. Brush with remaining garlic butter.
8. Cover with a clean, dry towel and let rise until puffy—about 20 to 30 minutes.
9. Bake at 375° F for 10 to 12 minutes, until golden.

Easy White Bread

1 loaf

While studying French cooking in the south of France, my teacher had us make a simple, versatile bread each night to enjoy with our *café au lait* in the morning. Sylvie's recipe required very little kneading and only a quick rise before baking. I frequently make this bread adding toasted walnuts or sesame seeds, rosemary, black olives, or raisins.

1 ½ teaspoons active dry yeast
1 teaspoon honey
1 teaspoon olive oil
1 ½ cups tepid water
3 ½ to 4 cups bread flour or all-purpose flour
1 ½ teaspoon salt

1. Dissolve the yeast, honey, and olive oil in ½ a cup of tepid water and allow to bubble.
2. Put the flour and salt in a large bowl; add the yeast mixture and remaining water. Knead by hand until dough is soft, adding any nuts or fillings toward the end of the kneading process. The dough will be very sticky.
3. Grease a loaf pan; fill with the dough; cover and allow to rise in a warm place until doubled in bulk.
4. Bake in a preheated 400° F oven for about 30 minutes.

Rich Sour Cream Yeast Dough

This recipe makes enough dough for a large group of people. It is very rich, but would be fabulous for a morning potluck for a big group.

4 packages dry yeast (3 tablespoons) dissolved in tepid water
½ cup sugar
1 teaspoon salt
½ cold milk
1 cup sour cream
2 teaspoons lemon juice
1 teaspoon vanilla
3 egg yolks
5 to 6 cups flour
1 ½ cups soft butter

1. Cream together the dissolved yeast, sugar, salt, milk, sour cream, lemon juice, and vanilla. Add the egg yolks.
2. Add enough flour to make a medium-firm dough. Beat in the soft butter.
3. Knead 10 minutes—until the dough is smooth and elastic—adding more flour as necessary. Place the dough in a large Ziploc bag or covered bowl and chill for at least 4 hours. (Punch the dough down when it rises in the refrigerator. After it has become thoroughly chilled it will only need to be punched down twice a day. This dough can be prepared up to three days in advance.)

Schnecken

5 dozen large or 7 dozen small rolls

¼ cup soft butter
1 ¼ cups brown sugar
1 tablespoon corn syrup
1 ½ cups coarsely chopped or whole pecans
1 recipe Rich Sour Cream Yeast Dough (above)
2 teaspoons cinnamon
1 cup currants or raisins (plumped in brandy)
1 cup finely chopped pecans

1. Cream together the butter and ½ a cup of the brown sugar. Beat in the corn syrup. Generously grease regular size or tiny muffin tins with this mixture. Place 2 or 3 pecans in each muffin cup.
2. Preheat the oven to 375° F.
3. Roll the dough into a long rectangle ¼-inch thick. Sprinkle with the remaining sugar, cinnamon, currants or raisins, and finely chopped pecans. Roll the dough tightly, jelly-roll style, sealing the seam. If the roll becomes much thicker than the size of the muffin tins, stretch it out. If it is too thin, compress it.
4. Slice the roll into pieces that will fill the muffin cups halfway up. Press the slices firmly into the cups.

Allow to rise only until the dough looks puffy. Bake for about 20 minutes, or until the tops of the schnecken are golden brown.

5. Immediately turn the muffin pans upside down on wax paper, to remove the schnecken; allow the glaze to run over the sides.

RapidRise Yeast Techniques

This recipe uses RapidRise Yeast, a Fleischmann product that is a completely different strain of yeast from regular active dry yeast. RapidRise Yeast has greater leavening power per cell and its particle size is smaller, so it disperses through the dough at a faster rate. It is also more resilient and less sensitive to temperature changes, making it more foolproof.

You can use the following steps to convert your favorite yeast recipes for use with RapidRise Yeast.

1. Set aside 1 cup of all-purpose flour from the total amount. Mix the remaining flours and other dry ingredients for dough (including yeast) in a large bowl.
2. Heat the shortening and other liquid ingredients (except eggs) until hot to the touch—125 to 130° F.
3. Stir the hot liquids into the dry mixture.
4. Mix in eggs (if required).
5. Mix in only enough reserved flour for desired consistency.
6. Follow directions for kneading, if required. Use additional flour, if necessary, until the dough is no longer sticky. Cover the dough; let rest 10 minutes. Shape or stir the batter down. Place the dough in a greased bowl; grease the top of the dough. Cover and let rise in a draft-free place until doubled in size. Most dough will require about half the normal rising time. Bake as directed.

Quick Mix Swedish Limpa

2 loaves

6 ½ cups all-purpose flour
2 cups rye flour
¼ cup firmly packed brown sugar
2 teaspoons salt
2 teaspoons fennel seeds
2 teaspoons grated orange peel
2 packages RapidRise Yeast
2 tablespoons butter
2 ⅔ cup hot water

1. Follow steps 1, 2, 3, and 5 in RapidRise Yeast instructions. Turn the dough out onto a floured board; knead until smooth and elastic. Set in a greased bowl and grease the top. Cover the dough and let it rise in a warm, draft-free place until doubled in bulk—about 30 to 40 minutes.
2. Punch down the dough. On a floured board, divide the dough in half and shape into loaves. Place in 2 greased loaf pans. Cover; let rise in a warm, draft-free place until doubled in bulk—about 30 to 40 minutes.
3. Bake at 400° F for 30 to 35 minutes or until done. Remove from pans; cool on wire racks.

Jalapeño-Cheddar Bread

2 loaves

6 ¾ cups all-purpose flour
2 tablespoons sugar
2 teaspoons salt
4 to 6 tablespoons chopped canned jalapeño chiles
2 ½ cups grated cheddar cheese
2 packages RapidRise Yeast
2 cups hot water (120°F to 130°F)

1. Follow steps 1, 3, and 5 in RapidRise Yeast instructions (page 184). Turn the dough out onto a floured board; knead until smooth and elastic. Cover and let rest for 10 minutes.

2. Divide the dough in half and shape into loaves. Place in 2 greased loaf pans. Cover and let rise in a warm, draft-free place until doubled in bulk—about 40 to 50 minutes.

3. Bake at 350°F for 30 to 35 minutes or until done. Remove from pans; cool on wire racks.

Sourdough Starter

I got interested in sourdough baking after tasting Barbara's sourdough bread one night aboard *Wanderjahr 2*. The next morning, Barbara showed up at my transom with two cups of starter and some recipes. She told me that the starter had been nurtured by a man named Jack McLaughlin in Long Beach, California, who passed it on to Mary Taylor aboard *Avventura*. It made its way to the Sea of Cortez and became a permanent galley item aboard *SpiceSea* several months later.

The best starter is one that is passed along to you by a friend. You can, however, make your own!

1 package active dry yeast
2 cups tepid water
2 cups unbleached all-purpose flour

1. In a clean, rigid-covered container (I use a hard plastic Tupperware container that fits easily in my refrigerator), dissolve the yeast in the water and stir in the flour. Don't use a metal spoon—use wood or a chopstick.

2. Leave uncovered in a warm place (80°F to 90°F) for four days to a week, or until the mixture bubbles and has developed a sour odor. Stir the mixture daily. If it smells bad or becomes discolored, discard and start again.

3. You can begin using the starter or store it in the refrigerator. If stored in the refrigerator, allow it to come to room temperature before using.

4. You should feed your starter every week. Always save 2 cups of this mixture for an ongoing starter. If you have your original 4 cups of starter, either give half away or use it in baking. To the remaining 2 cups of starter, add 1 cup of unbleached, all-purpose flour and 1 cup of tepid water. Allow the starter to ferment and bubble overnight at room temperature, then use or place in the refrigerator.

5. You can also freeze the starter for two to three months. Thaw at room temperature for 24 hours, feed it some flour and water, and it should start to bubble. If it doesn't, add a teaspoon of active dry yeast and let it ferment overnight.

6. If a gray liquid accumulates on top of the starter, pour it off. Wash your starter container every week with soap and water, then rinse and dry it.

7. To use the starter in any bread recipe: 2 cups of starter equals 1 package of dry yeast and the dissolving liquids in the recipe.

Sourdough French Bread

1 loaf

1 ½ cups room temperature starter
1 cup warm water
2 teaspoons salt
2 teaspoons sugar
4 cups all-purpose unbleached white flour

1. Mix together all the ingredients. Knead on a floured board until the dough becomes smooth and elastic. Add more flour if the dough is sticky.

2. In a warm, draft-free area, allow the dough to rise in a greased bowl covered with a cloth until doubled in bulk. Punch down and allow to rise another 45 minutes.
3. Shape the dough and place in a greased loaf pan. Allow to rise again.
4. Bake in a preheated 375°F oven for 45 minutes. Remove from pan when done.

Sourdough Rolls

12 rolls

1 cup room temperature starter
1 cup tepid water
1 tablespoon olive oil
1 teaspoon salt
4 cups water

1. Follow steps 1 and 2 for the Sourdough French Bread (page 185). After the first rising, roll the dough into a 12 × 16-inch rectangle and roll it jelly-roll style (If desired, fill with herbs, spices, nuts, brown sugar, and raisins.)
2. Slice lengthwise into 12 equal pieces and place on a greased baking sheet. Allow to rise for 90 minutes.
3. Bake in a preheated 375° F oven for 15 to 20 minutes.

Sourdough Biscuits

14 biscuits

½ teaspoon salt
1 tablespoon sugar
2 teaspoons baking powder
2 cups flour
½ cup butter
1 ½ cups room temperature starter

1. Mix together the salt, sugar, baking powder, and flour. Cut in the butter and stir in the starter.
2. Knead lightly, then roll out to a ½-inch thickness. Cut with a biscuit cutter and place on a baking sheet; allow to rise for about 30 minutes.
3. Bake in a preheated oven at 425° F for 10 minutes.

Sourdough Pancakes

4 to 6 servings

2 cups room temperature starter
2 tablespoons sugar
4 tablespoons oil
1 egg
½ teaspoon salt
¾ teaspoon baking soda dissolved in 1 tablespoon tepid water

1. Combine all the ingredients *except* the baking soda. Fold the dissolved baking soda into the batter; allow the batter to double in bulk.
2. Bake on a hot griddle until light brown.

Sourdough English Muffins

12 to 14 muffins

1 package active dry yeast
¼ cup tepid water
1 tablespoon sugar
1 cup warm milk
½ cup room temperature starter
¾ teaspoon salt
3 ½ to 4 cups all-purpose unbleached white flour
¼ cup yellow cornmeal

1. Proof the yeast (see page 179) in the water with the sugar. Add the milk, starter, and salt. Add the flour and knead on a floured board until smooth and elastic.
2. In a warm, draft-free area, allow the dough to rise in a greased bowl covered with a damp towel until doubled in bulk. Punch down.
3. Roll the dough to a ½-inch thickness on a board covered with cornmeal. Cut into 3-inch rounds.
4. Dip the other side in cornmeal and place on a baking sheet covered with a towel. Allow to rise about 45 minutes until puffy.
5. Toast in a lightly greased frying pan over low heat for about 10 minutes per side. Cool on wire racks.

6. Split the muffins open with a fork and toast in a hot frying pan (or toaster). Serve with butter and jam.

FOCACCIA

8 to 12 servings

1 recipe Easy Pizza Dough (page 188)

1. Follow steps 1, 2, and 3 for Easy Pizza Dough. Roll the dough into a large rectangle ¼-inch thick.
2. Place on a greased baking sheet and prick the surface evenly with a fork. Make small indentations in the surface of the dough with your finger or the end of a wooden spoon. Spread with the topping of your choice (see below).
3. Bake at 400° F for 20 minutes or until golden brown.
4. Cut into squares and serve warm.

Onion and Herb Topping

½ cup olive oil
1 ½ cups sliced onions
1 teaspoon crumbled rosemary leaves
1 teaspoon coarse salt

Cook the onions in the olive oil until soft. Spread over the dough. Sprinkle with herbs and salt.

Pine Nut Topping

¼ cup olive oil
¼ cup pine nuts
1 ½ teaspoons sage leaves
¼ cup freshly grated Parmesan cheese

Spread the oil over the focaccia; sprinkle on the nuts, sage, and cheese.

Gorgonzola and Walnut Topping

¼ cup olive oil
½ cup walnut pieces
1 cup blue cheese

Spread the oil on the focaccia. Press in the walnuts and sprinkle with the cheese.

STUFFED FOCACCIA

6 to 8 servings

1 ½ tablespoons pesto sauce
¼ cup sliced black olives
1 cup grated mozzarella cheese
1 tablespoon minced sun-dried tomatoes
1 egg
Sesame seeds

1. Follow the directions for Easy Pizza Dough (page 188) through step 3. Roll the dough into a large rectangle and place on a greased baking sheet.
2. Spread the pesto down the center third of the dough length. Sprinkle with the olives, cheese, and tomatoes.
3. Slice the dough in one-inch intervals along both sides, from where the filling stops, to the outer edge. Alternating sides, fold strips at an angle across the filling, completely covering the filling.
4. Allow to rise in a warm place for 30 minutes.
5. Make an egg wash by combining the egg and 1 tablespoon of water. Brush the top of the dough with the egg wash and top with the sesame seeds.
6. Bake at 400° F for 25 minutes or until done. Cool briefly before slicing.

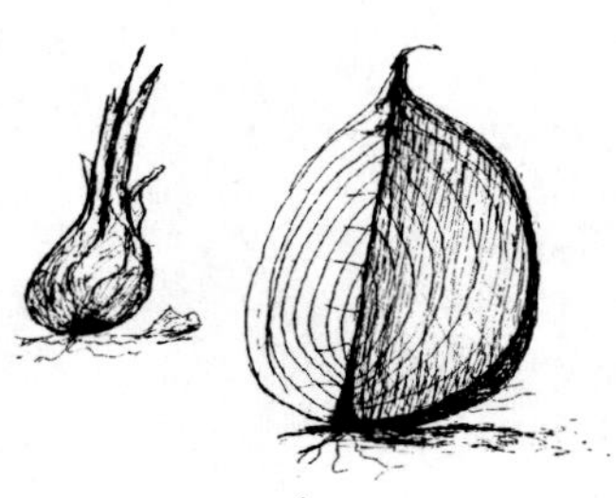

Pizza, Pizza

Before I went cruising for the first time, I remember talking to a friend who said that during her 42-day South Pacific passage, all she could think about was getting ashore and having a pizza. I, too, am a pizza lover and decided that it couldn't be that hard to make pizza while cruising aboard *SpiceSea*.

The first year we were in Mexico I provisioned with several prepackaged kits that included the sauce, cheese, and a mix for the crust. All you did was add water, mix, shape, and bake to make the crust. What a disaster!

I next tried the pizza crust that is sold like the pop-open refrigerator biscuits. Once again, it was awful.

So there I was making my pizza dough from scratch, kneading it, and letting it rise. It tasted great, but took all the spontaneity out of eating pizza.

And then someone introduced me to Boboli Bread—the perfect pizza crust. Boboli comes in a vacuum-sealed plastic wrapper. If you select only the rounds of bread that have a tight seal, they will keep long after the expiration date. For long-term storage, however, it is necessary to freeze the rounds.

There is another product from an Italian company called Parmalat that stays even fresher on board. They make both focaccia (a thicker crusted bread that is excellent for pizza) and pizza rounds (two per package) that are available in a specially sealed nondated package. They will keep for one year or longer on board. (For ordering information, see page 11.)

If I want a red sauce on my pizza, I use one made in a convenient squeeze bottle by Contadina if I don't make my own. (See pages 189 for sauce recipes.) The Contadina label says to refrigerate the sauce after opening, but I have been able to keep the open bottle many months without refrigeration.

And what is pizza without cheese? I like to sprinkle a little Parmesan over the tomato sauce. (Chunks of ungrated Parmesan, sealed in a FoodSaver Bag, will keep for months without refrigeration.) Mozzarella cheese, another key ingredient on a traditional pizza, can be bought in eight-ounce balls that keep for six to eight months in the refrigerator; they'll keep without refrigeration for at least a month in a cool place. For convenience you can purchase already grated cheeses which also have a long shelf life, but they take up too much space in the refrigerator if you are going to be on board for an extended period of time.

If you want some pepperoni on your pizza, buy the packaged kind but check the expiration date on the package. You can usually find packages that have a couple of months before they expire and most pepperoni keeps at room temperature until the expiration date. The oily film that may appear in the package is fat that comes out of the meat at room temperature. Blot it with a paper towel before using the sausage.

There are many great canned toppings that can be kept on board—black olives, marinated bell peppers, sun-dried tomatoes in olive oil, canned pesto sauce, and anchovies to name a few. Onions and garlic are also great on any pizza.

Easy Pizza Dough

2 pizza crusts, 8 slices each

1 cup warm water (105°F to 115°F)
1 package yeast
1 teaspoon sugar
2 teaspoons salt
2 tablespoons olive oil
2 ¾ to 3 ¼ cups flour

1. Dissolve the yeast in the water. Add the sugar, 1½ teaspoons of salt, olive oil, and 1½ cups of flour. Beat until smooth. Stir in enough additional flour to make a stiff dough and turn out onto a lightly floured board. Knead until smooth and elastic—about 5 minutes.

2. Place the dough in a greased bowl, covered with a clean, dry towel, in a warm, draft-free place until doubled in bulk—about 45 minutes.

3. Punch the dough down and divide in half. Cover and allow to rest for 10 minutes.

4. Roll out and stretch each half into a 10-inch circle; place on a greased baking sheet. Pinch the edge to fit the pan, forming a standing rim of dough around the perimeter. Allow to rest 10 minutes.

5. Bake at 375°F for 8 to 10 minutes. Top as desired and heat.

Tasty Pizza Combinations

Following are some great pizza combinations that you can mix and match. Brush the edges of pizza rounds with olive oil to prevent them from drying out if they're not completely covered with a sauce.

- Cheese: Italian Tomato Sauce (page 171), oregano, mozzarella, and Parmesan cheeses.
- Pepperoni, Italian Sausage, and Mushrooms: To the above, add sliced mushrooms, pepperoni, and cooked Italian sausage.
- Grilled Vegetable: Sliced eggplant, zucchini, bell peppers that have been grilled on the barbecue (see page 155), roasted garlic (see page 143), tomato sauce, and mozzarella.
- Pizza Margherita: 4 cups of Bruschetta Sauce (page 170), 8 ounces of mozzarella (preferably fresh), and ½ cup of Parmesan cheese.
- Barbecue Chicken: Use leftover barbecued chicken with smoked Gouda cheese, mozzarella, red onion, and cilantro.
- Caramelized Onion, Walnut, and Gorgonzola: 6 cups of sliced onions seasoned with 1 teaspoon of sage, slowly cooked in olive oil until golden. Top with chunks of Gorgonzola cheese and toasted walnuts.
- Thai Chicken: Chicken with Chunky Thai Peanut Sauce (page 94), cilantro, sprouts, a green onion, carrots, and mozzarella cheese.
- Cheese and Mushroom: 2 cups of sliced mushrooms and 2 teaspoons of chopped garlic sautéed in olive oil. Mix the mushrooms with Italian Tomato Sauce (page 171). Sprinkle with cheddar cheese and top with chopped sun-dried tomatoes.
- Avocado and Bacon: Bake a pizza with cheddar cheese and black olives. Top with diced avocado, sour cream, and chopped bacon.
- Brie and Smoked Salmon Appetizer: Top pizza round with thin slices of Brie, smoked salmon, and sliced red onions. Heat until the cheese melts, then serve.
- Herbed Cheese and Broccoli Appetizer: 1 recipe of Herbed Cheese Spread (page 39), 1 can of sliced black olives, 1 cup of chopped broccoli florets, sliced cherry tomatoes or chopped red bell peppers or marinated bell peppers, sliced pepperoni, and chopped green onion lightly heated.

Fresh Tomato and Goat Cheese Pizza

1 pizza

12 medium plum tomatoes, peeled, seeded, and diced
Freshly ground black pepper
1 teaspoon dried oregano
6 ounces goat cheese (Montrachet), crumbled
¼ cup chopped fresh basil leaves
⅓ cup sliced black olives
1 tablespoon olive oil
2 tablespoons Parmesan cheese
1 (10-inch) pizza crust, baked (see page 188)

Season the tomatoes with the pepper and oregano. Arrange on a crust with the goat cheese, basil, and olives. Drizzle with the olive oil and top with the Parmesan cheese. Bake in the lower third of the oven at 500°F for 15 to 20 minutes.

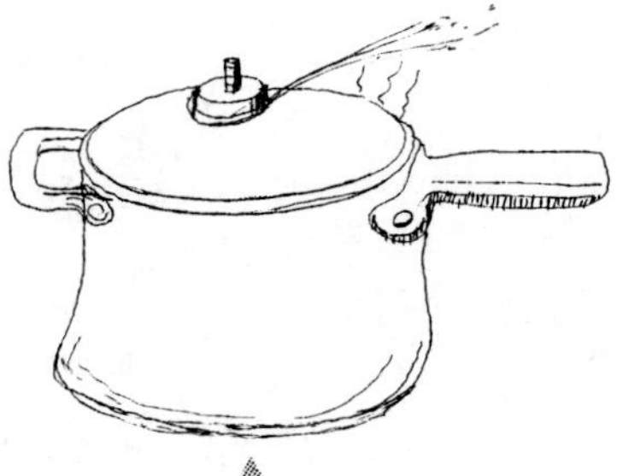

Pizza with Spicy Shrimp

1 pizza

2 tablespoons olive oil
4 cloves garlic, minced
½ pound uncooked shrimp, peeled and deveined
6 ounces grated Jack cheese
2 teaspoons dried basil or 2 tablespoons fresh, finely chopped
3 green onions, minced
Grated peel from 1 lemon
½ teaspoon dried hot red pepper flakes
1 (10-inch) pizza crust, baked (page 188)

Sauté the garlic and shrimp in the olive oil until the shrimp are barely cooked. Allow to cool; drain well. Assemble the pizza in the following order: cheese, basil, drained shrimp, green onions, lemon peel, and pepper flakes. Bake in the lower third of the oven at 500°F until the cheese is melted and starts to brown—about 12 minutes.

Tomato, Roasted Pepper, and Pepperoni Pizza

1 pizza

¾ cup Italian Tomato Sauce (page 171)
8 ounces grated mozzarella cheese
4 ounces pepperoni, sliced
1 (7 oz.) jar roasted peppers, drained, cut into strips
1 cup Italian olives, halved, pitted
¼ cup grated Parmesan cheese
1 (10-inch) pizza crust, baked (page 188)

Assemble the pizza toppings in the following order: tomato sauce, mozzarella, pepperoni, peppers, and olives. Bake in the lower third of the oven at 500°F until the cheese is melted and starts to brown— about 12 minutes.

Beer Bread

1 loaf

Beer breads, unlike yeast breads, can be mixed and baked without the time-consuming step of rising. When you want sandwiches in a hurry, or bread at the last minute for dinner, beer breads are the answer. They make excellent sliced bread for sandwiches and can be flavored with dried herbs and spices for a variety of flavors. The beer helps the bread rise; there is no residual flavor of beer after the bread has baked.

3 cups flour
1 tablespoon baking soda (check expiration date!)
1 teaspoon salt
3 tablespoons sugar
12 ounces beer, at room temperature

Grease a bread pan. Combine all the ingredients. Add any fruit, nuts, herbs, and spices that you desire. Bake at 350°F for 45 minutes. Allow to cool 15 minutes before slicing.

Variation
Cinnamon Breakfast Bread

Add 3 tablespoons of raisins, 1 tablespoon of cinnamon, 1 teaspoon of nutmeg, and 3 tablespoons of additional sugar to basic Beer Bread Recipe.

Variation
Apple Bread

Add 1 cup of chopped apples to the Cinnamon Bread Recipe.

Variation
Olive-Herb Bread

Add 1 cup of chopped onion, ½ teaspoon sage or thyme, ½ teaspoon of basil, and 1 cup of sliced black olives to the basic Beer Bread recipe.

Sandwiches

Tortillas, pita bread, bagels, and slices of homemade bread all make great sandwiches. Try some of these combinations when you are looking for new ideas.

- ***Avocado, Cashews, Chicken, and Alfalfa Sprouts with Sliced Tomatoes and Mayonnaise*** (Variations: Substitute bacon for the chicken and cashews; sliced turkey for the chicken and cashews; or sliced red onions for the cashews and sprouts.)
- ***Smoked Salmon, Cream Cheese, Thinly Sliced Onion, and Capers*** (Variation: Substitute avocado, sliced cucumber, and sprouts for the capers.)
- ***Grilled Eggplant, Roasted Peppers, Melted Mozzarella, and Bruschetta Sauce***
- ***Curried Tuna with Almonds, Raisins, Chutney, Lettuce, and Tomatoes***

Baking Bread in a Pressure Cooker

Several years ago I met a couple who had cruised the world for more than 30 years. They were on a new boat, their first powerboat, and it was equipped with a fine oven. Nevertheless, the lady of the boat was so accustomed to baking bread in a pressure cooker that she saw no reason to change her method just because she now had an oven.

To bake bread in a pressure cooker, the cooker must be made of a heavy gauge metal. If it is too lightweight, use a heat diffuser. Before the final rising, grease the cooker and spread a thin layer of cornmeal on the bottom.

Bake the bread over a medium-low flame, with the lid on but without setting the pressure—you want the steam to escape. Baking time will be about 40 to 45 minutes for a loaf of bread made with 3½ to 4 cups of flour.

Quick breads can be done in a separate pan in the pressure cooker. Grease a 4- to 6-cup pan that will fit into your pressure cooker. (I like to use a tin can because its round shape makes a nice shape for the bread.) Fill the can two-thirds full; cover with foil; and place on a rack in the pressure cooker. Add 2 cups of water, cover the cooker, and cook for 50 minutes at minimum pressure. Release the pressure following the manufacturer's instructions. Allow to cool slightly before removing from the pan.

Hot and Spicy Jalapeño Muffins

24 muffins

1¼ cups flour
1 tablespoon baking powder
1 teaspoon salt
2 tablespoons sugar
¾ cup yellow cornmeal
2 eggs, lightly beaten
1 cup milk
¼ cup melted butter
4 fresh jalapeño chiles, stems removed, chiles chopped
¼ teaspoon dried crushed red pepper
1 cup grated mozzarella cheese

1. Combine the flour, baking powder, salt, sugar, and cornmeal. Mix the eggs, milk, and butter; add to the

dry ingredients. Stir in the chiles and mix just enough to dampen the dry ingredients.

2. Grease and flour minimuffin pans. Fill the pans ⅔ full with batter.
3. Bake in a preheated 375°F oven for 15 minutes or until done. Sprinkle with cheese and place in the oven for an additional 2 to 3 minutes.
4. Allow the muffins to cool in the pan for 10 minutes before removing.

Pumpkin Banana Bread

8 to 10 servings

When we are making short hops, Hal usually does the piloting and I spend my time writing or, if it's calm enough, puttering in the galley. I look over the fruits and vegetables and separate anything that is getting too ripe. Being underway is also a good time to clean out the refrigerator or defrost the freezer because we have fully charged batteries.

On one such occasion, the fruit flies were circling some very ripe bananas and I had a can of pumpkin on board, so I made some quick bread.

⅓ cup butter or margarine
1 cup brown sugar, packed
1 cup banana pulp (2 to 3 very ripe bananas), mashed
2 eggs
1 teaspoon vanilla
1 cup pumpkin
¾ teaspoon cinnamon
½ teaspoon ginger
¼ teaspoon salt
2 ½ teaspoons baking powder
2 cups flour
¾ cup chopped nuts
½ cup currants

1. Cream together the butter and sugar. Add the bananas, eggs, and vanilla; beat well. Stir in the pumpkin.
2. Combine the cinnamon, ginger, salt, baking powder, and flour. Add to the pumpkin mixture and stir to combine. Do not overmix. Add the nuts and currants, if desired.
3. Pour the batter in a greased loaf pan and bake at 350°F for 1 hour and 10 minutes or until a toothpick inserted into the center comes out clean. (If using minimuffin pans, allow 30 minutes baking time.)

Cranberry, Pine Nut, and Banana Bread

8 to 10 servings

I bought a package of dried cranberries recently and found their delicious flavor and burst of color a tasty addition to many traditional recipes. They are ideal for keeping on board because they store so well. In this recipe you could, however, substitute raisins or any dried fruit for the cranberries, or just prepare a basic banana bread without the berries or nuts. If you happen to have pine nuts on board, try them in this recipe.

⅓ cup butter or margarine, at room temperature
⅔ cup sugar
1 to 2 cups banana pulp (3 to 5 medium bananas), mashed
Grated peel from 1 large lemon
2 eggs
1 ¾ cups all-purpose flour
½ teaspoon salt
2 ½ teaspoons baking powder
⅓ cup pine nuts
⅓ cup dried cranberries

1. Cream together the butter and sugar. Add the bananas, lemon peel, and eggs; beat well.

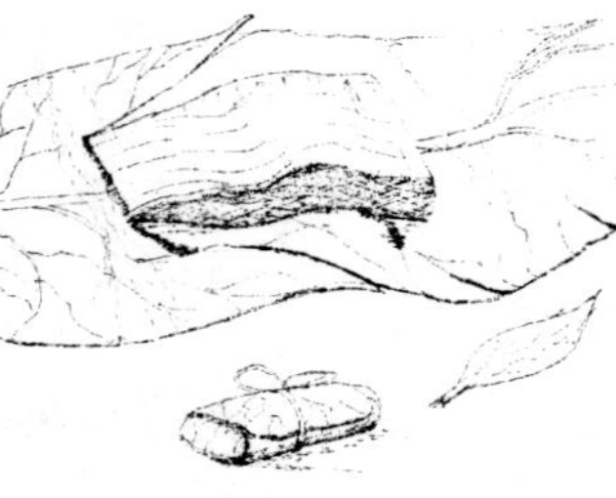

2. Combine flour, salt, and baking powder. Add to the banana mixture and stir to combine. Do not overmix. Add the dried fruit and nuts if desired.

3. Pour the batter in a greased pan and bake at 350° F for 1 hour or until a toothpick inserted in the center comes out clean. Cool before slicing.

LAVOSH

3 large rounds

Lavosh, or Middle Eastern cracker bread, keeps indefinitely in an airtight container.

1 package active dry yeast
1 cup tepid water
1 tablespoon sugar
2 ½ cups all-purpose flour
1 tablespoon salt
⅛ teaspoon cayenne pepper
3 tablespoons lightly toasted sesame seeds or poppy seeds

1. In a large bowl, proof the yeast in the water with the sugar until it foams. Add the flour, salt, and pepper and stir until the dough forms a ball.

2. Knead on a floured surface until the dough is smooth and elastic. Place in a greased Ziploc bag and chill for 1 hour.

3. Divide into 3 pieces. Roll each piece out on a floured baking sheet to about ⅛-inch thickness and sprinkle with seeds.

4. Bake the lavosh in a preheated 400° F oven for 12 to 15 minutes or until golden. (It will become crisper as it cools.)

The Versatile Tortilla

Flour tortillas are one of the most versatile foods that I carry aboard *SpiceSea*. I can easily store a couple of dozen tortillas in our small refrigerator and still find room for other necessities. Bread, on the other hand, molds quickly in the marine environment and doesn't stimulate my creative cooking juices like a flour tortilla. Perhaps it's my midwestern background where the standard fare was toast for breakfast, sandwiches for lunch, and rolls for dinner. When I left home in the sixties, Mexican ingredients were unheard of; tortillas still have an exotic connotation for me.

Today, bread is becoming more popular in Mexico while tortillas have become a standard item in most U.S. grocery stores! This exchange of cultures hit home when we were once cruising off of Santa Maria Bay on Baja's west coast. There is a lot of fishing for lobster in that area, and we were once asked if we'd trade a bucket full of lobster for a loaf of bread. But all we had on board *SpiceSea* was tortillas!

Living on our boat in Mexico for several years has permeated my cooking with a definite south-of-the-border flare. We enjoy fish, chicken, or beef fajitas for dinner, rolled in steaming hot tortillas; we eat quesadillas for lunch that are filled with the leftovers from the night; and for special breakfasts, I fix burritos.

FLOUR TORTILLAS

8 to 12 tortillas

When camping near small villages or boating in areas where there are primitive Mexican fishing camps, I have always been impressed with the ease and expertise with which the women, who live in remote areas, make their flour tortillas.

Although I don't think I'll ever regard making flour tortillas as an easy task, they do taste wonderful and are mighty handy when I've run out of bread.

2 cups flour
½ teaspoon salt
¼ cup vegetable shortening or lard
½ cup warm water

1. Mix the flour and salt. Add the fat and rub into the flour with your fingertips until the mixture resembles the texture of cornmeal. (This can also be done in a food processor.)

2. Add the water and stir until the dough forms a ball.
3. Knead the dough on a floured surface until it's smooth and elastic.
4. Cover with plastic wrap and allow to rest for 30 minutes.
5. Divide the dough into 8 pieces for 10-inch tortillas or 12 pieces for 8-inch tortillas. Roll each piece into a ball and cover.
6. Roll out each ball with a rolling pin on a floured surface, turning frequently until the desired sized circle is formed. Stack the tortillas between sheets of plastic wrap.
7. Heat an ungreased griddle or frying pan until water sizzles instantly. Place a tortilla in the hot skillet and cook until the top is bubbly and the bottom begins to get flecks of brown.
8. Turn the tortilla and cook until it is speckled with brown.
9. If the tortilla puffs up during the cooking process, press it down with a spatula.
10. Stack the tortillas and cover with a clean cloth, if serving hot.
11. If made in advance, allow to cool before stacking. Wrap tightly in aluminum foil. Tortillas can be frozen or stored in the refrigerator for several days.

Variation
Mama Cesena's Jalapeño Tortillas

When we first moved to San Diego, one of the live-aboards on our dock helped us into our slip and then brought over freshly made jalapeño tortillas. Nancy has gone on to produce these fabulous tortillas on a commercial basis. They are the best tortillas I have ever tasted.

3 cups flour
¼ cup vegetable shortening or lard
½ teaspoon baking powder
1 teaspoon salt
3 jalapeño chiles puréed in ½ cup water
½ cup additional water

Make the tortillas as directed for Flour Tortillas (page 193), adding the puréed jalapeños when you add the rest of the water.

Flour Tortilla Snacks

When you have stale flour tortillas or pita bread, cut them into wedges and bake at 400° F until they are almost crisp. Cover with a light mist of olive oil and sprinkle with dried Italian or Mexican herbs. Sprinkle with jack, Parmesan, or Swiss cheese and finish baking until they are crisp and the cheese is melted.

Papaya Quesadillas

6 servings

6 flour tortillas
⅓ pound cheese, such as jack, Brie, or Chihuahua, cut into thin strips
1 (4 oz.) can diced mild green chiles
1 ripe papaya, peeled, seeded, and diced (or mango)
1 onion, peeled, halved, thinly sliced, and wilted (see instructions)

1. Make the tortillas as directed in the recipe for Flour Tortillas (page 193), or use store bought tortillas.
2. Combine the cheese, chiles, and papaya; set aside. Wilt the onion by boiling 1 cup of water and allowing the onion to steep in the hot water until soft—about 10 minutes. Drain and combine with the cheese mixture.
3. Fill each tortilla with one-sixth of the ingredients and fold in half. Heat a nonstick skillet and brown the tortillas on both sides. Serve warm.

Variation
Chicken and Avocado Filling

6 servings

1 cup diced, cooked chicken
1 cup shredded jack cheese
4 tablespoons sour cream
1 diced avocado
¼ cup chopped green onion
4 tablespoons Mexican-style salsa

Combine all the filling ingredients and follow step #3 in directions for Papaya Quesadillas (page 194).

Variation
Squash Blossom Filling

6 servings

The beautiful flower from squash is often sold in Mexican markets. Lightly sautéed, it makes a tasty filling for tortillas.

18 squash blossoms, stems and green sepals removed
2 cloves finely chopped garlic
2 tablespoons finely chopped onion
1 tablespoon olive oil
2 tablespoons chopped green chiles
1 cup grated jack, Manchego, or Chihuahua cheese

Chop the squash blossoms and set aside. Sauté the garlic and onion in the olive oil until soft. Add the chiles and blossoms and cook, uncovered, until all the liquid has evaporated. Place one-sixth of the ingredients in each tortilla and fry as directed in the recipe for Papaya Quesadillas (page 194).

Calamari Tacos

4 servings

4 squid, prepared like abalone (page 80)
½ cup finely chopped onion
1 bell pepper, cut in thin strips
2 cloves garlic, finely chopped
2 tablespoons olive oil
2 teaspoons soy sauce
4 flour tortillas, heated

1. Cut the cooked squid into thin strips and set aside.
2. Sauté the onion, pepper, and garlic in the olive oil until tender. Season with soy sauce and add the squid to reheat.
3. Divide the mixture into warm tortillas, roll up, and serve.

Breakfast Burritos

4 servings

4 flour tortillas, heated
1 (8 oz.) can refried beans, heated
1 avocado, peeled and sliced
4 ounces grated cheddar cheese
1 (4 oz.) can Mexican-style salsa
1 (4 oz.) can sliced black olives
4 eggs, lightly scrambled

1. To assemble, spread each tortilla with ¼ of the beans. Top with ¼ of the remaining ingredients. Fold in one side, then the bottom, then the other side.
2. If made in advance, omit the avocado and wrap each tortilla in a piece of aluminum foil; add the avocado and reheat just before serving.

Apple Turnovers

4 servings

4 flour tortillas
Soft butter
4 cooking apples, peeled, cored, and chopped
Sugar
1 egg diluted with 1 tablespoon milk

1. Butter both sides of the tortillas. Place some of the chopped apple on half of each tortilla. Sprinkle with sugar. Fold the tortilla in half and seal with the egg wash.
2. Sprinkle the top of each tortilla with sugar and bake at 350° F until tortilla is golden brown—about 15 minutes.

Mexican Pizza

6 servings

½ pound homemade chorizo, cooked (page 106)
½ cup Spanish Tomato Sauce (page 171)
Vegetable oil for frying
6 (8-inch) flour tortillas
¾ cup chopped onion
2 cloves garlic, finely chopped
1 pound ground beef
1 teaspoon chili powder
½ teaspoon freshly ground black pepper
Salt to taste
½ cup chopped bell pepper or 4 ounces canned mild green chiles
½ cup sliced black olives
½ cup chopped green onions
6 ounces grated jack cheese
6 ounces grated cheddar cheese

Garnishes

1 ½ cups Mexican Salsa Fresca (page 165)
Sour cream
1 recipe guacamole (page 166)

1. Make the chorizo, tomato sauce, guacamole, and Mexican salsa; set aside.
2. Heat ½-inch of oil in a frying pan to 375°F. Fry the tortillas 30 seconds per side, until golden. Blot with paper towels. Discard oil.
3. Combine the chorizo, onion, and garlic in the frying pan and cook until the chorizo is lightly brown and the onion is soft. Add the ground beef, chili powder, salt, pepper, and tomato sauce. Cook until most of the liquid has evaporated.
4. Assemble each pizza by first layering the meat mixture; then add the bell pepper, olives, and green onions. Sprinkle with the cheeses and bake at 475°F until the cheese melts.
5. Pass the salsa, sour cream, and guacamole.

Sopaipillas

20 to 24

Sopaipillas, a New Mexican staple, are small pillows of golden fried bread that show up at breakfast, lunch, or dinner. Try serving them with butter and honey, sprinkled with cinnamon and sugar, or stuffed with refried beans.

2 cups flour
½ teaspoon salt
2 teaspoons baking powder
1 tablespoon shortening
¾ cup warm water
Oil for frying

1. Combine the flour, salt, and baking powder. Cut in the shortening. Add enough water so that the dough forms a ball.
2. Turn the dough onto a floured surface and knead until smooth—about 5 minutes. Cover with a towel and allow to rest 5 minutes.
3. At this point, the dough can be wrapped and chilled for up to 24 hours.
4. To prepare the fried bread, cut the dough in half and roll out into ¼-inch thick pieces. Cut each piece into 3- or 4-inch squares.
5. Pour oil 3 inches deep in a wok and heat to 400°F. Carefully drop the squares in one at a time. Cook until they are puffed and golden brown, turning once. If they do not puff immediately, the oil is not hot enough. Drain on paper towels.
6. Serve immediately. Any leftovers can be reheated in a foil packet in a 350°F oven for about 15 minutes. Just before serving open the foil so that the sopaipillas will dry on the outside.

SOUTHWEST CORN BREAD

8 to 12 servings

1 ¼ cups cornmeal (yellow or blue)
1 cup flour
2 tablespoons sugar
1 tablespoon baking powder
½ teaspoon salt
¼ cup powdered milk
2 eggs, lightly beaten
¾ cup oil
¾ cup water
1 cup grated cheddar cheese
1 (4 oz.) can chopped mild green chiles
1 (4 oz.) can corn, drained

1. Mix together the cornmeal, flour, sugar, baking powder, and salt. (Better yet, package the premeasured dry ingredients in a Ziploc to have on hand.)
2. Mix the eggs, oil, and water together; stir into the dry ingredients. Mix until moist. Add the cheese, chiles, and corn.
3. Spray a 9 × 13-inch baking pan with nonstick coating. Bake at 400° F for 25 to 30 minutes.

Variation

Eliminate the green chiles and cheese. Add ¼ cup of New Mexican dried chile powder, 4 cloves finely chopped garlic, and ⅓ cup chopped cilantro.

CHAPTER 11

Desserts

One of the complaints I hear most frequently from people who live aboard—especially from cruisers who enjoy baking desserts—is that boat ovens are too small and bake too unevenly. Too often, the result is burned cookies and cakes. Cushionaire baking sheets help correct this problem. The sheets, which are available in small sizes for boat ovens, are made with a double layer of aluminum and air space in between for additional insulation. The result is more even baking.

Living the casual life afloat, though, doesn't mean that I always have the time—or the inclination—to bake from scratch. That's why I keep an assortment of packaged mixes aboard. When I need a quick dessert, I can whip up a cake, brownies, pudding, or cookies in minutes. There are times, however, when I enjoy making special desserts from scratch.

There is nothing like homemade cookies to cheer up whoever's on watch—especially on a cold and dreary night. Two of my favorites are Crispy Orange Cookies (see page 202) and Oatmeal Cookies (and the varieties), on page 204. For entertaining, I've included suggestions for miniature tart fillings as well as some interesting Madeleine cookies.

If you have fresh berries on board, try Susan's Easy Berry Pie; if it's apple season, the Easy Crustless Apple Pie can be made in minutes. The Apple Cake and Carrot Cake are especially good for potlucks, and the Cream Cheese Raisin Cake is to die for.

I've included dessert recipes that can be made in the pressure cooker (Rice Pudding, page 210, and Lemon Chiffon Pudding, page 211); recipes for crêpes and soufflés that can, indeed, be made on board for special occasions; and even a recipe that uses stale bread—New Orleans Bread Pudding (see page 211).

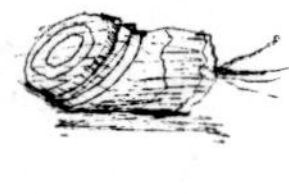

Lemon Bars

30 cookies

These are a big hit with kids of all ages and are easy to prepare—they can be whipped up in minutes. There's no need to roll the crust; just pat it firmly in the pan, cover with the rich lemon filling, and bake.

Crust

2 cups sifted all-purpose flour
½ cup powdered sugar
1 cup butter, at room temperature

Filling

4 eggs
2 cups granulated sugar
⅓ cup fresh lemon juice
¼ cup flour
½ teaspoon baking powder
Powdered sugar

1. To make the crust, combine the flour and powdered sugar, then add the butter. Beat with electric beaters, or by hand, until the dough forms a ball. Press into a 9×13-inch baking pan and bake at 350°F for 20 minutes.
2. To make the filling, beat the eggs until they begin to thicken. Add the sugar and lemon juice and beat until smooth. Stir in the flour and baking powder.
3. Pour the filling mixture over the baked crust and bake at 350°F an additional 25 minutes.
4. Allow to cool. Cut into squares and sprinkle with powdered sugar.

Variation
Easy Almond Tart

Filling

1 ½ cups sugar
1 ½ cups heavy cream or evaporated milk
2 cups sliced almonds
2 teaspoons orange flavored liqueur
¼ teaspoon almond extract
¼ teaspoon salt

Combine all the above ingredients for the filling; set aside. Make the crust as directed in the recipe for Lemon Bars (page 198). Spoon the filling onto the prebaked crust and bake at 375° F for 25 to 30 minutes or until golden.

Variation
Walnut Coconut Bars

Filling

4 eggs
2 ½ cups brown sugar
¼ cup flour
1 teaspoon baking powder
1 teaspoon salt
1 teaspoon vanilla
2 cups chopped walnuts
2 cups shredded coconut

Make the crust as directed in the recipe for Lemon Bars (page 198). Make the filling by beating the eggs until they begin to thicken. Add the brown sugar and beat until smooth. Stir in the remaining ingredients. Spread the filling onto the prebaked crust and bake at 350° F for 15 minutes or until set.

Variation
Pecan-Chocolate Chip Bars

Follow the directions for Lemon Bars (page 198), substituting the following filling.

Filling

4 eggs
1 ½ cups brown sugar
1 tablespoon flour
1 teaspoon vanilla
2 cups chopped and toasted pecans
8 ounces chocolate chips

Beat the eggs until thick. Add the brown sugar and beat until smooth. Stir in the flour, vanilla, pecans, and chocolate chips. Spread the filling onto the prebaked crust and bake at 350° F for 20 to 25 minutes or until set.

Variation
Lime-Pecan Bars

Follow the directions for Lemon Bars (page 198), substituting the following filling.

Filling

6 eggs
3 cups brown sugar
1 ½ teaspoons vanilla
2 ¼ cups flaked coconut
½ teaspoon baking powder
1 ½ cups chopped pecans

Glaze

3 tablespoons lime peel
5 tablespoons lime juice
2 cups powdered sugar

1. Beat the eggs and brown sugar until the eggs are thick and the sugar has dissolved. Fold in the remaining ingredients.
2. Spread the filling onto the prebaked crust and bake at 350° F for 20 minutes.
3. Make the glaze by combining the lime peel, lime juice, and powdered sugar.
4. Remove the bars from the oven and immediately drizzle with the glaze.

Dessert Tartlets

48 tartlets

By adding a little sugar to the appetizer tart recipe (see page 47), you can make a surprisingly easy crust. Using miniature muffin pans makes this a special dessert treat.

Dough

½ pound cream cheese, at room temperature
½ pound butter or margarine, at room temperature
½ cup powdered sugar
2 cups flour
2 teaspoons grated lemon or orange peel (optional)

1. Make the dough by beating together the cream cheese, butter, and sugar. Stir in the flour and lemon or orange peel. Chill the dough for one hour.
2. Divide the chilled dough into 48 pieces and press into mini-muffin pans so that each piece covers the bottom and sides of cups.
3. Fill with any of the following fillings.

Pecan Filling

2 eggs
1 ½ cups brown sugar
2 tablespoons butter or margarine, at room temperature
2 teaspoons vanilla
1 ⅓ cups chopped pecans

1. Beat together the eggs, brown sugar, butter, and vanilla.
2. Sprinkle half of the pecans in dough-lined mini-muffin pans. Spoon in the filling and top with the remaining pecans.
3. Bake at 325° F for 25 minutes. Cool briefly before removing from pans.

Almond Paste Filling

⅔ pound blanched almonds
1 ⅓ cups sugar plus ¼ cup sugar
⅔ cup water
⅓ cup orange juice
¼ cup flour
2 eggs plus 2 additional egg whites
1 ½ teaspoons almond extract

Frosting

1 cup powdered sugar
2 tablespoons milk

1. Finely grind the almonds.
2. Heat the sugar and water together until the temperature reaches 240° F. Add the almonds and orange juice and stir until creamy.
3. Mix in the flour, eggs, egg whites, and almond extract.
4. Place a tablespoon of the filling in each cup of the dough-lined mini-muffin pans, and bake at 350° F for about 30 minutes.
5. While the tartlets are baking, mix together the powdered sugar and milk; set aside.
6. Allow the tartlets to cool slightly before removing from the pans. While the tartlets are still warm, top each one with a ½ teaspoon of the powdered sugar and milk frosting.

Variation
Macadamia-Caramel Filling

Filling

½ recipe almond paste made with ¼ cup butter and
⅓ pound blanched almonds
¾ cup sugar
⅓ cup water
3 tablespoons orange juice
2 tablespoons flour
1 egg plus 1 additional egg white
¾ teaspoon almond extract

Topping

1 ⅓ cups sugar
¼ cup water
6 tablespoons unsalted butter
1 cup heavy cream
2 ½ cups macadamia nuts, lightly toasted and chopped

1. In dough-lined mini-muffin pans (see page 200), distribute the filling and bake at 350° F for 30 minutes or until just set. Allow the tartlets to cool and remove from shells.
2. Make the topping by combining the sugar, water, and butter in a heavy saucepan. Boil until the mixture becomes a deep caramel color. Remove from heat and carefully pour in the cream. Return to heat and boil over moderate heat until thick and smooth. Stir in the macadamia nuts.
3. Spoon the topping over the filling and allow to cool.

Variation
Chocolate Caramel Walnut Filling

4 ounces semisweet chocolate, melted
2 cups toasted walnuts
¾ cup sugar
1 ½ cups corn syrup
3 tablespoons butter
4 eggs
1 ½ teaspoons vanilla

1. In dough-lined mini-muffin pans (see page 200), distribute the melted chocolate and top with the walnuts.
2. In a heavy saucepan, cook the sugar until golden. Remove from heat and add the corn syrup. Cook until smooth. Add the butter.
3. In a mixing bowl, beat the eggs and vanilla. Gradually add the caramel mixture.
4. Top the walnuts with the caramel mixture. Bake the tartlets for 35 minutes at 325° F. Allow to cool before removing from pan.

Variation
Cream Cheese Filling

8 ounces cream cheese, at room temperature
1 egg yolk
¼ cup sour cream
2 tablespoons powdered sugar
2 tablespoons orange flavored liqueur
Fresh fruit
Jelly or preserves

1. Prebake the tart shells (see page 200) at 375° F for 12 minutes. Allow to cool before removing from pan.
2. Mix together the cream cheese, egg yolk, sour cream, powdered sugar, and liqueur, and fill the shells.
3. Arrange a piece of fruit, such as a pineapple square, a piece of date, or a section of mandarin orange, on top. Brush a glaze of warm jelly or preserves over the fruit and chill until firm.

Multipurpose Cookie Dough

4 dozen cookies

Changing a few spices or a technique in this master recipe gives you a wide variety of cookie possibilities.

1 cup butter, at room temperature
¾ cup sugar
1 egg
1 teaspoon vanilla or your choice of flavoring
2 ½ cups flour

1. Beat together the butter and sugar until fluffy. Add the egg and flavoring and beat until well blended.
2. Stir in the flour and mix well.

Variation
Chocolate Nut Logs

6 ounces melted chocolate
½ cup finely chopped toasted nuts

Make the cookie dough and shape into 48 logs about 3 inches long. Bake at 350° F for 15 to 20 minutes. When the cookies are cool, dip both ends in the melted chocolate and nuts.

Variation
Almond Topped Cookies

1 cup sliced almonds
2 ounces semisweet chocolate, finely chopped

1. Make the cookie dough and shape into 48 balls. Flatten each ball and press almonds onto the tops.
2. Bake at 350° F for 15 minutes or until golden.
3. Place the chocolate in a small Ziploc and heat in warm water until melted. Make a small hole in the corner of the bag and drizzle the chocolate in a zigzag pattern over the tops of cookies.

Variation
Peanut Butter Cookies

Make the multipurpose cookie dough (page 201) with the following additions: 1 extra egg, an additional 1¼ cups sugar (use a total of 2 cups of sugar—1 cup granulated and 1 cup brown), 1 cup peanut butter, ¾ teaspoon baking powder, ½ teaspoon baking soda, ½ teaspoon salt, and 1 teaspoon vanilla.

Form into 1-inch balls. Flatten slightly and crisscross the tops with the tines of a fork. Bake at 350° F for 10 to 12 minutes.

Variation
Cutout Cookies

36 three-inch cookies

Make the multipurpose cookie dough (see page 201), chill well, and roll to a ¼-inch thickness between 2 sheets of waxed paper. Cut into shapes and bake on an ungreased baking sheet at 350° F for 15 to 20 minutes, until golden.

Chocolate Cutouts

Make the multipurpose cookie dough (page 201), substituting ¼ cup unsweetened cocoa powder for the ¼ cup of flour and use an additional ¼ cup of sugar.

Spicy Cutouts

Make the multipurpose cookie dough (page 201), adding the following ingredients: 1 teaspoon ground ginger, ¼ teaspoon ground nutmeg, and 2½ teaspoons ground cinnamon.

Crispy Orange Cookies

3 dozen cookies

1 cup butter, at room temperature
½ cup brown sugar
½ cup granulated sugar
1 egg
1 ¼ cups all-purpose flour
2 tablespoons grated orange peel
2 tablespoons orange juice
¼ teaspoon baking soda
¾ cup chopped pecans

1. Cream together the butter, brown sugar, and granulated sugar until smooth. Add the egg and beat well. Add all the remaining ingredients and mix.
2. Drop small rounds of the dough 2-inches apart on an ungreased cookie sheet; flatten gently with finger tips.
3. Bake at 350° F for 8 to 10 minutes.
4. When cool, store in an airtight container for several weeks.

Mexican Wedding Cakes

3 dozen cookies

1 cup butter, at room temperature
⅓ cup powdered sugar, plus extra sugar for dipping
2 cups flour
1 ½ cups chopped pecans
2 teaspoons vanilla

1. Mix together all the ingredients; the dough will be very stiff.
2. Shape into round balls and flatten with the tines of a fork.
3. Bake at 350° F for 13 to 15 minutes or until slightly brown.
4. While the cookies are still warm, dip in powdered sugar.

Variation
Toasted Almond Wedding Cakes

Substitute 1 cup of finely chopped toasted almonds for the pecans; add 1 tablespoon of grated lemon or orange peel.

MADELEINES

30 Madeleines

A madeleine is a small, rich tea cake baked in a special pan that produces a shell-shaped pastry. When Hal and I moved aboard *SpiceSea,* I brought along some of the madeleine pans that I had leftover from my days as a cooking school teacher. Even the simplest of cakes, when baked in the special shape of a madeleine, never fails to elicit a glowing response from our guests. By the way—I also use my madeleine pans for baking corn bread and tiny muffins. (**NOTE:** The following madeleine recipes are designed for the size "80" madeleine pan.)

2 eggs
⅔ cup sugar
1 cup flour
½ cup butter, melted
2 teaspoons grated lemon peel
¼ teaspoon lemon or vanilla extract
Powdered sugar

1. Beat the eggs and sugar until the sugar dissolves. Add the flour and stir in the butter, lemon peel, and extract.
2. Butter the madeleine pans well. Fill with 1½ teaspoons batter. (You can substitute mini-muffin pans.)
3. Bake at 350°F for about 12 minutes or until the madeleines are lightly brown around the edges.
4. Cool on a wire rack for 5 minutes before removing from pan.
5. Sprinkle with powdered sugar before serving.

Variation
Orange Madeleines

Substitute grated orange peel for lemon peel, and use only vanilla extract. Add 1 tablespoon of orange juice to the batter.

Variation
Chocolate Madeleines

Add 1 tablespoon of unsweetened cocoa to the flour and substitute 2 ounces of finely grated semisweet chocolate for the lemon peel. Use vanilla instead of lemon extract.

Variation
Toasted Almond Madeleines

Substitute ¼ cup of finely ground toasted almonds for the lemon peel. Use vanilla instead of lemon extract, and add ¼ teaspoon of almond extract.

PECAN MADELEINES

48 cookies

The following recipe can be pressed into a madeleine pan for a rich, crispy cookie. The cookies taste equally as good rolled into small balls, flattened with the tines of a fork, and baked on a baking sheet according to recipe directions.

1 ¼ cups brown sugar, firmly packed
1 cup butter, at room temperature
½ teaspoon cinnamon
1 teaspoon vanilla
½ cup finely ground pecans or any other nut you have on hand
2 ¼ cups flour
Powdered sugar

1. Beat together the sugar and butter until light and fluffy. Add the cinnamon, vanilla, pecans, and flour. Stir until well combined.
2. Press about 1½ to 2 teaspoons of dough into buttered madeleine molds.
3. Bake at 350°F for 12 to 15 minutes. Allow to cool 2 minutes before removing from pan. Sprinkle with powdered sugar when cool.
4. Store in an airtight container at room temperature for up to a month.

Incredible Chocolate Chip-Oatmeal Cookies

48 cookies

There aren't many more inviting aromas than that of cookies baking in the oven. I store uncooked dough in the refrigerator and bake in small batches in the winter when the oven's heat is appreciated in *SpiceSea's* cabin. (Be sure you have adequate ventilation.)

When the weather is warmer or when I want to cook the entire recipe at one time, I cover my baking sheet with parchment paper to speed up the process and save on cooking fuel. Like most boat ovens, mine is small—I can only bake about 9 to 12 cookies at a time. While one batch is cooking, I prepare another on a second piece of parchment. When the cookies are done, I simply slide the parchment paper and cookies onto a flat surface to cool and then slide the next sheet of parchment and cookie dough onto the baking sheet—and I don't have to wait for the first batch of cookies to cool.

1 cup butter or margarine, at room temperature
2 cups sugar (I use 1 cup of white and 1 cup of brown)
2 eggs
2 tablespoons milk
2 teaspoons vanilla
1 ¾ cup flour
1 teaspoon baking soda
½ teaspoon salt
2 cups uncooked oatmeal
12 ounces chocolate chips
1 cup chopped nuts (optional)

1. Cream together the butter and sugar. Add the eggs, milk, and vanilla.
2. In a separate bowl, mix together the flour, salt, and baking soda; combine with the butter mixture. Stir in the oatmeal, chocolate chips, and nuts.
3. Shape the dough into 1 ¼-inch balls and bake on a greased baking sheet at 375° F for 10 minutes for chewy cookies, or 12 minutes for crisp cookies. Allow to cool before removing.

Variations

- For Chocolate Chip Cookies without the oatmeal, add an additional ½ cup of flour.
- For Oatmeal Raisin Cookies, substitute ½ cup of raisins for the chocolate chips.
- For Oatmeal Coconut Cookies, substitute 1 cup of flaked coconut for the chocolate chips.
- For Oatmeal Orange Cookies, substitute 1 tablespoon of grated orange rind for the chocolate chips.

Peanut Butter and Chocolate Bars

32 cookies

The following two sinfully delicious recipes don't even need to be baked! I prepare them in a 9 × 13-inch Tupperware container; the tightly sealed lid keeps them fresh for weeks. They should be stored in the freezer or refrigerator.

1 cup graham cracker crumbs
2 ½ cups powdered sugar
2 cups peanut butter
1 teaspoon vanilla
½ cup melted butter
8 ounces chocolate chips, melted

1. Mix together the crumbs, sugar, butter, vanilla, and butter. Press into a 9 × 13-inch pan.
2. Top with the melted chocolate and slice before the chocolate hardens.

Nanaimo Bars

32 cookies

Crust

½ cup butter
¼ cup sugar
5 tablespoons cocoa
1 tablespoon vanilla
2 eggs
2 cups graham cracker crumbs
1 cup shredded coconut
½ cup chopped nuts

Filling

¼ cup butter, at room temperature
2 cups sifted powdered sugar
3 tablespoons milk
2 tablespoons Bird's Custard (Or substitute 2 tablespoons cornstarch and 1 tablespoon vanilla. If doing so, reduce milk to 2 tablespoons.)

Frosting

3 ounces semisweet chocolate
1 tablespoon butter

1. To make the crust, melt the butter with the sugar and cocoa. Add the vanilla and eggs and beat well. Stir in the crumbs, coconut, and nuts. Pat the mixture into a 9×13-inch pan.
2. To make the filling, beat together the butter, powdered sugar, milk, and custard until the mixture is smooth. Pour over the crust and chill until firm.
3. To make the frosting, melt the chocolate and butter over low heat. Carefully spread the frosting over the chilled filling and score it with a knife into serving-size pieces before the chocolate hardens. Chill well and finish cutting before serving.

Brownies

Both of the following brownie recipes are rich beyond belief, use ingredients that store well on a boat, and will keep for many days without refrigeration.

For the cruising cook, finding a decadent chocolate dessert in a third-world country is often impossible. Being able to create your own indulgence just might save the day. Keep in mind, though, when making desserts, that sugar outside of the United States is often much coarser than what we're used to. If you have a blender or food processor, you can grind the sugar to break down the crystalline structure, which makes it easier to cream with the other ingredients.

Chocolate Truffle Brownies

3 dozen brownies

1 pound semisweet chocolate, cut up
⅔ cup butter, at room temperature
1 ¼ cups sugar
6 eggs
¾ cup flour
1 ½ cups coarsely chopped walnuts
Powdered sugar

1. Melt the chocolate in the top of a double boiler over hot, not boiling, water. (If you have a microwave, melt in a large mixing bowl for about 2 minutes.) Be careful not to overcook. Remove and stir. Allow to cool slightly.
2. Beat the butter into the chocolate until thick. Gradually beat in the sugar. Add the eggs, one at a time, beating well after each addition.
3. Fold in the flour, followed by the nuts. Pour into a 9×13-inch buttered pan that has been lined with foil or parchment paper. Smooth the top. Bake at 350°F for 30 to 35 minutes or until the brownies are slightly cracked on top.
4. Allow to cool before cutting. Sprinkle with powdered sugar before serving.

White Chocolate Brownies

16 brownies

½ cup butter
8 ounces white chocolate chips or coarsely chopped white chocolate
½ cup sugar
2 eggs
1 teaspoon vanilla
1 cup flour
4 ounces semisweet chocolate chips

1. Melt the butter, remove the pan from the heat, and add 4 ounces of the white chocolate. Allow the chocolate to melt in the hot butter.
2. Add the sugar and beat until dissolved. Add the eggs and vanilla and beat until the mixture is thick and creamy. Stir in the flour.
3. Stir in the remaining 4 ounces of white chocolate and the semisweet chocolate chips.
4. Pour into an 8-inch buttered baking pan that has been lined with foil or parchment paper. Smooth the top. Bake at 350° F for 35 to 40 minutes or until a toothpick inserted in the center comes out almost clean.
5. Allow to cool before cutting.

Susan's Berry Pie

4 to 6 servings

We have enjoyed so many wonderful meals through the years aboard *Limerick,* our friends' boat, on which the specialty is this pie, made with the profusion of boysenberries that grow in their shoreside garden.

Tom calls this recipe Mackerel Pie since he says the way you get lots of berries is to catch four mackerel, dig a hole in the ground, and plant a boysenberry bush! Whatever you want to call it, I like the ease of preparation and not having to precook the berries.

4 cups ripe berries
1 cup sugar or to taste
1 ½ cups oatmeal
½ cup brown sugar
¼ cup Bisquick
2 tablespoons cold butter

1. Combine the berries and sugar together in a 6-cup baking dish and allow to marinate for 15 minutes.
2. Combine the oatmeal, brown sugar, Bisquick, and butter, cutting in the butter with 2 knives. Sprinkle over the berries.
3. Bake at 450° F for 10 minutes; reduce heat to 350° F and bake another 30 minutes.
4. Serve with whipped cream or sweetened Nestle Crema if desired.

Fruit Crisp

4 to 6 servings

1 tablespoon butter
4 peaches, bananas, or apples, peeled and sliced
1 tablespoon grated orange peel
3 tablespoons white or brown sugar
½ teaspoon cinnamon or nutmeg
½ cup flour
¼ cup white or brown sugar
¼ cup cold butter

1. Grease a pie pan with 1 tablespoon of butter and layer the fruit in the pan. Sprinkle with two knives until the mixture has the texture of cornmeal. Sprinkle over the fruit.
3. Bake at 375° F for about 25 minutes or until the topping is crisp and the fruit is tender.
4. Serve with whipped cream or sweetened Nestle Crema if desired.

Easy Crustless "Apple" Pie

9-inch pie

This dessert looks like a pie, can be made in just a few minutes, and uses any fruit and any type of nuts. (Try pears and dried cranberries with pine nuts, or sliced peaches or nectarines with pecans.) It is also low in fat if you don't top it with whipped cream. A little canned Nestle Crema that's been sweetened with some powdered sugar almost makes you think you are eating ice cream.

1 egg
1 teaspoon vanilla
½ cup brown sugar
½ cup white sugar
1 teaspoon baking powder
½ cup flour
½ cup chopped walnuts
2 apples, peeled and chopped

1. Mix together the egg, vanilla, and sugars. Stir in the baking powder and flour, then add the nuts and apples.
2. Place in a 9-inch buttered pie pan and bake at 350° F for 30 minutes.

Ginger Chocolate Pie

6 to 8 servings

30 gingersnaps (or substitute vanilla wafers seasoned with ground ginger)
½ cup melted butter
12 ounces chocolate, coarsely chopped
1 egg, beaten
2 eggs, separated
1 can aerosol whipping cream

1. Finely grind the gingersnaps in a food processor or place the cookies in a plastic bag and crush with a rolling pin. Add the butter. Press into a 9-inch pie pan and bake at 375° F for 5 to 7 minutes. Allow to cool.
2. Melt the chocolate and cool slightly. Add the 1 beaten egg and the 2 egg yolks. Beat well.
3. Beat the 2 egg whites together until they are stiff; fold into the chocolate mixture. Pour the filling into the cooled ginger shell.
4. Chill the pie before serving. Garnish with whipping cream, if desired. (An aerosol can of whipping cream is easy to store and keeps well.)

Carrot-Pineapple Cake

8 servings

Carrot cake has always been a favorite of ours and, since we usually have carrots on the boat, I make this recipe frequently. It keeps well for a few days without refrigeration, but needs to be frozen or kept in the refrigerator for longer storage. If you don't have a can of pineapple on board, add another ½ cup of carrots.

2 eggs
1 cup sugar
⅔ cup cooking oil
1 teaspoon vanilla
1 cup flour
1 teaspoon baking powder
1 teaspoon baking soda
½ teaspoon salt
1 teaspoon cinnamon
1 cup grated carrots (⅓ pound)
½ cup crushed pineapple with juice

1. Beat the eggs and sugar until smooth. Add the oil and vanilla and beat until well combined.
2. Stir together the flour, baking powder, baking soda, salt, and cinnamon, and add to the egg mixture. Add the carrots and pineapple and mix together until well combined.
3. Pour the batter into a greased and floured 8-inch square baking pan and bake at 350° F for about 40 minutes; cool and frost if desired.

Cream Cheese Frosting

3 ounces cream cheese
2 tablespoons butter, at room temperature
1 teaspoon vanilla
2 cups powdered sugar
½ cup chopped pecans

Beat together the cream cheese and butter. Add the vanilla and sugar and beat until smooth. Stir in the nuts.

Spiced Apple Cake

12 servings

Potlucks are one of the easiest ways to meet other boaters while cruising. They are also lots of fun. Every boat gets a chance to contribute a favorite dish and, since potluck etiquette dictates that you bring more food than your crew can eat, they are a great way to get rid of leftovers!

It is nice to have a special potluck dish in your repertoire, one whose basic ingredients you can keep on board and one that you know will be enjoyed by your fellow cruisers. It doesn't have to be expensive—a great tasting dish of rice and beans is enjoyed just as much as a recipe using expensive cuts of meat or lots of costly cheese.

One of my favorite potluck dishes for many weeks while cruising the Pacific coast of Mexico was an apple cake. I started making it because we had a huge batch of apples that had been bruised and were starting to spoil. It has become a staple in my potluck recipe file.

½ pound butter or margarine, at room temperature
1 cup sugar
3 eggs
3 cups flour
1 ½ teaspoons baking soda
½ teaspoon salt
2 teaspoons pumpkin pie spice (cinnamon, clove, or ginger)
¾ cup raisins soaked in brandy
3 ½ cups (1 lb.) cooking apples (Pippin or Granny Smith)
1 cup chopped walnuts

1. In a large mixing bowl, cream together the butter and sugar until light and fluffy. Add the eggs and beat well.
2. Combine the flour, baking soda, salt, and spice and stir into the butter mixture. Stir in the raisins, apples, and nuts.
3. Spread the batter in a buttered and floured 9×13-inch baking pan and bake at 325°F for about an hour. (The cake is done when a toothpick inserted in the center comes out clean.)

Upside Down Cake

8 to 12 servings

This recipe typically uses pineapple, but any canned fruit will do—fruit cocktail, cherries, peaches, apricots, or others. I keep some powdered eggs on board for when I've run out of fresh.

½ cup butter
1 cup packed brown sugar
1 cup pecans
2 (14 to 15 oz.) cans fruit, drained
1 package yellow cake mix, mixed according to package directions

1. Dot the butter over the bottom of a 9×13-inch baking dish and sprinkle with the brown sugar. Arrange the pecans and canned fruit on top. Pour the mixed cake batter on top.
2. Bake at 350°F according to cake package directions. Test for doneness; you may need to add another 15 minutes to baking time.
3. Immediately upon removing the cake from the oven, invert it onto a large piece of foil, allowing the pan to remain over the cake briefly to let the brown sugar mixture coat the cake.

Cream Cheese Raisin Cake

8 to 12 servings

4 ounces cream cheese
½ cup butter, at room temperature
¾ cup sugar
2 eggs
1 cup plus 2 tablespoons flour
¾ teaspoon baking powder
½ cup chopped pecans
⅔ cup raisins, soaked in brandy or bourbon

1. Grease and flour a loaf pan.
2. Combine the cream cheese and butter and beat until fluffy. Add the sugar and beat until dissolved. Beat in the eggs.

3. In a separate bowl, combine the flour and baking powder; stir into the batter. Stir in the nuts and drained raisins.

4. Place the batter in a prepared pan and bake at 325° F until a toothpick inserted in the center comes out clean—about 1 ¼ hours.

TURTLE CAKE

Serves 16

1 package German chocolate cake mix
½ cup butter
½ cup evaporated milk
14 ounces caramels, unwrapped
1 cup coarsely chopped pecans
1 cup (8 oz.) semisweet chocolate chips

1. Mix the cake according to package directions. Pour half of the batter into a greased and floured 9×13-inch baking pan. Bake at 350° F for 20 minutes.
2. Combine the butter, evaporated milk, and caramels together in a saucepan over low heat; stir until melted. Pour evenly over the baked cake and sprinkle with the pecans and chocolate chips.
3. Top with the remaining cake batter. Bake an additional 20 to 25 minutes or until a toothpick inserted into the center comes out clean.
4. Cool before serving. Spread with frosting if desired and cut.

Frosting

½ cup butter
3 tablespoons unsweetened cocoa powder
6 tablespoons evaporated milk
1 pound powdered sugar
1 tablespoon vanilla

Combine the butter, cocoa, and evaporated milk in a saucepan and heat until the butter melts. Beat in the sugar and vanilla until smooth. Spread over cooled cake.

Variation
Turtle Brownies

Make the German chocolate cake mix with ¾ cup of melted butter, ½ cup of evaporated milk, and 1 cup of chopped nuts. Bake half of the batter for 8 minutes and top with 1 pound of caramels melted with ⅓ cup of evaporated milk. Top with 12 ounces of chocolate chips and the remaining batter. Bake for an additional 15 minutes. Cool and chill before cutting.

THAMES' CAKE

16 servings

2 cups flour
2 cups sugar
½ pound butter
4 tablespoons unsweetened cocoa powder
1 cup water
½ cup buttermilk
1 teaspoon baking soda
2 eggs
1 teaspoon vanilla

1. Mix together the flour and sugar.
2. In a saucepan, bring the butter, cocoa, and water to a boil. Mix with the flour mixture. Stir in all of the remaining ingredients.
3. Bake in a 9×13-inch greased baking pan at 375° F for 35 minutes. Frost while still hot.

Frosting

4 tablespoons butter
2 tablespoons unsweetened cocoa powder
2 ½ tablespoons milk
1 ¾ cups powdered sugar
½ cup nuts

1. Bring the butter, cocoa, and milk to a boil in a saucepan.
2. Stir in the sugar and mix until smooth. Stir in the nuts.

Eggless Chocolate Cake

Serves 6 to 8

This cake, which is mixed right in its baking pan, has had many names, including Wacky Cake and Crazy Cake. It is low in fat and deliciously moist.

1 ½ cups all-purpose flour
1 teaspoon baking powder
1 cup granulated sugar
¼ cup unsweetened cocoa powder
½ teaspoon salt
1 tablespoon vinegar
1 tablespoon vanilla
⅓ cup vegetable oil
1 cup water
Powdered sugar

1. Grease and flour an 8-inch square pan. Thoroughly combine the flour, baking powder, sugar, cocoa powder, and salt.
2. Pour the vinegar, vanilla, oil, and water in the pan and mix thoroughly.
3. Bake at 350° F for about 30 minutes or until a toothpick inserted in the center comes out clean. Allow to cool and dust with powdered sugar before serving.

Variation
Linda's Wok Method

Our friends on *Green Dolphin* have spent so much time in the tropics that they have come up with all kinds of clever ways to avoid lighting their boat's oven. This is Linda's version of the Eggless Chocolate Cake—it's a moist, light cake that always gets rave reviews.

Make the Eggless Chocolate Cake as directed above, substituting 2 tablespoons of rum for 2 tablespoons of the water. Place a vegetable steamer in a wok with 1 ½ cups of water. Put the cake pan on top of the steamer, cover the wok, and allow to steam on low for 50 minutes.

For a white cake, eliminate the cocoa and substitute lemon juice for the rum. (You might also add some grated lemon peel.) Steam as directed above for 1 hour. Linda suggests spreading some strawberry jam on top and coating with coconut.

Rice Pudding with Raisins and Molasses

6 to 8 servings

In Scandinavia, rice pudding is traditionally served on Christmas Eve—but I think it's great any time of the year. Folklore has it that whoever finds the almond in his or her pudding will have good fortune for the coming year.

Rice pudding is comfort food at its best—and a perfect dessert to serve on board. This recipe is especially handy for boats without ovens—it's foolproof and quick when made in a pressure cooker.

2 tablespoons butter
1 ½ cups long grain white rice
2 cups milk
2 cups water
½ cup raisins soaked in rum or brandy for 1 hour or until soft
⅛ teaspoon salt
1 teaspoon ground cinnamon
¼ teaspoon ground ginger
¼ teaspoon ground nutmeg
½ cup packed brown sugar
1 tablespoon molasses
2 teaspoons vanilla
2 teaspoons grated lemon peel
1 blanched almond

1. Heat the butter in a pressure cooker. Stir in the rice and make sure that all the grains are coated with butter. Stir in all the remaining ingredients and lock the lid in place
2. Bring to pressure over high heat. Adjust the heat to maintain high pressure and cook for 3 minutes. Allow the pressure to drop naturally, over low heat, for an additional 7 minutes. Quick-release any remaining pressure.
3. Carefully remove the lid and taste for doneness. If the pudding is too chewy, stir in a few tablespoons of water, replace the lid, and allow to steep for an additional 2 or 3 minutes.
4. Serve warm with whipped cream if desired.

Lemon Chiffon Pudding Cake

4 to 6 servings

This is a popular dessert that's delicious and easy to make. It's a light textured cake that rises to the top—and underneath is a lemon pudding sauce.

1 cup sugar
5 tablespoons flour
2 tablespoons butter, at room temperature
Pinch of salt
¼ cup lemon juice
3 eggs, separated
1 cup milk
Grated peel of 1 lemon

1. Mix together the sugar, flour, butter, and salt. Add the lemon juice and egg yolks and beat well. Stir in the milk and lemon peel.
2. Beat the egg whites until stiff. Fold into the above mixture.
3. Pour the batter into a buttered 2-quart baking dish. Bake as directed below and allow to cool before serving. Cut into servings and spoon the pudding over cake.

Microwave: Bake 9 minutes on high.

Conventional Oven: Place in a water bath (a pan of boiling water set in the oven) and bake at 350° F for 45 minutes.

Pressure Cooker: Cake should be placed in a metal bowl with a lid—a 2-quart Charlotte mold is ideal. Place on a rack inside the pressure cooker. Add 2 cups of water to cooker. Cook 17 minutes on high pressure. Allow pressure to release naturally. **Note:** When we are at anchor, the pressure cooker is my preferred method of cooking this recipe—a water bath is too dangerous unless you are in a marina. For ease in removing the baking pan from the pressure cooker, you need to have two foil straps that go under the baking pan and that are long enough to fold over the top of the pan.

New Orleans Bread Pudding with Whiskey Sauce

8 to 10 servings

This classic dessert from New Orleans is great when you want to use stale bread.

5 eggs
2 cups sugar
2 tablespoons vanilla
2 teaspoons cinnamon
2 teaspoons nutmeg
4 cups milk (or 2 cups milk and 2 cups cream)
4 tablespoons butter, melted
1 cup raisins, soaked in amaretto or brandy
1 cup pecans, coarsely chopped and roasted
1 10-ounce loaf very stale French bread, broken (8 cups)
1 recipe Whiskey Sauce (page 178)

1. Beat the eggs until they are very frothy. Add the sugar, vanilla, cinnamon, and nutmeg and beat until well combined. Gradually beat in the milk and butter. Stir in the raisins and nuts.
2. Butter a 9×13-inch ovenproof baking dish and spread the bread over the bottom. Pour the egg mixture over the bread and allow to marinate for 30 to 45 minutes, until almost all the liquid has been absorbed into the bread. (You may need to pat the bread down into the liquid occasionally.)
3. Bake at 350° F for 40 minutes, then increase the temperature to 425° F and bake until the pudding is well browned and puffy—about 15 to 20 minutes.

Puffy Pecan Meringue Crêpes

6 crêpes

6 dessert crêpes (page 33)

Pecan Filling

⅔ cup corn syrup
3 tablespoons unsalted butter, melted and cooled
1 egg yolk
1 teaspoon vanilla extract
1 cup chopped pecans, dry roasted until dark in color
¼ cup heavy cream or milk

1. Combine the corn syrup, butter, egg yolk, and vanilla; stir until well blended.
2. Add the pecans and milk, mixing well. Set aside.

Meringue

3 egg whites, at room temperature
½ cup powdered sugar
1 tablespoon rum

1. Beat the egg whites until frothy. Add the powdered sugar and beat until fairly stiff peaks form. Add the rum and beat another minute.
2. Fold about ¾ cup of this meringue mixture into the pecan filling.

To Assemble

1. Fill each crêpe with 2 tablespoons of pecan sauce and ¼ cup meringue. Fold the crêpes in half and place on a baking sheet.
2. Bake at 475° F until the meringue puffs up and is golden—about 5 minutes. Remove from oven and serve immediately, spooning about ¼ cup of additional pecan sauce over each crêpe.

Easy Chocolate Soufflé

4 to 6 servings

Soufflés have a reputation for being difficult to make, but I think they've gotten a bum rap. For best results, serve the soufflé immediately after you remove it from the oven so that it will be nice and puffy. If dinner is delayed for some reason, store the completed, but uncooked, soufflé away from any draft with a large Dutch oven or other pan inverted over the soufflé dish to protect it.

I have eaten this soufflé the next day—it had become a dense, moist chocolate cake. Granted, it was not puffy like a soufflé, but it tasted great. In hot climates when you don't want to turn on the oven after the sun comes up, you might think about baking the soufflé in advance and calling it cake!

2 tablespoons cornstarch
½ cup sugar
¾ cup milk
2 squares unsweetened chocolate
3 tablespoons butter
1 teaspoon vanilla
4 egg yolks
6 egg whites, at room temperature
¼ teaspoon cream of tartar or a couple drops of vinegar

1. Grease the inside of a 2- to 2½-quart soufflé dish with butter and sprinkle with granulated sugar. (I use a 2-quart Charlotte pan.)
2. Combine the cornstarch and sugar in a saucepan. Stir in the milk and cook over medium heat until the mixture boils and thickens.
3. Turn off the heat and add the chocolate and butter; stir until melted, then stir in the vanilla. Allow the mixture to cool before adding the egg yolks.
4. Beat the egg whites until soft peaks form. Fold the whites into the chocolate mixture and pour into the prepared dish.
5. Bake at 350° F for 30 minutes. Serve immediately with Whisky Sauce (page 178) if desired.

Cold Mango Soufflé

6 to 8 servings

This soufflé may sound like it's a lot of work in the confines of a small galley, but it can be made in the morning and, by the time you are ready to serve it, you'll have forgotten about how much work it was!

1 envelope unflavored gelatin
¼ cup cold water
4 egg yolks
½ cup sugar
¾ cup evaporated milk
1 cup pureed mango pulp
1 tablespoon lime juice
4 egg whites

1. Sprinkle the gelatin over the cold water and allow to soften.
2. Beat the egg yolks with ¼ cup of the sugar until thick; set aside. Heat the milk in a saucepan until bubbles form along the edge of the pan. Remove the pan from the heat and add the softened gelatin. Stir well to dissolve. Gradually beat in egg yolk mixture.
3. Return the pan to low heat and continue to stir until the mixture thickens enough to coat the back of a spoon. Do not let it boil. Beat in the mango pulp and lime juice. Chill the mixture until it starts to thicken, stirring frequently.
4. With a clean beater, beat the egg whites until frothy. Gradually add the remaining ¼ cup of sugar and beat until the egg whites form stiff, unwavering peaks.
5. Gently but thoroughly fold the egg whites into the cooled mango mixture.
6. Pour into a serving dish and chill until firm.

Variation
Lime Soufflé

1 cup strained lime juice
1 envelope unflavored gelatin
4 egg yolks
1 ¼ cups sugar
¾ cup evaporated milk
4 egg whites

Follow the directions for the Mango Soufflé (see above), softening the gelatin in lime juice instead of water and beating 1 cup of sugar with the yolks and ¼ cup of sugar with the whites.

Amaretto Peach Mousse

6 servings

2 pounds canned sliced peaches
2 envelopes unflavored gelatin
1 cup yogurt cheese (see page 37)
or 8 ounces cream cheese
1 tablespoon amaretto

1. Drain the peaches, reserving the juice. Add enough water to the juice to make 1 ¾ cups of liquid and heat to boiling. Add the gelatin and stir until dissolved.
2. Purée the peaches in a food processor or mash them with a fork. Combine the yogurt cheese with the peaches and mix well. Stir in the Amaretto and gelatin mixture. Chill in serving dishes until firm.

Fresh Mango Dessert

6 servings

8 ounces sweetened condensed milk
2 cups mango pulp
⅓ cup fresh lime juice
3 tablespoons orange liqueur
Pecan halves or lime slices

1. Purée the milk and mango in a blender or food processor. Add the lime juice and orange liqueur.
2. Serve in small bowls and garnish.

Oranges in Burgundy

8 servings

8 large seedless oranges, peeled and thinly sliced
Fresh mint

Syrup

$\frac{3}{4}$ cup sugar
1 $\frac{1}{4}$ cups water
1 $\frac{1}{4}$ cups red wine
2 cloves
1 $\frac{1}{2}$-inch length cinnamon stick
1 $\frac{1}{2}$-inch length vanilla bean
4 lemon slices

1. In a medium saucepan, combine all the syrup ingredients. Heat and stir until the sugar dissolves. Bring to a boil and simmer 15 minutes.
2. Strain the syrup and pour over the oranges while the syrup is still hot.
3. Serve chilled, garnished with fresh mint leaves.

Note: Don't throw away the cinnamon sticks and vanilla beans after using—they still have lots of flavor. Rinse and save.

Variation
Pears Poached in Red Wine

6 servings

6 small ripe but firm pears, peeled, cored, and halved
Syrup from Oranges in Burgundy (see above)

1. Add the pears to the hot syrup and simmer for 15 to 20 minutes, or until they are soft but not mushy. Cool the pears in the syrup.
2. Serve warm or chilled with a small amount of the syrup.

Ann's Fruit Dip

2 cups

This is great for dipping bananas, strawberries, or whatever fruit is at the market.

8 ounces cream cheese, softened
12-ounce jar marshmallow cream
$\frac{1}{2}$ teaspoon nutmeg

Beat the cream cheese until light and fluffy. Beat in the marshmallow cream, followed by the nutmeg.

Baked Bananas with Brandied Raisins

4 servings

I have a jar of raisins on the boat that I keep covered with brandy. The brandy keeps the raisins indefinitely and the flavor makes an interesting addition to many desserts. Rum also works well; amaretto is even better.

4 firm bananas, peeled and cut lengthwise in half
$\frac{1}{4}$ cup brown sugar
$\frac{1}{2}$ cup chopped walnuts
$\frac{1}{2}$ cup brandy-soaked raisins
2 tablespoons unsalted butter, cut into bits

1. Place the bananas in a buttered baking dish and sprinkle with the brown sugar, nuts and raisins. Dot with butter.
2. Bake at 350° F for 25 minutes or until lightly browned and tender.

(You can also bake these on the barbecue. Prepare as above and wrap tightly in buttered foil.)

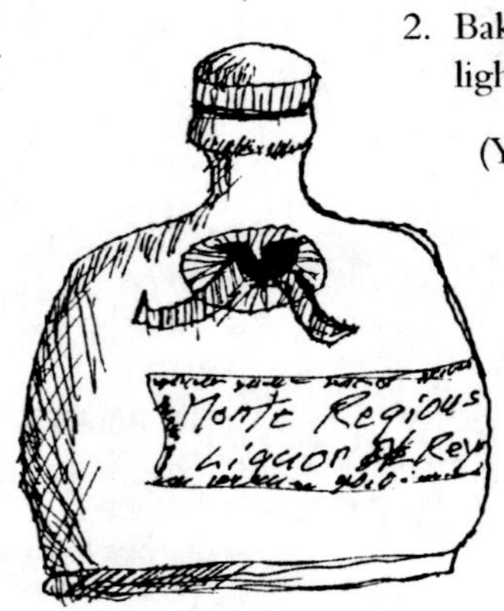

Variation
Baked Bananas with Cream Cheese

Another tasty way to use up a plethora of bananas, this recipe stands on its own or as a fabulous filling for crêpes.

Use an additional ¼ cup of brown sugar and substitute 8 ounces of cream cheese blended with 1 teaspoon cinnamon for the nuts and raisins. Mix together the cream cheese mixture and brown sugar until smooth and pour over bananas. Bake as directed above.

Better Than S'mores

Bananas stuffed with miniature marshmallows and chocolate are a special treat. Although this is a popular dessert for kids, I know lots of adults who can't resist the delightfully gooey, messy, yummy concoction! This is a great dessert that can be put on the barbecue as the coals are burning down.

For each person

1 ripe banana
1 small bar milk chocolate
12 miniature marshmallows

1. On the concave side of each banana, peel back one-third of the skin, leaving it attached at the stem end. Using the tip of a spoon, make a pocket in the banana for stuffing by scooping out about one-fourth of the pulp.
2. Place the chocolate in the indentation and top with marshmallows. Fold the banana skin back in place and wrap tightly in aluminum foil that has been sprayed with a nonstick coating.
3. If not barbecuing, bake the bananas in a 375°F oven for 15 minutes. Allow to cool slightly before unwrapping.

Reduced Cream Recipes

Having a few cans of reduced cream or Nestle Crema (see page 11) makes the following desserts a cinch.

Sweetened Whipped Cream

1¾ cups

2 egg whites
¾ cup powdered sugar
1 (225 gram) can reduced cream, chilled
1½ teaspoons lemon or lime juice

1. Beat the egg whites to soft peaks. Gradually add the sugar, beating to form stiff peaks.
2. Drain any liquid from the reduced cream. Beat the cream with the lime juice until fluffy. Lightly fold into the egg white mixture.
3. Chill until firm. Use as a dessert topping or on fruit.

Chocolate Sauce or Easy Mousse

2 cups

This delicious sauce can be served warm over ice cream or as a dessert topping for Easy Chocolate Soufflé (page 212).

6 ounces chocolate chips
1 can reduced cream (crema) or 8 ounces evaporated milk
2 tablespoons orange liqueur

Melt the chocolate and stir in the reduced cream and orange liqueur.

Easy Caramel Sauce

Approximately 2 cups

1 cup brown sugar
1 tablespoon butter
¼ cup water
1 can (225 grams) Nestle reduced cream or 8 ounces evaporated milk

Melt the brown sugar with the butter and water; simmer for 10 minutes. Stir in the reduced cream. Serve warm.

Easy Custard Flan

8 servings

1 (14 oz.) can sweetened condensed milk
2 (225 gram) cans Nestle reduced cream
4 eggs

1. Beat together all the ingredients and place in 8 custard cups or a 6 to 8 cup baking dish.
2. Bake in a water bath (see next recipe) in a 350° F oven for 40 minutes.
3. This is best when served chilled, but also tastes great at room temperature. Serve topped with sweetened fruit.

Creamy Flan

8 servings

A water bath is a way of gently cooking a custard so that the eggs do not overcook. When using custard cups, I pour boiling water into a 9×13-inch dish, until the water is halfway up the sides of the custard cups. If you don't have individual custard cups on board, use a 2 to 2½-quart container for the flan and a pot with a slightly larger diameter for the water.

Note: Only use a water bath in a calm anchorage or at a marina, since you don't want nearly boiling water sloshing out of your oven.

1 cup sugar
1 can evaporated milk
10 egg yolks
¼ cup light rum

1. In a heavy saucepan, caramelize a ½ cup of sugar by heating it without stirring until it's golden. Coat each of the 8 custard cups with the caramelized sugar and set aside.
2. Heat the evaporated milk and remaining ½ cup of sugar and stir until the sugar dissolves. Allow to cool before whisking in the egg yolks and rum.
3. Divide the flan into the custard cups, place in a hot water bath, and bake at 325° F for 20 to 25 minutes. Test for doneness by inserting a knife in the center—it should come our slightly coated. As the flan cools it will congeal a bit more. Chill before serving.

Chocolate Kahlúa Flan

8 servings

2 ¼ cups evaporated milk
½ cup sugar
Pinch of salt
1 ounce semisweet chocolate
2 eggs plus an extra yolk
½ teaspoon powdered instant coffee
3 tablespoons Kahlúa

1. Bring the milk, sugar, and salt to a boil. Allow to cool briefly and add the chocolate.
2. Beat the eggs and yolk together and gradually add to the milk. Add the coffee and Kahlúa.
3. Distribute the custard into 6 buttered custard cups. Place in a hot water bath and bake at 325° F for 45 minutes.
4. Chill before serving.
5. Serve with whipped cream and shaved chocolate if desired.

Caramel Flan in the Microwave

2 servings

If you have a microwave on board you can eliminate the need for a water bath when making flan.

Custard

2 eggs
3 tablespoons sugar
½ teaspoon vanilla
Dash of salt
¾ cup milk

Caramel

¼ cup water
¼ cup sugar

1. Beat the eggs, sugar, vanilla, and salt in a mixing bowl. Set aside.
2. In a microwave on high power, heat the milk for 2 minutes. Gradually add the heated milk to the egg mixture.
3. Divide the mixture into 2 custard cups, cover with wax paper, and microwave on low for 6 minutes or until the custard is set.
4. In glass measuring cup, make the caramel by heating the sugar and water on high for 6 to 7 minutes or until golden brown. Let the caramel cool slightly before pouring it over the custard. (As an alternative, you can pour the caramel in fine ribbons onto an ungreased baking sheet. Let it cool slightly, then crush it and sprinkle over the custard.)

Pie Crusts

Crustless pies and quiches are quite delicious and save both time and calories. For a special occasion, though, it's nice to spend the extra time to make a crust.

Easy Pie Crust

3 (9-inch) crusts

3 ¼ cups flour
1 ½ cups vegetable shortening
1 teaspoon salt
2 teaspoons sugar (for dessert crusts only)
1 egg
1 tablespoon vinegar
5 tablespoons cold water

1. Cut the flour, shortening, salt, and sugar together until you achieve a cornmeal-like consistency.
2. Beat together the egg, vinegar, and water; blend into the flour mixture with a fork. Do not overwork the dough.
3. Divide the dough into thirds, cover tightly, and allow to rest in the refrigerator for 30 minutes.
4. Roll out each crust on a floured surface with a floured rolling pin when needed. Dough will keep for one week if refrigerated.

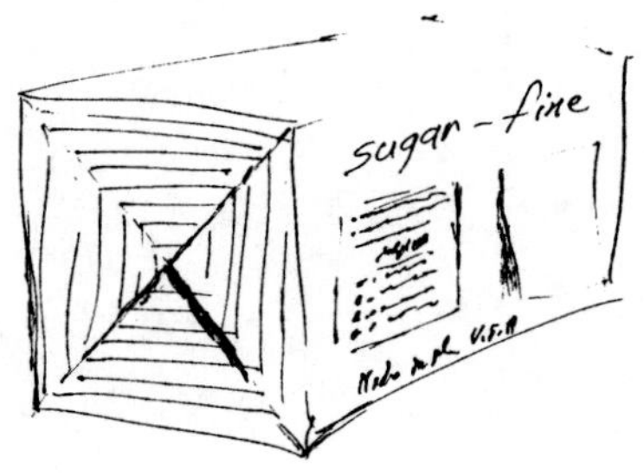

No-Roll Pie Crust

1 (9-inch) crust

For those cooks who don't like to spend the time rolling out a pie crust, this crust can be made right in the pie pan and patted into shape with your fingers.

1 ½ cups flour
¾ teaspoon salt
1 teaspoon sugar (for dessert crusts only)
½ cup cooking oil
2 tablespoons milk

1. Place the flour, salt, and sugar in a 9-inch pie pan. Mix the oil and milk and pour into the pie pan. Stir with a fork until uniformly mixed.
2. Flatten out the crust with your fingers, then squeeze the edges of the crust together with your thumb and index finger at evenly spaced intervals for a decorative effect.
3. Prebake the crust at 450° F for 10 minutes.

Crunchy Pie Crust

1 (9-inch) crust

1 cup finely chopped nuts (walnuts, almonds, peanuts, pecans, or coconut)
1 cup flour
½ cup melted butter

Combine all the ingredients and pat into a pie pan. Bake at 350° F for 15 to 20 minutes.

Index

A
Abalone, 4, 80
  Spaghettini with, 80
Abalone Picatta, 90
Abalonetti, 80
Achiote Paste, 72, 176
Acini di Pepe and Sausage Soup, 121
Acini di Pepe Stracciatella Soup, 120
African Sauce, 157, 164
Agua de Jamaica, 54
Aioli Mayonnaise, 157
Ailoi Sauce, 161
albacore, for jerky, 58
alfalfa sprouts, 10
All Clad Ltd., 20–21
Almond Paste Tartlets, 200
Almond Tart, Easy, 199
Almond Topped Cookies, 202
Almond Wedding Cakes, 203
aluminum foil, 15
  disposing of, 16
Amaretto Peach Mousse, 213
Amnesic Shellfish Poisoning, 59
Anaheim chiles, 140, 141
anchovies,
  Broccoli and Garlic with, 132
  marinated, 60
  safety using, 59
Anchovy-Herb Sauce, 168–69
Anchovy Sauce, 142
angel hair pasta, 116
Angel Hair Pasta Primavera, 117
Ann's Fruit Dip, 214
Appetizer Tarts, 47
appetizers, 38–53
  Bev's Favorite Party, 39
  Brie and Smoked Salmon Pizza Rounds, 189
  Cashew Brie, 45
  Easy, 38
  Herbed Cheese and Broccoli Pizza Rounds, 189
  Layered Cheese, 41
  Northern Thai, 50
Apple Bread, 191
Apple Crêpes, 34
Apple Pancakes, 34
Apple Turnovers, 195
apples, 4
  green, 6
appliances, electric, 23
Arlene's Crab Quiche, 29
Artichoke Tomato Pasta, Peppery, 118
Artichoke-Walnut Pesto, 157, 168
Artichokes, Grilled, 155
Australia, importation laws, 2
Avocado and Bean Dip, 43
avocados, 4, 6
  Pasta with Bacon and, 118–19
  storage of, 6
  with Spicy Corn Cakes, 44
Avocado and Bacon Pizza, 189
Avocado and Papaya Salad, 146

B
bacon, canned, 3
Bacon and Avocado Pasta, 118–19
bacteria, formation of in food, 4
bags,
  garbage, 15–16
  oven roasting, 16
  plastic, 15–16
  See also Ziploc bags.
Bahia de los Puercos Pescado con Tomatoes, 71
Baja California, seafood in, 62, 65, 82, 84, 86
Baked Bananas with Brandied Raisins, 214–15
Baked Eggplant, 142
Baked Herbed Chicken, 90
Baked Red Snapper with Salsa Esmeralda, 70
baking equipment, 22, 198
banana breads, 192–93
Banana Pancakes, 32–33
bananas,
  Baked with Brandied Raisins, 214
  Baked with Cream Cheese, 215
  storage of, 6
  use of, 6
banh trang, 4
barbecue,
  propane, 21
  vegetables grilled on, 155–56
Barbecued Baby Pork Ribs, 106
Barbecued Bistec, 99
Barbecued Chicken Pizza, 189
Barbecued Clams, Beach Party, 86
Barbecued Lobster Tails Santa Rosalillita Style, 65
Barbecued Parrot Fish, 72
barbecuing tips, 21
Barley, Roasted, with Wild Rice, 127
Barley and Wild Rice, 127
barracuda, ciguatera in, 58–59
Bars,
  Lemon, 198
  Lime-Pecan, 199
  Nanaimo, 205
  Peanut Butter and Chocolate, 204
  Pecan-Chocolate Chip, 199
  Walnut Coconut, 199
Basic Crêpe Batter, 33
Basic Omelette, 27
Basic Pancakes, 32
Basic Soufflé, 31
Basic Vinegared Rice, 88
Basic White Sauce or Béchamel, 162
basil, 6, 7
  storage of, 7
Basil-Parsley Vinaigrette, 175
Basil Pesto Sauce, 167
Basque-Style Chicken and Sausage, 93
bass,
  panfrying, 58
  with Pecan Cajun Coating, 73
  See also sea bass.
batter dough, 180
Beach Party Barbecued Clams, 86
bean, mung, 10
Bean Dip, Avocado and, 43
bean salad, 9
Bean Soup with Sausage, 108
bean threads, 124
  Pork with, 124
Bean Threads with Chicken Wrapped in Lettuce Leaves, 124
beans,
  Black Gazpacho, 114
  Cajun Red and Rice, 114–15
  Corn, 197
  Dilled Spicy Green, 152
  dried, 113
  Hal's SpiceSea, 114
  pasta and, 113
  White Tuscan-Style, 115–16
  White with Bruschetta, 170
  White with Sausage and Tomatoes, 114
Béarnaise Sauce, 159
Béchamel, 161, 162
beef,
  canned, 3
  Shredded in Pressure Cooker, 110–11
Beef Burgundy, Easy, 103
Beef Fajitas, 100
Beef Fillet with Sun-Dried Tomato Aioli Sauce, 99
Beef Stew, Playa Maria, 102
beer, 4
Beer Bread, 190
Bell Pepper Sauce, 169
Bell Peppers Stuffed with Orzo, 120
Berry Pie, (Susan's), 206
Better Than S'mores, 215
Bev's Favorite Party Appetizer, 39
Biscuits, Sourdough, 186
Bistec, Barbecued, 99

Black Bean Gazpacho, Easy, 114
Black Bean Salad with Garlic Soy Dressing, 137
Black Bean Sauce, Spicy, 68
Blackened Fish, Cajun-Style, 69
bleach, as disinfectant, 17
blender, electric, 23
Blender Hollandaise Sauce, 157, 158–59
Blender Mayonnaise, 160
boat, living on, 1–2
Boboli Bread, for pizza, 188
bonito, for jerky, 58
  Pacific, 78
Bonito Sauce, 78
Bratwurst Enchiladas, 107
Braun Hand Blender, 23
bread,
  about making, 179
  Apple, 191
  baking in pressure cooker, 191
  batter dough for, 180
  Beer, 190
  Cinnamon Breakfast, 191
  commercial mixes for, 11
  Cranberry, Pine Nut and Banana, 192
  dough for, 180, 183
  Easy White, 183
  flour for, 179
  Jalapeño-Cheddar, 185
  kneading dough for, 180
  Lavosh, 193
  Limpa, 184
  mail-order, 18
  No-Knead Yeast, 181
  Oatmeal-Wheat Germ, 182
  Olive-Herb, 191
  quick, 11, 191–93
  Pumpkin Banana, 192
  Rich Sour Cream Yeast Dough, 183
  rising, 180
  Rosemary with Smoked Gruyère Cheese, 182
  sea water in, 180
  shaping dough for, 180–81
  Sourdough English Muffins, 186–87
  Sourdough French, 185–86
  sourdough starter, 185
  Sourdough Stuffed with Clams, 46
  Sourdough Stuffed with Crab, 45–46
  Sourdough Stuffed with Dry Beef and Chiles, 46
  storing, 11, 181
  tips for making, 180–81
  White, 183
  yeast for, 179, 184
  See also rolls.
Bread Pudding, New Orleans with Whiskey Sauce, 211
Breaded Halibut with Almonds with Mango-Basil Sauce, 74
breadfruit, 7–8, 145
  Fried, 145
Breadfruit Vinaigrette, 145
breakfast, recipes for, 26–37
Breakfast Burritos, 195
Breakfast Puffs, Sweet, 36
Brie and Smoked Salmon Pizza Rounds, 189
broccoli,
  Stir-Fried Stems with Oyster Sauce, 131
  storing, 4
Broccoli with Anchovies and Garlic, 132
Broccoli with Red Wine and Olives, 132
Brown Sauce, 161, 162
brownies,
  Chocolate Truffle, 205
  Turtle, 209
  White Chocolate, 206
brunch, 26–37
Bruschetta, 7, 70, 170
Bruschetta Sauce, 77, 170
  uses for, 170
Bucatini alla Puttanesca, 119
Buckeye Beans and Herbs, 18
bugs, food, 3, 23
Burrito-Wrapped Sausages, 40
Burritos, Breakfast, 195
Burton Stove Top Smoker, 21, 94
butter, canned, 12

C

cabbage, 133
  napa, 4, 5
  purple, 5
  Stir-Fried Spicy, 134
  storage of, 4–5
Cabbage and Mint Salad, 135
Cabbage-Wrapped Dumplings, Mexicana, 52
cactus, prickly pear, 150
Cactus Leaf Salad, 150
Cajun Red Beans and Rice in the Pressure Cooker, 114–15
Cajun Spice Mix, 69
Cajun-Style Blackened Fish, 69
cake,
  Carrot-Pineapple, 207
  Cream-Cheese Raisin, 208–09
  Eggless Chocolate, 210
  Lemon Chiffon Pudding, 211
  Spiced Apple, 208
  Thames' Cake, 209
  Turtle, 209
  Upside Down, 208
Calamari, Abalone-Style, 80
Calamari all'Amalfitana, 60, 61
Calamari Tacos, 195
California Department of Health Services, 59
callaloo, 8, 149
Callaloo Rockefeller, 149
campfires, 16–17
canning jars, 16
Caper-Mayonnaise Sauce, 173
Caper Vinaigrette Marinade, 174
Caponata, 46–47
Caramel Flan in the Microwave, 217
Caramel Sauce, Easy, 215
Caribbean Jerk Marinade, (Jim Babb's), 177
Carnitas in the Pressure Cooker, 111
Carnitas Salad, 111
Carnitas Tacos, 111
Carrot-Pineapple Cake, 207
carrots, 131, 138
  Grilled with Vinaigrette, 155
  Honey Glazed, 138
  storing, 4, 5
Carrots Chinese-Style, 138
Carrots with Ginger, 138
Carrots with Mint, 138
Cashew Brie Appetizer, 45
Cashew Chicken, 96
casserole, Chile Relleño, 27
catarinas, 84
cauliflower, curried, 133
  storing, 4
  with Bruschetta, 170
Cauliflower with Garlic and Chile, 132
Cauliflower with Garlic Crust, 133
caviar, 87
  Eggplant, 142
celery, 4
  storage of, 6
cereal, price of, 3
Ceviche, 48–49
Chantal Speed Cooker, 24–25
  foil straps for, 25
  using, 25
chayote, 8, 150
  Meat-Stuffed, 151
  Shrimp-Stuffed, 151
Chayote with Corn, 150
cheese,
  Brie, 12, 45
  Camembert, 12, 45
  canned, 12
  Cheddar, 12
  cottage, 37

cream, 12, 40, 41
feta, 12, 137
Fried Mozzarella, 44
goat, 189
Kraft Parmesan, 115
Layered Appetizer, 41
making your own, 12, 37
Mozzarella, 40–41, 44, 62, 140, 188
Parmesan, 3, 12, 115, 188
Queso Anejo, 3
ricotta, 37, 62
Velveeta, 12
yogurt, 12
Cheese Rolls, 181
Cheese Spread, Herbed, 39
Cheese Strata, 30
Cheese-Stuffed Chile Relleños, 141
Cheese Wafers, 38
Chef's Choice knife sharpener, 22
chicken, 14
Baked Herbed, 90
canned, 3
Cashew, 96
Foil-Wrapped with Salsa, 91
Helen's, 91
Kung Pao, 95–96
salmonella and, 14
Spicy Orange Szechuan-Style, 97–98
Spicy Stir-Fried with Pine Nuts Wrapped in Lettuce Leaves, 97
Spicy with Peanuts, 95–96
Stir-Fried Thai in Coconut Sauce, 96
storage of, 14
Yucatecan-Style, 90
Chicken and Avocado Quesadillas, 194–95
Chicken and Sausage, Basque-Style, 93
Chicken Breasts, Sautéed, with Provençal Herbs, 92
Chicken Breasts with Chili Hollandaise, 93
Chicken Chunks, Spicy Pecan, 50
Chicken, Foil Wrapped, with Salsa, 91
Chicken Picatta, 90
Chicken Raviolis with Green Chile Pesto, 125–26
Chicken Salad, Tuscan, 10
Chicken Stock, 108
Chicken with Chunky Thai Peanut Sauce, 94
Chicken with Curry Mayonnaise, 91
Chicken with 40 Cloves of Garlic, 92
Chicken with Tomato and Feta Cheese, 93
Chilaquiles in Salsa Verde, 32
Chilcotin's Coffee, 54
Chile Cheese Appetizer Tarts, 47
Chile Relleño Casserole, 27–28
Chile Relleño Wontons, 43
Chile Relleños, 141
Cheese-Stuffed, 141
Crab-Stuffed with Curried Papaya Salsa, 141
chiles, 139
Anaheim, 140, 141
ancho, 140, 141
chipotle, 163
habanero, 140
how to handle, 139–40
jalpeño, 140
mild green, 3, 140
poblano, 140, 141
serrano, 140
chili,
Kay's Dynamite, 102–03
Stagg, 17
White, 115
Chili Hollandaise Sauce, 159
Chili Pasilla Marinade, 176–77
chili powder, 140
Chimichurri Sauce, 157, 165
Chinese Chicken Salad, 136
Chinese Fried Rice with Egg Pancake, 130
Chinese Noodles with Garlic Sauce, 125
Chinese Noodles with Spicy Peanut Sauce, 124–25
Chinese Vegetable Stir-Fry, 132
chipotle chile, 163
Chipotle Chile Sauce, 163
Chocolate Caramel Walnut Tartlets, 201
Chocolate Chip Cookies, 204
Chocolate Chip-Oatmeal Cookies, Incredible, 204
chocolate chips, 3
Chocolate Kahlúa Flan, 216
Chocolate Madeleines, 203
Chocolate Nut Logs, 201–02
Chocolate Sauce, 215
Chocolate Soufflé, Easy, 212
Chocolate Truffle Brownies, 205
chocolates, 83
cholera, 17
chorizo, 106
Chowder, Conch, 81
christophene, 8
Chutney, Sorcery's Papaya, 147
ciguatera, 58–59
cilantro, 6, 7, 42
and Avocado Spicy Corn Cakes, 44
Garlic, and Chile Purée for Salsa, 165–66
Stir-Fried Lobster with, 49
storage of, 7
Cilantro-Garlic Marinade, 177
Cilantro-Lemon Sauce, 173
Cinnamon Breakfast Bread, 191
Cioppino,
Diver's, 62
Ratatouille, 63
Circulan, 20
Citrus Vinaigrette, 157, 173
Clafouti, Puffy Fruit, 35
Clam Chowder San Ignacio, 84
Clam Sauce, Linquine with, 84–85
Clam Sauce with Porcinis and Pesto, 83–84
Clambake,
Easy, 86
New England, 87
Clams, 83
Barbecued, 86
butter, 84, 86
in salad, 61
safety in using, 59–60
Sourdough Bread Stuffed with, 46
Spaghetti with Mussels and, 60
Stuffed, 83
Cocido, 101–02
Cocinita Pibil, 110
Coco Locos, 55
coconut, 8
Coconut Sauce, 96
cod, rock, 58
coffee, 54
Chilcotin's, 54
iced, 54
cola syrup, 22
Cold Mango Soufflé, 213
Cold Marinated Shrimp with Cilantro and Garlic, 66
Cold Tuna Sauce, 76
coleslaw, 131
Jalapeño Pineapple, 133
Lemon-Olive, 134
Papaya, 147
Raisin-Ginger, 133
conch, 4, 81
Conch Chowder, 81
Conch Fritters, 82
Conch Salad, 81
Conch Stew, 81
Contadina pizza sauce, 188
containers,
food, 3
storage, 15–16
cookbooks, local, 3
Cookie Dough, Multipurpose, 201–02
cookies, 198
Almond Topped, 202
Almond Wedding Cakes, 203

Chocolate Chip, 204
Chocolate Chip-Oatmeal, 204
Chocolate Nut Logs, 201–02
Crispy Orange, 202
Cutout, 202
Madeleines, 203
Mexican Wedding Cakes, 202
multipurpose dough for, 201
Oatmeal Coconut, 204
Oatmeal Orange, 204
Oatmeal Raisin, 204
Peanut Butter, 202
Spicy Cutout, 202
cooking in foil, 153
Corallini alle Violette di Mare, 60
Corelle Dinner Wear, 22
Corn,
Chayote with, 150
Red Pepper, Black Bean, and Feta Cheese Salad, 137
Corn Bread, Southwest, 197
Corn Cakes, Spicy, with Cilantro and Avocado, 44
Cornish Game Hens in the Pressure Cooker, 112
costillas, 106
Cottage Cheese, 37
counter space, 23
Crab, Sourdough Bread Stuffed with, 45–46
Crab Linguine, 121
Crab Quiche, Arlene's, 29
Crab-Stuffed Chile Relleños with Curried Papaya Salsa, 141
crabs,
Dungeness, 62
safety using, 59
cracked wheat, 126
cranberries, dried, 3
Cranberry, Pine Nut, and Banana Bread, 192
Cranberry, Pine Nut, and Chile Relish, 178
crayfish, 62
cream,
reduced, 11–12, 215–17
Whipped, 215
Cream Cheese, Fast and Easy, 40
Cream Cheese Frosting, 207
Cream Cheese Raisin Cake, 208–09
Cream Cheese Spread, Lemon Pepper, 40
Cream Cheese Tartlets, 201
Creamy Flan, 216
Crema, 11–12
Creole Sauce, 128, 171–72
Crêpe Batter Using Dried Ingredients, 33
crêpes, 26
Apple, 34
basic recipe for, 33
Pear, 34
Pecan Cranberry, with Fresh Peaches, 33
Puffy Pecan Meringue, 212
using dried ingredients for, 33
Crispy Orange Cookies, 202
cruising lifestyle, 1–2
Crunchy Pie Crust, 218
Crustless "Apple" Pie, Easy, 206
Crustless Quiche, 29
Cucumber Salad, Oriental, 135
Cucumber Salad with Mint-Yogurt Dressing, 135
cucumbers, 4
hothouse, 135
storage of, 6
Cuisinart Little Pro food processor, 23
Curried Cauliflower, 133
Curried Goat, 107
Curried Papaya Salsa, 141, 157, 166
Curried Plantains, 145
Curried Rock Scallops, 68
Curried Tuna Sandwich, 191
Cushionaire baking sheet, 22, 198
custard, baked, 27
Custard Flan, Easy, 216
Cutout Cookies, 202

D

Daiquiri, 55
Deep-Fried Vietnamese Spring Rolls, 53
Del Verde Company, 122
Delicious Scalloped Potatoes, 144
Demoic Acid Toxicity, 59
Dessert Tartlets, 200–01
desserts, 198–218
Dijon Vinaigrette, 174
Dilia Corporation, 24
Dilled Spicy Green Beans, 152
Dinty Moore, 17, 20
Dip,
Avocado and Bean, 43
Porcini Mushroom, 41
Spinach, 39
dipping sauces,
Lime, 165
Spicy Soy, 164
dishes, 22–23
dishpans, plastic (for storage), 16
dishwashing detergent, 15
Diver's Cioppino, 62
dorado,
for jerky, 58
Smoked, 73
dough, 180
Rich Sour Cream Yeast, 183
Downwind Marine, 4, 10
dressings,
Garlic Soy, 137, 174
Lemon Garlic, 157, 174
Lime, 124
Mint-Yogurt, 135
Papaya Seed, 174
Tarragon-Cilantro, 174
Walnut Blue Cheese, 157, 174
See also under vinaigrette.
dried foods, mail-order, 18–19
drinks, 54–56
Dry Beef and Chiles, Sourdough Bread Stuffed with, 46
Dry Pancake Mix, 32
Dumplings,
Cabbage-Wrapped, Mexicana, 52
Steamed Meat, 51
See also Pot Stickers.
Dutch Babies, 35

E

East Coast Lobster, 66
Easy Almond Tart, 199
Easy Appetizers, 38
Easy Beef Burgundy, 103
Easy Black Bean Gazpacho, 114
Easy Caramel Sauce, 215
Easy Chocolate Soufflé, 212
Easy Clambake, 86
Easy Crustless "Apple" Pie, 206–07
Easy Custard Flan, 216
Easy Lasagna, 122–23
Easy Mousse, 215
Easy Oatmeal-Wheat Germ Bread, 182
Easy Pie Crust, 217
Easy Pizza Dough, 188
Easy Seafood Soup, 85
Easy Spinach Quiche, 30
Easy White Bread, 183
eating habits, 1, 3
eel, ciguatera in, 58–59
Egg Pancake with Chinese Fried Rice, 130
egg salad, 27
egg-based sauces, 157
Eggless Chocolate Cake, 210
eggplant (Caponata), 46, 142
Baked, 142
Grilled (sandwich), 191
Grilled Oriental, 155
Hot Garlic with Pork, 105–06
Eggplant and Tomato Pasta, 117–18
Eggplant Caviar, 142
Eggplant Salad, Roasted, 10

Eggplant with Anchovy Sauce, 142
eggs, 12–13, 26–30
  casserole, 27
  Cesena, 28–29
  fried, 27
  frittatas, 28
  garlic pickled, 26
  hard boiled, 13, 26
  Huevos Mexicanos, 27
  Huevos Rancheros, 27
  omelettes, 27–28
  pickled, 13, 26
  pink pickled, 26
  poached, 26
  powdered, 13–14, 27
  scrambled, 27
  storage of, 10, 13
  strata, 30
  washing, 13
  yolk of, 13
Enchiladas, Bratwurst, 107
  New Mexican Green Chile, 98
Enchiladas Oaxaceñas, 99–100
Enchiladas Suisse, 99–100
English Muffins, Sourdough, 186
Ensenada Fish Tacos, 79
equipment, galley. *See* galley equipment.
Escabeche, 78
Espagñole Sauce, 162
Evert-Fresh Bags, 4
Exquisitos, 107

F

Fajitas, Beef, 100
fan, galley, 24
Ferrara Foods, 11
Fillet of Beef with Sun-Dried Tomato Aioli Sauce, 99
fish,
  baking, 58
  barbecuing, 57–58
  broiling, 57
  Cajun-Style Blackened, 69
  Ceviche, 48–49
  cooking in foil, 57
  deep-frying, 58
  filleting, 57
  panfrying, 58
  pickled, 78
  poaching, 58
  raw, 59
  Steamed Chinese Style, 72
  storage of 14, 15
  with tomato sauce, 71
Fish Jerky, 58
Fish Stew, Hazard's Cove, 64
Fish Tacos, Ensenada, 79
flan,
  Caramel, in the Microwave, 217
  Chocolate Kahlúa, 216
  Creamy, 216
  Easy Custard, 216
flounder, 62
  ciguatera in, 58–59
flour, 179
Flour Tortilla Snacks, 194
Flour Tortillas, 193–94
Focaccia, 187
  Ferrara Foods mix, 11
  Parmalat, 188
  Stuffed, 187
Focaccia with Black Olives and Cream Cheese, 41
foil, cooking in, 153
Foil-Wrapped Chicken with Salsa, 91
Foil-Wrapped Ratatouille, 154
Foil-Wrapped Veggie Pack, 154
  with Bruschetta, 170
fondue, 45
food,
  canned, 3
  cost of, 2–3
  difficult to find, 3
  dry, 3, 18–19
  from street vendors, 17
  importation of, 2
  mail-order, 17–19
  master list of, 3
  substitutes for, 4
Food Chopper, The, 23
food processor, 23
FoodSaver, 23–24
Foodways (catalog), 18
French Toast, 27, 35–36
Fresh Mango Dessert, 213
Fresh Tomato and Goat Cheese Pizza, 189
Fresh Tuna Steaks with 40 Cloves of Garlic, 77
Fresh Tuna Steaks with Olives and Capers, 76
Fresh Vietnamese Spring Rolls, 53
Fried Breadfruit, 145
Fried Mozzarella, 44–45
Fried Rice, Chinese with Egg Pancake, 130
Frittatas,
  Miniature, 47–48
  Puerto Vallarta, 28
Fritters, Conch, 82
frosting, 209
  Cream Cheese, 207
Fruit Crisp, 206
Fruit Dip, Ann's, 214
fusilli, 116

G

galley equipment, 20–25
galley fan, 24
garlic, 4, 5, 143
  Roasted, 143
Garlic and Oil Pasta, 117
Garlic-Lemon Sauce, 52
Garlic Potatoes, 154
Garlic Sauce, 125
Garlic Soup, Toni's, 143
Garlic-Soy Dressing, 137, 174
Garlicky Dinner Rolls, 182
Gazpacho, 148
  Easy Black Bean, 114
  White with Sunflower Seeds, 148
Georgia's Marlin with Italian Mayonnaise Marinada, 74
ginger, 6
  storage of, 6
Ginger Chocolate Pie, 207
glasses, wine, 22–23
Glaze, Yogurt, 173
Glazed Carrots, Honey, 138
goat meat, 14
  Curried, 107
  roasted, 14
Grand Gold Margarita, 55
Greek Salad, 131, 134
Green Beans, Dilled Spicy, 152
Green Chile Enchiladas, New Mexican, 98
Green Chile Pesto, 71, 125–26, 154, 168
Green Papaya Salad, 147
Green Peas and Angel Hair Pasta Soup, 120
Green Rice, 129
Green Sauce, 167
Green Tomato Sauce, 166
Grilled Artichokes, 155
Grilled Carrots with Vinaigrette, 155
Grilled Mozzarella Kabobs, 44
Grilled Oriental Eggplant, 155
Grilled Tomatoes, 155
Grilled Salmon with Green Chile Pesto, 71
grilled vegetables on the barbecue, 155–56
Grilled Vegetables with Rosemary, Mixed, 156
grilling tips, 21
grouper, 71
  ciguatera in, 58–59
Guacamole, 42, 166
guava, 8

H
habanero chiles, 140
hachas, 84
halibut,
  Breaded with Almonds with Mango-Basil Sauce, 74
  in tacos, 79
  poaching, 58
Hal's SpiceSea Beans, 114
Handi-Wipes, 15
Hazard's Cove Fish Stew, 64
Hazard's Cove Spaghetti, 119
Healthy Living, 23
Heart Interface Inverter, 23
Helen's Chicken, 91
Herbed Cheese Spread, 39
Herbed Chicken, Baked, 90
herbs, fresh, 6–7
Hibiscus Flower Juice, 54
hollandaise-based sauces, 157–59
  problem-solving, 158
  tips for making, 158
  See also under sauces.
Hollandaise Sauce, Traditional, 158
Hominy and Pork Stew in the Pressure Cooker, 109
honey, 2
Honey Glazed Carrots, 138
Hot and Sour Shrimp Soup, 67
Hot and Spicy Jalapeño Muffins, 191
Hot Buttered Rum Mix, 55
hot dogs, 107
Hot Garlic Eggplant with Pork, 105–06
Hot Spiced Olives, 39
Huachinango Veracruz, 58, 70
Huevos Mexicanos, 27
Huevos Rancheros, 27

I
Iced Coffee, 54
importing restrictions, 2
Incredible Chocolate Chip-Oatmeal Cookies, 204
Independent Micro Diet Advisor, 19
Insalata di Mare al Limone, 61
Isla San Francisco, Mexico, 62
Italian Bean Soup with Fresh Chard, 108
Italian cooking, 115
Italian Mayonnaise Marinade, 74
Italian Potato Salad, 144
Italian Sausage, 106
Italian Tomato Sauce, 171

J
jack, ciguatera in, 58–59
Jalapeño-Cheddar Bread, 185
Jalapeño Muffins, Hot and Spicy, 191
Jalapeño Pepper Jelly, 42
Jalapeño Pineapple Coleslaw, 133
jalapeños, 140
Jambalaya, 128
jars, canning, 16
jelly, 4
  Jalapeño Pepper, 42
Jerky, Fish, 58
jicama, 5
Jim Babb's Caribbean Jerk Marinade, 177
Joy, 15
Joys of Pressure Cooking, The, 109
juice,
  Hibiscus Flower, 54
  orange, 36

K
Kay's Dynamite Chili, 102–03
kid meat, 14
kneading bread, techniques for, 180
knife sharpener, 22
knives, 22
Kung Pao Chicken, 95–96

L
Lamb Shanks with Orzo, 109
lasagna, 122
  Easy, 122–23
Lasagna Instanti, 122
Lavosh, 193
Lawry's Lemon Pepper, 3
laws, importing, 2
Layered Cheese Appetizer, 41
Lemon Bars, 198
Lemon Caper Rice, 129
Lemon-Caper Sauce, 173
Lemon Chiffon Pudding Cake, 211
Lemon Garlic Dressing, 157, 174
Lemon-Olive Coleslaw, 134
lemon pepper, 3
Lemon Pepper Cream Cheese Spread, 40
Lemon-Worcestershire Marinade, 176
lentils, 113
lettuce, storing, 4, 5
Lime Dipping Sauce, 165
Lime Dressing, 124
Lime-Chili Butter, 172
Lime-Pecan Bars, 199
Lime Soufflé, 213
Lime Syrup, 54–55
Lime Wine Punch, 55
Limeade, 54, 55
Limpa, Quick Mix Swedish, 184
Linguine, Crab, 121
Linguine (Spinach) with Bonito Sauce, 78
Linguine with Clam Sauce, 84–85
Linguine with Tuna, Olives, and Capers, 76
Linguine with Tuna Sauce and Lemon, 77
liquor, prices of, 3
Lobster,
  East Coast, 66
  Stir-Fried with Cilantro, 49
  Stir-Fried with Shrimp, 64
Lobster Tails,
  Barbecued, Santa Rosalillita Style, 65
  Sautéed, 65
Los Pelicanos Smoked Dorado, 73

M
Macadamia-Caramel Tartlets, 200
mackerel,
  ciguatera in, 58–59
  Escabeche, 78
  Spanish, 58
  with Tomatoes and Peppers, 60–61
Madeleines, 203
  Chocolate, 203
  Orange, 203
  Pecan, 203
  Toasted Almond, 203
Magma Marine Cuisine Barbecue, 21
magnet bars, for storage, 23
mahimahi, barbecuing, 57
mail-order supplies, 17–19
Maki Sushi California-Style, 88
mango, 4, 8
Mango-Basil Sauce, 74, 178
Mango Dessert, Fresh, 213
Mango-Lime Sauce, 177
Mango Soufflé, Cold, 213
Manicotti, Seafood, 123
Maple-Flavored Syrup, 178
Marbella Farmers' Market, 11
Margarita,
  Grand Gold, 55
  Santa Fe, 55
Marinade Dijon, 157, 175
Marinade Tomas, 175–76
marinades, 157, 175–77
  Caper Vinaigrette, 174
  Caribbean Jerk Marinade (Jim Babb's), 177
  Chile Pasilla, 176–77
  Cilantro-Garlic, 157, 177
  citrus, 72, 157
  fajita, 100
  Italian Mayonnaise, 74
  Lemon-Worcestershire, 176
  Mustard-Soy, 175
  Red Wine, 176

Marinated Mozzarella, 44
Marinated Mushrooms, 152
Marlin, Georgia's with Italian Mayonnaise Marinade, 74
Mashed Plantains, 145
mayonnaise, 4, 159
  Aioli, 157, 161
  Blender, 160
  curdled or separated, 160
  Italian, 74
  Traditional, 160
mayonnaise-based sauces, 159–61
  tips for making, 159
meat, 90–112
Meatballs with Tomatillo Sauce, 103
Mediterranean Magic Pizza Bases, 11
Mediterranean Salad, 10
Mediterranean Vegetable Soup, 148
Melon Cooler, 55
menus, simplicity of, 1
Mexican Pizza, 196
Mexican Salsa Fresca, 156
Mexican Wedding Cakes, 202–03
Mexico,
  drinking water in, 17
  prices in 3
Microwave Hollandaise, 159
Microwave oven, 23
Milton Waldbaum Company, 14
Miniature Frittatas, 47–48
Mint-Pineapple Tea, 55
Mint-Yogurt Dressing, 135
mirliton, 8, 150
mixer, electric, 23
mold, 3
mollusks, safety using, 59
Mornay Sauce, 162
Mousse,
  Amaretto Peach, 213
  Easy, 215
Mozzarella,
  Fried, 44–45
  Grilled Kabobs, 44
  Marinated, 44–45
Mozzarella Prosciutto Spread, 40–41
muffin pans, mini, 22
muffins, Hot and Spicy Jalapeño, 191–92
  See also English Muffins.
Multipurpose Cookie Dough, 201–02
mung beans, 10
Mushroom Cheese Sauce, 163
Mushroom Cream Sauce, 163
Mushroom Dip, Porcini, 41
Mushroom Green Peppercorn Sauce, 163
Mushroom Sauce, 163
Mushrooms,
  Dry, 163
  Marinated, 152
Mushrooms with Chipotle Chile Sauce, 157, 163
mussels,
  in salad, 61
  pasta with, 60
  safety using, 59–60
  steamed, 60
Mussels in Orange Sauce, 49
Mussels Punta Cabras, 82
mustard, 4
Mustard Sauce, 157, 172
Mustard-Soy Marinade, 175

N

Nachos, 42
  Potato, 42–43
Nanaimo Bars, 205
New England Cheese Making Supply Company, 12
New England Clambake, 87
New Mexican Green Chile Enchiladas, 98
New Orleans Bread Pudding with Whiskey Sauce, 211
New Zealand, laws of, 2
newspaper, for wrapping produce, 4
Nigiri Sushi, 89
NOAA broadcasts of shellfish quarantines, 59–60
No-Knead Yeast Bread, 181
No-Roll Pie Crust, 218
nonskid, 16
noodles,
  bean threads, 124
  Chinese with Garlic Sauce, 125
  Chinese with Spicy Peanut Sauce, 124–25
  lasagna, 122–23
nopales, 150
Norcold refrigerators, 7
Nori, 3
Northern Thai Appetizer, 50

O

oatmeal cookies, 204
Oatmeal-Wheat Germ Bread, Easy, 182
Octopus,
  finding, 69
  Los Frailes, 69
olive oil, 115
Olive-Herb Bread, 191
Olives,
  black, 188
  Hot Spiced, 39
omelette, basic, 27
onions, 4, 144
  storage of, 5
  stuffed, 144
Orange-Butter Sauce, 178
Orange Chicken Szechuan-Style, Spicy, 97
Orange Chile Salsa, 167
Orange Cookies, Crispy, 202
Orange Hollandaise Sauce, 159
Orange, Jicama, and Cilantro Salad, 135
orange juice squeezer, 23
Orange Madeleines, 203
Orange Slurpies, 36
Oranges in Burgundy, 214
organizing preparation, 1
Oriental Cucumber Salad, 135
Oriental Eggplant, Grilled, 155
Oriental Sauce Mix, 164
Oriental Vinaigrette, 175
Orzo, Bell Peppers stuffed with, 120
  Lamb Shanks with, 109
Orzo with Sun-Dried Tomatoes, 120–21, 167
oyster sauce, 131–32
oysters, safety using, 59

P

Paella, Seafood, 63
pancakes,
  Apple, 34
  Banana, 32–33
  basic, 32
  clafouti, 35
  dry mix for, 32
  Egg with Chinese Fried Rice, 130
  Sourdough, 186
panko, 48
pans, Charlotte, 22
  disposable roasting, 15
  See also saucepan *and* skillets.
papaya, 146
  Sautéed Green, 146
  Stuffed Green, 146
Papaya and Avocado Salad, 146
Papaya Chutney, Sorcery's, 147
Papaya Coleslaw, 147
Papaya Quesadillas, 194
Papaya Seed Dressing, 174
Papaya Slaw, 147
Papaya Quesadillas, 194
paper, parchment, 15
paper plates, 15
paper towels, 15
pappardella pasta, 117
Paralytic Shellfish Poisoning, 59

parchment paper, 15
Parmalat, 188
Parrot Fish, Barbecued, 72
parsley, Chinese, 7
Party Appetizer, Bev's Favorite, 39
pasta, 76, 116–17
  acini di pepe, 120
  angel hair, 116
  and beans, 113
  cheese-filled shells, 118
  cooking, 116
  Eggplant and Tomato, 117–18
  fusilli, 116
  Garlic and Oil, 117
  instant, 122
  mail-order, 18–19, 122
  mussels with, 60
  pappardella, 117
  penne, 116
  pennette, 121
  Peppery Artichoke Tomato, 118
  sauce, 60, 169
  spaghetti, 117
  storing, 116
  ziti, 116
Pasta DeFino NoBoil Lasagna, 122
Pasta e Fagioli, 113
Pasta Primavera, Angel Hair, 117
Pasta Shells Filled with Three Cheeses, 118
Pasta with Bacon and Avocado, 118–19
Pasta with Mussels, 60
pastries, 35–36
Patsalis, Toula, 109
pawpaw, 145
peaches, 4
Peanut Butter and Chocolate Bars, 204
Peanut Butter Cookies, 202
Peanut Sauce, Spicy, 124–24
peanuts, 10
Pear Crêpes, 34
pears, Asian, 4
Pears Poached in Red Wine, 214
Pecan Chicken Chunks, Spicy, 50
Pecan-Chocolate Chip Bars, 199
Pecan Cranberry Crêpes with Fresh Peaches, 33–34
Pecan Madeleines, 203
Pecan Meringue Crêpes, Puffy, 212
Pecan Pilaf, 128–29
Pecan Tartlets, 200
penne, 116
Pennette with Zucchini, 121
peppers, 4, 139
  bell, 6, 139
  peeling, 139
  Pickled, 151
  Roasted Red with Garlic and Tomatoes, (Toni's), 143
  roasting, 139
  seeding, 139
  See also chiles.
Peppery Artichoke Tomato Pasta, 118
perch, ciguatera in, 58–59
Pescado con Achiote, 72
Pescado con Tomatoes, Bahia de los Puercos, 71
pesto sauce, 3, 83
  Anchovy-Herb, 168
  Artichoke-Walnut, 157, 168
  Basil, 70, 167
  Green Chile, 71, 125–26, 154, 168
Pesto Swordfish in Foil, 70
philosophy of cooking, 1
pickle weed, 9
Pickled Peppers, 151
pickled vegetables, 151
pickles, 4
pickling, 11
pie,
  Easy Crustless "Apple," 206–07
  Ginger Chocolate, 207
  Susan's Berry, 206
pie crusts, 217–18
  Crunchy, 218
  Easy, 217
  No-Roll, 218
pine nuts, 10
Piperade, 169
pizza, 188
  Boboli Bread for, 188
  Contadina sauce for, 188
  Fresh Tomato and Goat Cheese, 189
  Mexican, 196
  Parmalat products for, 188
  Tomato, Roasted Pepper, and Pepperoni, 190
Pizza Dough, Easy, 188
Pizza Margherita, 189
Pizza with Spicy Shrimp, 190
plankton, harmful, 59
plantains, 6, 8–9, 145
  Curried, 145
  Mashed, 145
plates, paper, 15
Playa Maria Beef Stew, 102
poblano chiles, 140
Pompano with Onions and Salsa, 74
Popcorn in the Pressure Cooker, 48
popovers, 35
Porcini Mushroom Dip, 41
Porcini Mushroom Sauce, Pork Chops with, 105
Porcinis and Pesto, Clam Sauce with, 83
Pork,
  Hot Garlic Eggplant with, 105–06
  Yucatecan Steamed, with Banana Leaves, 110
Pork Chops with Apple-Yogurt Sauce, 104
Pork Chops with Crispy Potato Crust, 105
Pork Chops with Olives and Fennel, 105
Pork Chops with Porcini Mushroom Sauce, 105
Pork Ribs, Barbecued Baby, 106
Pork Tenderloin Pasilla, 104
Pork Tenderloin with Orange Sauce, Stuffed, 104
Pork with Bean Threads, 124
Posole, 109–10
pot, six-quart, 20
Pot Stickers, Shrimp and Spinach, 52
Potato Salad, Italian, 144
Potato Nachos, 42–43
potatoes, 4, 144
  Garlic, 154
  Scalloped, 144
  storing, 5
  See also sweet potatoes.
poultry, 90–112
preparation, organizing, 1
preserving, 2–19
pressure cookers, 24–25, 109–12
  for baking bread, 191
  for dried beans, 113
  for rice, 128
  making soup in, 107–08
  popping corn in, 48
  Risotto in, 128
Prevention magazine, 14
prices, food, 2–3
produce,
  storing fresh, 4
  wrapping, 4
propane barbecue, 21
  tips for using, 21
propane bottles, 21
  disposing of, 16
propane torch, 22
provisioning, 2–19
  estimating, 2
pudding,
  New Orleans Bread, with Whiskey Sauce, 211
  Rice, with Raisins and Molasses, 210
Puerto Gato Salad with Raisins and Cheese, 135
Puerto Refugio Scallops, 68
Puerto Vallarta Frittata, 28
Puffy Fruit Clafouti, 35

Puffy Pecan Meringue Crêpes, 212
Pumpkin Banana Bread, 192
Punch, Lime Wine, 55
purslane, 9

Q
Quesadillas,
  Chicken and Avocado, 194–95
  Papaya, 194
  Squash Blossom, 195
Queso Fundido, 45, 106
Quiche,
  Arlene's Crab, 29
  Crustless, 29
  Easy Spinach, 30
  Shrimp, Appetizer Tarts, 47
  Zucchini, Sausage, and Spinach, 29–30
Quick Loaf (breads), 11
Quick Mix Swedish Limpa, 184

R
Raisin-Ginger Coleslaw, 133
RapidRise Yeast Techniques, 184
Raspados, 56
Ratatouille, Foil-Wrapped, 154
Ratatouille Cioppino, 63
raviolis,
  Chicken, with Green Chili Pesto, 125–26
  Shrimp, with Tomatillo Sauce, 126
  Wonton, 125
records, 3
Red Beans and Rice, Cajun, 114–15
Red Rice, 129
red snapper,
  Baked, with Salsa Esmeralda, 70
  baking, 58
  Escabeche, 78
red tide, 59
Red Wine Marinade, 176
reduced cream recipes, 215–17
refrigeration, avoiding need for, 1, 4
refrigerator, planning use of, 4
Relish, Cranberry, Pine Nut, and Chile, 178
Remoulade Sauce, 77, 161
rice, 128
  Chinese Fried, with Egg Pancake, 130
  Green, 129
  Lemon Caper, 129
  Red, 129
  vinegared, 88
  wild, 127
rice paper, Vietnamese, 4
Rice Pudding with Raisins and Molasses, 210
Rich Sour Cream Yeast Dough, 183
Ricotta Cheese, 37
Risotto in the Pressure Cooker, 128
Roasted Barley and Pine Nuts, 127
Roasted Garlic, 143
Roasted Pepper and Mozzarella Salad, 140
Roasted Red Peppers with Garlic and Tomatoes, (Toni's), 143
Rockfish, Stir-Fried Curried, 73
Rolls,
  Cheese, 181
  Garlicky Dinner, 182
  Rosemary Bread Pizza, with Pepperoni, 182
  Schnecken, 183
  Sourdough, 186
Rosemary Bread Pizza Rolls with Pepperoni, 182
Rosemary Bread with Smoked Gruyère Cheese, 182
roux, 161
Rubbermaid products, 23
Rum, Hot Buttered, 55

S
salad,
  Black Bean, with Garlic Soy Dressing, 137
  Cabbage and Mint, 135
  Cactus Leaf, 150
  Carnitas, 111
  Chinese Chicken, 136
  Conch, 81
  Corn, Red Pepper, Black Bean, and Feta Cheese, 137
  Cucumber, with Mint-Yogurt Dressing, 135
  egg, 27
  emergency, 9–10
  Greek, 131, 134
  Green Papaya, 147
  Italian Potato, 144
  Lemon-Olive Coleslaw, 134
  Mediterranean, 10
  Orange, Jicama, and Cilantro, 135
  Oriental Cucumber, 135
  Papaya and Avocado, 146
  Potato (Italian), 144
  roasted eggplant, 10
  Roasted Pepper and Mozzarella, 140
  seafood, 61
  Spicy Thai, with Roasted Peanuts and Cilantro, 136
  Thai, 131
  Thai Shrimp, 67
  tostada, 10
  Trigger Fish, 75
  tuna, 10
  Tuscan Chicken, 10
Salad 16 Days Out, 134
salmon,
  barbecuing, 57
  eating raw, 59
  Grilled, with Green Chile Pesto, 71
  poaching, 58
  Smoked, with Brie, Appetizer, 189
  Smoked, Sandwich, 191
Salmon Fillets in Foil with Dill and Mandarin Orange Sauce, 71
salmonella bacteria,
  on chicken, 14
  on eggs, 13
  poisoning from, 13
salsa, 139
  cilantro, garlic, and chile puree for, 165–66
  Curried Papaya, 141, 157, 166
  Foil-Wrapped Chicken with, 91
  Orange Chile, 167
Salsa de Tomatillo, 79, 166
Salsa Esmeralda, 70, 167
Salsa Fresca, Mexican, 79, 165
sand dabs, 62
sandwiches, 191
Santa Fe Margarita, 55
sashimi, 88
saucepan, 22
sauces, 157
  African, 157, 164
  Aioli, 161
  Anchovy, 142
  Basil Pesto, 167
  Béarnaise, 159
  Béchamel, 161, 162
  Bell Pepper, 169
  Blender Hollandaise, 157, 158–59
  Bonito, 78
  Brown, 161, 162
  Bruschetta, 77, 170
  Caper-Mayonnaise, 173
  Caramel, Easy, 215
  Chili Hollandaise, 159
  Chimichurri, 157, 165
  Chipotle Chile, 163
  Chocolate, 215
  Citrus Vinaigrette for Seafood, 157, 173
  Clam, 83–85
  coconut, 96
  cold tuna, 76
  Contadina pizza, 188
  Creole, 128, 171–72
  egg-based, 157
  Espagñole, 162

Garlic, 125
Green Tomato, 166
Hollandaise, Traditional, 158
hollandaise-based, 157–59
Italian Tomato, 171
Lemon-Caper, 173
Lime Dipping, 165
Mango-Basil, 74, 178
Mango-Lime, 177
mayonnaise-based, 159–61
Microwave Hollandaise, 159
Mornay, 162
Mushroom, 163
Mushroom Cheese, 163
Mushroom Cream, 163
Mushroom Green Peppercorn, 163
Mushrooms with Chipotle Chile, 157, 163
Mustard, 157, 172
Orange-Butter, 178
Orange Hollandaise, 159
Oriental Mix, 164
Oyster, 131–32
pasta, 60, 169
pesto, 3, 83
Piperade, 169
Remoulade, 77, 161
seafood, 172–73
Spanish Tomato, 171
Spicy Black Bean, 68
Spicy Peanut, 124–25
Spicy Soy Dipping, 164
starch-based, 161
Sun-Dried Tomato Aioli, 99, 157, 161
Sun-Dried Tomato and Basil, 119–20
Teriyaki, 177
tuna, 76, 77
tomatillo, 66, 103, 126
tomato, 171
Tomato, Garlic, and Wine, 172
Tomato-Mushroom, 171
Velouté, 161, 162
Veracruz, 166–67
Whiskey, 178
White, 161, 162
Whore's, 119
Worcestershire, 3
See also under salsa *and* pesto sauce.
Sausage and Chicken, Basque-Style, 93
Sausage Stuffed Wontons, 50–51
sausages,
Burrito-Wrapped, 40
cantimpalo, 18
chorizo, 108
Italian, 106
mail-order, 18
Soria, 18
Sautéed Chicken Breasts with Provençal Herbs, 92
Sautéed Green Papaya, 146
Sautéed Lobster Tails, 65
Sautéed Shrimp with Feta Cheese, 66
Scalloped Potatoes, Delicious, 144
scallops,
Baked in their Shells, 68
Curied Rock, 68
in Spicy Black Bean Sauce, 68
Puerto Refugio, 68
rock, 62, 68
safety using, 59–60
Skewered Shrimp and, 66
Schnecken, 183–84
Scotch Bonnets (chiles), 140
sea bass,
ciguatera in, 58–59
Escabeche, 78
in tacos, 79
poaching, 58
sea spinach, 9
seafood, 57–90
cooking, 57–58
local, 62
parasites in, 58–59
poisons in, 58–59
preparing, 57
sauces for, 172–73
storage of, 14–15
substitutions, 57
Seafood Manicotti, 123
Seafood Paella, 63
Seafood Soup, Easy, 85
sealing foods, 3
serrano chiles, 140
Shade Pasta Inc., 18–19, 122
shark, in tacos, 79
poaching, 58
thresher, 58
shellfish, safety using, 59–60
sherry, 6
Shredded Beef in the Pressure Cooker, 110
shrimp,
Cold Marinated, with Cilantro and Garlic, 66
in salad, 61
Sautéed, with Feta Cheese, 66
Skewered, with Scallops, 66
Stir-Fried, Lobster and, 64
Stuffed with Cheese and Wrapped in Bacon, 67
Shrimp and Spinach Pot Stickers with Garlic-Lemon Sauce, 52
Shrimp Quiche Appetizer Tarts, 47
Shrimp Raviolis with Tomatillo Sauce, 126
Shrimp Salad, Thai, 67
Shrimp Soup, Hot and Sour, 67
Shrimp Stuffed Chayote, 151
Shrimp with Mango-Lime Sauce, 50
Siu Mai, 51
Skewered Shrimp and Scallops, 66
skillets,
cast iron, 21
Teflon, 20–21
slurpies, 26
Orange, 36
Smoked Dorado, Los Pelicanos, 73
Smoked Salmon Sandwich, 191
Smoked Salmon with Brie, 189
smoker, stove-top, 21, 94
smoking, tea, 93
S'mores, Better Than, 215
snapper, ciguatera in, 58–59
soda siphon, 22
Soligen knives, 22
Sopaipillas, 196
Sorcery's Papaya Chutney, 147
Soria, 18
Soufflé,
Basic, 31
Cold Mango, 213
Easy Chocolate, 212
Lime, 213
Soup,
Acini di Pepe and Sausage, 121
Acini di Pepe Stracciatella, 120
Bean with Sausage, 108
Chicken, 108
Easy Seafood, 85
Garlic, 143
Green Peas and Angel Hair Pasta, 120
Hearty Vegetable-Beef, 101–02
Hot and Sour Shrimp, 67
Italian Bean with Fresh Chard, 108
Mediterranean Vegetable, 148
pressure-cooker for, 107
Tortilla, 108
Vegetable (Mediterranean), 148
White Bean, 108
White Bean Chicken, 108
See also Gazpacho.
Sour Cream Yeast Dough Bread, Rich, 183
Sourdough Biscuits, 186
sourdough breads, 185–87
Sourdough Bread Stuffed with Clams, 46
Sourdough Bread Stuffed with Crab, 45–46
Sourdough Bread Stuffed with Dry Beef and Chiles, 46

Sourdough English Muffins, 186–87
Sourdough French Bread, 185–86
Sourdough Pancakes, 186
Sourdough Roll-Ups, 40
Sourdough Rolls, 186
Sourdough Starter, 185
soursop, 9
Southwest Corn Bread, 197
Soy Dipping Sauce, Spicy, 164
spaghetti, 117
  Hazard's Cove, 119
Spaghetti con Vogole, 60
Spaghetti with Mussels and Clams, 60
Spaghetti with Tuna and Tomato Sauce, 77
Spaghettini with Abalone, 80
Spanish mackerel, ciguatera in, 58–59
Spanish Tomato Sauce, 171
spice rack, 23
Spiced Apple Cake, 208
Spiced Olives, Hot, 39
spices, 3
Spicy Black Bean Sauce, 68
Spicy Corn Cakes with Cilantro and Avocado, 44
Spicy Cutout Cookies, 202
Spicy Orange Chicken Szechuan-Style, 97–98
Spicy Peanut Sauce, 124–25
Spicy Pecan Chicken Chunks, 50
Spicy Soy Dipping Sauce, 164
Spicy Stir-Fried Chicken with Pine Nuts Wrapped in Lettuce Leaves, 97
Spicy Thai Salad with Roasted Peanuts and Cilantro, 136
spinach, 149
Spinach Dip, 39
Spinach Linguine with Bonito Sauce, 78
Spinach Quiche, 30
Spinach Rockefeller, 149
Spread,
  Herbed Cheese, 39
  Lemon Pepper Cream Cheese, 40
  Mozzarella Prosciutto, 40
Spring Rolls,
  Deep-Fried Vietnamese, 53
  Fresh Vietnamese, 53
sprouts, 10
Squash Blossom Quesadillas, 195
squid, 4, 60, 61
  in salad, 61
Squid Picatta, 90
staples, listing, 3
starch-based sauces, 161
Steamed Fish, Chinese Style, 72
Steamed Meat Dumplings, 51
steamer, bamboo, 20
stew,
  beef, 102
  Conch, 81
  Fish, 64
  Hominy and Pork, in the Pressure Cooker, 109–10
Stir-Fried Broccoli Stems with Oyster Sauce, 131–32
Stir-Fried Chicken with Pine Nuts Wrapped in Lettuce Leaves, Spicy, 97
Stir-Fried Curried Rockfish, 73
Stir-Fried Lobster with Cilantro, 49
Stir-Fried Lobster with Shrimp, 64
Stir-Fried Spicy Cabbage, 134
Stir-Fried Thai Chicken in Coconut Sauce, 96
stir-frying, 95
stocking up, 15–16
storage,
  bags for, 1, 4
  dishes, 22–23
  dry food, 3
  pots and pans, 22–23
  space for, 22–23
Strata, Cheese, 30
Stuffed Clams, 83
Stuffed Focaccia, 187
Stuffed Green Papaya, 146
Stuffed Pork Tenderloin with Orange Sauce, 104
Sturgeon, 87
substituting ingredients, 4, 109, 131
sugar, brown, 3
Sun-Dried Tomato Aioli Sauce, 99, 157, 161
Sun-Dried Tomato Seasoning, 167
Sun-Dried Tomatoes and Basil Pasta Sauce, 119–20
sunflower seeds, 10
sunflower sprouts, 10
Susan's Berry Pie, 206
sushi, 88–89
  Maki, California-Style, 88
  Nigiri, 89
sushi party, 89
Sweet Breakfast Puffs, 36
sweet potatoes, 144
Sweetened Whipped Cream, 215
swordfish,
  barbecuing, 57
  with Pesto in Foil, 70
Syrup,
  Lime, 54
  Maple-Flavored, 178

T

Tabbouleh, 126
Taco Tarts, 48
Tacos,
  Calamari, 195
  Carnitas, 111
  Ensenada Fish, 79
Tagliatelle with Cold Tuna Sauce, 76
taro, 8, 9, 149
Tarragon-Cilantro Dressing, 174
tartlets,
  Almond Paste, 200
  Chocolate Caramel Walnut, 201
  Cream Cheese, 201
  frosting for, 200
  Macadamia-Caramel, 200
  Pecan, 200
  See also tarts.
tarts,
  Almond, Easy, 199
  Appetizer, 47
  Chile Cheese, 47
  Shrimp Quiche filled, 47
  Taco, 48
  See also tartlets.
Tea, Mint-Pineapple, 55
tea cake, 203
tea kettle, 22
tea smoking, 94
Teriyaki Sauce, 177
Thai Appetizer, Northern, 50
Thai Chicken, Stir-Fried in Coconut Sauce, 96
Thai Chicken Pizza, 189
Thai Salad with Roasted Peanuts and Cilantro, Spicy, 136
Thai Shrimp Salad, 67
Thames' Cake, 209
thermometers, 22
thermos, wide-mouth, 22
Toasted Almond Madeleines, 203
tofu, 1
tomate verde, 9
tomatillo, 9
tomatillo sauce, 66, 103, 126, 166
Tomato and Goat Cheese Pizza, Fresh, 189
tomato sauce, 171
Tomato, Garlic, and Wine Sauce, 172
Tomato, Roasted Pepper, and Pepperoni Pizza, 190
Tomato Vinaigrette, 175
tomatoes, 4
  canned, 3, 115
  Grilled, 155
  Italian plum, 5
  Roma, 5

storage of, 5
sun-dried, 3
Tomato-Mushroom Sauce, 171
Toni's Garlic Soup, 143
Toni's Roasted Red Peppers with Garlic and Tomatoes, 143
tools, small galley, 22
toothpicks, 16
spaghetti as, 16
Tortilla Soup, 108
tortillas,
Flour, 193–94
for sandwiches, 191
Mama Cesena's Jalapeño, 194
snacks, 194
Traditional Hollandaise Sauce, 158
Traditional Mayonnaise, 160
trash,
burning of, 17
disposal of, 16
Trigger Fish Salad, 75
tuna,
canned, 76
Curried (sandwich), 191
Escabeche, 78
salad, 10
with Linguine, Olives, and Capers, 76
Tuna Bonito Salad, 78
Tuna Sauce,
Cold (with Tagliatelle), 76
and Lemon, Linguine with, 77
Tuna Steaks,
with Olives and Capers, 76
with 40 Cloves of Garlic, Fresh, 77
Tupperware, 7, 23
Turkey Breast with Curried Papaya Salsa, 99
Turkey Mexicana with Cherry Tomatoes, 98
Turkey Picatta, 90
Turnovers, Apple, 195
Turtle Brownies, 209
Turtle Cake, 209
Tuscan-Style White Beans, 115–16

U

Upside Down Cake, 208
U.S. Food and Drug Administration, 60

V

Veal Picatta, 90
Vegetable-Beef Soup, Hearty, 101–02
Vegetable Soup, Mediterranean, 148
Vegetable Stir-Fry, Chinese, 132
vegetables,
grilled, 155, 156
Mixed Grilled, with Rosemary, 156
washing, 17
Veggie Pack, Foil-Wrapped, 154, 170
Yam Los Frailes, 154
Velouté Sauce, 161, 162
Veracruz Sauce, 166
verdolaga, 3, 9
Vietnamese Spring Rolls,
Deep-Fried, 53
Fresh, 53
Vinaigrette,
Basil-Parsley, 175
Citrus, 157, 173
Dijon, 174
Oriental, 175
Tomato, 175
See also dressings.
vinegar, wine, 10–11
Vinegared Rice, Basic, 88

W

Wafers, Cheese, 38
waffle iron, stove-top, 22
waffles, 33
wahoo, for jerky, 58
Wakefield Scrambled Egg Mix, 13–14
Walnut and Blue Cheese Dressing, 157, 174
Walnut Coconut Bars, 199
walnuts, 10
wasabi, 88
Washington State University Creamery, 12
water, purifying, 17
Wedding Cakes,
Almond, 203
Mexican, 202
wedge shells, 83
weevils, 23
wheat, cracked, 126
Whiskey Sauce, 178
White Bean Chicken Soup, 108
White Bean Soup, 108
White Beans, Tuscan-Style, 115–16
White Beans with Bruschetta, 170
White Beans with Sausage and Tomatoes, 114
White Bread, Easy, 183
White Chili, 115
White Chocolate Brownies, 206
White Gazpacho with Sunflower Seeds, 148
White Sauce, 161, 162
Whore's Sauce, 119
wild rice, 127
Barley and, 127
Wild Rice Stuffing, 127
W.J. Clarke and Company, 18
wok, flat-bottom, 20
Wonton Raviolis, 125–26
Wontons,
Chile Relleño, 43
Sausage Stuffed, 50–51
Worcestershire sauce, 3

Y

Yam Veggie Pack Los Frailes, 154
yams, 144
yeast, 179
RapidRise techniques, 184
yellowtail, barbecuing, 57
yogurt, making on board, 36–37
yogurt cheese, 12
Yogurt Glaze, 173
Yorkshire Pudding, 35
Yucatecan Steamed Pork in Banana Leaves, 110
Yucatecan-Style Chicken, 90

Z

Ziploc bags, 1, 5, 15
ziti, 116
Zucchini, Pennette with, 121
Zucchini, Sausage, and Spinach Quiche, 29–30
Zucchini with Green Chile Pesto in Foil, 154